THE LIBRARY OF HOLOCAUST TESTIMONIES

Who Are You, Mr Grymek?

Who Are You, Mr Grymek?

NATAN GROSS

Translated by William R. Brand

VALLENTINE MITCHELL
LONDON • PORTLAND, OR

Originally published in Hebrew as *Mi ata adon Grymek?*
by Moreshet, Israel, 1990 and © Natan Gross
Published in Polish as *Kim Pan Oest, Panie Grymek?*
by Wydawnietwo Literackie, Cracow, 1991 and © Natan Gross

Published in 2001 in Great Britain by
VALLENTINE MITCHELL
Newbury House, 900 Eastern Avenue
London, IG2 7HH

and in the United States of America by
VALLENTINE MITCHELL
c/o ISBS, 5804 N. E. Hassalo Street
Portland, Oregon 97213-3644

Website: http://www.vmbooks.com

British Library Cataloguing in Publication Data

Gross, Natan
    Who are you, Mr Grymek. – (The Library of Holocaust
    testimonies)
    1.Holocaust, Jewish (1939–1945) – Poland – Krakow
    I.Title
    940.5'318'094386

ISBN 0-8530-3411-7
ISSN 1363-3759

Library of Congress Cataloging-in-Publication Data

Gross, Natan. 1919–
    [Mi atah, Adon Grimek? English]
    Who are you, Mr Grymek? / Natan Gross; translated by William R. Brand.
    p. cm. – (The Library of Holocaust testimonies)
    ISBN 0-85303-341-17 (pbk.)
    1. Jews–Persecutions–Poland–Krakâw. 2. Holocaust, Jewish
(1939–1945)–Poland–Krakâw–Personal narratives. 3. Gross, Natan, 1919– 4.
Krakâw (Poland)–Ethnic relations. I. Title. II. Series.

DS135.P62 K682513 2001
940.53'18'02–dc21
                                                              00-054548

Printed in Great Britain by
MPG Books Ltd, Bodmin, Cornwall

Contents

To the memory of my parents
– to my heroic mother, who saved her
children's lives and risked her own to
rescue another mother's Polish daughter
following her to Auschwitz
– to my father, who met with his tragic
death alone, far from his beloved wife
and children, killed in the cruel liquidation
of Sarny ghetto in the East of Poland.

The Library of Holocaust Testimonies

It is greatly to the credit of Frank Cass that this series of survivors' testimonies is being published in Britain. The need for such a series has long been apparent here, where many survivors made their homes.

Since the end of the war in 1945 the terrible events of the Nazi destruction of European Jewry have cast a pall over our time. Six million Jews were murdered within a short period; the few survivors have had to carry in their memories whatever remains of the knowledge of Jewish life in more than a dozen countries, in several thousand towns, in tens of thousands of villages, and innumerable families. The precious gift to recollection has been the sole memorial for millions of people whose lives were suddenly and brutally cut off.

For many years, individual survivors have published their testimonies. But many more have been reluctant to do so, often because they could not believe that they would find a publisher for their efforts.

In my own work over the past two decades, I have been approached by many survivors who had set down their memories in writing, but who did not know how to have them published. I realized what a considerable emotional strain the writing down of such hellish memories had been. I also realized, as I read many dozens of such accounts, how important each account was, in its own way, in recouting aspects of the story that had not been told before, and adding to our understanding of the wide range of human suffering, struggle and aspiration.

With so many people and so many places involved, including many hundreds of camps, it was inevitable that the historians and students of the Holocaust should find it difficult at times to grasp the scale and range of the events. The publication of memoirs is therefore an indidspensable part of the extension of knowledge, and of public awareness of the crimes that had been committed against a whole people.

Martin Gilbert
Merton College, Oxford

Biographical Note

Natan Gross was born in November 1919 in Cracow, Poland. He studied Law and Art, attended the Polish Film Institute and has been a Film Director, Journalist, Poet and Translator. He is a member of the Film Critics Section of the Association of Israeli Journalists, the Film and TV Directors Guild, Israel and Chairman of the Publishing Committee Cracow Organization in Israel. Natan Gross has written numerous books and articles and won many awards, including the Leon Lustig prize for *Who Are You, Mr Grymek?* (Hebrew version) in 1986 and the *Echo Krakowa* newspaper's award for the best book of the year on Cracow for the Polish version of the same book in 1991. He lives in Israel.

Foreword

In one respect the Germans were unlucky in their choice of victim. The Jewish people were determined to leave a trace of their fate, at whatever cost. Feeling abandoned by God and man they were haunted by the thought that the world would not know how they lived and died. Writing made dying easier. The last entry in Chaim Kaplan's diary before his deportation to Treblinka was his anguished cry: 'If I die, what will happen to my diary?'

Primo Levi, in *The Drowned and Saved* imagines members of the SS taunting their victims: 'However this war may end, we have won this war against you. None of you will be left to bear witness and even if someone were to survive, the world will not believe him. There will perhaps be suspicion, discussions, research by the historians, but there will be no certainties, because we will destroy the evidence together with you. And even if some proof should remain and some of you survive, people will say that the events you describe are too monstrous to be believed; they will say that they are exaggerations of Allied propaganda and will believe us, who will deny everything, and not you'.

Well, things have not turned out as in this Primo Levi scenario. Because of these writers and scribblers the truth has been recorded and has become known to the world, the Germans have not denied it, and no one but a maniac or a pervert will try to deny it.

I must declare an interest. The author of this memoir is a fellow Cracovian and a life-long friend. His mother, the true heroine of this story, is de domo Scharf, her brother's first name is Szulim, the same as my father's. This cannot be a pure coincidence and, no doubt, there is here a close family relationship. But beyond the family bonds, what keeps us close together is our attachment to Crakow, our birthplace, which despite the passage of time and memories which are not all endearing remains close to our hearts.

A substantial portion of the book is devoted to Crakow. Natan Gross was born into a well-to-do family, his father an owner of large stores of china, porcelain and decorative glass, landmarks in the very centre of the city. He had a care-free childhood and youth and the detailed recollection of that time, of his parents, siblings, teachers and friends gave him faith in human nature which was not easy to maintain in the light of what has happened. Overnight that world crashed around him.

When the Germans sentenced the Jews to death, one way to escape was to pretend not to be Jewish. Not many Jews could even try to play that game convincingly – it was easier, of course, for women than for men. First to be considered were the so-called 'good looks' (in the language of the time it meant 'lack of semitic features'). Further, and of equal importance, was the manner in which one spoke Polish. Correct grammar was not enough; one's speech had to be free of the slightest trace of the 'Yiddish' accent. Now many Jews, even if they spoke Polish, grew up in homes where Yiddish was commonly spoken – and it showed. Polish is distinguished by sharp, clearly articulated vowels – Yiddish is not fussy in that respect. The Poles were very sensitive to these 'accents', as well as to the many gestures and mannerisms which they deemed specificallly Jewish. The Germans, left to themselves, could not distinguish a 'real' from a 'not real' Pole, but the local population had a very sharp eye and nose for those distinguishing marks, which became a matter of life and death.

Those who felt that they could merge with the crowd needed documents to 'prove' their non-Jewish origin, – a birth and baptismal certificate issued by church authorities, the so-called 'Aryan papers'.

The acquisition of such documents, genuine or faked, and life on the strength of such documents provides material for human stories which are heart-rending. Altogether, this phenomenon of a group of people, a section of society, trying to become invisible must be unique in history. It is only due to the survivors, eye-witnesses like Natan Gross, with his total recall and astonishing ability, many years later, to record it in minute detail that the contemporary reader can familiarise himself with those unbelievable events. It makes for difficult reading but we must not shirk from the truth about man, about ourselves and about those consummately hideous times.

Rafael F. Scharf

Preface

When I set about writing my memoirs, I intended to limit myself to the 'interesting' wartime events, offering my readers only highlights, episodes full of suspense and danger, situations with no way out, and the experiences of my extensive family during the five years of war – the Second World War with its adventures and tragedies in the cities, towns, and villages, in the ghettos and 'on Aryan papers', on both sides of the River Bug. There was material enough for a thick novel. I intended to spare my readers any gilded or idyllic descriptions of pre-war life and images from my home town. Who, in our turbulent times, has the patience for such reading? Today, readers want emotion and high tension. Naturalism, or even hyper-naturalism, are running wild in the cinema and on stage. There is no time for reading books. We have television.

Nevertheless, once I had put the majority of my material down on paper, it no longer struck me as honest to describe the fall and ruin of a house without showing what that house once looked like. And I must candidly admit that this had to do with more than readers or literature. People have grandparents and parents. They also have children and grandchildren. Therefore, even if these reminiscences were to add nothing noteworthy to history or the literature of memoirs (and I am immodest enough to feel that they do contribute something), I still think that my grandchildren deserve such a description. It is highly fashionable these days to search for roots. My grandchildren should know where they come from. I also believe that my parents, well-known and respected citizens of the city of Cracow, deserve to be remembered. If they have not 'gone down in history', that is only because they belonged to no party, took no part in public life and were not presidents, patrons, or activists. Even though they formed part of the major league of commercial Cracow, they were not active in any merchants' association. They were involved and influenced the way various matters worked out, supporting – and not only financially – a range of institutions. Yet they never sought honors, titles or chairmanships. That was not their ambition. They did not go to meetings and did not sit on boards. They had contacts with highly placed, influential personages, and they intervened in community and individual matters – but they did so behind the scenes. Professional activists took the credit for what my parents achieved.

My intention, as I went back to my childhood years to describe my mother's and father's families, the shop, and my home, neighbors, schools, friends and teachers, was to include it all in an introductory chapter before my war memoirs. Yet the subject grew, under my pen, to such dimensions that it would have constituted one-third of the book I was planning. I felt that such a proportion was improper. The childhood idyll and local color, which might be of interest to a restricted circle of readers from Cracow, contrasted starkly with the dramatic and suspenseful wartime portion of my memoirs. I decided to divide the portrait of the Cracow of my youth from the tempestuous wartime period. Thus arose this contribution to some sort of memorial composed of memoirs of Jewish Cracow. I live in the hope that such a memorial will arise.

It seems to me that the collection of the memoirs of the Jews of Cracow is more than a matter of honoring the memory of families annihilated by Nazism. It is also a matter of primary importance to the history of the city of Cracow. The Jews were an integral part of that history. It is impossible to write the history of Cracow without taking account of the great Jewish contribution to the cultural, economic and social development of the city. I think that my memoirs, too, describe an episode in that history. In them, historians may uncover some name, some figure, some element of folklore or characteristic information on the life of the Jewish middle class, the life of Jewish families in that city.

I would be happy if my notes inspired other survivors of Jewish Cracow to write down their recollections of their family homes.

Natan Gross, 2000

Acknowledgements

The author acknowledges with thanks the support received from the Irena Kozlowski Fiszel and Edmund Kon Fund, London, and thanks Mr Rafael F. Scharf, London, Mr Ben Helfgott, London, Mrs Iris Greenberg-Smith, Berkley USA, Yoram Gross, Sydney, Australia and everyone else who contributed to the publicationof this book.

Note to the English Reader

It may help the reader who is unfamiliar with Polish to know how certain letters are pronounced.

ś is pronounced *sh* as in *sure*

ć is pronounced *tch* as in Tchaikowsky

ą is pronounced *om* as in *Sombrero*

PART ONE

Such a Home it Was …

To Shulamit,
my spouse, with her origins in Grodno,
I offer these flowers from a Cracow garden
– as a keepsake

1. Introduction

A NAME OF MY OWN

My first name was of decisive significance for my life. If, instead of Natan, I had been named Jozef or Jerzy like my brothers, then I would probably not have stuck with Judaism and would not be a Jew today. Natan … introducing myself to anyone was like showing them my birth certificate with 'of the Mosaic faith' entered on it. I am an Israelite. This is the name of a Jewish prophet. There is no room for doubt … even though there was an occasion, during a film makers' ball, when the girl I happened to be dancing with asked me (there are some girls so naive as to defy belief!), 'Who was that Saint Natan, anyway?'

I did not like my first name. Not because it gave me away – that only mattered later, when I registered at the university in Cracow. Until then, I lived in the Jewish community, attending Hebrew elementary school and then Hebrew secondary school. Until the war, I had only Jewish friends. Yet I disliked the name. It bothered me somehow – perhaps because I was so deeply immersed in Polish culture. Or perhaps it was because I did not like the sound of 'Natan'. People often used the diminutive form 'Natek', which sounded like … well, it didn't sound like anything at all. Natek rhymed with *patyk*, Polish for 'stick'. The sound of two sticks knocking together. What kind of sound is that? A dull sound. Only in Israel, when the Hebrew poet Shimshon Melcer began calling me Natán with the accent properly placed on the last syllable, and in addition emphasized the final 'n' with his melodious Lwow pronunciation, did it sound like two iron bars ringing together, like the gong heralding the beginning and the end of the work day at a construction site. I am not sure that I was immediately aware of this, but when my year-and-a-half-old granddaughter began calling me 'Tatan', I was convinced of the true sound of my name. Tan-tan-tan-tan! I love the sound of that mellifluous name!

My wife sometimes calls me 'Natinka', tenderly, with the accent on the first syllable. She comes from Grodno. In those parts, all masculine first names end in 'a' – Jasha, Sasha, Grisha, Mula (from Shmuel) or Iska (from Isaac). In Grodno, people named Natan are called Sania. On what grounds? The path from Natan to Sania is short but complicated. There are two principal forms of pronounciation in the Hebrew language, Sephardic and Ashkenazy. In Sephardic, which is used in Israel, my name is Natan, but in Ashkenazy, as used by eastern European Jews when they pray, it is read as 'Nosn' (in Vilna) or 'Nusn' (in Galicia). Sania, like Munia or Lonia (from Leon), shows the Russian influence.

My mother called me Natuś (with the final letter pronounced 'sh' as in Polish), and at school I was Natek. Later, girls showed their affection by turning my name into Polish diminutive forms to suit my face or the way they felt about me. Niusia and Franka called me 'Nateczku'; for Pola I was 'Natik', for Renia I was 'Nat', and Rachela Auerbach, a writer from Lwow, addressed me as 'Panie Natasiu'. For Wilek, I was 'Natanek'. Nunek, who coyly remade his first name Edmund into 'Eddy', had a whole range of names for me, ranging from Naciu (pronounced 'Natch'), through Naścislaw, all the way to Nataniel (which is a completely different name). When I visit my brother in London, I am 'Uncle Natan'. I remember how an aunt of my mother who had a shop selling dried mushrooms on Nowy Square in Cracow used to call me Nute. She even had that name stamped in golden letters on the book she gave me on the day of my barmitzvah. Aunt Tyla, on the other hand, liked to summon me with the rhyming Yiddish ditty 'Nute–mishpute'. I have asked the eminent folklorist Dr Dow Sadan, who comes from Brody, to explain this rhyme, but he was familiar with a different version. In his hometown, people chanted 'Nute hot harute' (Nute has regrets), while 'Nute–mishpute' would have meant something along the lines of 'Nute, king of galoshes'. In any case, Nute is *de facto* a completely different name. The son of the Nute who shined the poet Tuwim's shoes in Lodz was no son of Natan.

In Hebrew, Natan means 'gift' or 'given' (the Latin Donatus!). Nuta (in Sephardic: nata) means 'grafted' or 'engrafted'. The names Natan and Nata (or Nusn and Nuta) often form a pair and are given to children born on Shavuot, the day when God gave ('natan') the Torah to the people of Israel, or at Sukkoth (the Feast of Booths), which culminates in Simchat Torah (the Joy of the Torah). This is the day when the yearly cycle of Torah readings in the synagogue ends and a new cycle begins. Before beginning each chapter, the man called to read the Torah recites a short

4

prayer: 'Blessed be Thou, God, Lord of the world, Who hast given ('natan') us the teachings ('Torah') of the truth and engrafted ('nata') in us eternal life'. The combination of the words 'natan' – 'nata' was made into a first name. This was the name of the great Cracow cabbalist Natan Nata Spiro, 'The Discoverer of the Depths', as he was called eponymously after the title of his works.

I was not born on Shavuot or Simchat Torah, but rather inherited the name Natan from my mother's brother. He had died at 16. As my parents' first child, I was given this name in order to perpetuate his memory. This is a Jewish custom. Children are named after deceased grandfathers and grandmothers or relatives, and sometimes in honor of heroes, great rabbis, or dear friends. The custom was passed down from time immemorial, but not from biblical times.

In biblical times, a child was named according to some sign accompanying the birth. Isaac's name came from the fact that his mother Sara laughed at the news that she was going to have a child at her advanced age (80); Esau's from the fact that he was born covered with hair; Jacob's because he was born clutching his twin brother Esau by the heel ('Yaakov' – 'akev', Hebrew for heel), and so on and so forth. Throughout the Bible, which consists of more than a dozen books containing long lists of names in the genealogical trees of the generations, it is hard to find a name that recurs. The tradition of passing names down from one generation to the next developed afterwards, when the Jews were dispersed throughout the world. My son is named Jacob after my father, and my daughter Aliza after my wife's mother. However, my children never knew their grandparents. They gave their children newly invented Hebrew names that are not found in the Bible: Maoz (fortress), Peled (steel), Sheli (mine) and Hili (she belongs to me). Aliza's oldest son is named Achi (my brother), in memory of her husband's brother, a splendid 18-year-old boy, a soldier in an armored unit, who fell in the Sinai. His name was Yaakov. In order to avoid making the child 'unlucky' through this venerable biblical name, they called him Achi (which is, nevertheless, a biblical name itself – Benjamin named his son Achi in memory of his own deceased brother Joseph!).

It is now the fashion in Israel to invent 'original' names that follow the poor child for the rest of his or her life … And the worst thing is that these names generally have no past, and will therefore have no great influence on their bearers. My name has a past; it has a literature. Although there was a time when I did not like the name, I learned to bear it with dignity, if not with pride. The idea of changing it never crossed my mind. In those pre-war times, changing one's name was not such a simple matter. In moral terms, I mean, not technical. People who bore the name Mojzesz or Mendel might ask to be called Marcel, Marek or Mundek, but the name written in their documents, in their identity cards, was still Mojzesz.

Gross is a very popular surname. 'Grosses by the gross', as mama used to say. That is the answer that I give when asked, 'which Grosses?' Sometimes, if someone is from Cracow, I say, 'the Grosses in china'. Then they know: 'Jakub Gross, China, Crystal, Glass and Lamps' was a firm on the Main Square in Cracow. Everyone in Cracow knew it ... There were so many well-known Grosses from Cracow: the physician Ludwik Gross, and the prominent socialist Adolf Gross. There were painters: one French (Antoine) and the other German (Georg). Today in Israel, when I say that my name is Gross, people take me for a Hungarian. There were even more Grosses in Hungary than there used to be in Poland! It is simply a standard name from the series of adjectives: Gross, Klein, Breit, Kurz, Lang. Until the nineteenth century, Jews did not have surnames. Not all of them, at least ... There were some who had surnames and others who, being affiliated with some sort of landowner or count, were identified according to that affiliation: Mojsie Potocki, Szyja Zamojski. Others were identified by the names of one of their parents: Berek son of Josel, or Berek Joselewicz. Berek's son, who was named Jozef after his grandfather, bore the surname Berkowicz. Surnames derived from Yiddish first names were polonized in Wielkopolska. In Lithuania, they took a purely Yiddish form: Chajes means son of Chaja, Ryfczes is the son of Ryfka, and Surkis is the son of Sura. Where Russian influences were stronger, the endings were also Russian: Malkin (son of Malka), Frumkin (son of Fruma), Chajkin, Dworkin – all based on the name of the mother, not the father.

In Germany, it was Frederick the Great who ordered that all Jews be given surnames. His court adviser, the great poet E. T. A. Hoffman, was responsible. At first, he thought up the names personally, and they were very poetic: Rosengarten, Rosenkranz, Rosenblum ... nothing but roses. However, Hoffman soon designated local officials to take over the work. They did not put themselves to so much trouble. They sometimes accepted suggestions from the interested parties standing in line, sometimes thought up something based on their 'first impression' of a given person, and sometimes followed a series. Colors, for instance: Weiss, Braun, Schwarz, Roth, Grün, Gelb, Blau, or even shades of colors, like Dunkelblau or Himmelblau – thousands of such names! Sooner or later, all other states followed Frederick the Great's example. The Jews of Galicia obtained their names under Austrian rule, which explains the prevalence of German names in Poland.

At this point, I recall a familiar Jewish anecdote. A certain merchant was setting off to register a surname for himself at city hall. His wife admonished him: 'Just make sure you get me something nice!' When he returned, she was waiting anxiously at the door: 'So, what is our name?'

'Schnitter', he replied, crestfallen.

'What kind of a name is that? Couldn't you think up anything better?'

'Stop complaining, Sara. That 'n' in the middle cost me a fortune!'

Short and inelastic, Gross is a very unexceptional surname. It might sound strange, but I must say that I have suffered from this name in a certain sense. It is somehow solid – and I am not thinking of its meaning. My friends had surnames that could be changed easily into something that became a nickname. If someone was named Peterseil, he was called Pecio; someone named Pinkas became Pikuś; Wiesenfeld became Wiśka. There was a tendency to shorten surnames, but nothing could be shorter than Gross. Many of the boys in my class had nicknames: this one was Gorilla and that one King Kong, one was Plague and another Siberia (from the Polish, *sila bez rozum* – strength without common sense), or Fountain, or Batty. To me, no nickname stuck. I felt disadvantaged. Such a clanging, inelegant name and surname, devoid of fantasy. Immediately after the war, Nunek – who could never forgive me for the fact that we had attended kindergarten together, since he thought that this fact made it impossible for me to appreciate his talents as a composer – called me alternatively either 'Natano Grosso' or 'von und zu Gross', but no one had ever given me a nickname during our school days. This resulted in such a complex that a joined a university fraternity solely in order to get a *kneipname*, the nickname given to every pledge. Imagine my disappointment when I was invited to choose my own *kneipname*! That wasn't why I had joined. The fraternity featured a 'Zbik' (Polish for wildcat – he had been Gorilla at school), a Diva (whose uncle ran a cabaret), a Simon (who was in love with the actress Simone Simon), and a Lopek (who had a big nose). They pondered and pondered and finally gave me the Latin name Ridens, meaning 'laughing', because I supposedly had a highly developed sense of humor. I knew how to laugh in those days. At myself, as well, but mostly at others. Today, I seldom laugh. Later, I used that Ridens as one of my pen names; I had several – Geen, F. Enge, Negro, Hagrizi, but that was after the war …

My surname seemed meaningless to me, which made me all the more determined to seek models among historical characters who had borne the same first name. The prophet Natan – this hermit had been a man of spotless reputation who lived modestly and feared no one except the Lord. He gave King David a very hard time. David was a prodigious sinner, which did not prevent him from being a great poet and a great king. And Natan crushed him. He cursed and threatened, raged, and thundered until poor David was humbled to the point that he began writing imploring psalms. These psalms turned out to be pearls of poetry, so the final effect was positive. I, however, did not like and was even repelled by the fanaticism of the prophet. I had no choice but to turn to Nathan the Wise. 'Natan der Weise' was a robust, likeable old man who knew that he knew nothing. Even if he knew more than others, he preferred to take no notice of the fact, since not all knowledge produces peace and love – and the only thing that Nathan the Wise wanted among people of different races, religions and nationalities was love. Love, and leaving each other in peace. By the time I was old enough for philosophy, just as the Second World War was breaking out, I wanted to be a wise man, a Nathan the Wise. That sounds pretentious, doesn't it? What did it mean? I surrounded myself with books and practiced a stoical indifference to the storms raging around me. I tried to put my ideas into practice (anyone who wants to go on living should avoid doing this!), and people clung to me.

I graduated from a *gimnazjum*, a secondary school, that imbued in me the spirit of humanism, broadly conceived: a faith in humankind. With that faith, I went to war against Hitler. My faith never wavered during the time of contempt. It permitted me to endure every horror and emerge with a healthy soul. I created my own philosophy in those days. Today I am aware that it requires revision. With today's eyes – experienced eyes – I see things differently. Back then, I believed that the world was built on love, and that love was a basic human characteristic. Today, I only stick to this philosophy out of inertia. I simply have neither the time nor the strength to think things out again from the beginning, so I will probably die in my beliefs. I was Nathan the Wise despite the war and despite all the horrors happening around me. Or perhaps because of them. I was able to keep people's spirits up. I was able to speak to them about a beautiful world, about art, literature and philosophy, and I could help them to escape, even briefly, from a terrifying reality. I believed that this helped them to endure in the faith that good always vanquishes evil. That was what they had taught us at school. And then my world suddenly came crashing down. The dreadful news arrived that Jews were being asphyxiated in gas chambers in Chelmno. My mother's healthy instincts had prompted her to furnish the whole family with Aryan papers, Christian birth certificates and identity cards. The official who supplied us with those documents at a high price filled them in by hand according to authentic entries in the registry office, where he worked. He did not put himself to much effort or thought in copying the certificates. Or perhaps he did it maliciously, with premeditation. It later turned out that he hunted down the people for whom he had produced identity cards – or the people who were sheltering them – in order to blackmail them and rob them of everything. Only later, however, did I become aware of this. I was disenchanted and enraged on first reading my new name and surname: Franciszek Grymek, journeyman cobbler – *Schustergeselle* – born in Czulice, 1910 – in other words, ten years older than me! I was supposed to embark on a new, Christian life among the Poles with such a document. If I had ever had any sort of complex on account of my Jewish name and unremarkable surname, then this new Polish identity made things a hundred times worse. Franciszek Grymek – talk about a proletarian name! A journeyman cobbler – and where was that Czulice, anyway? At least it was in Cracow province.[1] Those ten additional years were the final straw.

I had to change my face and my occupation. I grew a drooping mustache and decided to learn the shoemaker's craft. Yet no matter how many times I tried to draw needle through shoe leather, the white hands of the intellectual betrayed me. No. I was definitely

9

not cut out to be a cobbler. Yet I could not afford to change identity cards, and so, like it or not, I remained Franciszek Grymek.

The name Franciszek did not much appeal to me – what a wild sound, a disorder of hard and soft consonants. As for the nicknames Franek and Franuś … these homely names whistled like organ music through bad teeth … (I am not sure where that association comes from, but it seemed apt). As little as I liked the name, I began searching through the Catholic calendar to find out when my saint's day fell. I found three or four of them: Francis à Paulo, Francis de Sales … and, of course, I chose Francis of Assisi. Hagiography had never been my strong point, but I had read *The Little Flowers of St Francis*. Saint Francis was a poet who preached sermons to the birds! Furthermore, he gave everything he possessed to the poor and set out barefoot in search of God and the Truth. This was a figure after my own heart, and I decided to be Brother Francis. I did not, of course, tell this to anyone. Nevertheless, I embodied myself in the figure of a saint who was more a product of my imagination than of anything I really knew. To a degree, this was an extension of Nathan the Wise, operating among the little ones. I was then living (in the spring of 1943) among the lumpenproletariat on Ciasna Street in the Old Town in Warsaw. I had a great deal of feeling for these poor people. I taught them things and told them tales and parables. They felt good with me. I know that they felt good.

I became good friends with the renowned geographer, Professor Wuttke. He never called me anything except 'Brother Franciszek'.

'Brother Franciszek, I spent ten days with the Ursuline Sisters in Lublin. They spoke about you each evening and we prayed for you.'

Did he know that I was a Jew? He never mentioned it. We read Norwid aloud and analyzed the poems of Leśmian …

As in Cracow, so also in Warsaw, and later in Otwock, people clung to me. Even though they soon became convinced that I was a Jew, they did not desert me. There was no falsehood in me. I behaved in such a way that, should my Jewish background become known, no one would ever be able to accuse me of deceit: I never avoided talking about the Jews, and always took the Jewish side. At times, these were acrid discussions.

I therefore came to terms with 'Franciszek'. With 'Grymek', things were worse. I could not swallow that name. What is a *grymek*? A small *grym*, of course. But what is a *grym*? I did not have Brückner or

10

any other Polish dictionary at hand, and I was depressed and enraged by the fact that I bore a name that meant nothing to me. Only on the day the war ended – 8 May 1945 – when I was on my way from Otwock to Cracow and had stopped in a village near Radomsko, did I hear the word 'grymek' for the first time, as something other than my name … I spent the night in a barn, and when I went outside in the early morning to enjoy the sunrise, shake the straw out of my trousers, and sigh longingly for the coming freedom, I overheard two peasants sharing their impressions from the previous day's market. 'And I bought three *grymeks* and a dress for the old lady … ' I was dumfounded. A moment later, I began delicately quizzing the mustached peasant about those *grymeks*. He did not understand what I wanted from him. To buy the *grymeks*? He wasn't going to sell them. Finally, whether he understood me or not, he pointed to the nearby dovecote, where the *krymeks* – Crimean pigeons (or so I interpreted it) – were going industriously about their morning toilet and breakfast, cooing merrily.

The *krymki–grymki* were harbingers of peace for me. Oh, if only I had known two years earlier! I would have felt so much better.

As soon as the Red Army entered Otwock, followed by the Polish Army, I decided on an immediate return to my old name. Perhaps, had I been called Zieliński, Staniszewski, Sawicki or something of that sort, I would not have been in such a hurry to go back to Gross. Perhaps, like many 'Aryans', I would never have returned to Jewishness at all. When I announced to the provisional authorities in Otwock that I was a Jew and intended to return to my own name, they unexpectedly objected. They said that it was dangerous, that there was no need to hurry, and that I should continue to call myself Grymek for the time being. On returning to Cracow immediately after the end of the war, I was again Natan Gross (although I entered an oratorical contest under the name Wiśniewski and won first prize, only to 'drop out of sight'). I enrolled in the Film School as Natan Gross and, as Natan Gross, was second assistant director to Stanislaw Wohl on the feature film *Two Hours*. The credits for that film consisted of nothing but non-Polish-sounding names: Wohl, Szancer, Hechtkopf, Gross. Even where we had the most authentic of non-Jews, he too bore a non-Polish name: Wojtek Has. Like me, he was an apprentice second assistant director … Only our initials appeared instead of our first names: N. Gross, W. Has. Sensing a certain consternation at such a foul assembly of names (*nomina sunt odiosa!*), I decided to 'sacrifice myself'.

I declared to the others: 'I'm not particular about my name. Being second assistant director is no great honor, and I can see that something is bothering you. You can put me down as "F. Grymek".'

My offer was accepted with satisfaction. A quarter of an hour later, there was a phone call from the office: 'Does the F stand for Florian?'

'No. Franciszek. Nice, huh?'

Everyone's first name thus appeared in the opening credits: Stanislaw, Wojciech, Henryk – and Franciszek Grymek.

When I arrived in Israel in 1950 and went to the *ulpan*, the special language course for immigrants, a renaming operation was underway. My teacher, the gray-haired Itzak Livni, gave everyone a Hebrew surname. He attempted to maintain the greatest phonetic resemblance to the original. Thus Efraim Kishon, the outstanding humorist who emigrated from Hungary as Kisont, obtained a new name that is known all over the world today. I waited patiently for my turn, but the weeks passed and Mr Livni never came forward with a proposition. Finally, I went to him to complain: 'What about me? Haven't you got a name for me?'

'Wait a while, and we'll think of something …'

Two weeks later, I confronted him again. He reflected for a moment, and then said, 'You don't need to change your name. You already have a Hebrew name.'

'What?'

'That's right. *Gross* means to interpret, to state, to think. "*Gros lecha et girsatcha, ani gores she gros ze shem ivri*"'(Think what you like, but I state that Gross is a Hebrew name.)

And so I never managed to escape from my surname. Instead, I have passed it on to my children and grandchildren – but with a new significance. I always emphasize that: names and surnames have importance. They can have significance – they need to be borne in such a way that they make sense.

NOTE

1 Only some 40 years later, in Israel, did my friend Dr Józef Haubenstock inform me that part of his family sprang from Czulice, which was known for producing the best butter in the region. That butter could be had in Cracow at Macherski's (run by the father of Cardinal), Allerhands, Ogorzaty and 'Bar pod poczty' – a restaurant run by Haubenstock's father.

2. Having Been Born in Cracow

Everyone loves their home city or hometown, from beloved Belz to 'Warsaw, my Warsaw'. So why shouldn't I love my Cracow? Is it possible, at all, to fail to love Cracow? Even the blue River Vistula fell in love with Cracow at first sight, and wrapped itself around the city like a ribbon as a proof of love. Note well how the motive of the ribbon recurs: 'And everything was striped as if with a ribbon among the green ...'

Aside from the blue ribbon of the Vistula, Cracow has a border of green, planted not with pear trees but with chestnuts, growing densely. The 'Planty' – the circular park around the old town of Cracow – the chestnuts of Cracow. My childhood and my youth were somewhat gloomy, somewhat silly, and somewhat exalted. To this day I can hear the way the bombs of the chestnuts exploded in the autumn, and my eyes still seek out the gleaming veneer of those brown nuts with the pale patches on them. The chestnuts were like eyes looking out from their thorny nests. Those chestnuts were collected and threaded like corals in long chains to adorn the booths at the holiday of Sukkoth, or used in children's home-made billiard games. Little girls made them into furniture for their doll houses.

The autumnal chestnuts on the Planty strewed a rusty carpet on the walkways. The chestnut trees in springtime, all white and green, brimmed handsomely with joy and hope. Since my childhood, the Planty have led me towards Wawel. Before my young feet first buffed the royal chambers in the felt protective covers that one had to pull over one's shoes at the entrance, before I mused over the monuments to fame in the cathedral with all the enthusiasm of a young Cracovian, before the mighty tolling of the Zygmunt bell had anything to say to me – before all of that, I had already shed many a tear over the fate of Wanda, who had not wanted to marry a German or any other foreigner. When I walked with my nanny near the Dragon's Cave, my little heart hammered at the thought of the dragon who lived there after arriving from parts unknown. Had he come from Greece? From Asia Minor?

Perhaps some Perseus had driven him out of Asia Minor? The dragons from those parts had a taste for breakfasts of lovely young maidens. What a terrifying tale for the imagination of a poet or a small child! To go back to Wanda: the pride of those female Cracovians! They spurned the wooing even of kings who came with six pair of horses; the girl who gathered leaves beneath the linden tree preferred to offer her fair neck to the executioner, rather than give herself to an unloved king. Even the angels had wept when her head was cut off, so how was I supposed to forebear from crying over her fate? Yet Esterka, for example, obviously came from the Kazimierz district, rather than Cracow. As an adherent of the faith of the Old Testament, she must have had religious scruples. Still, she did not run to drown herself in the Vistula, and she enjoyed herself with King Kazimierz – who had a tender spot for feminine charms.

Here, my Wawel crosses paths with the Old Synagogue, the legends of royal Cracow with the legends of Jewish Kazimierz. I listened to them as I strolled with my father along Waska and Szeroka Streets during the Yom Kippur fast, on the way to visit the little cemetery of the great Remuh.

The two shops belonging to my father Jakub Gross on either side of the Main Square were closed on Yom Kippur, although they stayed open Saturdays – for my father, this must undoubtedly have represented a certain betrayal of the traditions of his devout parents. Yet, as he said, he could not afford to limit himself to a five-day trading week. While the Jewish merchants in Kazimierz kept their shops shut Saturdays, customers could enter on Sundays 'through the back door'. The police, those guardians of the law, hardly turned a blind eye! On Sundays, lookouts stood on every intersection along Krakowska Street. When a policeman came in sight, the word was relayed: '*zeks, zeks*'. Customers in the shop had to hold their breath until the danger passed, and then the normal Cracow bargaining resumed.

Such maneuvers were unthinkable on the Main Square, at least in Jakub Gross's prestigious shops with their two display windows. That is why his firm was closed Sundays and open Saturdays. On the Jewish high holy days, however – Rosh Hoshana, Yom Kippur and the first day of Passover – the shop stayed shut. We went with father to the Tempel, the progressive synagogue on Miodowa Street, where we listened in an exalted

14

mood to the golden-tongued orator Ozjasz Thon, who sometimes wove political themes among his religious preaching and admonitions, pointing towards Zion as the solution of the Jewish question. 'They do not hate us for our faults, but for our virtues!,' he thundered from the pulpit. He was a member of parliament and spoke beautiful Polish – as did the majority of Cracow Jews, even those with beards and side locks. When Dr Thon mounted the pulpit after the last notes of the choir faded away and after the *Kol Nidre* prayer, a thrill ran up the spines of the faithful who had come here to cast off the sins and blame of the year past. In silence, he looked for a long moment around the congregation packed into the chamber. Then he adjusted his fringed garment and began softly: 'My pious friends ...' He immediately cast out some rhetorical question or quotation from the liturgy as if he had been ruminating over it. He raised his voice slowly, developing his theme, and soon he reached the high tones of exhilaration as he cast wrathful accusations on the denouncers of Israel. Like a prophet, he rained thunderbolts down on the enemy – and also on the Jewish aristocracy, the gentlemen in top hats who came to the Tempel once a year to hear the *Kol Nidre* – assimilation in frock coats, he said. Doctor Thon's sermons were the main attraction. They were listened to in openmouthed enthrallment and then quoted and discussed at length in Jewish homes afterward. Finally, they appeared the following day in *Nowy Dziennik*, the newspaper read by every respectable Jewish family in Cracow.

As a member of the Polish *Sejm*, or parliament, Dr Thon was a dignified representative of Polish Jewry and the interests of the national minorities. Liked and respected, he fought uncompromisingly for the constitutionally guaranteed equality of all citizens, which was knocked out of equilibrium when the influence of antisemitic elements grew. Thon's sharp tongue was famous; various anecdotes circulated about his cutting rejoinders. People told about how the National Democrat member of parliament, Father Zongolowski, had invited Thon to the buffet in the parliament building and offered him a ham sandwich.

'Is it possible', Thon inquired civilly, 'that the Reverend Father is unaware that we Jews may not eat ham?'

'Too bad', Father Zongolowski replied with false sympathy. 'It's so good.'

'Well, please give my warmest regards to your wife!'

'Isn't the Honorable Member aware that priests are not allowed to marry?'

Thon spread his hands: 'Too bad. It's so good!'

*

Father fasted on Yom Kippur and so did I – even though mother tempted me to sin. To avoid being led into temptation, I did not return home during the afternoon break in the Yom Kippur prayers. Instead, father and I made a walking tour of the prayer houses of Kazimierz. Yom Kippur falls in mid- or late September, and there was always fine, sunny weather. The golden Polish autumn trailed falling leaves, the sadness of the dying summer, through the Jewish streets. There was neither sight nor sound of any buggy, cart, or automobile. In their glistening coats, with their prayer garments draped over their arms, the Jews stood in the doorways of the Wysoka or Kupa prayer houses, hurried home to rest before the afternoon prayers that closed the holiday, or stood taking in the courtyard of the Remuh synagogue.

Father and I looked in on the beautiful frescoes of the Popper-Bocian prayer house, and on the Old Synagogue that had sunk a meter below the level of the square. On those walks, I heard the legends that clung to the stones. I shall write a few of them down here, for there is no one left to pass them in spoken form, from father to son.

There were legends and religious traditions native to Cracow, and others borrowed or adapted to local realities. The tradition of the Old Synagogue, the most ancient Polish prayer house still standing, is strangely interwoven with the tradition of the *hejnal*, the trumpet call played from the tower of the Church of the Blessed Virgin Mary.

A fireman played that *hejnal* from the windows of the higher of the two towers each hour, and at 12 noon it was broadcast throughout Poland by radio – as it still is today. The trumpeter could be seen from my parents' bedroom window and from the kitchen balcony. Repeated four times, the *hejnal* carried across the city. The trumpeter indulged in minor variations and trills from time to time, and sometimes played a whole recital, the *majowka*, during the month of May. I enjoyed those concerts very much, and sometimes leaned from the balcony on a cold May morning with my gaze fixed on the golden trumpet flashing in the rays of the rising sun. The chestnuts all around were in blossom and the Ursuline sisters in their garden next door were tending their pears and plums. The air was clean and fragrant, and the pristine melody graced the soul with a sort of angelic sweetness ...

Everyone knows that the *hejnal* ends with an interrupted note in commemoration of the Tatar invasion: an arrow from a Tatar bow pierced the watchman's heart straight through.

This legend has its counterpart in the tradition of the Old Synagogue.

On Simchat Torah (The Joy of the Torah) – the last day of the feast of Sukkoth, the Jews joyously and ceremoniously read out the final chapter of the Bible and begin reading it from the start: 'In the beginning, God created the heaven and the earth.' They dance and sing. Traditionally, all those at prayer join in dancing a circle around the prayer house with the Torah in their arms. There are seven such circles – *hakafoth*. In only one prayer house in the world, in the Old Synagogue of Cracow, do the people suddenly break off the waves of joy and celebration in the middle of the fourth circle and begin reading the Psalms. This tradition is associated with a tragic event. The Tatars burst into the synagogue in the middle of the fourth circle and slaughtered all those at prayer. Historians state that the Old Synagogue was built on this site in 1356 (having stood previously in the place now occupied by St Anne's Church), so there is a chronological problem with the 1341 Tatar invasion. Yet there can be no doubt that the massacre of the Jews at prayer is a historical fact.

Today, three-and-a-half circles are no longer danced around the Old Synagogue on Simchat Torah. There are no *hakafoth*. The Old Synagogue has been turned into a museum.

An interesting history and numerous legends are linked with the Ajzyk prayer house – *B'Ajzyk Shul*, as the Jews of Cracow used to call it. It was built by Reb Ajzyk Jekeles, Ajzyk son of Jakub, a rich banker who wielded enormous influence at the court of King Wladyslaw IV. The Catholic clergy firmly opposed, and repeatedly blocked, the construction of synagogues. Nevertheless, Ajzyk managed over six years (1638–44) to erect a beautiful Baroque edifice and to furnish it richly with silver and golden crowns, 'pomegranates', artfully embroidered *rodal* covers, and other treasures that constituted a grain of salt in the eyes of the mob that was hostile to the Jews. Various gangs tried repeatedly to force their way into the synagogue, but its treasures were well guarded against the rabble. The Jewish district of Kazimierz was surrounded by a high wall and the gates were closed at dusk. Easier access could, however, be had from the cemetery side, where low walls bounded the Jewish city to the east.

Before the grand inauguration of Reb Ajzyk's prayer house, word indeed reached the Jews that the organized riffraff intended to plunder the new synagogue that night. The attackers intended to come through the cemetery. Dread seized the residents of Kazimierz. They were helpless and defenseless. Word of the planned assault also reached the ears of Reb Ajzyk. He immediately made his way to the Head Rabbi of the community, Rabbi Yom-Tov Heller, a great scholar in the Scriptures. An hour later, Ajzyk emerged with a plan of his own.

That night, the Jews barred the doors of their households and peered out through cracks in the shutters. When the bell in the nearby church struck midnight, drunken voices, laughter and ribald songs could be heard in the distance. The merry band was lighting its way toward the cemetery with several lanterns. When the mirthful company was approaching the wall of the Jewish district, 'spirits of the dead', all in white, sprang up from behind the tombstones and, brandishing thick clubs and raising infernal screams, rushed towards the intruders. The trespassers turned on their heels and took flight, convinced that the dead had risen from their graves. The 'spirits' were *yeshiva* students; they had wrapped themselves in sheets and hidden among the gravestones on the rabbi's advice. From that time on, there were many years of peace in the Jewish streets, and no further attempts to loot Reb Ajzyk's synagogue.

Today, the beautiful prayer house is a ghastly ruin. The remnants of those who prayed there, those who survived Hitler and his death camps, are scattered throughout the world. They remember the beautiful liturgical melodies of Lejzerka Goldenberg, who conducted the synagogue choir here.

Another version of this defensive operation is extant. It holds that, on Rabbi Heller's advice, the *yeshiva* students stood in a row behind the cemetery wall; at the appropriate moment, as the attackers approached, they lighted candles. In the misty winter night, the effect was uncanny. The drunken band fled, and the candles glimmering in the fog formed the basis for a new Hanukkah legend.

How had Reb Ajzyk accumulated such a great fortune and such exceptional respect? He was indeed the son of the wealthy merchant Reb Jekele, known as Jakub the Rich. But Reb Ajzyk exceeded his father in fame, affluence, and standing – for 40 years, he headed the Jewish Community of Cracow. It seems that, when he was taking his first independent steps as a young merchant, he had an eerie dream about a treasure buried beneath a bridge in the distant city of Prague. Man should trust in God, not dreams. But when that treasure appeared in his dreams a second and a third night, Ajzyk provisioned himself for the journey, heaved a sack over his shoulder, took up a shovel and set out for Prague. After the torments of a long journey he found himself at last under the bridge across the Vltava and began his search. He dug here, he dug there, until he was noticed several hours later by the city watchman. The watchman inquired threateningly about what he was looking for under the bridge. Frightened, Reb Ajzyk decided to tell the whole truth. He recounted his dream.

The gentile smiled and said: 'Silly Jew! What if I told you that I dreamed that a certain Jew in Cracow found a treasure in his kitchen stove? What then? Would I leave my home and set out on a long journey because of this dream?'

Reb Ajzyk listened to his words, thought for a moment, and then set out on the journey home. On his return, he pried loose a tile in his kitchen stove, and his eyes beheld a pot full of golden *denar* coins! Thus do many seek happiness and riches in distant lands, unaware that these lie close at hand in their own homes.

Father and I often visited the little cemetery next to the prayer house of Remuh – Rabbi Moshe Isserles, a great Scripture scholar. His father, banker to King Zygmunt August, built him this prayer house in 1553 so that he could devote himself without a care to study and prayer. Remuh died on the holiday of Lag Ba'omer and pilgrims came to his grave on that day from all over Poland – no, from all over the world. To this day, *hasidim* from America visit the grave of Remuh to tuck letters, asking for solutions to their greatest problems, in the cracks of the gravestone.

Before the war, 47 gravestones were known in that cemetery, as described by the historian Balaban: the graves of great rabbis, physicians, leaders of the community and aristocratic families.

During the war, the cemetery was devastated. The broken gravestones were used as paving stones on the roads. By coincidence – or could it have been a miracle? – Remuh's family grave survived.

When the JOINT representative in Poland, Dr Akiba Kahane, a Cracovian himself, visited the city in the 1960s, he was surprised to find himself invited by Jewish community chairman Maciej Jakubowicz to a meeting with the veteran socialist, Boleslaw Drobner. Little aside from his family background linked Drobner to the Jewish community. In his declining years, however, and following the Great Tragedy of the destruction of the Jewish people, what had been dammed up for so many years in Drobner's heart finally overflowed. He waited for Akiba Kahane in the small Remuh cemetery on a drizzly November afternoon. Drobner himself had chosen their meeting place.

'Dear sir', said the old socialist, worn down by life, 'if something is not done in the nearest future to save this hallowed place, then in a month or two a playground and a kindergarten will be built here.'

Yet Drobner could not say what should be done. Perhaps a few gravestones could be brought from the cemetery on Miodowa Street, he mused. Then the City Council would have to treat the location as a religious site. As Drobner, Kahane and Jakubowicz paced the muddy grounds, they noticed a bulge in the earth. They wondered if digging in one place or another might not lead to the uncovering of some sort of ancient remains ... Thus, in an instant, the idea was born of organizing an archaeological excavation. Kahane assented immediately and pledged two million dollars' worth of financial backing.

The work soon began with the help of JOINT, the Religious Congregation, and the Cracow city government. It led to a sensational discovery. More than 800 sixteenth- and seventeenth-century memorials emerged, including the gravestones of famous rabbis and physicians to the royal court who had been summoned from Italy by the Polish kings. Most of the markers featured rare, striking Renaissance and Baroque ornamentation. The archaeologists were surprised to discover memorials in the form of sarcophagi, known from western and central Europe but not in the east, where upright *stele* markers predominated. One theory, not yet conclusively proven, holds that a thick layer of soil was laid down over most of the cemetery to protect the graves from devastation and profanation during the period of the Swedish invasions – and that the existence of the old graves buried underneath had later been simply forgotten.

Each stone in the small pre-war cemetery had a tale to tell and contained a fragment of the history of Jewish Cracow. A tourist attraction today, the restored Remuh cemetery holds many mysteries in its inscriptions. Historians will spend many more years connecting all those inscriptions to concrete events.

As a small boy, I was touched by the story of a great rabbi who was buried next to the fence, in a place usually reserved for suicides, sinners, and others unworthy of respect. This is the grave of Rabbi Jehoszua ben Josef (1590–1648), the author of *Megina Shlomo (The Shield of Solomon)*. I was surprised to find a story about him in *Beyond the Wall* by Shay Agnon, the Nobel Prize laureate. Here is what the legend says:

A wealthy but terribly miserly Jew lived in Cracow. He was in the habit of driving away poor people who asked him for assistance. He sent away empty-handed every *yeshiva* delegate who came collecting contributions for the school. People held the miser in contempt and hated him for his hard-heartedness. One day, the rich miser died. No one mourned him. Some even wondered how to preserve his notoriety. They turned for advice to Rabbi Jehoszua ben Josef. He thought for a short time and declared that there was no place for the miser among respectable citizens, and that he should therefore be buried next to the fence, among the beggars. And so he was interred shamefully, to the bitter disgrace of his relatives.

In that same district lived a respected Jew whose heart and purse were always open to those in need of assistance. No poor man ever left his home without sating his hunger and being given something for the road. The respected Jew supported the *yeshivot* and synagogues; everyone loved him and praised the magnanimity of his heart.

After the death of the wealthy miser, poor people appeared as usual at the home of the charitable man to ask for assistance. This man who had been known for long years for his generosity suddenly sent them away empty-handed.

'I have no money left', he explained.

People grew concerned and began collecting donations all over town for the charitable man who had lost his fortune – but he refused to accept the sum.

'The money that I distributed to the poor, the orphans, and people in need did not belong to me', he said. 'I received it from the man whom you buried near the fence … He extracted an oath from me that I would not betray even a word of what I knew about his good deeds.'

These were thus nameless donations, anonymous contributions – the highest virtue known to Jewish ethics. When Rabbi Jehoszua ben Josef heard about this, he sank into profound dejection, and harsh remorse tore at his heart. In his will, he ordered himself to be buried next to the man who had never revealed his good deeds; it would, after all, be a great honor for the rabbi to lie at the fence, next to the Righteous One.

*

I became aware of many of the traditions of Jewish Cracow – which was one of the most important cultural centers of European Jewry – only when those traditions were lost irretrievably. To tell the truth, even though I went to Hebrew school and grew up among Jews, the Yiddish language grated on my ears. To put it delicately, I did not approve of the traditional garb of the Jews of Kazimierz: the *kapot* coat, the yarmulke, and the *shtraimel* – the cap of fox fur copied centuries before from the bourgeoisie. This disaffection for 'Kazimierz Jews' – however similar they may have been to my own grandparents, whom in any case I respected (I saw them too seldom to be attached to them, to speak of them with love) – was also due to my rather scant interest in the history of the Jews of Cracow. Only after the war – haphazardly, but lovingly – did I fill in my knowledge about the status of my city, the 'Jerusalem of Galicia', in the history of the Jews. I have no intention of loading down my personal recollections with the ballast of history. This has already been done by Professor Majer Balaban and other Jewish scholars. I prefer to tell about the Cracow that I knew and loved, about the people with whom I strolled the walkways of the Planty and the streets of the city. When I write about them, it will be like writing about a Cracow diaspora. Will their names mean anything to my readers? To the older generation of Cracovians, perhaps yes. These may not be people of the stature or from the circles of those immortalized by 'Boy', yet these too are a part of Cracow and its history – like the stones from which Wawel Castle is built.

I sometimes peruse the recollections of various more or less known Cracow memoirists, sometimes literary figures and sometimes not, and I have come across many a name that means nothing to me. These are the memoirs of people who lived above all within the Polish community. They could hardly, of course, fail to notice the 60,000 Jews of Cracow, some of whom were an integral part of the city landscape. In these memoirs, we thus encounter the booksellers and antiquaries, the Taffets, Seidens and Himmelblaus, in proportion to the role they played in the social life and interests of one memoirist or another. I read and re-read these memoirs in search of some trace of my own youth in the two decades between the World Wars – and am surprised to find none of the 'institutions' that are unforgettable *to me.*

Quarts of ink have been consumed on the subject of the Hawelka restaurant – and rightly so, for that was almost a historical institution among the landowning and literary classes. I myself went there for the *maczanka* – steak sandwiches in delicious gravy. My father's shop was nearby, so I would stop in there for 'second breakfast', even though the Pod Ratuszem (Town Hall) restaurant was closer at hand. The latter bar features less prominently in memoirs than Hawelka. I used to love to go there for May bread sticks with fresh *bryndza* cheese, abundantly sprinkled with salt crystals and exquisitely topped with sliced red radish. Jews went to the restaurant infrequently, perhaps once a year. The owner once asked my father: 'Mr Gross, could you please tell me when those holidays are when Jews can eat *treyf*?'

He was thinking of Yom Kippur, the day of the great fast when all Jewish restaurants were closed. Young people who did not observe the rituals and who got no dinner at home that day would visit small restaurants like the Town Hall *en masse.*

I understand how the Town Hall could fall into oblivion, but how can the culinary landscape of central Cracow be described without mentioning the 'sausage on the fork' served at the Pod Jutrzenka (The Dawn) restaurant on Sienna Street? I have never come across The Dawn in memoirs of Cracow. And what was 'sausage on the fork'? Snip, snip, snip – kilometer after kilometer of kielbasa went into the kettles that steamed there from morning until late at night, and the plates flew through the air. Never in my life, and in no other restaurant in Cracow, have I tasted such cabbage (what was it seasoned with – tomato sauce?). Yet no one writes about The Dawn. Is this because the eatery was favored by the working classes, secondary school students, or at best by Jewish university students? In any case, it has waited in vain for its panegyrist. Polish gourmands from certain spheres cherish tender memories of Thorn's restaurant on Krakowska Street, where they sometimes went – or could they have been invited there? – for gefilte fish. The residents of the Stradom and Kazimierz districts bought kosher sausage there. We bought krakauer sausage and brisket at Groner's on Dominikańska Square, and later fat wursts or thin wieners (steamers or sausages) at Apollo's, which was the shop that occupied the same premises after Groner. If the face of that sausage-maker perpetuated a family resemblance, then it is easy to understand why a malicious official, in charge of assigning surnames to the Jews, entered the great-grandfather in the city books under the name of the Greek god. There was indeed something of a Greek sculpture, something of Scopas, about that face, although the years had gnawed at it somewhat.

The house where we lived stood on Zielona (now Sarego) Street. This was not in Kazimierz proper, but directly adjacent; the street was inhabited entirely by Jews. I attended the Hebrew Secondary School and perforce associated only with Jewish friends. My parents had a great many Polish acquaintances who were, I would say, quite cordially disposed. Yet they did not maintain what are called 'social relations', which means that they did not go to visit them or receive them in our home. I thus lived in a sort of isolation from Polish society – yet this did not prevent me from absorbing Polish culture, Polish poetry, or Polish music and art in the depths of my being. We spoke Polish at home. My parents knew Yiddish, of course, but they used it when they wanted us children to be unable to understand what they were talking about. Mother loved Cracow above all else, and I suppose father did, as well. Mother loved the theatre and sometimes quoted Slowacki and other poetry that she must have remembered from school. Yet my love for Polish culture came not so much from home, as from the Hebrew school that I attended, and especially from my beloved professor – a humanist, Polish teacher, poet, writer, and above all a charismatic teacher – Juliusz Feldhorn.

24

What he imbued in me has remained until today.

Cracow and Polish culture are an inseparable part of my identity, no less than Tel Aviv and Hebrew culture.

Everyone has a Cracow of his or her own, and the image of that beautiful, beloved city continues to emerge in ever-richer and more interesting ways from numerous memoirs. However, the image will not be complete or authentic until some memoirist who spent his youth in Kazimierz fills it with the names, shops, institutions, and customs of its Jewish residents. I will not be that memoirist, unfortunately, but perhaps some small contribution, the image of a Jewish family in Cracow, can be provided by my point of view.

3. Branches of the Family Tree: the Shop on the Corner of Szewska Street

As far back as my memory reaches, father's parents lived in Rzeszow. I was there once, or perhaps twice. Through the mist, I remember my grandfather Eliezer Gross as a slender Jewish man in a gray Hungarian frogged coat with a long black beard containing silver threads. I cannot remember my grandmother. One of her daughters – my aunts – might have taken after her. Nor do I even know my grandmother's first name. She might have been called Guta or Giza, because that name was given to one of the girls in father's family. Grandmother's maiden name was Mühlstein and that was father's surname until my grandparents took out a civil marriage license. At that point, Jakub officially assumed his father's surname.

I never learned much about my grandmother, but the little I knew has always been a signpost, a light that has illuminated my way all my life. She was a woman of extraordinary goodness, as Aunt Tyla recalled her. On the day of Esther's Fast, preceding Purim, she ran around town giving the poor *shlachmunes*, the Purim gifts of cakes, *hamantashe*, and wine, so that their holiday could be merry. On returning home in the evening, she said, 'I'm a little tired. I'm going to lie down for a moment to rest.' She lay down – and never got up again. That is the way I should like to die, I have told myself more than once. I never laid eyes on her, but I have always remembered her tenderly.

I cannot say what Grandfather Eliezer was like, but my father, Jakub, inherited his mother's heart. He was the second child in the family, after Mojsze. Next came Rozia, Henek, and Thila – or Tyla. None of them ever had a career; they all depended on and worked for their brother Jakub. He found wives and husbands for them, furnished their dowries, and tried to set them up on their own. He opened a shop for Henek in Krynica, one for Rozia (after finding her a husband) in Cracow, and one for Mojsze in Bochnia. Somehow, they could never make a go of it and returned to the care and support of their wealthy brother.

Tyla worked in the shop as a sales assistant, and later – after Aunt Mala, mother's sister, married – sat behind the cash register in the 'old' shop. She was my favorite of all father's family. She was merry and played the mandolin. She often quietly sang a sad Scandinavian song:

> Far off the echo carries
> Sound of a forgotten melody,
> Echo of a song about a girl
> And the boy she loved …

Or she sang the then-fashionable cabaret number 'Well, I'm Afraid of Getting Fat Both Here and There', the opening lines of which I still remember:

> Years back the world loved ladies fat and great;
> Old-time beauties were like butcher's shops:
> Abundant hips, flesh beneath the chops,
> They lolled about reading, and gaining weight …

Tyla herself was plump, giggly, silly, and read a lot. Aunt Rozia, older and more intelligent, was lame in one leg. Uncle Henek was short, with an athletic build, and loved to tell jokes that we termed 'popular' – which was our way of saying 'not terribly wise'. Mojsze, father's eldest brother – the one who lived in Bochnia – was taciturn and eternally worried: he had a wife and three children to support.

All of them, the whole family – over time, one after another, they married and had children – were annihilated during the Second World War. Most of them gathered in Zakliczyn, where I believe Rozia's husband came from, and from there they went to Belzec extermination camp. Not a trace of them is left.

The uncles and aunts on father's side of the family were good people, but unresourceful. I am not sure that father was any different, but he had a resourceful wife. That fact determined the course of his life, and the success and satisfaction that he gained from it.

Father was born in Kolbuszowa, or perhaps in Majdan Kolbuszowy. His parents moved to Rzeszow afterwards. Young Jakub came to Cracow in search of work several years before the First World War. I do not know the circumstances in which he met mother. I only know that they went to dance evenings at the Sokol Hall, which mama sometimes remembered tenderly. In any case, it was not an arranged marriage. The courtship dragged on for several years because it got mixed up with the First World War. Jakub was drafted and sent to the front lines. He was a handsome young man with large dark eyes and a small black mustache. He looked beautiful in an Austrian uniform with a high, stiff collar on which there were two buttons – or were they stars? I do not know. I do not know if they marked the rank of corporal or of an ordinary private. That is how I remember father in a photograph from those days. In another photograph – those photographs are gone now – I saw him in a hospital in Kiev, with his head bandaged. Wounded near Zhytomir, he was taken prisoner by the Russians. He wrote sentimental pages full of longing from captivity to his fiancée, Sala Scharf, in Cracow. These pages did not fail in their effect. An energetic person who was not the sort to wait for things to work out on their own, Sala undertook a dangerous journey to Kiev in order to rescue her fiancé from captivity. My sister Klara remembered many of mother's amusing anecdotes – mother would never have shared such accounts with me! Particularly memorable was the story of how mother, small, green – that was her own term – and looking much younger than her 25 years, finally stepped off the train at the Kiev station after her long and harrowing journey. She inquired about the way to the toilet. Someone pointed the way, and she then spent a long time searching in vain for any sort of recognizable facility. It finally turned out that the toilet was an open hole with nothing to screen it from view. Anyone in need of relief simply squatted over the hole, facing the passersby. Sala Scharf did not avail herself. Such an act was more than she was capable of.

She hunted down the hospital where the slightly wounded Jakub lay, and bribed the baker who delivered bread every day to smuggle our future father out of the military complex in his sack. Kerensky's revolt occurred just on the day that Jakub regained his freedom, and the young couple had to hide in a cellar instead of joyously celebrating their reunion.

Jakub and Sara tied the matrimonial knot after the end of the war, a knot of close cooperation in which they built a home and developed a business, only to be separated again 20 years later. Once again, it was war that divided them – this time, forever.

Sara, or Sala, was the second daughter in the Scharf family, after her sister Lana. Later came a sister, Mala, and a little brother, Szulim, or Selm. There had been one more brother, the firstborn, but he died of skeletal tuberculosis as a 16-year-old boy. It was after him, Natan, that I was named.

My mother was a born Cracovian. I seem to remember her father, an official of the *kahal*, the Cracow religious community, through a fog: a well-built *hasid* with an abundant beard. The Scharfs lived in Kazimierz, at 44 or 46 Krakowska Street, in the same building as the community board offices, or next door. Mother sometimes took me there, but aside from an old-world atmosphere and some sort of paintings in golden frames, I recall only the great Baroque-looking glass in the bedroom. I loved to climb up and sit on it, to the despair of my grandmother, who feared that I would break the priceless mirror.

One heirloom from my grandparents' house remains in the family today. It is a large painting by Tomkiewicz, signed 1883 and representing a romantic young lady in a blue dress and a straw hat, seated on the Planty on an old-fashioned railed bench. She is holding a bouquet of flowers in one hand, and a book in the other. At her feet lies a large dog whose dam or sire must have been a setter. This painting hung over the piano in our dining room. Polish acquaintances hid it during the war and were very eager to purchase it, but mother would not part with the family heirloom and carried it with her to Israel.

On pictures from her younger days, Sara looks like a graceful and lively person, an undoubtedly winning young lady of the sort that it is a pleasure to flirt with. A charitable observer would note, philosophically, that she may not be pretty, but certainly looks intelligent. That was always my impression when looking at that photograph – for I do not remember my mother as a young person. Neither as a child nor later did I ever think about her beauty or lack of beauty. Her face was not young-looking, and while she was not ugly, she was also unmarked by 'the vestiges of yesterday's beauty'. I would say that she had a wise owl's face, with lively, pale-blue eyes. She lost her hair at the birth of her second child (I was the firstborn), my brother Jozek, and wore a wig afterwards. Her older sister Lana was regarded as a beauty and enjoyed great success among the men. Perhaps Sara envied her a bit, although she, too, seems to me to have had success. In any case, her life's motto was, *'Wer is sheyn, bin ich klug'* – 'Someone else may be beautiful, but I am wise'. She repeated this, with a chuckle, more than once. She was therefore wise, clever and resourceful. She was a classic example of the Jewish older sister – not necessarily older in years – who takes care of the whole family, makes all the decisions, marries off her younger siblings, and takes pains about her own relatives and her in-laws. She had never been beautiful but always paid attention to her appearance and was always carefully dressed, elegant, but not *auffalend* – as people said – never loud. She always bought the best material (and she knew her material!) and had her suits sewn by the best ladies' tailors. She had good taste. And she paid the same attention to the way her husband and children looked. When I was already the father of a family, she was still adjusting my jacket or tie before I went out and checking to see that my shoes were shined, my heels weren't run down, and that I didn't need my shoes fixed or need to buy a new pair. In this regard, she was pedantic, if not nagging. She insisted on perfection in everything that she did and everything that she had done – it had to be done to a t. To this day, I wish I were her equal in that regard.

Mother's older sister, the beautiful Lana, was a tall, blue-eyed blonde with a highly developed sense of her own good looks: she loved herself more than she loved her neighbor. As she told it – and I am not totally disinclined to believe her – boys from the best homes were ready to kill for her. She finally settled on a very handsome husband from Sanok, Jozef Steinmetz. My father set him up in a china shop on Bracka Street. The Steinmetzes had a son named Gustek and a daughter, Nata, a fiery brunette who was no less successful among the boys than her mother had been.

When the war broke out, Uncle Steinmetz and Gustek wandered eastward to Lwow, but only Gustek – deported into the depths of Russia – survived the wartime maelstrom. Aunt Lana and Nata stayed with us throughout the occupation, until the Warsaw Uprising. When peace came, Nata married her pre-war boyfriend, Nardelli, who had survived the war in a POW camp in Germany. She died giving birth to her second child. Gustek had already arrived in Palestine with Anders's army; Aunt Lana soon emigrated there. She lived out her days, remembering to the end the beauty she had in her youth.

Mother's younger sister Mala was a kindly, naïve young lady

from a good home. She had a noble spirit and a tendency, which she could never overcome, to put on weight. She lived with us until she married, running the cash register in the shop. She never parted company from Heksa, a beautiful example of a pedigreed German shepherd. Mala travelled to Krynica every summer, obviously counting on the Kryniczanka or Zuber mineral waters to help her in some way. In what way? I cannot say. But this helped mother to solve the problem of vacations for us children without our parents having to close the shop. So we holidayed with our aunt each year, gathering golden caterpillars, blueberries, and wild strawberries in the woods – and hating that beautiful resort town with all our hearts. We dreamed of Zakopane or even of a school camp in Rabka. With its promenade and spa orchestra, Krynica bored us. We were fed up with the place. Only when I neared my graduation from secondary school did I look back on Krynica from a different perspective. By then it was too late to be able to savor its charms …

Aunt Mala's wedding, around 1928, was a grand family event. As an eight- or nine-year-old boy, I danced at the reception with Giza Vogler, who was even younger. Her father, Szymon Vogler, a goldsmith, was the brother-in-law of the bridegroom, Jozek Grünberg. In the eyes of the wedding guests, the sight of such young children dancing together was some sort of portent … There was nothing then to foreshadow what lay ahead – the way that all those beautiful families would be broken up, lost, scattered, with their homes collapsing like houses of cards.

We enjoyed cordial relations with the Grünbergs (which is more than I can say of the Steinmetzes). Jozef Grünberg was a handsome, dark-haired man with bushy eyebrows, a Polish Army lieutenant in the reserves, and as straightforward as his wife. He played chess with his brother-in-law Vogler and took me to a soccer match each Sunday. He was a diehard Cracovia fan. He apparently earned a good living as a salesman for a tea company. When he left Cracow with his family in September 1939, his oldest daughter Sientka (Sientka was a diminutive form of Klarusieñka, which in turn was derived from the name Klara) was ten, Janek was two years younger, and Adam was six. As they fled from the Germans, they had no idea that a fourth child was on the way. Krysia was born in Lwow and, as an infant, joined the whole family in a column deported to Sverdlovsk *oblast*. Not all of that

31

family returned from there to Cracow in 1947. Jozef, that splendid man, an athlete and a born officer, died at the reins of a horse cart during a blizzard, trying to earn bread for his wife and four children. That was when naïve, good-hearted Mala, who had lived comfortably before the war bearing children and putting up preserves that the whole family ate through the winter, showed what a courageous woman she was. She brought her children back from the Urals to Cracow, and then moved with them to Israel, where she raised them and made human beings out of them in the incredibly difficult conditions of a *maabara* (a transit camp for immigrants). She watched with pride as they grew and developed in their homely way – and then fate stepped in. Her oldest daughter, the fair-haired and universally beloved Sientka, died of some sort of post-partum infection after giving birth to her second child. The hapless physicians were too slow to catch on to the reason for her mild but persistent fever. 'I'm going to die on you and you won't even know what of,' she joked. And she died. That was enough to bring a stroke and partial paralysis on Aunt Mala. Unable to speak and limited in her mobility, she nevertheless lived on for several more years until the children were all married and had started families. Janek served in the air force and then studied electronics, becoming an assistant professor at the university of Tel Aviv before being 'snatched away' to Los Angeles. Adam began as a black-market employee in the Geva film laboratories, made a career for himself as a film cameraman, and is now a top-notch Israeli cinematographer who circulates between Hollywood and Tel Aviv. Krysia is married to the director of a vocational school and works at the Histadrut. Each of the surviving Grünbergs has two daughters and a son ...

Mother's youngest brother, Szulim or Selm Scharf, developed his abilities first in Germany and then in England. When he came to Cracow to visit the family from time to time, it was a great family holiday. The sisters idolized their elegant, well-situated brother, who was always full of humor and ready to help. We children also loved this uncle above our other uncles, especially since he always slipped a fiver or a chocolate bar into our pockets. He was a person of undeniable charm. His wedding has not stuck in my mind like Aunt Mala's wedding, but I fondly recall his sweet little daughter Vila, who was four when the war broke out. Today, that little girl is a professor of American literature at the Sorbonne. The war caught

Uncle Szulim in Poland, while his wife Rega and Viola were in Italy (Rega's sister was married to the Italian consul in Poland). Resourceful and foresightful, on friendly terms with the family of the Lubomirski princes, Szulim tried to cross the border during the first year of the war – and fell into the hands of the Gestapo. He somehow got out of their hands, having had a taste of German interrogation, and then spent the rest of the occupation sticking close to his sisters. Perhaps he supported them. In any case, the Scharfs stuck together, of which I shall have occasion to say more later. The husbands of the Scharf sisters died during the war and their brother Szulim also failed to survive, but the chain of generations was not broken. Branches of the Gross and Scharf trees are blowing in the wind and bearing fruit.

*

Jakub Gross's shops – China, Crystal, Glass and Lamps – were located on either side of the Cloth Hall that stands in the Main Square in Cracow. The old shop, at 8 Grodzka Street (where that street extends into the Square), was advertised on the street only by a small, round display window. To reach it, customers had to walk down a long passageway and across an elongated courtyard. There was no possibility of straying, since customers were accompanied along the whole way, over 100 meters, by more than a score of display cases that were always carefully arranged and featured new merchandise. The second shop, the new one that was opened in the 1930s, stood at 30 Main Square, at the corner of Szewska Street. It had previously been occupied by the Sperber brothers and had sold wholesale velvet goods. Aside from five big display windows in the front, it teased the eye with the perspective of more than a score of display windows in the adjacent passage, which led back to the Town Hall restaurant.

However, as the saying goes, Cracow was not built in a day! Jakub Gross inherited no fortune from his parents. He began, according to the aphorism, with the ten fingers on his hands. He was an apprentice at Rubinstein's porcelain emporium on Stradom Street. After the First World War, having put aside a few *groszy* and added Sara Scharf's dowry, he bought a tiny shop buried deep in that enormous courtyard – and developed it over time into a large, splendid store.

I know little about the beginnings of the shop. My sister Klara has shared mother's account of how there was no merchandise available after the First World War. My parents traveled to Czechoslovakia to purchase something. They were greeted at the faience factory by a sign reading *'Wie man macht ist falsch'*. Mother broke out laughing: 'What fools!' However, the motto turned out to be accurate. The Grosses returned happily to Poland, satisfied at having been able to lay their hands on some merchandise. In the meantime, the faience factory at Chodziez, Poland, was opened. By the time the shipment from Czechoslovakia arrived, it had lost its value. Faience mugs with little laughing faces on them were still taking up space in the company's warehouses at the outbreak of the Second World War.

Jakub Gross started small, but he was hard-working and lucky, and above all he had a wife with a head on her shoulders and extraordinary business sense. Year after year, step by step, display by display, premises by premises, floor by floor, that palace of china, ceramics and crystals, glass, lamps and figurines, grew for 20 years. And then it all came crashing down in a single day under the force of a storm of history.

Jakub Gross was not a 'born merchant'. By no means. He was an artistic soul, a man of ideas with a love of art and of life (but not in the practical sense!). He had a beautiful voice and sang Ukrainian *dumki* beautifully, as well as he sang *chazunes*, the *hasidic* liturgical melodies. He collected the records of Josele Rosenblat, whose *kopfstime* – melodic variations of the highest tones – he could imitate masterfully. He drew beautifully, and his artistic impulses found an outlet in the arrangement of the window displays that he stayed up nights to work on. The window displays in the shop on the corner of Szewska Street were a feast for the eye. When he traveled abroad on business, he always brought home the newest advertising gimmicks – attention-getting, making surprisingly inventive use of simple techniques: some sort of intersecting mirrors, running texts, or neon effects. Jakub Gross's neon sign had, after all, been one of the first on the Main Square. For holidays, and especially national holidays, he ornamented a shop window with a large new painting by Wojciech or Jerzy Kossak. That was a tradition. Such displays always drew a crowd. *Marching Out of Oleandry*, *The Charge of the Ulans at Ostrolêka*, etc. The central figure in these panoramic paintings was usually Marshal Jozef

34

Pilsudski on his chestnut mare. (Could this be the reason that memoirists describing the Cracow Main Square usually omit the firm of Jakub Gross from their accounts?)

The store was father's work of art. He plowed all his energy and all his income into the business. Getting rich was not the point. In a small city like Cracow, the 'physical' size of a business – the number of showrooms, floors or displays – was out of all proportion to its earnings. A tiny shop in Kazimierz might yield more income for its owner than Jakub Gross's extensive business. Who needed two shops, one across from the other, on the Main Square? The cost of running such a business, with a staff of 36 and high taxes, was enormous. How much effort did it cost him to run two shops and keep them at a high standard?

Jakub Gross did not employ an advertising agent; he was his own agent. He had a certain literary gift. I remember how, rummaging through old papers, I found a brochure for the Achduth Socialist–Zionist organization that he had written (and signed). This does not mean, however, that he wrote all his own advertisements. When he needed a longer text, he sometimes turned to Adam Polewka; I think that he also did so in order to help that poet who always went about without a cent to his name.

Father was a merchant who followed the new trends in his profession. The Gross firm promoted itself through filmed commercials shown in the cinemas (as confirmed by the literature on film history!), signs on tram cars and, of course, newspaper advertisements. During a certain period, an advertisement in each week's illustrated supplement to the Cracow *Kurier* featured a photograph of some service, Giesche for instance, or a glass set from Stolle Niemen, 'Jakub Gross exclusive distributor in Poland'. Father adapted – but never copied! – various novelties that he introduced to the Polish market with great success, like for instance the 'Grossowka', a little glass cabinet with nine transparent glass drawers to replace the china containers labelled 'flour', 'salt', 'kasha', 'tea', etc., or the 'Groja' percolator – the name of which, after a protest by a citizen who bore that name, had to be changed to 'Jagro'. After the advertisements in *Kurier* came the idea of a richly illustrated catalogue sent all over Poland, which produced more and more new customers. The Gross Company cooperated with the china factory in Cmielow and the Giesche factory in Silesia, as well as the Zawiercie and Stolle Niemen glass factories, on the basis of exclusive rights to certain lines for the Cracow firm. Such contracts were salt in the eyes of the competition. Abroad as well, and particularly in Czechoslovakia, Gross guaranteed himself special crystal styles, for instance in the 'Royalit' and 'Alexandrit' lines manufactured by Moser, where he was a valued client. The inventory included lovely French Baccarat glass, Gallé multi-layered designer glass, English Wedgwood china, Japanese porcelain and Meissen figurines. However, Jakub Gross favored Polish factories and doubtlessly contributed to their growth and the improvement in the quality of their products. Until 1933, he travelled to the Leipzig Trade Fair each year and always brought back the latest designs. He passed these on to the local glass and china manufacturers. He made several trips to Niemen, and I believe that he made a significant contribution to the development and market presence of this little-known glass factory. I also think that the Cieszyn Crystal Factory owed more than one success to its cooperation with Gross's.

*

If father was the heart of the business, then mother was its driving force, its soul. Father took care of the appearance of the shop, and mother took care of the business. This was an extraordinary and harmonious partnership in which each partner had absolute trust in the other and knew the other's strengths and shortcomings. Father had a big heart and an open hand. Supplicants knew about this and tried to take advantage of him. Mother was not petty or miserly – by no means! She taxed herself for all charitable campaigns, but she hated parasites and *schnorrers*. Alms-seekers – the ones who had a marriageable daughter, or who needed an unsecured loan because they had hit on a sure money-making idea, or who had someone sick in the family and could not afford a doctor – were always hanging around outside the shop waiting for a moment when mother was absent. If they saw her, they did not even bother to enter; it was clear that they would receive nothing. They feared her like fire. But they converged on father when he opened the shop in the morning or at the end of the noontime break and gnawed at him until they had extorted a few *zloty* – and sometimes more. Mother came to the store later – things needed doing at home, as well.

The Jakub Gross company never sold on credit or installments, only for cash. This, of course, was Sara Gross's decision. However, there were exceptions for government clerks and teachers. This was a social class that mother sympathized with and supported. There was obviously a basis in 'materialistic realism': clerks and teachers lived on the edge of poverty, but they were assured of a salary on the first of the month and could be counted on to pay five *zloty* against their account. Mother was grateful for such an agreement. When hard times came for the Grosses, this gratitude assumed concrete expression. It was worth maintaining good relations with clerks because, at times, they were indispensable. But teachers? That was a matter of pure sentiment. Mrs Gross liked intelligent customers, and they appreciated, respected and liked her in return. They trusted her wisdom and good taste, sometimes coming to her for advice on a gift for the superintendent. Mrs Gross knew how to give good advice, and she never tried to unload junk or hard-to-sell, non-standard merchandise on her customers.

And then there were the actors. How could I ever forget about the actors! They were mother's best and favorite customers. The whole Slowacki Theatre bought from us. When young Miecio Wegrzyn walked in with his wife Suchecka, all the salesgirls rushed forward. Or Alicja Matusiak (Radulska by her first marriage and Tarczalowicz by her second) – what a beautiful woman and what a splendid actress. The whole shop lit up when she walked in wearing a broad smile and a wide-brimmed hat. Or Zygmunt Modzelewski (for whom, by the way, mother arranged a passport so that he could get out of Poland during the war). And Kazimierz Szubert, an outstanding comic actor who intended to quarter Klara and mother at his apartment in Warsaw – except that the Gestapo showed up a few hours before they did. I shall write about that later. Or Janina Wernicz, a red-haired Jewish woman – that is how I remember her from the beginning of the war – who was perfect in the chiseled roles for which she often had to put up a brave fight.

Ninety per cent of the customers of the Gross Company were Christian Poles, and the list could begin with the Civil Chancellery of the President of the Republic of Poland. Lines of Cmielow china bearing golden eagles and chalices with the state coat of arms engraved on them were the pride of the Cmielow Factories. That firm was contending for an order from the president's kitchen, but could not make the sale and had to be content with selling its goods through the intermediacy of Gross's. This success can be put down to Sara Gross's diplomatic abilities; as people said of her, she had a ministerial head. Gross's supplied army garrisons, monasteries, city and national institutions, guest houses, and hotels; the National Democrat slogan 'buy from your own' had very little influence on purchasing agents. National Democrat organizations themselves were steady customers; the firm's competitors clearly had trouble keeping up. They could, for lack of anything better, smash the display windows. This happened two or perhaps three times. I remember how pale father's face was when demonstrators shattered a centimeter-thick pane of Belgian glass during an antisemitic tumult. The window pane was insured, of course, but it was a very hurtful experience for father.

*

As children, we sometimes visited the shop with our nanny. Later, when I was in the seventh or eighth grade, and especially in the pre-holiday period (before the Christmas vacation!), I occasionally sat at the cash register. The shop was full of clients. There wasn't room to turn around. Wealthy people were buying new table settings for the holidays; poor people were buying plates only; school teachers were buying a present – a Moser vase – for their principals; boarding-school girls were buying modest presents – something made of Viennese china – for their mothers.

The shop girls dashed back and forth and were everywhere at once. The good-looking Irena Mucha was married to a painter and had once told me, in secret, about how beautifully he had painted her in the nude. There was the blonde woman called Stasia, and there were Gizia, and Aunt Rozia, Thila, Mala, and the orphan Genia, who had grown up with us and worked in the shop. Even the bookkeeper, Mania Hoenig, helped out with sales. Mr Ziembinski helped – he was the head electrician in the company that was responsible for lighting in the shops and the dozens of window displays; he later married the good-hearted Stasia. All of these were long-term employees or associates. We also had schoolgirls working part-time, and, of course, there were mother and father. Mother had an eye for 'the better sort' of customers, most of whom she already knew well. Klara, Jozek and I helped with the cash register. Sometimes I went over to help a customer who looked lost and was not being waited on.

The large warehouse in the basement of the building had its own staff: Pawel with the harelip, Antoni with his enormous mustache, dark-haired Jan, and Wladek with his round, laughing face. We called him 'Mug' because he resembled those Czech mugs with their smiling-face folk motif. Father's brothers Mojsze, with his philosophical–pessimistic expression, and Henek, the strongman who was always telling his 'popular' jokes, expertly packed shipments of china in wood shavings. Packing a 144-piece table setting in such a way that it arrived unbroken was a sort of art, especially if the package itself was also supposed to look elegant. 'Mug', handy at everything, helped with the packing at peak periods, but he was essentially the firm's carpenter. He had a well-equipped workshop in the basement, where he built the wooden structures, sometimes quite complicated, that were used in the displays. Engineer Czeslaw Wallis, a licensed architect, was our interior designer; I believe that he also helped Szyszko-Bohusz to lay out the new restaurant at Wawel Castle. Wallis was best known for having remodelled and modernized the Artists' House, installing an auditorium and designing the backdrop for the avant-garde Christmas cabaret. When he was asked from time to time, he would deny categorically being any sort of relative of the prominent art critic Mieczyslaw Wallis, who was in fact Jewish and was named Walfisz. While agreeing to the use of 'Mieczyslaw Wallis' as a pen-name, Czeslaw Wallis did not want to accept the critic 'into the family' and blocked Walfisz's efforts to change his name legally. 'That Walfisz is a decent man', he would say, 'but who knows how his children will turn out? He can borrow my name as long as he's alive, but his children? – No!' I remember him as a handsome, elegant character who came to the shop to discuss the designs for the holiday displays with father. His first act on arriving was invariably to pick up the telephone and call his wife to ask: 'Hello, Bronia. What's Bonzo doing?' Bonzo was his beloved white poodle. Under father's direction, Mug was capable of designing simple constructions on his own. But the holiday display had to be a hit that would set the whole city talking. That was why Wallis was needed.

I liked to go down to the warehouse when crates of new merchandise were opened. New lines, new fashions, figurines, ceramics and crystals emerged from clouds of wood shavings to dazzle the eye. Before the first customers arrived in the morning, I enjoyed walking around the upstairs showrooms. I would ping the crystal with my finger and listen to the way it resonated. I could tell the sound of French crystal from Czech with my eyes closed – they were pure bells with different tones. Zawiercie crystal had a rather dull tone, and it's better not to say anything about the wares from Piotrkow. In any case, we didn't carry Piotrkow china, which looked like green bottle glass. The Zawiercie glass was clear and relatively thick, but the cut-glass chalices were not unattractive. Yet how they fell short of the delicacy of the French Baccarat! I also had a soft spot for Viennese ceramics, and slowly became something of a connoisseur of china.

While other Jewish parents dreamed that their sons would study medicine and open their own doctors' offices, mine wanted me to stay in the shop. Of course, they wanted me to be an educated businessman. Mother had her own ideas about a diplomatic career and believed that she could use her connections to get me accepted in the Higher School of Diplomacy. After my matriculation exams, however, I put my name down for the law faculty at the university – and went on sitting in the shop.

I had no intention of and no interest in staying at the shop, and did not expect to do so. However, I did not want to disappoint my parents. I used those diplomatic abilities that mother had sensed to try to back out gracefully. What I wanted was to become a painter. Before entering the Fine Arts Academy, I served an apprenticeship with the outstanding landscape painter Abraham Neumann.

The war released me from my conflicts with my parents and myself. When I came back to my hometown of Cracow in 1945, I stopped at the shop. The woman who worked as the janitor in the building looked at me in wide-eyed surprise: 'Are you alive?'

I thought that I sensed disappointment in her voice. The shop was still there, but it no longer existed. For me, it no longer existed.

I was not even interested in who had taken over the premises or what would be there. When mother came back from the camp, she complained with some justice that I had not even attempted to claim our rights in our firm. I was not interested in property laws or compensation. I am hardly proud of myself. I regret having disappointed mother. Such, however, was the egoistical philosophy of life that I had adopted.

4. Home, Sweet Home

A home is more than walls. But it includes the walls. All the more so because the walls grow. New walls are added, wall space grows, walls are covered with pictures, walls are painted a new color. My color was green. Our nursery was green when we were children, and its window looked out on Zielona Street, which means 'green' in Polish, and led to the green Planty, and there was a green garden behind the house surrounded by the gardens of the neighboring houses. And those were green years.

The Gross apartment house at 12 Zielona Street, today called Sarego Street. My parents did not obtain it as an inheritance or dowry. When they got married in December 1918, they rented one of the eight rooms on the third floor. Over time they rented an additional room after a neighbor moved out, and then another room and yet another room, until only the Tigners were left. The Tigners occupied three rooms and a kitchen, and they lived across from us. Samuel Tigner – 'Samek' – was a gruff, squat man with an abundant brushy mustache who was always in a good mood, but spoke loudly in tones that indicated he did not tolerate being talked back to. His wife Marysia was slightly hard of hearing. Their three children were more or less our age. Julek was one grade ahead of me. Rysio was Klara's age, and their youngest daughter, Celinka, who was great friends with Klara, must have been two years younger than Rysio. I once met Julek, who now lives in London, and we reminisced about the building on Zielona Street. To this day I can see the large-format portrait of Samuel Tigner by a painter named Czaj. I watched him paint it. I can still hear the harsh, throaty way that Mr Tigner pronounced the letter 'r'. I remember a vulgar army song that Mr Tigner sang, although I may only have heard my father parodying it: 'Maciek Grela was in the Fortieth Regiment – And everyone said it was a good thing – Boom-tra-di-ra-di-ra'. The song had to do with the acoustic after-effects of the consumption of beans by the said Maciek Grela, and the refrain took the place of a rhyme after each line. Julek was absolutely incapable of recalling that song. Mr Tigner obviously never sang it in front of his children; anything of the kind would have been unthinkable in a self-respecting bourgeois family ...

The Tigners were a clan! They were a large family who lived together and ran a joint business, a large furrier's shop on Grodzka Street, with their own lovely prayer-house adjoining the shop. It had been founded by Markus Tigner, the head of the family. Samek's brother Menasze had a wife named Laura. She chaired the parents' committee of the Hebrew school that we all attended. Laura Tigner was a good-looking woman of considerable personal charms. She was helpful, active, and quite likeable from my childhood perspective. Since she had a great deal of influence over matters like reduced tuition fees, and was additionally a member of the wealthy Tigner clan, some of the less affluent parents of children attending the Hebrew school had a less favorable opinion of her than I did. Her two sons, Olek and Henek, were several grades ahead of me. They carried themselves with such pride that I was afraid to speak to them. Later, when the war crashed down on all our heads, things changed and we became dear friends. I remember how they invited me to the first Passover *seder* after the war ...

There were only a few survivors from that large family. The gruff Samek, the docile Marysia, the intelligent Rysio and the kind-hearted Celinka all died tragic wartime deaths. Fate pursued even those who managed to slip out of Hitler's hands into the haven of the Soviet Union. Olek, who married a Polish woman, died of a heart attack during a police search of the shop he opened after the war – his parents' old shop on Grodzka Street. His wife emigrated to Israel with her little daughter and her mother-in-law. Henek and his wife joined them shortly afterwards. He was already terminally ill and died soon after arriving.

I met Mrs Laura Tigner, the mother of those boys, by chance on a bus in the 1950s. She recognized me. As always, she was elegantly but modestly dressed, and she was carrying a small parcel. 'It's a Christmas present for my daughter-in-law, Olek's wife. Today is Christmas', she said with a sad smile.

Of that whole family, only Julek is alive today.

When the Tigners built their own four-story house a couple of doors down, in the garden at 8 Zielona Street, my parents had no choice but to take over their apartment and occupy the whole floor. Later, they bought the whole building and became the owners of the apartment house and its garden. In time they liquidated the wooden balconies and outside toilets and put up a small building at the back of the lot ... All that happened between the two World Wars. The building was an apartment House with a capital 'H' when Hitler came along and changed it back into indifferent walls. Those walls did not stop developing. The administrator designated by the municipal authorities came to the conclusion that it was worthwhile to add one more floor. No one asked the owners for their consent; no one cared if they were alive. The house was mortgaged to cover the costs of the work. After returning from Ravensbrück, mother was of course unable to pay off the debt, and so her house – our house – no longer belonged to us. Formally, however, we were the owners. That is, we were obliged to pay the taxes. And since we did not pay them – what were we supposed to pay them with? – there were more and more liens against the mortgage. When mother died in Israel, neither I nor any of my siblings opened inheritance proceedings. This was surely unwise, and mother would not have praised my indifference to the family property, but to me it did not seem worth the trouble. It was not so much a matter of costs (although the costs would not have been inconsiderable) as of time, bother and running back and forth – and for what? Some of the tenants were interested in purchasing the house, and they wrote me long letters from Cracow. 'Dear Sir', one of them assured me, 'this will not cost you a cent ...' He was ready to cover all the debts outstanding against the house, and to take possession of it. I assume that he would even have been willing to cover the costs associated with the inheritance proceedings and the transfer of the house to the heirs. Another tenant asked to rent the attic. He was a trumpeter in a jazz band, and the attic would be an ideal place to rehearse in. As it was, his neighbors were complaining about the noise ... I would gladly have rented the attic to him, but I could not do so. Formally, the house belonged to Jakub and Sara Gross, and they were no longer alive. The biggest bone of contention among the tenants was the garden with its summer house. I have no idea how that one turned out.

I would like to be able to write that the present building is a matter of indifference for me, and that the home from before the war is the one that remains alive. But that is not the case. That building, with all new tenants, would still move me if I ever walked up to its front door. Perhaps I shall have the courage to do so someday …

*

I cannot recall all the stages in which rooms were added and my parents' standard of living changed. I recall images and episodes involving some of the tenants, who changed seldom. One was named Horowitz and played the piano. Vladimir Horowitz he was not, however, and this may be the reason that his concerts drove me crazy. I must have been three years old at the time. Was my reaction an early expression of my musical abilities? In any case, as mother told me, I refused to cross the threshold of Mr Horowitz's apartment. Could I have been frightened by the black coffin of the piano? I remember him, how I remember! I screamed and refused for all the world to visit 'Uncle' Horowitz. Father was so enraged that he spanked me. That was the only time he ever raised his hand to strike me. He never forgave himself as long as he lived … for I was regarded as a 'good child', a good pupil. Everyone praised me – teachers, parents, aunts, uncles, neighbors – but I wasn't good at all! My reputation grew in proportion to the growth of the notoriety of my brother Jozek. He was the 'bad child', the black sheep.

Jozek was dark-haired and had a bulging forehead. He was regarded as an ugly child (although he later became a 'handsome man'). Mother was infuriated by the delusions of people she met while walking with Jozek along the Planty. They would smile tenderly and say, 'What a lovely little boy'. So perhaps he was not so ugly after all. But my brother howled and let out blood-curdling screams at night, preventing my parents from sleeping … One way or another, the opinion emerged that we were opposites, and this opinion persisted all the time, right up to the war. On the basis of this opinion, I grew in the eyes of my teachers, while Jozek, who was one grade behind me in the same school, sank deeper and deeper into their bad graces. Jozek was a rascal, he had a great imagination, he loved playing jokes. No one knows how it happened, but if he appeared at one end of the long school corridor, then someone at the other end would immediately bruise themselves or start bleeding from the nose. During gym class, he once rearranged everybody's shoes so that no one could find their pair and half the next lesson was lost. And that only happened because the gym teacher ejected him from class for making trouble. It was boring there in the locker room, so he had to find some way of passing the time ... Jozek had a heart of gold and always told the truth. When he came home in the afternoons, he would barely open the door before admitting, 'Mama, I had to stand in the corner as punishment', or, 'I was kicked out of class', or, 'Teacher wants you to come to school tomorrow, mama'. Jozek's pranks were too much for father. Father did not have the patience for such a troublesome son and would have preferred to give him an immediate whipping for his bad behavior. Jozek fled under mama's wing; she loved him very much and sheltered him against father's ire. She also felt a certain resentment towards teachers who, instead of bringing up the boy and teaching him something, kept sending him home and requesting that she come to school. She did not have time for that. She always sent one of our aunts to the parent–teacher conferences.

I was well aware of the injustice of the fate to which my younger brother fell victim. I was hardly the ideal student that I was taken for, and Jozek was not the fierce devil he was made out to be. Dynamic, full of fantasy and imagination, he could not deal with the school regulations – while I had a free ride on the reputation maintained by constant comparisons: 'Look at them, two brothers, sons of the same mother, and so different!' I knew how to take advantage of the situation and get what I wanted, even if my plans conflicted with those of our parents or the school lessons. I am unable to banish the impression that this situation engendered certain complexes in my brother. Jozek, of course, did grow up to be an artist of the highest order and a man of great charm. He never lacked for charm. It was only the limitations of teachers for whom discipline was everything that prevented them from seeing the diamond under the scruffy shell.

We were good brothers, despite what I should term certain glaring differences in temperament. We had pillow fights in our green room on Saturday mornings when we did not have to go to school, and on occasion a shoe flew out the window into the street. In our secondary school years, we cooperated in composing humorous verses for the school Purim program, and we rehearsed acts together, jumping and bending in unison to music in front of the big mirror in the foyer ... When Jozek began taking an interest in art (no less than I did), he had me approach father about acquiring expensive books like the Van Gogh album published by Phaidon. Father never refused me, but then my requests never exceeded modest boundaries of finances and common sense. An unwritten agreement existed between my parents and me: they trusted me entirely, and I never abused their trust. I knew the limits. I would not disappoint my parents for all the world. However, this does not mean that I refrained from gradually widening my prerogatives, the way that a placid brook gradually erodes its banks. We were accustomed to a modest life; even when we were older we always received the same allowance, one *zloty* per week. We could hardly 'go wild' on such a sum – but, on the other hand, did we ever want for anything at home? In such circumstances, asking father for 25 *zloty* for a book required a certain daring and diplomacy. Jozek would never have been able to succeed, given his impulsive directness. Van Gogh was a revelation and an ideal to him, and I became infected with my younger brother's enthusiasm. I had my own abilities at drawing, and while remaining active on stage – I recited fairly well and took part in all school performances as author, actor and director – I still regarded painting as coming first of all, and intended to dedicate myself to it. Yet in the end, it was Jozek, and not I, who became a painter.

First came two sons. Then a daughter, Klara, was born to the Grosses. Father tenderly referred to her as 'the only daughter of the King of Big Money'; he seems to have taken this nickname from an operetta. Little Klara had her pink room and wanted for nothing; she must have been badly spoiled. Lively and sociable, she had many girlfriends and also became friends with Rysio Apt, a conceited but very handsome and unusually gifted boy that all the girls in Klara's class had a crush on. She took dancing lessons – and after the war, she ran ballet schools in Poland and in Israel. Klara went through life joyfully, but in the spring of her years she had to stem the waves of the deluge like all of us; the experience may have been more painful and difficult for her.

The youngest of the Grosses was Jerzyk. When he started school, the teachers were soon convinced that 'Jozek was an angel in comparison to Jerzyk'. We older siblings had been raised in a home that was still developing, with all the effort and money going into raising the standards at home and in the shop, and not into luxury or high living. Jerzyk entered the world under objectively improved circumstances and it was only natural for him, as the youngest, to be spoiled the most.

By the early 1930s, our apartment already encompassed a whole floor of the building: eight lovely rooms tastefully furnished. I think that this was more mother's doing than father's. Father's fifth child was the store. I can still recall the deep-red wallpaper with gilded wreaths being torn from the walls when we moved into the apartment that the Tigners had vacated. I remember how Cygielman painted garlands by hand on the walls of the Rococo living room, and the furnishing of father's dark-green study with its beautiful carved mahogany bookcase, and the delivery of the piano and the dark walnut furniture for my parents' bedroom ... I remember how our Home came into being.

Jerzyk was born when all of this was already in place and the consciousness of prosperity may have influenced his cheekiness. When his first-grade teacher threatened to summon mother to school, he retorted, 'Oy vey, I'm quaking in my trousers', and backed up his words with the appropriate gesture. On another occasion, he assured an irate teacher that his parents had enough money to buy the whole school, including the teachers that worked there. There was no way to handle him.

When I was young – I was seven or eight – our parents sometimes took us to the Bizanc café on the Planty for sour milk and a 'squabble', the name given to a dish consisting of sardines, cottage cheese, onion and paprika; to this day I enjoy making myself a 'squabble'. For us children, such a Sunday outing was a grand occasion. A red pedal-driven car was on display, or perhaps for sale, at the Bizanc. I dreamed about it, but it never crossed my mind to ask my parents to buy me such a car, which must have been terribly expensive! So I thought. Who knows – if I had asked, they might have bought it for me. When Jerzyk was old enough to reach the pedals, father bought him a real little two-wheeled bicycle. It was probably Jerzyk's idea to use this bicycle in races around the dining-room table. We held our watches and checked the time to see who could complete the most laps in one minute. It was a big dining room. On the floor below us lived other Grosses – Bernard Gross and his wife. They were both old and hard of hearing. But when they saw their ceiling lamp dancing on its chain, they realized that something was going on upstairs. They telephoned to say that the plaster was falling on their heads. What could we say? That our home was our castle? We interrupted the races, and then started up again an hour later.

*

Of all our neighbors, the tenants in our building, the ones I remember best are the Ginsbergs from the second floor. Of course, I have not forgotten Salomea Gross, the old lady on the ground floor, or her grandson Janek, a law student, or the imperious Grynszpan, a senior accountant who supplemented his income by running courses in bookkeeping, or the Pempers, who always set up a Sukkoth booth in the courtyard, or the Walersteins who moved in after the Pempers moved out. Yet Captain Pinkas Ginsberg was in a class by himself. He always wore an elegant uniform with everything buffed and gleaming, and his saber at his side on a wide belt. He was a senior professional officer from Austrian times, disciplined and strict in his deportment. And yet he was broken in his old age. Having been promoted to lieutenant-colonel after the outbreak of the war, he ended up famished and ill at Katyń. After three months in that camp, he asked a Soviet officer acting as his escort to shoot him: 'I'm no use to anyone any more. I can't go on. I'm an old Jew …'

After consultation with the general in charge of the region, the suffering Ginsberg was sent to Stanislawow. And thus he was saved. He nevertheless had to wander around the Siberian wilderness and he buried his wife Mania somewhere along the way, but he returned to Poland after the war and died in his Cracow.

I well remember Mrs Ginsberg (a Haubenstock by birth), a petite, lively woman who was always calling her youngest daughter 'Lonka! Lonka!' Lonka was older than us, already in her teens, but she preferred playing with us in the courtyard to doing her homework. Her older sister Cesia was a much more solid character. Tall and neat, her soft hair was always flawlessly combed. Fate did not spare her. The Germans shot her daughter in the hospital in the Cracow ghetto, her husband died in Auschwitz, and in the last days of the war, Cesia herself was drowned in the sea by the Germans along with the other prisoners of Stutthof concentration camp.

Dawid, known as 'Witek', was the apple of his parents' eye and the Ginsbergs' great hope. He died in 1932. I recall how he was studying for his examinations in the second year of law school. He wore out a path in our garden next to the wooden fence that divided it from the Ursuline sisters' property. Back and forth, back and forth he paced with his friend, Maks Ferstendig, from morning to night, with short breaks for meals. Then, suddenly, he developed gangrene in his leg while recovering from the flu. What a tragedy! The best specialists were consulted. Professor Hladij was regarded as the best in Cracow. Glatzel and Rutkowski may have been just as good; in any case, the last named, a splendid diagnostician, was more delicate and more humane. Various anecdotes circulated about Hladij's professional manner and approach to his patients. He was said to be a 'butcher' who never began operating without first downing a quarter-liter of vodka in order to prepare himself for a master stroke of an incision.

After examining Witek's leg, he told the boy's parents: 'Go to the prayer house and cry out to Him not to take away such a golden boy.'

Of the whole beautiful Ginsberg family, only Lonka is alive. She lives in Israel with her husband and three children. She married young. Her husband is an agronomist named Machles. They emigrated to the agricultural settlement of Nachalal. She came to visit her parents in 1939. She returned to Israel – but only after the war, and by way of Siberia.

*

As far back as my memory reaches, we always had a maid, a 'nanny'. This is understandable when we remember how mother worked in the shop and had no time to look after her children, who came into the world one after the other. They came into the world at home. In those days, only poor women gave birth in the hospital. Mother retained her mistrust of hospitals to the end of her life, and refused even after the war to allow her daughters to give birth there. I remember Jozek's wet nurse, Leośka, only from anecdotes. She was a simple village woman who colored her cheeks with beet juice and did not avoid alcohol. Such a wet nurse was a paid terrorist in the house; when she began nursing the baby, her every whim had to be met. It was forbidden to upset her. We had to put up with everything until the baby had its fill.

The domestic help, the servants, worked from several to more than a dozen years, until they got married. Tosia served us for 15 years, staying with us after she got married. She even stayed with us during the war, although she lived in her own home then.

There were always three auxiliary forces at home: the cook Ludwisia, Tosia for cleaning (she later took over the function of cook), and the nanny – first, fat Berta, and then Frieda Cierniach from Sosnowiec (there were hopes that Fräulein Frieda might help us at our German). When Fryda married Alojzy Swoboda, she sent her younger sister Truda to replace her. They were both good-looking girls.

I associate fat Berta with the memory of homemade dumplings in hot milk. We did not like either milk or homemade noodles, and by the time we learned to like them, they were gone. By some strange coincidence, there were always homemade dumplings for supper when Berta had a visit from a girlfriend who was just as fat as she was. This sent us into gales of laughter. We howled and squealed and poured the milk on each other. Poor Berta did not know what to do: uncontrollable children who had it too good.

When Fräulein Frieda arrived, tanned dark brown, we were a little older. Frieda had a Silesian accent, but not a bad one, and was a zealous Polish patriot. She knew how to take charge. She taught us to tie knots and inculcated the Scout's Oath: 'A scout's word is as reliable as Zawisza' (a Polish hero – years later I added, 'and you'll end up like Zablocki' – the symbol of starting out wealthy and going bankrupt). She taught us sentimental, melancholy songs: 'The campfire is burning and the forest is soughing', or 'Fare thee well my mother dear, I'm off to bloody war, All your teachings I revere, And of wisdom could not ask for more'. There were also German ditties that I only understood when I began learning German in school: '*Fuchs, du hast die Gans gestohlen*', or '*Goldene Abendsohne*'. Her sister Truda was 18 when she came to act as nanny to Jerzyk. By then, we older boys were interested in more than her educational expertise. One should not, however, read too much into that remark …

If it is plain to see why nannies were needed at home, the presence of private tutors is explained in part by our laziness and lack of internal discipline. We were all lazy, which is why we all

50

chose artistic careers ... That, however, is another matter. I have no doubt that we were bright enough to pass from one grade to the other on our own. I was generally regarded as a good pupil and always had a decent report card. Klara was also a good pupil and could pass unaided. And Jozek? Jozek, it seems, was beyond help. A tutor could, however, make sure that he finished his homework. And once a tutor was employed for one child, he could supervise the others for the same money. We were all inclined towards the humanities and had no gift for mathematics. As for myself, I must regretfully submit that I gave up. I simply refused to learn mathematics or to do my homework. At best, I would copy a friend's mathematics assignment under the desk during history class.

Mother hired some tutors on the basis of acquaintance. Rafal Mahler, the eminent historian, was some sort of distant relative of mother. When his brother Jozek came to Cracow, he lived with us and was incidentally expected to help us with our lessons. He was an intelligent boy, but showed little interest in applied pedagogy. Still, it was pleasant to pass the time with him. Mrs Braun, wife of the teacher Majer Braun, had pedagogical talents. However, even when we were in the first and second years of secondary school, her fund of knowledge proved inadequate. Young Zunik, who came from Lida to study in Cracow, was colossally provincial and spoke with a dreadful Lithuanian accent that struck us as extraordinarily ridiculous, disqualifying him in advance as a tutor. He was the son of a salesman for the Stolle Niemen glass factory. His father wanted to set him up as well as possible in Cracow. My dear father was terribly anxious to help. He ended up taking him on as an apprentice at the shop; Zunik was a lost cause.

When the time came for me to prepare for my matriculation exams in mathematics, after having studied the subject for eight years, I took private lessons with our physics teacher's sister, whose name I cannot recall. She knew what she was doing. She may not have succeeded in teaching me much, but at least her intelligent approach to the subject inculcated a deep respect for mathematics in me. That respect has remained until today.

Two or three more names could be added to this list of helpers who attempted to boost us fortuitously from one grade to the next, such as Miss Berkwic. She gave us piano lessons and taught me Mozart's sonatas and Chopin's mazurkas (this was at my personal request, since I knew that I would never be a pianist, but still wished to learn the etudes, preludes, nocturnes and mazurkas of Chopin, my favorite composer). There was also Mrs Spiro of the Spiro Institute, who gave us violin lessons. What a nightmare! What screeching!

As reflected in the foregoing compilation, our afternoons were full of lessons and little time remained for a social life. Supper was served at seven, and one did not go out afterwards.

*

The kitchen was Tosia's kingdom. Her elder sister Anielcia had been in service to our parents for several years. When Anielcia found a good match and got married, she brought Tosia to us. That was in 1923, when Klara was born. Tosia was then 16 and, as mother told the story, stood crying at the window all the time. Anielcia was still with us, and mother advised her to take Tosia home to Bochnia because she was still a child, but Anielcia assured her that her younger sister would get used to things. And she got used to things. All week long, Tosia did the shopping, cleaned the apartment (and there was a lot to clean!). Before we got a nanny, she dressed us, fed us, and served meals while helping the cook, Ludwisia. Later, when Ludwisia had married and set up housekeeping on her own, Tosia assumed her functions. She had her culinary instruction from mother: she made very good stuffed pike on Fridays and a traditional yeast cake on Saturdays. On the other hand, the chicken in her everyday chicken soup was always tough, perhaps because we sat straight down at the table when we came home from school; we had lessons at three. The chicken had no time to cook properly. I derived no pleasure at all from these hurried dinners with their unvarying menu. Only on Saturdays and Sundays, when mother took a personal hand in preparing a feast for us, did I understand that eating, too, could be a pleasure. During the war, when mother made our dinners 'from nothing', I could appreciate what a good cook she had been.

Tosia had her own room (although I can remember the times when she slept on a folding cot in the kitchen). In that room, she read *The Leper, A Novel a Week*, and even *Secret Detective*. The latter magazine was blood-curdling; my hair stood on end at the very sight of it and it was not without reason that the courts closed it down. Tosia had a day off once a week, on Sundays. She went to the movies – and where else, and with whom? I do not know how she ended up with a rather gloomy fellow called Janek who was a communist. It must have been 1938 when he began visiting Tosia in the evenings. Finally, they got married. Mother gave her a hope chest fit for her own daughter; although she was on her own, Tosia continued to work for us during the war.

Tosia was merry and had an idiosyncratic sense of humor. We split our sides when she did an imitation of an old Jewish woman. She bought herself a tree at Christmas time and sang carols. The lovely Polish carols with their varied rhythms and melodies were catchy. I hardly suspected that the time would come when I would sing them as an 'Aryan', and even teach *The Lord is Born* to children and young people.

Mother had learned traditional Jewish cooking at home. She was not religious, and the fact that our cook never made pork resulted more from an attachment to Jewish specialties than from keeping kosher. I sometimes accompanied mother to New Market Square, where she selected a chicken that was then subjected to ritual slaughter and plucked on the spot – a rather horrifying sight for a child. Later in my life, I would see a few more things that were even more horrifying. Aunt Rifka – mother's aunt – had a shop with dried mushrooms at this Square. The aroma! I still remember it. I also remember Aunt Rifka, a small Jewish woman who was as clean and dried-up as her mushrooms, and who spoke beautiful Polish. Her children were frequent guests at our home: the energetic Mańka with her layabout husband and three successful children (none of whom survived), Oskar the furrier who had a shop in Katowice, and their younger brother Leon, who worked for Oskar. Oskar survived the war in terrible conditions, hiding in an attic with his wife and several other Jewish people. He emigrated to America afterwards. Leon found shelter in Russia and then went to Vienna, where he is in wholesale furs. His son is studying medicine, and his daughter graduated from the university in Jerusalem in political science and got married. Leon complains that none of his children wants to go into the business. He thinks about closing it down – he is no longer young and has heart problems – but then what would he do? What would he live for? So he goes on opening up the warehouse each morning and travelling to auctions in London, New York, and Leningrad. The very image of a man from those bygone times … Sometimes we reminisce together over that Square and those mushrooms.

Mother bought her butter and cheese at Leśniak's on the Small Market Square. She went there evenings, once the china shop was closed. I often accompanied her there, too. The fresh dessert butter, yellow or cream, came straight from the village wrapped in cabbage leaves. A vigorous woman with a pug nose, Mrs Leśniak offered samples of butter on the tip of her knife, praising her merchandise and then whispering a tidbit of gossip into mother's ear. She would wink and wrinkle her sharp chin in a meaningful way – she had customers of a high class and knew more than a little about them! Mother tried the different types of butter. This one was bitter, that one was salty – and then she ordered that the best be packed for her. Now came the turn of the cottage cheeses, wrapped in white cheesecloth and fragrant of sour milk. Again: this one was too dry, that one was too fresh, that one was too old – she repeated the sampling procedure while Mrs Leśniak served other customers.

We bought aromatic bread with fennel seed at the shop belonging to a man called Rajter, a traditional Jew with a black beard that the Germans later cut off, along with some skin. He also carried fresh, dark plum jam in flat wooden crates, sprats, and pickled herring. When 'the lady' was absent, Tosia bought whatever she needed at Rajter's 'on the book', which means on credit.

A woman from Bochnia brought eggs by the dozen in a big wicker basket. Mr Sroka, who owned a big delicatessen business on Dluga Street, sent sacks of flour and sugar to us at home. This Sroka was a tiny mustached man who wore a pince-nez; his colossal wife called him 'Daddy'. I remember them well from before the war – and even better from wartime. They were our customers, and we were theirs. I shall have more to say about the Srokas.

Mother kept all her foodstuffs under lock and key in the pantry. Each day, she gave Tosia what was needed for dinner and supper. The pantry was well-stocked. My mother was quite a housekeeper. And now that I've mentioned it, she was also an excellent cook. She tried to train Ludwisia and Tosia, but they could never match her. When a lot of guests were coming – on the occasion of a wedding in the family or one of Uncle Szulim's visits from abroad, for instance – she would be busy beforehand at the table in the kitchen and around the stove. Her youngest sister Mala was perhaps even more adept at the culinary arts. Mala specialized first and foremost in compotes, which she put up in jars by the dozen all summer and fall. Pears, sour cherries, blackheart cherries, gooseberries, plums, greengages – and then there were the currants, and then there was the raspberry juice, and then there was the raisin wine in gigantic demijohns for Passover ...

My parents were modest people. Success never went to their heads. They never went out dancing, they never hit the night spots, they did not lead an extensive social life. Their life consisted of their home and their shop, and everyday hard work. If they went to a restaurant, they usually took us along. We went to Weisbrot's on Starowislna Street for tripe with black pudding or for veal 'crumbs'. Or we might go, for a change, to Weisbrot's 'milk bar' for chulent with black pudding. Those stuffed black puddings were as broad as plates! Never since have I seen the like, anywhere. For us children, a visit to Weisbrot, whom we nicknamed 'Wajsprod', was a holiday. In my mind's eye, I can see the large arch-shaped dining room with a vast number of tables covered with snow-white tablecloths. I recall the obliging waiters with pencils behind their ears. I met one of them, Leon, in Tel Aviv, and he remembered me. At 'Wajsprod's' he might have been a busboy of the second category; in Israel, he rose to the rank of head waiter at the Acadia, one of the most elegant hotels in Herzliya. He remembered our whole family well. What he regretted was the decline of the profession of waiter in Israel: 'It's not the same as back home in Cracow, Mr Gross!'

I am inclined to agree. Tripe tastes different here and you have to go around with a candle looking for a restaurant that serves it. Cracow chulent is something I've never seen here, let alone black pudding. Chulent is the national specialty of Jewish cuisine. It comes in so many varieties that it is difficult to conceive of how they can all go under the same name. The one common characteristic, theoretically at least, is that they are prepared on Friday, kept overnight in the stove, and served for dinner on Saturday. Everything else is optional. Some people make chulent with roast potatoes and big chunks of meat, others with beans, others with some sort of buckwheat, and others still with hulled barley, *farfelki*, or even vegetables – take your pick.

We went to 'Wajsprod's' for chulent, and sometimes we took chulent home with us in a pot. Saturday was Saturday – not in the religious sense, but in family tradition. We ate separately all week; the times of the children's meals were not coordinated with those of our parents. Only on Saturday and Sunday did we sit down to a fully set table. And of course there was Friday supper. As I have mentioned, my parents both came from devout families and carried on the tradition after their own fashion. Friday supper was a holiday occasion. Mother did not go shopping on Fridays; she was already 'at work on Saturday'. She braided loaves of *challah*, boiled the fish, stuffed the pike, baked the goose. She was familiar with the rituals, although she had perhaps only an instinctive understanding of their significance. Father tried to close the shop a little earlier. When he returned home, washed, and changed clothes, mother lighted the candles – at an hour, of course, when it was already forbidden to light them. Father said *kiddush* and we children, dressed in clean clothes and washed, stood ceremoniously around the table, which was covered with a white tablecloth. Father celebrated *kiddush* (which we pronounced 'kiddish') over a chalice of golden Lęcka slivovitz – I can feel its sharpness on my tongue to this day. Afterwards, Tosia brought in two platters of fish.

I have never eaten stuffed pike since those days. Gefilte fish (interestingly enough, I never heard this traditional name at home, where it was called 'stuffed fish'), like chulent, tastes different in different places. At home, the fish was served sweet. People from Warsaw, where they ate their fish salty, called ours 'compote'. Lithuanians like their fish spicy. My wife comes from Grodno; her fish (perhaps for my sake) is a compromise version.

Julek Tigner once invited me to Friday supper in London. His wife is from Warsaw. They served fish, of course; Julek generally keeps the tradition. The fish balls looked like the ones back home, although they were on the small side and as white as dumplings. No one warned me that it was not pike, and not even carp. When I had taken a substantial mouthful, I suddenly felt that I was not going to be able to swallow it. I chewed and chewed, and somehow I triumphed and finally managed to get it down. I wanted to compliment the lady of the house, but the words stuck in my throat, just as that fish had stuck in my throat. Dear Lord, I thought, how poor Julek, raised on Tigner cooking, must suffer!

Home, Sweet Home

The Tigners were gourmets. When we lived next door, I envied the way that Jozia's cracklings came out – so good, crisp, and elegant, a treat for the palate – while Tosia's were always flaccid, soggy, oozing fat, and undercooked. I remember how Julek and Rysiek used to fight over the 'goose's pipe', which is when I learned that this is the tastiest part of the fowl. On Passover at the Tigner's I had *aufgefrishte* matzo, which is matzo freshened in water and deep fried in lard; in general, they consumed a lot of lard, which was apparent from one look at that well-fed family.

*

When I talk about Israeli children with other people who, like me, come from Poland, we often accuse them of being too uninhibited, with no sense of limits and too much *chutzpa*. Not like we were at their age. We were polite and obedient. It may be true, as the saying goes, that the bull does not remember what the calf was like, and we were certainly no angels, but there was still a difference. I always said that it all came from the differences in architecture. Houses in Israel have neither attics nor basements. Nor do they have doorkeepers' booths or porters. Attics and basements have a great influence on a child's imagination. I sometimes ventured up into the attic during the day to dig around among junk covered with a thick layer of dust, but in the evening – not on your life! You could only go there with a candle or an oil lamp. Attics were terrifying. And it was also terrifying to climb a dimly illuminated staircase at dusk, even as far as the third floor – anyone could jump out of the shadows, couldn't they? A thief, a criminal … a cloak murderer! This atmosphere was due in part to *Secret Detective* magazine, which I have already mentioned, with its greenish pages and blood-curdling photographs, with its descriptions of bloody crimes and unsolved mysteries, and its suitably embellished courtroom reports. 'The Werewolf of Düsseldorf' – a vampire, a blood-drinker, a pervert who attacked young girls! Kärtner! The search was on for a home-grown Kärtner right here in Cracow. He was allegedly a 'cloak murderer', who hid around corners or in the shadows of passageways in apartment buildings, threw his cloak over his victims' heads – a strangler! I raced up the stairs to the third floor and held my breath until the moment when Tosia opened the door! A happy childhood – with a dark passageway, an attic, a cellar full of terrors.

The watchman or watchwoman – that was a different story. The woman who guarded the door of our building was called Mrs Jozef. She liked her alcohol and always gave off an odor of vodka, but she kept her little room clean. Mrs Jozef was responsible for the cleanliness of the courtyard, and this led to conflicts. She sometimes chased us with a stick when we played too noisily or dragged a branch in to use in our games. Illiterate, she had a son who was a policeman somewhere in the provinces. She sent him long letters beginning 'Praise be to Jesus Christ'. Her amanuensis was Lonka, who also read out the letters that arrived from her son. Mrs Jozef hated it when she was called on to open the door after 'curfew'; she locked up on the stroke of ten. Sometimes you had to wait a long time, ringing and ringing, before – cursing like a sailor – she turned her massive key in the heavy, oaken door. Then she went back to her room, pausing along the way to relieve herself at the sewer grating in the middle of the courtyard. At New Year's she came around with 'best wishes', holding up some sort of picture and showering the tenants with oats for good fortune in the coming year. Then she went off with her pals to drink herself into a stupor in her little room in the afternoon. She kept wonderful company.

Before the building came into the possession of my parents, we played under the spreading chestnut in the courtyard, kicking first a rag ball and then one made of rubber. How often Jozek (why was it always Jozek?) broke the Pempers' ground-floor window! It was always fun in the courtyard and something was always about to happen. There were even set days for the courtyard singers, organ grinders or Gypsies. 'Fats', a stout Jew in a dirty Hungarian frogged coat belted with a string, in muddy, torn boots, perhaps not quite right in the head, always came on Sundays. He always sang the same *hasidic* melody – a *zmires* – livened up with a sort of Austrian march: 'Ram-tatata-ramta tam-trarara-rarara …'. Compassionate women threw him a *grosz* wrapped in a scrap of newspaper. It should be noted that the generosity falling from the windows and balconies of the apartment building was a measure of the artistic level of the guest performer. When a group of musicians came, the five- and ten-*grosz* pieces fell like rain. During the Depression (1936 or 1937?), when musicians lost their jobs in the cafés of Cracow, there was a sudden boom in courtyard ensembles that played to a very high standard. On the initiative of the city council, I seem to recall, a contest was organized for courtyard orchestras. Each of these orchestras had its own specially designed uniforms; it was a pleasure to watch and a pleasure to listen. We children, however, understandably preferred the Gypsy fire-eaters and circus acts, the occasional bear on a chain, or the organ-grinder with the parrot Lora who drew lucky lottery numbers for the cooks and serving maids. The greatest attraction of all was Caesar, a pederast with disgusting blistered lips who specialized in obscene rhymes of his own authorship. He sold copies of them in thin brochures or on single sheets. If you read them, the weakness of the rhymes was apparent, but when they flowed from the mouth of Caesar, it was another matter altogether. He was always followed around by a band of school kids that he chased away when they became bothersome – they all wanted to touch him for good luck – which is not to say that he did not basically enjoy their company. It was said that he had been a student (he wore a student's white cap on the days when he did not have his paper crown on his head) who had flunked an examination on Caesar and gone crazy – thus the nickname. Caesar could often be found on the Blonia meadow or in the Planty, but he also made regular rounds of the courtyards in various districts of the city. He would not begin his performance until he had collected a certain minimum sum. At times when too little was thrown to him, he would walk away obscenely cursing the miserliness of the tenants. We children regarded his as a demanding profession. At the end of his performance he waited for a few more *groszy*, and then gave his trademark farewell: 'To those who gave money, I bow down low; To those who didn't, my behind I show', which he proceeded to do in a grandiloquent manner.

The ragmen came: 'I'll trade glasses for old rags and shoes! Glasses for rags!' The tinkers cried, 'Pots soldered! Holes plugged!' – a text that could have come from one of Zegadlowicz's naturalistic novels. The whetstone man came with his workbench on his back: 'Knives to sharpen!' We peered in curiosity as the sparks flew from the stone when one of the tenants gave him a pocketknife to hone – or even a kitchen knife.

Sometimes, a touching orphan girl would appear in the

courtyard, dressed in rags, singing her woes in a plaintive little voice. My heart broke, but the windows did not open for the likes of her. Someone might toss out a slice of bread – what times those were. To give a beggar a slice of bread! Later, many of these same wealthy people would beg for a slice of bread, for a little water, as they stretched their hands out of the sealed cattle cars or stole a bread crust in a camp. They died of hunger …

*

While keeping the courtyard in order, Mrs Jozef jealously guarded access to the garden. And what a beautiful garden it was: 200 *sążni*, people said, although I never tried to convert this old Polish measure, equalling two cubits, into acres, hectares or square meters … It was separated from the courtyard by high lilac bushes that were dazzlingly fragrant in May. And what a treat for the eye! There was a mass of them, perhaps 15 bushes the size of young trees. With the entrance to the garden being next to Mrs Jozef's little room, you had to sneak past on tiptoe or wait until she had gone out shopping to pluck a few cherries or gooseberries (the gooseberry bushes were at the edge of the garden). Afterwards, when the garden became ours, such problems ended. We could knock pears down at will, aiming stones at the thickest clumps of red vitarnia, or shake the branches, or climb the beurre tree. The vitarnia pear tree was too high to climb, while the crown of the beurre was relatively low. Those were the sweetest, juiciest and most delicious of the pears … And then there were the sweet summer pears with their mealy fruit – although they were full of worms – and the winter pears: as hard as rocks, but they had an incredible taste if allowed to ripen for five weeks. The most attractive trees, however, were not ours, but those of our neighbors …

At the back, our garden abutted on the vast garden of the Ursuline sisters. We flirted through a hole in the fence with the young schoolgirls until the nuns chased them away. Then, standing on each other's shoulders, we used a stick to try to knock down the violet and dark-blue plums in the convent garden. There were other gardens at the sides of ours. Siodmak's wall, at 10 Zielona Street, was too high for any fruit from that garden to tantalize us. On the Steigler side, however, the wall was lower and we were tempted by greengages and huge red Santa Rosa plums – aside from this, Steigler had seven daughters.

The garden was rather neglected when it came into our possession, but it soon became the center of social life for us young Grosses. Mother hoed the ground and planted flower beds. She loved flowers so much that she always devoted Sundays to the garden. Then there was the summer house against the side wall of the apartment building, next to Mrs Jozef's little watch-room. Built by 'Mug' from the shop according to a design by Wallis, it featured a circular veranda and two built-in couches that folded away into the walls. The summer house was linked to our kitchen on the third floor by a 'cable car'. Squeaking and screeching, a box containing a pitcher of coffee, cups, and a complete supper ran down the thin cable. Once this apparatus had been installed, suppers in the garden became a tradition. Previously, our parents had sometimes stopped at Weisbrot's or Apollo's for supper; now, they returned home each evening and we all ate together in the garden. As Lonka told me recently, the Ginsbergs were not enamored of the racket Tosia made when she sent our supper down the cable. For us, however, it was the greatest fun in the world. Those suppers abounded in piquant novelties. Father loved delicacies, the fruits of distant seas, and tropical fruit. He also loved tomatoes, which we children would not touch. I remember how, when food shortages loomed at the beginning of the war, I announced that I would eat everything, even tomatoes. I was more reluctant to accept other delicacies of father's, such as fresh-water bull-heads in tomato sauce, or mackerel. Later, all these things began tasting good, when father was gone.

We had a ping-pong table in the summer house and a miniature billiard table, custom-made (by 'Mug', of course) with steel balls, and another Japanese-made billiard set that took tokens – all these different attractions for my friends, and Jozek's, and Klara's, and Jerzyk's. It was pleasant to sit playing bridge on the veranda and, in general, those were the times of our lives … Later, those times changed, and the garden and the summer house took on new significance. When there were no movies, no theatre, and even no school, more and more boys and girls began coming there seeking a refuge from the street and from their own homes, from the growing anxiety and the uncertainties about the future. We could be together there. That meant a lot.

Such a courtyard and such a garden favored the growth of the domestic menagerie.

Father loved animals. And, of course, he loved children – who also loved animals. There was always a menagerie at home: mammals, birds and goldfish. The first mammal that I remember was a hedgehog. It strolled around under my bed. It had probably not been brought in for me to play with, although I loved its endearing face peeping out from under the quills, with eyes like black pinheads. It seems to me that the purpose of the hedgehog was to catch mice, although I cannot say what success it had. In any case, it was followed by cats, divine creatures with character. A cat is no slave, not like a dog that comes apologizing and wagging its tail beseechingly even after being threatened with a stick or bombarded with shoes. Not a cat. A cat gets offended. I remember gray Puszek with black stripes. He was a very good cat, although he had too much of a liking for gefilte fish, to the point that he infuriated our Tosia. She inadvertently left a bowl of fish on the kitchen table. Puszek obviously caught the scent, found the temptation too great, and was on the table in an instant. He gulped it down in one bite and had not even managed to lick himself when Tosia was at his head with a ladle, whack! whack! She chased him around the kitchen until the miserable beast managed to slip out the door at the moment that someone happened to come home. Puszek never again returned to our apartment. Not that he disappeared. He came to the door each morning and meowed and meowed until one of us put out a saucer of milk. At the sight of Tosia, however, he took off down the stairs in a cloud of dust. He never forgave and never forgot her unseemly behavior.

There were goldfish at home and in the shop. They did not meow, but they died systematically, despite having a regular supply of oxygen and never going without food. We kept our squirrel in a cage at first, until we felt sorry for it. We decided that it was tame – after all, it ate from our hands – and let it out. It raced around the apartment like a madman. It took nuts from our hands, but since there were never enough nuts, it began gnawing all the furniture. Perhaps it was all an escape plan. In any case, it succeeded: we released the squirrel into the garden.

In the garden, next to the Ursuline sisters' wall (erected as a successor to the wooden fence), two splendid peacocks paced back and forth, back and forth, destroying all the flowers and wearing out a path exactly where Witek Ginsberg, blessed be his memory, had crammed with his friend.

There were chirping canaries, blue parrots, and guinea pigs. Then there were the pigeons. They perched in the chestnut tree that grew towards the window, and built nests in the holes that the builders of the house next to ours (on the western side) had deliberately left in the wall for just that purpose. We loved to listen to those pigeons cooing at dawn. They had only one drawback, which sealed their fate: they turned the lovely parapet outside my parents' bedroom window and the kitchen balcony into their toilets. Someone – I do not know who – decided one day that the best thing would be to eat them. Lord, what lamenting! They might as well have slaughtered us children. It turned out to be impossible for us to eat those roast pigeons. Never again were pigeons served to us, and I cannot say whether I would be capable of ordering such a delicacy in a restaurant today. Please note that those pigeons seem to have been *grymki*. Who knows? My wartime 'Aryan' name may have been their revenge.

*

In *Polish Flowers*, Julian Tuwim devotes a chapter to the Warsaw dogs that died and suffered among the ruins of the burning city. The poet mourns the dogs blown to bits by exploding bombs and those that pined away in sorrow for their owners, and the puppies left behind in abandoned apartments that, half-alive among the choking smoke, still believed that their masters would return – a dog always waits.

Some people reacted with distaste to such descriptions and criticized the poet who shed tears over the sad fate of the dogs at a time when people were dying. Those critics had probably never had a dog, or perhaps had never known anything about what a friend is ... Having witnessed every circle of the inferno of the occupation, I often feel emotional about the memory of our beautiful bitch, Dina. She went through a long succession of torments together with our family, until we had to part with her. We left her with Poles whom we knew – and fled. To this day it weighs on my heart to think of the wrong we did our faithful Dina. Only someone who has had a dog will understand.

Father bought Dina for us after Heksa died. And Heksa had not died a natural death. She committed suicide. Have you ever heard of a dog committing suicide out of longing for her master? That is what Heksa did.

She was a pedigree German shepherd bitch, similar to a wolf. Uncle Szulim brought her to Aunt Mala as a present, and Mala lived with us, so the dog was 'ours'. But Heksa was wise enough to know who her mistress was and whom she belonged to. In her time, she had been a police dog. During a manhunt, she had been shot. The wound had not been serious, but it sufficed for Heksa to be retired from the force. From then on, she hated people in uniform. Children could ride horseback on her or poke their fingers in her eyes – she was angelically imperturbable. Obedient and patient, she made friends with everyone – but let her catch sight of a soldier, policeman, or even a uniformed mailman, and her hackles rose, she showed her fangs, and she growled deep in her throat in a way that bode no good. The only way to avoid unfortunate occurrences in such cases was to take her away rapidly.

I have no intention of writing at length about Heksa. I will only note that her love for Aunt Mala, whom she accompanied from morning to night, was great indeed. One day, Aunt Mala departed for a month abroad. Heksa went down the stairs, lay down in the middle of the courtyard, and refused to come back inside. Not on her life. What is more, she turned her snout away from all food and would not take even a drop of water. We tried everything to get her to come in. We bought her kielbasa, ham, and other treats – she would not even sniff at them. She lay sadly on the courtyard paving stones, with her head down and her tail curled around her, and all she did was to let out a soft moan from time to time. No one could budge her. We looked on with broken hearts and a feeling of powerlessness as she faded away and suffered. Ten days after her mistress's departure, Heksa died of longing.

Father bought us Dina to console our sorrow. She was an Airedale terrier with short, curly fur, black spots on her back, and bright, merry eyes. How gentle and happy, how wise, how fun-loving are dogs of this breed! When I spoke to Dina, she eloquently nodded her squarish head and looked me in the eye. I had no doubts that she understood. Sometimes she let out a strange, throaty cry – I would swear that she was speaking. She was a faithful companion in our games, and our joy knew no bounds when she gave birth to six puppies. According to the ways of the world, we gave five away to acquaintances and kept one – Terry – for ourselves. Terry grew manly and beautiful until he was bigger than his dam; he was a splendid dog in all respects.

We loved our dogs very much, and they had it good with us. They were lacking nothing for canine contentment.

Then the war broke out and the German army entered Cracow. Everything changed in the course of one night. Father and Jozek went eastward, across the River Bug. Mother, Klara, my youngest brother Jerzyk and I remained at home.

Not many days passed before the Germans requisitioned our spacious apartment. They occupied all the rooms except one, which they left for us. Like all Jews, we were forced to wear the 'yellow patch', a white arm band with a blue Star of David. We were made to do forced labor each day. Things were so bad that we did not even stop to think that they could be worse …

In those gloomy times, the dogs were the only bright spots in our sad lives. When I returned home after a day of arduous slave labor, they leaped on me, licked my face and hands, and jumped for joy. They never complained about overcrowding. But the Germans who were living in our rooms grew worried about the way the beautiful dogs had to live in such inhuman conditions, in such overcrowding. They decided to give them to their boss in Tarnow as a present. At first, they attempted politely to convince us. Germans love animals, they said, and our dogs would never have it so good as with their boss. When they understood that their persuasion was in vain, that we would never voluntarily part with Dina and Terry, they stopped urging us. An army truck pulled up in front of our building one day. Two soldiers jumped out and, without asking anyone's permission, simply took our dogs away, despite their fierce resistance and the bitter tears of Klara and little Jerzyk. We were plunged into mourning for seven days. Our lodgers tried to cheer us up: the dogs are well off, they said. They have space to run and good food. There's no reason to be upset. They were probably right, since the Germans treated dogs much better than people. But who can understand a dog's soul? Exactly seven days after being kidnapped, Dina returned! She was dirty and exhausted, and a fragment of rope hung from her collar. She must have been tied up somewhere, before escaping and running 80 kilometers from Tarnow to Cracow. She was too tired to be happy. She wagged her short tail and panted, with white foam on her snout. Only when we had bathed and combed her did she go back to being as merry and pranksterish as ever. At night, however, we sometimes saw how she showed her teeth and barked quietly in her sleep. She was having bad dreams.

So Dina stayed with us and went wherever they made us go. Her son Terry never returned.

The situation in the occupied territory grew worse by the day, until they finally drove the Jews into ghettos. We tried to avoid the ghettos like the plague, and wandered for as long as we could from place to place through the suburbs and outlying villages. Yet the German noose tightened systematically. The Jews living in the villages were concentrated in small towns and sent in transports to the death camps. In the summer of 1942, everyone in Grêbalow, where we were, was carried in carts to Wieliczka. Dina, our faithful companion in suffering, did not leave us for a moment. When we arrived in Wieliczka, it turned out that there was no way in the world to escape. We were surrounded; they had put up roadblocks everywhere. It seemed like a trap with no exit. And yet we managed to get away in spite of everything.

A group of Jews doing forced labor at the airport bribed their German boss, who sent two trucks to Wieliczka under orders to return immediately with all his employees, under the pretext that they were being retained illegally. News of the trucks flew through Wieliczka faster than a bird. Mother, Jerzyk, Klara and I were in different corners of the town then, and to this day I cannot explain how it was that we were all standing next to the trucks within a few minutes – and Dina was there, too, of course.

A moment later the trucks were packed to overflowing. When people noticed a dog among the roiling crowd, they began protesting sharply. Someone grabbed Dina by the scruff of the neck and threw her into the street! My heart broke at the sight of the poor beast standing facing the truck, holding her head up in a silent question: are you going to leave me here? Jerzyk could not tolerate such a situation. He jumped down from the truck, picked Dina up, and threw her back in. I tried to hide her, holding her in my arms, but to no avail. People were furious, and they tore her away from me and threw her back into the street. A cry of despair arose from Jerzyk's breast: 'Noooo!' He threw Dina back to us like a ball. And so it went on until I finally managed to conceal the dog on the floor of the truck bed. Jerzyk jumped in at the last instant and the truck roared off at high speed toward Cracow.

Dina lay stretched out on the floor as we raced along. People stepped on her as if she were not there and, as if she understood the situation, she did not let out a peep … When we drove into the Cracow ghetto, we ran off immediately in different directions to avoid falling into the hands of the police, since we were there illegally. That was a time of great overcrowding in the ghetto. People were living ten or 12 to a room – and these people were strangers to each other who often did not share even a common language. And we had to keep a dog in one of those rooms. But Dina was so good and friendly that she soon made friends for herself, even among people who did not like dogs.

There was nothing to eat in the ghetto. Fortunately, Dina could fend for herself and did not require our aid. She looked here, dug there, and hung around the courtyards. There were times when we feared that she would get into trouble somewhere, but she always returned home before the curfew. This state of affairs did not continue long. After a month, there were new reports about another deportation. It was a dark day for everyone. One rumor followed another, and the ghetto hummed like a beehive. It was still possible to come in through the gate, but leaving through that same gate was out of the question. Everyone knew by then that deportation meant annihilation in the death camps.

We wandered from one gate of the ghetto to the other without any clear goal. Even if we could escape – where to? Yet that vital force, from which mother was able to draw new strength and ideas in the worst of moments, came to our aid once again. A 'Blue Policeman' stood guard at one of the side gates of the ghetto. He was afraid to take a bribe and afraid to let us out. Yet he turned a blind eye when, in the falling darkness, we walked straight through the gate and broke into a mad dash to escape along the barbed wire ghetto perimeter fence. How we ever made it is hard to explain.

The first door we knocked at was Tosia's. We could not spend the night there. The Germans had decreed a death penalty for Poles who sheltered Jews, and Tosia was afraid to take the risk. But she did agree to take Dina in. Dogs, after all, are not Jewish. The Germans left them alone. Far from representing a risk, Dina would serve as a watchdog.

An hour after our escape, the Germans surrounded the ghetto. Over the next two days, they deported tens of thousands of Jews to the death camp at Belzec. When that operation was over, we returned to the ghetto – we still had no definite place for ourselves on the 'Aryan' side. The boundaries of the ghetto were shrinking. We moved often from one place to another, from one apartment to another, from one hideout to another, because we had no permission to stay there. We took comfort in the thought that Dina, at least, was in good hands.

One evening, as we lay down to sleep on the floor of someone else's apartment, we suddenly heard a scratching at the door, and then quiet whining. It was Dina. How she found us, after we had moved several times, must remain her mystery. Our joy was boundless. The only thing we could not understand was why Dina had left the quiet home of Tosia, whom she knew well, to seek us with all our troubles … Only a dog can be so faithful.

Once again, there was no alternative but to prepare to leave the ghetto – for good, this time. To escape beyond the wall, to the Polish side, where we would live like the rest of the Polish population – except that we would have false 'Aryan' papers. We decided to leave Dina at Tosia's once again – we could not dream of a better place for her. But she did not want to part from us. She could feel that we intended to leave her and disappear. We had no choice but to lock her in a room at Tosia's before we left. We could hear her jumping against the door and barking, as if she was bitterly accusing us: I don't want to! I don't want to! – like a small child who has been wronged. We felt like traitors. We had betrayed our most trusting friend.

When we visited Tosia after the war, Dina was not there. She had escaped from the house at the first opportunity and never returned. Perhaps, alone and downcast, she had wandered the streets looking for us in the abandoned apartment houses of the ghetto. Might a German gendarme have shot her as a stray? Or could she have died of remorse and longing, like Heksa?

Whenever I remember Dina, I am overcome with sadness. Could she understand our actions? How is it possible to leave a beloved friend, to escape from that friend, to leave that friend in strange hands? A dog cannot understand that …

5. Learning Came Easy

How did the Hebrew school differ from the Polish school? In the Polish school, a Jew had to be a good student, perhaps better than the others, whereas in the Hebrew school he could allow himself to be a poor student, to assume an attitude of indifference towards lessons and teachers, to goof off to his heart's content, and to cut class. It was an oasis, an island isolated from Polish reality – and yet Poland and Polishness, in all their manifestations, were better represented and conveyed in our Hebrew school than was Jewishness.

The Hebrew school – everyone called it the Hebrew school, but its official name was the Jewish Coeducational Secondary School (or, after 1936, the Chaim Hilfstein Private Coeducational Secondary School) of the Jewish Primary and Secondary School Association in Cracow. And so it was a Jewish school, although perhaps due to the strength of some sort of complex, nobody paraded that Jewishness. Everyone called it 'Hebrew'. Nor was Yiddish heard in the corridors. The truth is that Hebrew was not heard either, unless a student was talking to a teacher from one of the Hebrew subjects. The prevailing language was Polish. As opposed to the schools in the Tarbut network – where Hebrew was the language of instruction and even mathematics, biology and history were taught in that sacred language – we had only four subjects in the language of the forefathers: Hebrew (language and literature), the Bible, religion, and Jewish history. Everything else was taught in Polish. Those Judaistic subjects meant that we had ten more hours of lessons each week than our counterparts in Polish school. That difference aside, we had all the other accoutrements of a Polish school: branches of the Anti-Aircraft Defense League and the Maritime League and of the Red Cross, along with literature, history, philosophy and drama clubs. There was a school military training unit with Polish commanders, a *Hatzofeh* scout organization, a sports club, Student Government (I was the last president before the war!), Student Aid society, and the orchestra under the direction of the Czech composer Karaś, who was later replaced by the Jewish musicians, Schleichkorn and Wendum.

The school orchestra! Second only to that of the Sobieski Secondary School, the proud Jewish ensemble had a regular place at the marching reviews held on the national holidays in May and November next to the Church of St Wojciech on the Main Square. All Kazimierz turned out to watch the school parade at the Makkabi stadium on Lag Ba'omer![1] At their head marched the gleaming tambourine-major, a drum on a carriage brought up the rear, and in between shone the trumpets, French horns, and trombones. The strains of the *Standard March* brought servants and shop girls out of the nearby shops, and Jews in *chalat* coats and *shtreimles* to the entrance ways and windows. Flocks of children tagged along after the orchestra, which was preceded by bicyclists with crêpe paper decorating the spokes of their wheels. And, of course, there was the beautiful silk banner. A holiday on the Jewish streets. Crowds on Krakowska Street, crowds on Dietla, on the roofs, atop the kiosks, on the balconies. What happiness, what pride! Did any public school in Cracow know such emotions?

Did I say that learning came easy? Not in the case of Hebrew, which I regret to this day. Perhaps this had more to do with the teachers than with me. My class was unlucky when it came to Hebrew teachers, or so it seemed to me. I was taught in primary school by Beniamin Jeruzalimski, a large, well-fed man with bulging eyes who never got through to me. When a young lady cannot dance, then either the floor is uneven or her slippers are too tight. In secondary school, I came up against Naftali Rubinstein. We called him 'Daft' – he was 'nervous' and could not handle his pupils. He was in fact an intelligent man and wrote articles on pedagogy for the *Jewish Almanac* and *The Link*, but he clearly had no idea of how to apply his theories to an uproarious classroom. I grew closer to him when he no longer taught us (he had lessons only with the lower classes), and even closer during the war. Among our teachers, he was the first victim of Nazi brutality, and was among the first people sent to the camp at Pustkow near Debica, where he was subjected to incredible torments.

Dr Wolf Blattberg, 'Flap-Ears', taught us Jewish history. Aside from his prominent ears, he had a deep bass voice that seemed to rumble from his belly. I could not bring myself to pay attention to his monotone lectures, preferring instead to play battleships under

the desk with a friend. The bearded Benzion Rappaport –
'Rapciuch' or 'the Old Man' – was a philosopher and a good soul
who preferred to converse with me in Polish. He obviously could
not bear to listen to the way I mangled the beautiful Hebrew
language – how I ever managed to pass my matriculation exam in
Hebrew, God only knows. Even before graduation, I regretted my
ignorance and said more than once that I would have surely been
a good Hebraist if I had been taught by Szmulewicz or Katz (who
taught the girls' classes). This seems, however, to be self-deception
or a delusion … when I arrived in Israel 12 years after graduation,
I attended *ulpan* to try to improve my Hebrew a bit. Here, too, I
learned little, although I had good intentions and a fine teacher: I
simply knew too much in relation to the level of the *ulpan* class, so
I was once again unmotivated. I did, however, pick up a few
elegant Hebrew turns of phrase, of the sort that no one in Israel
would ever use in an everyday context and which are dead give-
aways that make each *ole* (immigrant) recognizable.

And so, all through school, Hebrew did not come easy. I did not
understand the words of the prayers that we mumbled each day
before the start of the first lesson. As to spelling, I am ashamed to
admit, I am still lost, despite having written columns, reviews and
stories in Hebrew for the Israeli press for 20 years.

*

Nachman Mifelew. How I envied the classes that had Hebrew with
him. He came from Skidel, near Grodno. I did not know this at the
time, except that his 'Litwak' accent stood out in Galicia. He was
one of the first three teachers at our Hebrew school (which had
been founded in 1907 or 1908). He was a small man with a deeply
lined, weatherbeaten face, and he enchanted the pupils with his
imagination. His historical novel for young people, *The Valley of the
Ten Palms*, was favorite reading for those who knew Hebrew. He
also supervised the programs for the Hanukkah and Purim school
assemblies. The Mifelews lived five doors away from us, on Jasna
Street, and he prepared me for my barmitzvah when I turned 13. I
knew his son Chananel, or 'Nanek', who was one grade ahead of
me even though he was three months younger, but not until after
the war, in Israel, did we become friends. By then, he was the only
one of the Mifelews left. His father had died in 1937. I saw his

mother and his sister Lala (Cypora) for the last time in the Cracow ghetto. They were both tall, good-looking blondes and could have found refuge on 'Aryan' papers – they were on the first transport to Belzec. After graduating in 1937, Nanek enrolled at the Jagiellonian University and then tried his hand at a theatrical career. He appeared alongside Lolek Wojtyla in the academic theatre and in Jarema's avant-garde Cricot group. Having emigrated to Palestine just before the war, he enrolled in the Hebrew University, took off as one of the first Jewish flyers with the Royal Air Force in Palestine – and landed as Chan Canasta, a magician who enjoyed tremendous popularity in the 1950s and 1960s. For 20 years, he delighted and amazed live audiences and television viewers in England and America, using no other props than a deck of cards and the pages of a book. His act did not depend on telepathy, parapsychology or a sixth sense, but rather on his brilliant memory, his imaginative abilities, and his deep knowledge of human instinct. He said that he inherited the taste for show business from his father, who had wanted to be an actor and had ended up playing the role of a Hebrew teacher. When Nanek grew bored with his stage appearances, he took up painting – and here, too, he could not complain of a lack of success. He has never built himself a home and lives like a Gypsy, wandering around the world. He comes to Israel to visit his friends; he is highly sentimental and eagerly returns in his reminiscences to the Hebrew school. He also republished his father's book (which has gone through three printings).

The first year of school is usually associated with a child's first love – the love for a teacher. In my case, it was the golden-haired Mrs Zofia Leinkram. I was also a favorite of hers – surely not the only one – and that love of ours survived the tempests of the war. We continue to enjoy each other's company in Israel, to which Mrs Leinkram managed to travel immediately after the outbreak of war. She founded a kindergarten here, the famous Gan Zahava, or Garden of Zahava (Zofia means Zahava, which means Golden), and has helped raise the children of many people from Cracow and Tel Aviv.

I must have had no problems with writing, reading, and arithmetic, since no adventures in those subjects have stuck in my memory. Or perhaps I have a porous memory. By evening, I have often already forgotten what I had for dinner. Yet episodes from 50 years ago are lodged in the recesses of my brain and suddenly pop up without my knowing why or how. The fact that I recall the slender, ephemeral, ever-so-delicate Niusia from primary school (she looks different today) is perhaps explained by the fact that I had a crush on her. I remember Lusia, who blushed for the slightest of reasons – and still does; I see her regularly at reunions. I recall Hela because she was so big and Bronia because she was so sweet. Yet how to explain the miracle that occurred when a stout, short woman in the fullness of her years, with no characteristic features at all, came up to me on Allenby Street? She said, 'You surely won't remember me.' Yet without a moment's hesitation I cried out, 'Erna!' She herself was surprised; we had not laid eyes on each other since primary school, more than 50 years earlier. I omitted to tell her that I remembered her because she used to drink ink, and always had a blue mouth – not now, not on Allenby! That's the way it is with memory.

I remember the drawing instructor Zygmunt Seiden, who turned up for class one day with an iodine stain on his bald pate. That was enough to earn him the nickname 'Redbird', but he only sent us into worse convulsions of laughter when he explained: 'Don't laugh. A pocketknife fell from the fifth floor and hit me on the head.'

'Take up Pilsudski's shoulder with your pencil and set it down on the paper', Seiden taught us. Everybody laughed at him except for me. Perhaps this was because I loved drawing. And yet, interestingly enough, I was not handy and am still unable today to drive a nail properly … Seiden liked me very much. When I drew an Englishman on a horse and a Sioux Indian in a headdress, he led me to the teacher's room in order to show off such a capable pupil. He predicted a future as a painter for me, and it is not his fault that nothing ever came of it. In any case, my love of the paintbrush stayed with me and grew over the years. One more unfulfilled love.

Another unfulfilled love was music. Our singing teacher, Baruch Sperber, noticed that I was musical. Not blessed with a lovely voice, I at least enjoyed singing and could avoid the wrong notes. I used to say that I would have become a composer if I had known solfeggio. I played the piano and went to concerts, but never learned solfeggio. I composed symphonies in the clouds and conducted great orchestras in my sleep or walking down the city streets, which left me at risk of being run over, or at least walking into telephone poles. I never became a composer. As for Baruch Sperber, he knew how to maintain discipline. And his ear was sharp enough to catch even the slightest wavering in the choirs that he conducted – and he conducted splendidly. God forbid that he should hear a whisper during singing lessons. He twisted the offender's ear in a way that was painful even to those watching.

*

Sperber was friends with the great folk singer Gebirtig and even wrote the music to several of Gebirtig's lyrics. It was Sperber who first brought the Yiddish language on to our school stage, in the form of the duet *Ver der ershter vet lachen (Who Will Laugh First)*, by Gebirtig. I can still see that skit, and I remembered much of the text thanks to listening to the rehearsals, even though I did not know Yiddish. A boy from a wealthy home makes a bet with a pal who is poor – that the rich boy will be able to make him laugh. The poor boy is hardly in a risible mood, since his stomach is empty, and he has just had a whipping from the *rebbe* at the *cheder* for not doing his homework, which he was unable to do because his father is lying at home sick. However, it turns out in the end that the rich boy has an infallible method for raising a smile, and he is carrying it in his pocket: a buttered roll with a herring's head – the poor boy cannot help smiling at such a treat … this duet was my first encounter with Gebirtig.

In the *Yidisher Bande* revue theater many years later, I saw the excellent actress Chajele Gruber performing Gebirtig's thieves' ballad *Avreyml marvicher (Little Abraham the Pickpocket)*, about a Jewish robber with golden hands and a warm heart who does not ply the market places like most thieves, but lies in wait instead for the filthy rich. However, his career ends when he comes down with tuberculosis. He only asks that his gravestone be inscribed: 'Here lies Abraham the pickpocket, who could have been a decent man and a good citizen, perhaps even a great artist, if only he had had a mother and father instead of growing up on the streets'.

Later, during the war, I heard the song *S'brent–Gore (It's Burning)*, which Gebirtig wrote after the bloody Prytyk pogrom of 1936, and which became the anthem of the Jewish Combat Organization (JCO) in the Cracow ghetto several years later. It was translated into Polish by Gusta Dawidson, 'Justyna', a fearless partisan, the wife of the JCO leader Symek Drenger, and the author of *The Memoirs of Justyna*, which she wrote on scraps of toilet paper while imprisoned in the Helclow Prison. I was unaware of her translation when, at the request of Michal Borwicz (Boruchowicz), I translated *S'brent* for the anthology of Holocaust poetry titled *The Song Survives*. That is why my translation, rather than Justyna's, is always quoted, even though it is no better than hers. *S'brent* recounts a fire in a *shtetl*, which the inhabitants stand watching even though it is consuming their possessions and will soon consume them. In the last stanza, Gebirtig calls on them to come to their senses and save their little town. 'Don't stand inertly, with your hands at your sides! Take up a bucket and douse the flames. Show that you can douse them with your own blood!' It seems like a prophecy of the great conflagration of the Holocaust. And one more forgotten detail, of which those who sing this most popular Yiddish song from the Holocaust period are often unaware. Gebirtig copied the opening notes of *S'brent* after the characteristic siren of the Cracow fire company, which was used to clear the streets as the trucks rushed to a blaze: 'So-do, so-do!' 'Es-brent! Go-re!'

I knew about Gebirtig, an impoverished Jewish carpenter from Wielopole, from my earliest years. This was because we had a record at home with *Kinderyorn (Years of Childhood)* on one side and *Huliet, huliet Kinderlach* ('Make merry, children, while you're young, for it's only a short leap from spring to winter') on the other. These were the songs that first made Gebirtig popular, and everyone knew them. He wrote them for a minor operetta, *The Rumanian Wedding Feast*. I sang them along with the record, and also heard them occasionally from the courtyard musicians, without understanding the words. Gebirtig thus entered my consciousness by various routes. But only when I met Jews in Lodz after the war whose first language was Yiddish, and when I frequented the Yiddish Theatre, did I develop a true taste for Gebirtig. You might say that I learned Yiddish and discovered Jewish folklore from his songs. They were a revelation for me: I grew closer to and learned to love that Yiddish culture that I had instinctively (what sort of instinct was that?) rejected.

Let us return once more to Baruch Sperber. As I watched the outstanding conductor Stanley Sperber of Canada lead the 100-

voice choir of the Israel Philharmonic, I thought that he must be some sort of relative of our singing teacher. I went to see him backstage at the Tel Aviv Palace of Art after the concert. He had indeed heard of a relative in Cracow and was quite moved when he learned that his relative had composed the music for several of Gebirtig's songs. The next day, I copied them out for him from Gebirtig's book *Mayne Lider*. When he founded the Zamir (Nightingale) choir in Montreal, Stanley Sperber could not have known that his relative Baruch had founded a choir under the same name in Cracow, fifty years earlier.

*

In Cracow, we called secondary school teachers 'professors', according to the Austrian custom. People from Warsaw laughed at this. Our teachers differed little from those in the public schools. Some of them could hold a class spellbound through their lectures and others were bores whose monotonous voices could turn students against even the most interesting subjects. Some were disciplinarians, feared like fire, while others could be mistreated with impunity. They had their vices and habits, their likes and dislikes. Some were witty, making remarks that went over the heads of the duller students, while others were totally devoid of a sense of humor – and those were the dangerous ones! There were some whom we loved, others whom we respected, and some – the rare cases – whom we could not stand. In a word, they were a multi-colored assemblage. We generally knew little about the private lives of our teachers. In those days, distance was regarded as an indispensable element of education. Today, it seems to me that closer contacts between teachers and students could be beneficial for both sides.

The distance, the 'Yes, Professor', the fear of failing grades or of having one's parents summoned to school or of being sent to the principal's office – none of these factors diminished the criticism of teachers by students or discouraged the students from playing April Fool's Day pranks, often in bad taste, on the teachers.

I have been unable to assess the degree to which teachers were subjected to 'official' satire on the school stage, during assemblies, before my time. Students do seem to have expressed criticism or even malice in the school newspaper and the newsletters from summer camp. 'Scholastic realism' was a prominent inspiration in my days as an author, actor and director at school. I would never have staged a one-act play by Molière when instead I could write a song or poem on current school themes, with teachers and students as the protagonists. I usually composed couplets to the tune of folk songs or the popular hits of the day. These were woven together with patter from the master of ceremonies. My brother Jozek sometimes helped me. Together, we wrote duets for the Winter Relief Campaign spectacle, where fat Rysio Rechen played the accordion and Nunek Halpern the piano.

All of this was a sort of introduction to the great showdown with the faculty that came in the production I prepared along with my friends for Purim in 1937. I cannot remember exactly how the idea was born for a large-scale revue on the school stage, or how we won the acceptance of the teachers who were responsible for the drama club and under whose aegis the Hanukkah and Purim assemblies were staged: Feldhorn, Low and Rubinstein. They themselves often wrote and supervised such performances ... In any case, these influential advisers turned out to be quite liberal, had a good time, and lent a hand where necessary. Furthermore, they had too many other duties to interfere in our production, and their help consisted above all in providing us with written excuses from lessons so that we could hold rehearsals. We followed the letter of the law in using those excuses: half the class was 'featured', for this was a grand revue with a big chorus-line finale, in the manner of the Bagatela Theatre. No one was too lazy to win a lesser or greater role. We started rehearsals first thing in the morning, keeping an eye on which sections had class in the gym. We invaded those classes and, whether there was a rehearsal or not, sat out an hour that should have been given over to math or German.

The production was called *The Judgement of the Professors*. It was set in hell, in the year 2000. Arraigned by the district attorney of hell, our teachers confessed the sins that they had committed against their students, and other sins as well – such as we students were aware of. Some of the criticism was well-founded and some of it was venomous joking based on facts. The district attorney addressed Feldhorn in a paraphrase of the hit song *Zimny drań (Cold-hearted Guy)*:

His nanny by his cradle
Sang whenever she was able:
'Your fortune's good as made,
You'll leave others in the shade.'
She almost got it right
But for one small oversight:
His book made a star of him,
But he went by a pseudonym!
He is such a very strange Jew
Ashamed of his name old and true,
And if I may beg to dissent,
It does make a difference –
He's an extraordinarily strange Jew …

This was an allusion to Feldhorn's 1937 novel, *Cienie nad kolysk (Shadows over the Cradle)*, which he published under the pen-name of Jan Las.

We did not do things by half-measures. Tolek Senft's father owned the Bagatela movie house and revue. Tolek got a small role (which allowed him to skip classes) in return for a promise (which he kept!) of 'artistic support'. A real curtain and backdrop were brought from the Bagatela, along with experts to install them. We also had the aid of a professional make-up artist, although we did not need one, since our teachers Seiden and Rubinstein were more than up to the task. They knew how to glue on a false nose or false ears that really stuck out. Rubinstein lent his jacket to Lusek Daniel, who played him, and made Lusek up so well that when he walked on stage I heard somebody cry out in merriment, 'Look, look! Daft's come out in person to make a fool of himself!'

It was craftsmanship of a high standard, and the entrance of each 'professor' evoked salvos of laughter. Our Latin specialist Barasz wore a pince-nez, and he laughed so hard that he had to hold them in place with his finger. When he came back for the second night, he wore regular glasses to avoid missing anything.

The teachers were not impersonated under their own names, of course. We thought hard about a stage name for Dr Stendig, our German teacher, who had a whole row of titles printed on his business card: 'Ph.D., Professor, Director (Commercial School), Editor (*The Link*)'. Feldhorn himself suggested a pseudonym: Hippolit Polyglot, or Hipek Pipek. Stendig loved to confiscate whatever anyone hid under the desk during his lessons, and also had a habit of borrowing books and forgetting to return them. In the revue, he stood accused of borrowing a new book from a student and returning it torn and dog-eared. His circuitous defense went something like this: '*Primo*, when you lent me the book it was already dog-eared; *zweites*, I gave it back to you intact; and in the third place, you never lent me any book at all!' These texts were not always terribly intelligent, but the effect came from the make-up and the acting, the skilful imitation of the way the professor moved and spoke. Stendig was played by Olek Rubin, who impersonated him so well that each gesture brought the house down: he hitched up his trousers with an exaggerated movement, picked his nose, and talked and gestured just like Stendig … which is not to say that Olek's portrayal brought him any benefit. Stendig tried to put a good face on things, but was clearly offended. 'That pulling up the trousers may have been within boundaries,' he criticized Olek, 'but picking your nose was going too far.'

We thought that would be the end of it and that the matter would be forgotten, but Stendig proved to be more vengeful than he looked. He harried Olek mercilessly for the rest of the year, although he gave him a passing mark in the end.

The Judgement of the Professors ended with a grand parade of show girls and the whole cast, to a song with a rather awkward refrain borrowed from a number that someone had heard in the revue at the Bagatela:

> Our school is a grand old school
> The only one for us, and what a school!
> How I love it, that one and only school of mine.

I remember how it ended:

> When you finally manage to graduate
> You'll find hard times lying in wait,
> And one truth will prove undeniable,
> As you ponder nostalgically
> You'll say enthusiastically
> Our school indeed is a grand old school …

Those hard times came more quickly than we had anticipated.

Of the 55 members of the faculty of our primary and secondary school, eight survived the war. Today, as I write these words, only one is alive: Meir Bosak, who began teaching there in the 1938/39 school year.

Benzion Katz (Ben Szalom), the Jagiellonian University instructor who taught us Latin and the Judaic subjects during the time when he was translating the Latin and Greek classics into Hebrew, died in Israel. He was rector of the Tel Aviv University, in the founding of which he played no small part. He is buried in the Cemetery of Merit in Tel Aviv.

Our reunions in Tel Aviv were attended faithfully by the physicist Emil Waldman, who passed, on his stiff leg (because of which we called him Hephaestos), through all seven circles of the Nazi inferno, and Albert Reder, our physical education instructor who survived the war in Russia. They maintained hearty contacts with the alumni until the end, as did Zosia Leinkram, who greeted each surviving former student with tears in her eyes.

Our principal, the physician and Zionist Dr Chaim Hilfstein, was an active member of the Jewish Social Self-Help organization in the General Government. He died in Tel Aviv in the early 1950s.

Our teachers were intelligent and creative people. Many of them held doctorates. Their history deserves to be recounted – perhaps by the Teachers' Union in Poland, or perhaps in Israel. Within the scope of my account, I would like to offer more extensive portraits of three teachers whose work outlasted the Era of the Furnaces, although not all of them survived. Someday, I do not know when, a historian of literature might take an interest in them and seek out the 'sources' connected with the names Feldhorn, Rappaport, and Przemski ...

NOTE

1   Lag Ba'omer is a semi-religious Jewish holiday that falls in the spring. According to tradition, this was the day on which a plague came to an end after raging among the pupils of Rabbi Akiba, the spiritual leader of the Israelites in their revolt against Rome in the first century CE. According to another tradition, it is the camouflaged anniversary of a victorious battle against the Romans.
    On Lag Ba'omer, *cheder* pupils and school students make excursions outside the city and play with bows and arrows. In Cracow tradition, the holiday is connected with the memory of Remuh, who died on that day. *Hasidim* from all over the world travel to Cracow where they place pieces of paper, bearing their supplications for health and success, into the cracks in the gravestone of the great rabbi.

6. Portraits

A MANUSCRIPT FOUND IN A CELLAR

Juliusz Feldhorn's book *Artists and their Works*, written 25 years earlier, was published in Poland in early 1962. In the introduction 'About the Author', Feldhorn's friend Leon Przemski regarded it as appropriate to thank the publishers for their decision to bring the book out: 'It took some courage. The author is hardly a popular figure …' These thanks struck me as out of place. Rather, Poland and the publishers owed a debt of gratitude to an author whose book was 'intended to fill a yawning gap in the popularization of art and its history – a gap that existed then [that is, before the war] and that still exists', as Stefan Kozakiewicz noted in his foreword. 'Until now, there has been a need for a book written in a manner accessible to everyone that treats the history of art in general outline, from ancient to contemporary times, and that allows the reader to approach art in the proper way, through interpretation.'

Throughout the two decades between the wars and in the 15 years after the Second World War, no one in Poland had written (or published) a popularized scholarly history of art. It must nevertheless be noted that, as opposed to the inter-war period, a relatively large number of books on the fine arts did appear in communist Poland. These, however, were narrow studies and biographies on selected, specialized themes.

It is no easy matter to encompass the history of art and narrate it in an interesting way in 500 pages. It takes an author with special talents and knowledge to do so. Juliusz Feldhorn had such knowledge and talents. He was a humanist in the best sense of the word: the author of three volumes of poetry and the novel *Shadows over the Cradle*. He was also a superb translator from the Italian (Dante's *Canzonieri* and Boccacio's *Fiametti*) and the German (he won the *Literary News* second prize for his translation of Goethe's *To Delfina Potocki*); he also translated the *Song of Songs* from Hebrew. He had great accomplishments as a popularizer (having written five books for young people) and an art critic (as the regular exhibition reviewer for *Nowy Dziennik* in Cracow). Above all, however, he was an outstanding teacher and brilliant authority on Polish literature. He was a member of the faculty and vice-principal of the Jewish Coeducational Secondary School in Cracow.

There was nothing routine about Feldhorn's lectures, which diverged markedly from the school program. He did not confine himself to Polish literature, which was his main subject. He ranged far into the 'territory' of the other arts while teaching the analysis, composition and interpretation of literary works. He taught his pupils how to see and listen. He used the phonograph for classroom concerts of classical and contemporary music, and the slide projector to introduce masterpieces of art. When lecturing on Kochanowski, he spun an enthralling vision of the Italian Renaissance, full of palaces, sculpture, paintings, beautiful poetry and bloody revenge, humanists and *condottieri*, people and art. He was capable of spending a whole hour on one painting or one statue. He particularly enjoyed analyzing works on similar themes, like *The Offering of Isaac* by Brunelleschi and Giberthi, the *Betrothal of Mary* by Raphael and Perugino, or the statues of David by Donatello, Verocchio, Michelangelo and Bernini. He used such examples to teach us to distinguish craftsmanship from genius, compositional skill from profound experience, the classic from the Baroque. Such analysis filled page after page in *Artists and their Works*. He regarded depth as more important than breadth.

In literature, Feldhorn's passion was poetry. A poet himself, though not on a grand scale, he had a rare ability to inject the bacillus of poetry into his students – the bacillus of craving beauty, the imperative of seeking beauty. He recited poetry splendidly and demanded that we enunciate verse with comprehension and feeling rather than merely rattling it off from memory, which was enough to satisfy most teachers.

Hearing Feldhorn recite verse was an extraordinary experience. He had a warm, deep voice and impeccable diction, a rare ease in gliding from low to higher tones, a feeling for the rhythm and melody of verse. He controlled his voice like a virtuoso at the keyboard: sudden leaps, variations in tension, feeling and color, loud fortissimo and then pianissimo, an unexpected avalanche of onomatopoeic words, and then a folk ditty fit to dance to – he was amazing and hypnotic. When he finished reciting, the students sat petrified, holding their breath, entranced as if they had been transported into another world by the magic of poetry. Then, with an eloquent gesture and an expressive smile, Feldhorn signalled that breathing was now allowed, that the analysis could begin ... hundreds of his pupils remember those recitations and the soft timbre of his voice. What has stuck in my memory is that *silence* when the verse was at an end.

Feldhorn was a strict teacher. Students feared him like fire, and no one ever dared to interrupt a lesson. It was no easy thing to earn the status of 'good pupil' with him. Learning passages by heart was not enough. In his pupils, Feldhorn looked not so much for knowledge as for intelligence and independent thinking. A pupil's intelligence was measured by 'class work', the essays written during lessons. There were pupils whose report cards consisted of nothing but 'C's but who earned a sole 'A' from Feldhorn. There were also 'straight A' high-flyers whose records were punctured by a 'C' from Feldhorn. I could go a whole year without consulting 'Chrzan' – Chrzanowski's *History of the Literature of Independent Poland*. Feldhorn's lectures sufficed. I always earned 'A's from him even though, to tell the truth, my knowledge of the history of literature was undoubtedly inferior to that of more than one pupil who had difficulty passing. I would not like to bet that I could have told what year Slowacki was born or died. On the other hand, I could recite that poet's *Bieniowski* without difficulty. And I recited decently, which counted for a great deal with Feldhorn.

I was one of those pupils who enjoyed Feldhorn's trust and friendship. When I was in the sixth grade, he gave me a copy of Dante's *Canzonieri* with a warm dedication – the summit of happiness. I had been working at cataloguing the school library, which he was in charge of. I was able to draw close to the revered teacher in the 'unofficial territory' of the library. He sometimes told me about his literary work and his plans. He spoke about the recently published *Shadows over the Cradle*, a novel that described the feelings, experiences and development of a child from birth to the age of five. Critics, who were generally aware of the true identity of its author, 'Jan Las', wrote favorable reviews and predicted a great future for the 'young author'. Feldhorn laughed heartily as he showed me that term in a highly positive review in a National Democrat journal. *Shadows over the Cradle* was planned as the first volume of a trilogy. In the second volume, the hero was to discover suddenly that he is the son of assimilated Jews, and in the third volume, when he was at the university, his national consciousness was to crystallize finally amid racist persecution.

This cycle may have been intended as a reply to Jewish circles, including fellow teachers and the school administration, who viewed Feldhorn as an assimilationist. They discerned risks in his great influence over young people. Actually, Feldhorn was proud to be Jewish. He was progressive, engaged in community affairs, and conscious of the path he was following, and of his humanistic ethics. When he was offered a chair at the Jagiellonian University on the condition of baptism, he turned it down without hesitation. When a wave of antisemitism resulted in ghetto benches, he organized university-level courses, a sort of open university, at the Hebrew secondary school. They were highly popular (I remember two Catholic priests who regularly attended Feldhorn's lectures on contemporary literature). He wanted to establish a chair of Slavic languages at the Hebrew University. At the same time, he was working intensively on his translations (including Thomas Mann's *Magic Mountain*) and a book on his favorite poet, Norwid. He also published *Information for the World*, a popularized and excellently written history of postal and telegraph services. I came across that book in Israel at a publisher who intended to translate it into Hebrew, but the colossal progress in communications technology since the time of writing torpedoed this idea: it would have been necessary to update it with a second volume. I therefore took this cherished tome from the publisher and presented it as a gift to the Israeli post and telegraph minister, Elimelech Rimalt, who had himself been Feldman's pupil at our school. It is worth noting that Dr Rimalt had ordered, or was planning, a series of postage stamps depicting the most famous synagogues in the world. He chose the Cracow Old Synagogue for the most popular stamp, the one that would carry Rosh Hoshana greetings. The Cracow old-boys' network …

To return to Feldhorn's books for young people, we should mention those that he published (with Palas publishers), *The Strange Adventures of Coal*, *The Iron Dragon* (on railroads), *People Grow Wings*, and *The Alphabet Conquers the World*. Who can say whether these are covered in the histories of literature for young people? In 1938, Seiden's Popular Library ordered a history of art from Feldman. He set to work with his usual energy and organization. He knew the material off the top of his head – much of it came from his secondary school lectures; he would have to shorten it somewhat to fit within the publisher's space requirement, polish the style, and furnish it with the appropriate reproductions. Feldhorn sometimes read me particular chapters, wondering out loud whether or not to excise wide-ranging aesthetic deliberations that might overburden the historical material with philosophy. Some chapters stuck in my memory so well that, when a commemorative meeting about Feldman was held in Israel, I recounted them to my friends. I had no idea then that the manuscript had survived. The book had been scheduled for printing in the autumn of 1939.

I ran into Feldhorn on the street in Cracow in November 1939. Mobilized in August, he had been captured along with his whole regiment by the Germans near Lublin. He had returned to Cracow after being released from the POW camp by some miracle, but he had found his family missing.

'Tomorrow, I am setting out for the other side of the River Bug,' he confided. 'The only thing that I am taking with me is the manuscript of *The History of Art*.'

He expected to publish the book in Lwow. But he was too optimistic. From the Soviet point of view, the book had serious shortcomings. Attempting to secure a teaching position, the author himself had problems with his examination on Stalin's *Short History* of the Communist Party and was reprimanded sharply by the woman from the school authorities who was examining him: he tried to interpret in his own words a text that was supposed to be recited word for word. In the end, however, he won a license to teach in a vocational school.

When the German–Soviet war broke out, Feldhorn did not manage to be evacuated into the depths of Russia. After the Germans occupied Western Ukraine, he travelled with his family to the General Government, to Wisnicz near Cracow. We conducted a brief but intense correspondence at this period.

In Wisnicz, Feldhorn established contact with the Jewish underground, specifically with Dolek Liebeskind's group from the Cracow Akiba, which was receiving 'agricultural training' in nearby Kopaliny. When the deportations grew more and more ominous, Feldhorn furnished himself with 'Aryan' papers and moved to the Cracow suburb of Swoszowice with his wife and nine-year-old daughter. There, after being informed on, he fell into the hands of the Gestapo. He died together with his wife, Stella Lande, an accomplished translator of English and German literature. Their death is wrapped in legend. I heard the following version after the war on Polish Radio: Feldhorn came home from work to find that Stella was gone, and he learned from neighbors that the Gestapo had taken her away. In despair, he could see no other course of action than to surrender himself. They were executed publicly on the town square in Swoszowice. This version undoubtedly contains a certain amount of literary coloration. Knowing Feldhorn, however, I am inclined to regard it as authentic. In it, I discern Feldhorn's sense of pathos and his consistent humanism. Could he have saved himself while permitting his life's companion to die alone, leaving her without a word of consolation, a word of solidarity in her final hour? In the death of the two of them, there was something of the protest embodied two years later in the shared death of Stefan Zweig and his wife. That is how humanists die.

After the war, Feldhorn's sister, Dr Cecylia Szarzyńska, returned to Cracow and began seeking contact with people who could tell her something about her brother. It turned out that Feldhorn had maintained clandestine contacts with the poet and critic Ignacy Fik (who died together with his own wife). Szarzyńska found that there were papers stored in the attic at the home of Helena Wielowiejska, where secret meetings had been held. There, she discovered some of her brother's books and his notes on Norwid. At this time, the publisher Seiden was moving back into his old bookstore. The storage rooms in the cellar were full of papers, old books, manuscripts and typescripts from before the war. At Dr Szarzyńska's urging, Seiden agreed to sort out the confused mass of material – and the manuscript of the *History of Art* turned up! However, it could not be published. Leon Kruczkowski, by then minister of culture, had known Feldhorn well; he was prepared to publish the book, but only after thorough revisions in line with the research methodology of dialectical materialism. The author's sister would not agree to this. Following the October 1956 'thaw', Leon Przemski took up the cause of the book. Przemski was then editor of *New Culture*; the book finally came out under the imprint of Common Knowledge publishers. The print run of 10,000 copies sold out in the course of three weeks ...

'If *Artists and Their Works* was preserved, then perhaps *Ruslan* and his other translations are also extant', I wrote in a memoir of Feldhorn that I published in 1962 on the occasion of his book on art. Soon afterwards, I learned that the translation had indeed survived. Dr Szarzyńska sent me the manuscript only after a long delay. It turned out to be, apparently, only the first draft, in a very rough state, of a translation of this extraordinarily difficult poem by Pushkin. I decided, in memory of my beloved teacher, to work on that raw material. It was not easy: Tuwim had beaten his head against the wall in attempting to translate the opening expressions ('Four verses on craft') and had given up without ever finishing the translation. I was lucky: a lovely version of Pushkin's poem by Brzechwa was published just at that time. There was no way that I could compete with it, and I gave up.

I carried on an extensive, cordial correspondence with Dr Szarzyńska, who taught English and German at the Mining Academy in Cracow. From her, I learned about the fate of Dr Feldhorn's daughter, Marysia. The little girl ran from the house when the police came to arrest her mother. She had very 'bad looks', and had been instructed by her parents how to behave and where to go if they were arrested. She took refuge in a convent, where her mother's family found a place for her. Szarzyńska located her there in a dreadful state and took her to relatives in Warsaw. She lives there to this day. I never managed to get in touch with Marysia while Dr Szarzyńska was alive. Feldhorn's sister lived, alone and embittered, in the suburbs of Cracow. Cleaning house before the holidays, she fell from a chair or ladder and never got up. Only after several days was her death discovered. Marysia came from Warsaw for her aunt's funeral, discovered a bundle of my letters, and wrote to tell me the touching story of the tragic death of Juliusz Feldhorn's sister.

THE TWO FACES OF LEON PRZEMSKI

before the war: Chaim Low, teacher at the Hebrew Secondary School; after the war: Leon Przemski, Polish writer and editor of literary magazines

Leon Przemski, a writer, historian and journalist, died in Warsaw at the age of 75 on 13 September 1976. The Union of Polish Writers paid tribute to the writer with a notice summarizing his career and accomplishments:

An outstanding writer and essayist, author of books for young people, long-term and worthy member of our Union, winner of the State Prize, officer in the First Polish People's Army, member of the editorial staff of *New Culture*, managing editor of that magazine in 1953–54, holder of the Gold Cross of Merit, Officer's Cross of the Order of *Polonia Restituta* and many military distinctions.

His family and friends, who announced the details of his funeral at the Powązki public cemetery (formerly the military cemetery) in Warsaw, included his military rank: Lieutenant-Colonel (Reserve). Further information about Leon Przemski can be found in the *Dictionary of Contemporary Polish Writers* and Leslaw M. Bartelski's guide, *Contemporary Polish Writers 1944–1970*.

According to the *Dictionary*, Leon Przemski, the son of Emil and Maria (née Tyszler), was born into a craftsman's family in Przemyśl. After graduation from secondary school, he studied in the humanities faculty at the Jagiellonian University. In 1927, he earned a doctorate with his dissertation *The Tragedy of Personal Experience in the Dramas of Norwid*. He worked as a Polish teacher in Czêstochowa until 1928, and then in Cracow until 1939. During the Second World War, he was in Przemyśl and Lwow until June, 1941. He traveled into the depths of the Soviet Union after the capture of Lwow by the Nazi army. He worked as a German teacher at Volsk on the Volga and then at Novosibirsk until 1942. He joined the Polish army formed in the Soviet Union in 1943 and served as a journalist with the front-line newspapers *Soldier of Freedom* (1943) and *We Shall Triumph* (1943–44). He settled in Warsaw in 1946. He remained in the army until 1953, writing for *Armed Poland* and *Soldier of Freedom*. He joined the staff of *New Culture* in 1953. He was awarded the State Literary Prize (Second Class) in 1950, for his novel *Henryk Kamieñski*. He published some 20 books, mostly historical novels for young people but also including popularized sketches on linguistics.

I have never read any of Przemski's books, except for one. Nor have I read the articles and memoirs published in Poland after his death. I do not know how he is regarded by his readers, or what the people with whom he worked on the staffs of the military and literary journals think or know about him. I knew Przemski before 1939, when he was still named Chaim Fajwel Low and taught Polish literature at the Jewish Coeducational Secondary School in Cracow. I was hardly the only one who knew him. A teacher who works at a school for 12 years has many acquaintances and pupils. There must still be many people who remember him from Przemyśl as one of the six children of the tinsmith Mendel Low and his wife Miriam Tischler Low. The children received university educations thanks to their mother's special devotion. Natives of Przemyśl also remember Chaim's wife Rozia (née Fojer) and their two lovely daughters. When the Russian–German war broke out, Rozia and the girls were murdered bestially by the Nazis after they occupied Przemyśl. Chaim Low was then in Lwow on business. Unable to return home, he was evacuated into the depths of the Soviet Union. There, he opened a new chapter of his life as Leon Przemski.

Both of the Polish teachers at the Hebrew Secondary School in Cracow, Juliusz Feldhorn and Chaim Low, came from Przemyśl. Feldhorn was seen as an assimilationist with leftist views, distant from Jewishness. Low, on the other hand, was a known Zionist. While still a Ha-Shomer ha-Tsair student in Przemyśl, he learned Hebrew well enough to write poetry in that language (as well as in Polish), and when he had become a teacher, he co-authored a secondary school Hebrew textbook with Nachman Mifelew.

Chaim Low was always well-groomed and elegant, with smoothly combed blond hair and horn-rim glasses. He kept us on a short leash. Although he maintained his distance and did not fraternize with his pupils, he was generally respected. It is true that he lacked Feldhorn's inspiration, but he manifested intelligence and a breadth of knowledge: aside from Polish, he taught Latin, German, and even mathematics.

As a member of the socialist-right Hitachduth Zionist organization, Low edited their Polish-language journal, *Our Struggle*. He lectured in Yiddish, and at the literature club, as one of his teaching colleagues recalled, he read fragments of the *Iliad* that he had translated into Yiddish. His articles in *The Jewish Monthly* and *Opinion* and elsewhere were always connected with Jewish themes, and in particular with the Jewish contribution to Polish culture. When he wrote about Wyspiański, it was

'Wyspiański and the Jews' (1932); if he wrote about *Pan Tadeusz*, it was *'Pan Tadeusz* in Hebrew Robes' (a review of Lichtenbaum's translation). When he re-published his article 'Jews in the Poetry of Independent Poland' (originally printed in *The Jewish Monthly*) as a book, he gave it the significant title *The Dragon in the Nightingale's Nest*. He wrote the chapter 'The Participation of Jews in Polish Literature' for the collaborative book *Jewish Participation in Culture*, published in Cracow in 1938. However, his interests extended beyond Jewish–Polish relations. In issues from 1930 and 1931 of *The Jewish Monthly*, the tribunal of Jewish culture, we find his articles on 'Hebrew Avant-Garde Poetry' (which discusses the work of Uri Zvi Grinberg, Lamdan, and Szlonski) and 'Books for Young People' (on Hebrew and Yiddish books).

The only pre-war publication of Przemski in the bibliography in *The Dictionary of Polish Writers* is his book for young people, *Objects, Countries and Customs* (Warsaw–Cracow, 1939). Its second printing, edited and amended, came out in Lodz in 1947 – with the author's name now listed as Leon Przemski.

According to an account by the writer and historian Michal Borwicz (who died in Paris in 1987), Low-Przemski completed his novel *The Gray Jacobin*, which exhibits radical leftist tendencies, immediately before the war. Its author carried it to Soviet-occupied Lwow in the hope of finding a publisher. Despite highly positive reactions from those who read it, the book was never printed and the manuscript perished in the whirlwinds of war. Przemski rewrote it from memory after the war, and it went through five printings in communist Poland. In September 1962, Leon Przemski paid a short visit to his brothers in Israel. One of them, Josef, had come here back in 1920 with the *hakhshara*, the pioneers preparation camp for agricultural work before immigration to Palestine. The other, Adam Low, an engineer, arrived in 1960. Chaim's former pupils invited him to a reunion at a café. Adam Low learned that Chaim met with Dr David Lazer of blessed memory, one of the editors of *Maariv*. Lazer offered him a job in Israel. Przemski decided not to make a decision until his wife (a non-Jew) had visited Israel and expressed her opinion on emigrating. However, he suffered a heart attack shortly afterwards, and then his wife died. Leon Przemski remained in Poland for the next fourteen years, until the moment of his own sudden death.

Chaim Low's post-war life created the misleading impression that he had separated himself from the Jews and Jewishness. This view was supported by his intense literary activity, his military rank, and the public and literary status that he achieved in communist Poland. In the article that I published after the death of Przemski-Low, I emphasized – perhaps unjustly – the metamorphosis of this Hebrew school teacher. I obtained a sheaf of letters stating that he had never concealed his origins after the war, had kept Jewish company, and had been closely interested in the fate of the Jews in Israel and around the world. Mr M. Barac of Melbourne wrote:

> I have just had a chance to see the January 14 1977 issue of the newspaper, which contains your article 'The Second Incarnation of Leon Przemski'. I lived in Warsaw from 1950–1969, and in this period I met Leon very frequently at his home and at ours, where we talked long and cordially about the matters and problems that interested both of us … After returning from his trip to Israel, he shared his extraordinary impressions of the country at length and in detail. He experienced the Six-Day War no differently than the 10 million Jews scattered in the Diaspora who, while living outside the borders of Israel, have never in the least stopped being and feeling themselves to be Jews.

I also received reports indicating that Leon Przemski hung up his uniform and resigned from his work on the army newspapers and at *Culture,* in reaction to the wave of antisemitism in Poland and the intrigues mounted against his Jewish colleagues after March 1968. He ended up so thoroughly in the bad graces of the authorities that he was denied permission for some time to publish his books (on the pretext of a paper shortage).

While visiting Israel, he traveled the length and breadth of our country and was as delighted as a child when he recovered his fluency in Hebrew. He remained in contact with the country, by post, until his death.

This information comprises a different portrait of Leon Przemski from the one sketched in the article in *The Dictionary of Polish Writers*.

THE DEATH OF A PHILOSOPHER AND THE HISTORY OF A MANUSCRIPT

or the fates of people and books

Numerous Palestine Brigade soldiers, with the Star of David stitched on their epaulets, visited Poland in the early months of 1946, searching for their relatives or trying to learn something about their tragic fates. One such soldier, whom I have never met, happened to be in Katowice when his watch stopped. He made his way to the nearest watchmaker.

When that craftsman realized that his customer was a Jewish soldier, he invited him into his living quarters. Having bolted and locked the door, he admitted that he himself was a Jew who was still living on 'Aryan' papers, just as he had during the war. More importantly, the watchmaker pulled a scroll of papers from a hiding place. It was a manuscript written in Hebrew, with a cover letter in Polish that read as follows:

> This manuscript, along with some articles already published, constitutes a philosophical work in the Hebrew language. It has nothing to do with current events. In these uncertain times, the author has decided to conceal his manuscript in order to preserve it from destruction.
>
> The author urges the respected finder of the manuscript to be so kind as to forward this work to the Hebrew University in Jerusalem, to the address of the former rector of that university, Dr Hugo, or to Dr Hecheskel Kafmann in Haifa (Palestine) or to Dr Benzion Katz (pseudonym Benzion Ben Shalom) in Palestine (exact address unknown). By doing so, the respected finder will earn the deep gratitude of the author and will render a great service to scholarly literature in Hebrew.
> Benzion Rappaport
> Nowy Sacz, 16 August 1942.

The author of the letter and the enclosed manuscript was a philosopher and teacher at the Hebrew Secondary School, and a well-known figure in Cracow. 'The Old Man', as the students called Rappaport, was more cut out to be a university professor than a schoolteacher. He had the heart of a dove and enjoyed the love and affection of his pupils, but his goodness also produced a familiarity and directness that emboldened the tyros in the freshman and sophomore classes to take his classes on Judaistic subjects lightly. Yet unexpected horizons of ideas and beauty, of Hebrew literature, philosophy and culture in the context of world culture, opened to those who wanted to learn something and who knew how to pay attention to Rappaport's lectures. Benzion Rappaport, a self-taught man, possessed extraordinarily broad humanistic knowledge. His whole apartment at 7 Sarego (Zielona) Street was an immense library, and its owner knew every volume in that library by heart.

Rappaport maintained a lively correspondence with the most eminent living European philosophers, including Theodore Lessing, who was later murdered by the Nazis. Rappaport published two philosophical studies, *Cognition and Reality* and *Thinkers and Ideas*.

The outbreak of the war found him at work on a new book, a collection of philosophical essays titled *Teva ve'ru'ach (Nature and the Spirit)*. He finished it a month or so before his death at the hands of the German myrmidons and, as is indicated by a second enclosed letter, copied out the whole text in the hope that at least one copy would survive.

The Katowice watchmaker who ended up in possession of the manuscript of Rappaport's philosophical work refused either to give it to that soldier from the Palestine Brigade or to entrust it to the post. He agreed to give the soldier the Polish-language letter quoted above, while stating that he would only hand the manuscript over to one of the addressees named therein, or to an emissary from the Hebrew University. The soldier delivered the letter to the Hebrew University delegate Abraham Jaari, who was then in Paris. Jaari contacted Dr Ben Shalom and Dr Bergmann immediately, and they set about trying to secure the manuscript. Rappaport's former student Moshe Arie Kurz was travelling to Poland at that time on behalf of the Jewish Agency. He took the manuscript to Jerusalem. Only seven years later was Rappaport's work published in book form by the firm of Mosad Bialik.

In 1955, *Yediyot Yad Vashem* published a facsimile of Benzion Rappaport's Polish letter and an article by Abraham Jaari, who still had possession of the letter, describing the history of the manuscript.

In his conclusion, Jaari advanced various hypotheses about the road the manuscript must have followed before ending up in the hands of the watchmaker, and also about the death of the author. Since Katowice is not far from Auschwitz, there was a supposition that Rappaport may have thrown the manuscript from the train carrying him to his death, or may have given it to someone he met along the way. Jaari attempts to disprove the assertion of Hilel Zajdel, who writes in his memoir *Adam ba'michwan (Man in the Time of Trial)*, under the date 12 January 1943: 'My friend Saul Wolf of Bielsko has informed me from Tarnow that Prof. Benzion Rappaport has been killed there; he had written a great work of philosophy in these days of persecution, placed it in a bottle, and buried the bottle in the ground'. Jaari questions this assertion on the grounds that Rappaport was still in Nowy Sacz in September 1942, and that the manuscript was found in Katowice. The editors of *Yediyot Yad Vashem* supplement these suppositions with the information that the ghetto in Nowy Sacz was liquidated at the end of 1942, and the remaining Jews were transported to Tarnow, from which they were subsequently deported to the death camp at Belzec in several 'operations'. Only after the final liquidation of the Tarnow ghetto were those who remained alive transported to Auschwitz.

I learned about the theories concerning the death of Benzion Rappaport and the fate of his manuscript from the article cited above. I was amazed that such a serious institution as Yad Vashem would be spinning out suppositions and hypotheses ten years after the end of the war, when there were many witnesses who could offer reliable information. Of course, someone has to collect this information. I therefore sought out Dr Kurz in Jerusalem, but all he could remember was the name of the watchmaker: Sarna. So he thought. Perhaps that man had come to Israel? I placed an advertisement in the Polish-language newspaper. I wrote one article in Polish and another in Hebrew, and requested the assistance of Michal Borwicz, the director of the Jewish Historical Commission that had been set up in Cracow immediately following the war. Borwicz had also attempted in his time to find the chance possessor of the manuscript. No one knew, or no one remembered, how Benzion Rappaport's manuscript had ended up with the watchmaker in Katowice.

The manuscript had obviously been written in order to become a legend …

ABRAHAM NEUMAN – THE PORTRAIT OF A JEWELER

a citizen of the world enamored of the Polish landscape

A well-known painter before the war, Abraham Neuman was not a professor at the Hebrew Secondary School in Cracow. Nevertheless, I count him among my teachers. I have preserved him in memory as a silver-bearded giant with a great sense of humor. He had sharp reactions and could not remain indifferent to anything that happened around him. He was a favorite pupil of Jan Stanislawski, one of the finest of Polish painters. Stanislawski was another bearded giant with temperament. He too had a heart of gold. He painted miraculous miniature landscapes. Neuman borrowed the light in his paintings from Stanislawski. On larger canvases, Neuman's works radiated the same flashes of light – especially in his impressionistic period. For him, painting represented an escape from a reality that was growing gloomier by the day in the 1930s, with the rise of antisemitism.

That was when I made his acquaintance. When I decided to study at the Fine Arts Academy in Cracow, I asked Neuman to give me a few lessons in painting with oils. I well remember his bright, spacious studio with paintings stacked against the walls. Yet I cannot recall the address. Nor can I recall all the anecdotes that spilled out of him. Most of them concerned his clients and the way he sold his paintings.

There is one story that has stuck in my memory. 'There are occasions', he told me once, 'when a painting doesn't come out. Well, I simply don't like it. I have a place in the attic for such paintings. Once I had a boring woman client, and I knew within five minutes that she had not come to buy, but simply to bother me. She was turning my studio upside down. This picture was too big, that one too small, the one over there was too bright for her living room, the other one would have been good if only it had been horizontal instead of vertical. An hour later, I was tired and she was too, and for some reason I said, in spite of myself, `I have one more painting, but it is not for sale.'

"'Oh, show it to me, please, sir!"

"'No, no. There's no point, because I have no intention of selling it."

"'But please, just let me see it."

95

'"No. What's the point? I've already said it's not for sale."

'But the woman went on insisting, and I slowly softened.

'In the end, I brought that piece of kitsch down from the attic. The client burst out: "Oh, that's it! Why didn't you show it to me earlier? That's the picture that would go perfectly in my living room!"

'"But, my dear lady, it's not for sale."

'"You simply must sell it to me! I won't budge from here without that painting!"

'It might sound like a comedy routine, but believe me, that's the way it happened,' Neuman concluded. 'She paid through the nose for that painting. She got what she wanted, and I was rid of a canvas that I couldn't stand.'

Born in Sierpiec, Pomerania, Abraham Neuman was a citizen of the world. He treated Cracow as a jumping-off point for his journeys. I do not know why his memory is not cultivated in Poland. Perhaps there are none of his paintings left there. If they were anywhere, they would be in the National Museum in Cracow. Not even the prestigious album *The Jews of Poland* featured a single reproduction of a painting by Neuman. Many of his works are in Israel. When the local Union of Polish Jews brought them together for a retrospective exhibition, it was clear to Israeli critics that this was splendid art. It is also worth noting that the exhibition featured an intriguing and exceptionally beautiful portrait of Neuman by Samuel Hirszenberg.

*

Neuman painted a great deal and sold a great deal, and his paintings did not go cheap. Nevertheless, he was always short of cash. His constant journeys were the main reason for this. He was incapable of staying in one place. He sold everything he had and went to Palestine. He returned, started over from scratch – and then took off for Paris. Then he traveled to America, and back to Palestine, and over and over again. He would sometimes bring us a picture to sell before the paint was even dry – but he was not always prepared to sell his talent.

One day, a Cracow jeweler appeared in Neuman's studio and attempted to order a portrait. He was a short, pudgy man with a fringe of reddish hair around his bald pate. Not a particularly appealing model. Neuman fixed him with his gaze and sighed. 'A portrait? What do you need with a portrait? If you're so determined, then I advise you to go to Rosner's. He's an excellent photographer, and he'll make you a superb portrait.'

'But I want a portrait in oil, and I want it to be a Neuman!' replied the client determinedly.

'And I'm advising you to go to the photographer. He'll do the job much more quickly and it will cost far less. I'm very expensive.'

'I can afford it,' the jeweler retorted. 'I pay, and you paint. What will it cost?'

'If you insist … My price is $3,000.'

'What! So much! Why?'

'That's my price. 2,000 in advance, and the rest when I finish.'

In those days, that was a fortune, but the jeweler's ambition was prodigious. He wanted a Neuman portrait, and cost was no object. They fixed the first sitting for the following Sunday. When the model came at the agreed time, the painter ordered him to walk back and forth while watching him carefully. Then Neuman pronounced: 'Strip!'

The jeweler did not understand at first, so Neuman explained. 'Take your clothes off. Right down to the flesh. Take it all off, because I want to see you the way God made you.'

'But why?' the jeweler asked. 'I ordered a portrait, not a nude.'

'Do you intend to tell me how to paint portraits? What do you know? I must be familiar with my model's anatomy, in all its aspects and physical characteristics. That's the way I paint portraits! Take your clothes off!'

The client swallowed his pride and began undressing. Neuman ordered him to walk back and forth some more. Then he shook his head, not terribly pleased with the sight. 'Get dressed', he ordered.

They worked for four hours and fixed the next sitting for four days later. The second time, they went through the whole routine again. The jeweler's protests were of no avail. He complained, cursed, gritted his teeth, but finally had to give in.

Neuman tormented the poor jeweler at each sitting, for three months. Finally, the portrait was finished. It presented the jeweler seated at a table covered with precious stones, with one hand stretched out and the fingers spread, as if he were counting his money – or demanding payment.

'Why this?' the jeweler lamented. The gesture was not at all to his taste.

'Questions, questions! This is the way the Renaissance masters painted goldsmiths and jewelers. Look at Holbein, Titian. This is the mark of your guild. So it must be!'

I am not sure if Neuman managed to convince his client.

The portrait became the sensation of a retrospective exhibition of Neuman's work held in Cracow in 1938. Anyone who thinks that its owner loaned it willingly for exhibition, however, would be mistaken!

When Abraham Szenker, then the secretary of the Union of Jewish Artists in Cracow (he died in Israel in 1965), learned that the jeweler owned several Neumans, he asked for permission to see them. He was delighted with the portrait described above: 'This is just what I'd like to have at the exhibition!'

'But why that one? So many excellent Neumans, and you pick that one? I'm afraid I can't let you have it.'

'Why not?'

'I just can't. It's too valuable. I'm afraid it could be damaged. Besides, it's a personal matter. I never allow it to leave home.'

'But sir, we will guarantee its safety. We'll insure it. Everything will be covered, 100 percent.'

The jeweler kept objecting. Finally, after a long discussion, he told Szenker how it had been painted – which Szenker already knew, in any case.

'And that outstretched hand,' the jeweler said. 'What do you say to that hand?' asked the unfortunate subject. 'I refuse to let that painting leave my home.'

'No one is forcing you,' Szenker said in an unexpectedly conciliatory tone. 'It's your painting, and you can do with it as you please. But for my part, I cannot guarantee that some reporter will not decide to write a story tomorrow titled "How Abraham Neuman Painted the Portrait of a jeweler".'

The poor man caved in.

'Take the painting and go to the devil,' he cried in despair. 'I never want to see you again.'

Szenker, may the Lord shine upon his soul, told me that story. He was no great painter, but what a character! Someday, I will tell more about him.

I never saw Abraham Neuman again after the outbreak of the war. He went to the ghetto, and I went to the countryside.

Even if I had never heard or read accounts of his life in the ghetto, I would be capable of imagining the feelings of that citizen of the world, a painter who was proud of being Jewish. Lieberman had shown his works in Berlin when he was very young. For long years, he had been an inseparable part of the Montparnasse scene. He had traveled the world from north to south and east to west. He was a man of champagne temperament who loved life and was full of enthusiasm for all beauty and charm.

Caged in the ghetto, he starved. He fell ill and suddenly discovered that he was an old man. He was in the habit of saying sarcastically that he was the richest man in the ghetto, because his apartment was full of paintings that no one needed any more. But he never stopped painting. His last work was a self-portrait, showing him painting his friend Gebirtig, the folk poet. Those two artists both met their end in the June 1942 deportation operation. Fate was kind to Neuman. Shot dead in the ghetto, he was spared the humiliation and infernal suffering of the transport to the Belzec death camp.

A ROMANTIC STORY

or two Cracow spirits in Tel Aviv

Many people of my generation recall Bernard Zimmermann's romantic novel *Tirsa*, the only Palestine novel written in Polish. Published in Cracow in 1930, it has never been translated into Hebrew, although its true place is undoubtedly within the history of Israeli literature. It was probably never translated because the author died shortly after writing it. Later, there was no one to take an interest in having it translated. In Poland, however, it was 'required reading' for Zionist youth.

The book is a romantic and psychological study of a young woman student from Vienna named Tirsa. Wanting to extract her father, a widower, from a relationship with 'the wrong woman', she persuades him to emigrate to Palestine. She breaks off her own relationship with her cousin. The young people had been planning to get married, but he must finish his studies first. In the young Palestine of the 1930s, Tirsa's father goes bankrupt after investing unwisely. The girl experiences a new, unhappy romance. She falls for a young *kibbutznik* who is against marriage on principle. Her cousin's arrival in Palestine leaves Tirsa facing the decision of her life. Unable to solve the dilemma, she commits suicide.

So much for the plot. The background is more important. Bernard Zimmermann is an excellent reporter and faithful observer; furthermore, his heart is bursting for love of Israel and its people. The realistic description of the country – its poverty and struggle, its hope and faith, the life of the cities and *kibbutzim* – make this novel an authentic, unfalsified document of its time.

Bernard Zimmermann was a young Cracow engineer, but he knew the wider world. He first travelled to Palestine for the opening of the Hebrew University, and fell in love with the country at first sight. He brought his young wife Regina, a Jagiellonian University student, here a year later. Shortly afterwards, he was named Chief Municipal Engineer of Tel Aviv. He played a role in the development of the parks in the city, especially the Shderot Rothschild. The image of the Cracow Planty was engraved in his heart, and he made plans for a similar ring of green space around Tel Aviv.

The doors were always open – literally – at their home on Bugrashov Street. Regina once came home to find a man she had never seen before stretched out on the floor, asleep. He was one of the people who, in those days, were called *yomaim b'shavua* ('two days a week'), because the employment bureau had been able to find only part-time jobs for them. The Zimmermanns were among the few people in Tel Aviv who could then afford a high standard of living. Benek, as his friends called him, kept a splendid car. He was, however, too modest to drive it often. He preferred to get about on foot or, when he had to go to Jaffa, by public transportation. He walked around Tel Aviv like a starry-eyed lover, rejoicing at each new building and sign of development, each concert or open-air theatrical performance at Beit Haam, each sign portending the birth of a new culture. His young wife, however, looked upon the Levantine city from a different perspective. She found herself unable to adapt. She longed for European culture and wanted to finish her university studies. She finally issued an ultimatum to her husband: Tel Aviv or me.

Bernard Zimmermann returned broken-hearted to Cracow, where his brother Juda was a member of the city council and a prominent Zionist. Bernard never renounced the dream of Palestine and believed that he would return there some day. He expressed his affection in a series of 'Palestinian Sketches' that he published in the Cracow *Nowy Dziennik* newspaper, and also in *Tirsa*. He kept the writing of the novel a secret from his wife. In the spare time from his professional duties, he worked actively for Zionist causes, including the construction at his own expense of a beautiful Jewish recreation center near Bielsko. His home was a stopping point for all emissaries who came from Palestine to Cracow.

Then he suddenly died, at the age of 36, as a result of a totally unnecessary appendicitis operation. On his deathbed, he had his beloved wife swear that she would return to Eretz Israel after he died.

Regina kept her promise. Half a year after the death of Bernard, she arrived in Tel Aviv. She threw herself into a whirl of volunteer work. In time, she became head of the local branch of WIZO, the Women's International Zionist Organization, where she inspired whole generations of community activists. She worked at the University in Tel Aviv until 20 April 1982, the day of her death.

FACES FROM OUR CLASS PHOTOGRAPH

In class VIIIB, during the final school year before our matriculation exams, there were 54 of us boys. We were the last class to follow the old pattern of four years of elementary school followed by eight years of secondary school. When the winds of war stopped blowing, there were 25 survivors. This is a relatively high rate of survival, and is explained by the fact that, after graduating in 1938, a good many of us set off to study in other parts of the world: in Palestine, England and France. Those who remained in Poland studied in Plaszow, Auschwitz, and many other concentration camps in Germany and Austria, or in Siberia and similar picturesque locales that would have surely fascinated them had they gone there as tourists. How many of those who perished even have marked graves? Tadzio Szerer, who starved to death in Russia, may have been buried in the traditional way, but who can say where his grave lies? Who visits that grave?

Fifty-four of us took the matriculation exam. Not all had received their entire education in the same school, as I had. Few had been there for the whole 12 years. All the classes were coeducational in those first four years of elementary school. The invasion of students from the Mizrachi and Tachkemoni religious schools began in secondary school, and grew more intense with each passing year. The religious parents wanted their children to have an equal chance. The matriculation examination was a prerequisite for further studies, and of all the Jewish schools in Cracow, ours was the only one that offered that examination. New students kept transferring in; three orthodox boys, including two bearded ones, joined us in the eighth and final class. They intended to study at the Warsaw Judaistic Institute, and there, too, the matriculation examination was required. The moloch of the Holocaust consumed two of them, Stiglitz and Rotenberg. Aron Blaser survived in Russia and completed his legal studies, only to die young in Israel.

The students from the religious schools were intelligent and mature. They did well in school and, of course, stood out in the Judaistic subjects. They spoke Hebrew fluently, knew their Bible, and could engage in give-and-take with Rubinstein, Blattberg and Rappaport. We assimilated students could only look on in envy. Almost all of them belonged to Akiba, the largest pioneer organization in Cracow for prospective settlers in Palestine. Their religious roots combined with their political and ideological grounding to endow them with an air of seriousness.

They formed a cohesive group. Some of them had troubles with Polish. Not so much with the Polish language, as with Feldhorn – when he got his hooks into one of them, Lord have mercy! Take, for instance, Lolek Lewkowicz. In an hour foreboding ill, his father – a respected merchant in the ironware line – went to record his son's birth at the municipal offices in Podgorze. Mr Lewkowicz happened on an antisemitic clerk who was familiar with his religious roots. When the father attempted to register his son under the name 'Leon', after his grandfather, the clerk scoffed: 'Who's Leon? Your father's name was Lejb, sir! You're not ashamed of your own father's name, are you, sir?'

In consternation, Lewkowicz thought that the clerk might be right. 'Well, then, let it be Lejb,' he agreed.

'Lejb?' the clerk sneered. 'Such a tiny baby is supposed to be Lejb? He, at the most, is Leibuś', he said, using a comical diminutive form.

And, despite the father's protests, he recorded the child's name as 'Leibuś'. He could be enrolled at school only under this diminutive, absurdly inappropriate for a grown young man. Lolek was hardly proud of the appellation, and always replied 'Leon' when asked his name. Until he ran up against Feldhorn. From Feldhorn he received no quarter, especially because we had two Lewkowiczes in the class for several years. Aside from Leibuś, there was Izrael Lewkowicz from the village of Igolomia (the name of which, literally meaning 'broken axle' in Polish, was derived – as Feldhorn never failed to mention – from the lamentable state of the roads leading to that Galician backwater). When Feldhorn called Lolek Lewkowicz to the blackboard to recite, he always enunciated, with a sadistic leer, 'Leibuś Lewkowicz!' Leibuś therefore had no choice but to remain Leibuś. Today, Lolek is called Jehuda, the Hebrew equivalent of Lejb, which means 'Leon', or 'Lion', in Yiddish. He survived five concentration camps. He is a master of the Polish language, able to rattle off all the poetry and the most arcane grammatical rules. For his attempt at renouncing the beautiful name 'Leibuś', however, Feldhorn never gave him more than a 'C', which blotted the straight 'A's filling the rest of his report card.

Another of Feldhorn's victims was Izio – Izydor Borgenicht, another good student. Here, the problem was different. Izio played the piano and loved Chopin, which did not mean that he necessarily loved Polish poetry. In fact, he was rather mechanical in his recitation. Or perhaps what Feldhorn really disliked was Izio's bourgeois family, who had made a fortune in the coal trade. Or perhaps he was offended by the name Borgenicht ('no loans' in German), with its implied taste for miserliness and capital accumulation. In any case, Feldhorn had no sympathy for Izio.

I would like to stress here that family religious attachments had no influence on the children's social ties at school. Students who belonged to the same organizations did, of course, tend to stick together, but the most important factor in defining the 'pack' was one's address. Izio was therefore the only 'devout' boy in our pack; Janek Zimmerman, Wilek Nachhauser. Tadzio Szerer, Benek Halberstadt and I had attended school together since the first grade. We lived near each other and always walked home together.

To return to the Mizrachi students. What can I say about those who perished during the war? They all had well-trained minds; who can predict what they would have made of themselves?

A few survived.

Lolek-Arie Brauner was the son of a tailor whose clients included Wojciech and Jerzy Kossak, Wodzinowski, Uzięblo and others – the outstanding painters in Cracow. They paid for their suits with painting. Today, he is director of the Polish and Russian department in the Tel Aviv university library. He himself wields no mean pen, translating Polish poetry from Tuwim to Ficowski, Szymborska and Lipska into Hebrew. He has also rendered several volumes of Polish and Yiddish prose into the language of the Bible.

Moniek Hammer, who emigrated to Palestine before the war, is today Dr Moshe Dotan, a Hebrew University professor and prominent Israeli architect. He had a stunning head of black hair in his youth, just like Rudolf Valentino. When we met by chance after the war in Beer Shev, I must have recognized the bald man before me through some sixth sense. He displayed a similar instinct in regard to me …

Chanina Mandelberger was the son of a tanner, and also the class blockhead. After the war, which he survived in Russia, he was sent to England by his father. After finishing his studies and spending many years tanning hides in Leeds, he emigrated to Israel. Meniek, or Dr Emanuel Melcer, had a father who was active in the Zionist-religious Mizrachi organization in Cracow, and was one of the founders of the Tachkemon and Cheder Iwri religious schools (as noted on a memorial plaque in the courtyard of the Remuh synagogue). After passing his matriculation exam, he went to Jerusalem for his studies. He graduated in history and served in the Palestine Brigade. When I ran into him in Cracow in 1945, he was wearing the British uniform of the Brigade. Today, he is assistant principal of the Tel Aviv Municipal Secondary School (where the principal is another alumnus of our school, Dr Mosze Landau, three years our senior). Melcer has published a distinguished historical study in Hebrew, *Political Contention in the Jaws of the Trap: Polish Jews, 1935–1939*.

All those named above belonged to Akiba. That organization produced two active members of the Jewish Combat Organization in the Cracow ghetto: Maniek (Malachi Ajzensztajn) and Idek (Jechuda Tennenbaum). They died with rifles in hand, in the unequal struggle against the Germans. Another Tennenbaum from our class, Izydor, also belonged to Akiba. After studies in the Nazi concentration camps, he landed in Tel Aviv as a Jewish Agency official. It is worth noting that many Cracovians, including numerous graduates of our school, hold official posts, generally high ones, in Tel Aviv, Jerusalem and Haifa.

Our classmate Henek Bornstein survived the war on 'Aryan' papers and cooperated with the Polish resistance movement. He holds a directorate in the Water Department of the Tel Aviv Municipal Authority. Salek Schönberg of Akiba, who emigrated to Palestine as long ago as 1934, is the longest-serving staff member at Tel Aviv City Hall, where he began working at the age of 14, as a messenger. One more Akiba member, Moniek Borowski, runs a shop that makes eyeglass frames in Tel Aviv.

*

The Akiba members sat on the right side of the classroom, nearest the windows. To the left, nearer the door – perhaps because it was easier to sneak out from there – sat the boisterous members of the Revisionist El-Al fraternity. They represented an element that was the opposite of the Akiba members in ideology and temperament. Not that they were any less capable – not by any means! They were capable of anything, but simply had a rather negative attitude towards education. They cracked the books out of necessity, and only at the end of the year, before final examinations, did they sit to the point of numbness, cramming all the material into a few weeks. Whenever they could, whenever they had the opportunity, they slipped away from the school singly, in pairs, or in whole groups. There were selected lessons that they cut systematically; some teachers did not call roll and instead simply copied the absences noted by the teacher of the previous lesson.

Tolek Senft was absent all year from physics lessons with 'Hephaestos' – Professor Waldman. When Tolek suddenly came to class six weeks before the end of the school year, Waldman did not even recognize him. 'Who's that?' he asked.

At first, he threatened to refuse to examine Tolek at all and thus to block him from taking the matriculation exam. Later, he relented and called on Tolek to stand up for an oral classroom examination on the whole year's work. Tolek was incredible: he began answering

105

before Hephaestos had even finished his questions. Tolek answered precisely, without stammering, as if he were reading from a book. The class fell silent in awe, following this duel between teacher and student with bated breath. An hour passed and the bell rang. Out of breath, Tolek cast a triumphant glance around the classroom, wiped the sweat from his forehead, and sighed in relief. However, physics was the only subject in which we had two classes back to back. As soon as the bell rang again, the professor summoned Tolek back to the center of the classroom and resumed confronting him with increasingly convoluted questions. Waldman finally achieved what he had been aiming for: Tolek stood facing a complicated problem and did not know where to begin. Perhaps he was too tired, or perhaps this was a problem that was not even part of the course material; perhaps it was not even in the textbook. At that point, Waldman began to sneer vengefully: 'And you expect to be allowed to take the matriculation exam? You don't know anything! You don't have the slightest idea about the material! Your grade is D!'

Tolek broke down crying. He sobbed so pathetically that every one of our hearts broke!

'Sit down, you bumpkin from Mościce! Forget about matriculation! This is a school, not a cabaret!'

That was an allusion to the Bagatela Cinema-Revue, owned by Tolek's father, Gotlieb Senft. Probably following the example of some Warsaw cinemas, the Bagatela featured an hour-long revue as a supplement to the film showings. Good actors like Lawiński, Wyrwicz and Jankowski, and singers like Lena Zelichowska and Hanka Runowiecka sometimes appeared there. They were accompanied by chorus girls and second-rate but passable actors performing sketches. Tolek far preferred being backstage at the Bagatela to being in school. He watched rehearsals and spied on the soubrettes in their dressing room. In the fraternity, he was given the nickname 'Diva'. The father lavished the boy with protection, although I am not sure that protection is exactly the right word. In any case, his mother was completely at a loss with this son who was worldly-wise beyond his years, who 'felt God's will before his time' and sometimes had to be defended against expulsion from school. A long line of friends, the admirers of the Bagatela, followed him everywhere.

In the end, Hephaestos allowed Tolek to take the matriculation exam and he passed without difficulty. I do not know how he came to be in Palestine during the war. Perhaps the family had conferred and decided to get him as far away from the Bagatela as possible, for his own good. In any case, this daredevil who had previously swaggered through everything suddenly turned out to be helpless. He did manage to marry into the family of a very wealthy Tel Aviv industrialist and tried to set himself up in the café line, but nothing turned out right. The country was decidedly too small, too poor, and not at all suited to his style. As soon as communist Poland 'went into business', he signed up in the pro-government Union of Polish Patriots, hoping to return to Poland. As luck would have it, few people were interested in the Tel Aviv branch of the Union, and Tolek's name was at the head of the list. He ended up having a diplomatic career, undoubtedly surprising even himself in the process. As soon as Poland established its official diplomatic post in Tel Aviv, Tolek was promoted to the post of vice-consul in the Consulate General of the People's Republic of Poland. He soon took his wife – when his in-laws discovered whom she had married, they made her choose between her husband and the family fortune, and disinherited her when she refused to divorce Tolek – back to Poland with him. I met him for the first time after the war in Warsaw in 1948; he was director of the internal department of the Foreign Affairs Ministry. Later, he was ambassador to India. I met him in Vienna in the early 1960s, when he was the Polish representative to the International Atomic Energy Commission. As we sat in a café, he directed my attention to a shady-looking type sitting in the corner with a newspaper in front of his face. 'He's watching me,' Tolek chuckled.

They watched him and watched him until, one fine day, they summoned him to Warsaw. Then, just to be on the safe side, they took away his passport. Shortly thereafter, he died of a heart attack. That was in 1964. Tolek Senft, or Witold Lisowski, was the only one of our class to achieve a 'political career' – and in communist Poland, to boot. Could anyone who knew him at school have ever guessed?

*

... And who would ever have predicted that Aleksander Zala, or Olek Rubin, known as 'Gorilla', would become director of a secondary school, and a Hebrew one at that, in Melbourne, the capital of Australia. You would need to have some sort of extra-sensory perception. Olek was older than the rest of us and came from the small town of Dzialoszyce. Not without reason did the nickname 'Gorilla' stick to him. Olek was athletically built and, not to put too fine a point on it, abused his physical superiority. His *knajpname* in the fraternity was 'Wildcat'; his fraternity brothers obviously feared to offend him. Had Olek been a member of a Polish fraternity, he would without doubt have been one of the hoodlums who carried clubs and threatened their Jewish colleagues with brass knuckles and razor blades. He moved in an aura of awe and terror. Not belonging to his sphere of influence and authority, I had no reason to fear Olek. All the more so in that I chose in the tenth or eleventh grade to sit right next to him in a vulnerable position in the first row, exposed to the vigilant gaze of the teacher. (Did I do so out of some self-destructive impulse?) The third person in the row was Shmil Chil Fajgenblat of Wolbrom. He was also a character, but different: intelligent and clever, he stood apart from the rest of the class through his small-town mentality – and his poor command of the Polish language. The waves of the Holocaust swept him away, together with his family. I sat in the middle, between Olek and Shmil, and I had nothing in common with either of them except for the bench we sat on. We had different backgrounds, kept different company, and had different interests. I never visited them at home and knew nothing about their families. Why did I choose to sit between them? Let the psychologists say why …

Olek had his own pack in the fraternity, and as for the opposite sex, he seems to have sought out more mature and experienced company than the delicate girls in class VIIIA. He did not belong to the Bagatela crowd, and worked off his excess energy in boxing, fencing, and the other disciplines favored by the fraternities. Tales about his deeds circulated. I met him in Israel many years after the war, when he was visiting from Australia. My first impression was shattering: a short, elderly gentleman (I do not know why he had seemed such a giant in school) with a gray mustache, well-mannered, economical in speech, choosing his words with great care. I looked long and hard at him and failed to discern the slightest vestige of 'Gorilla'. When he told me that he was the principal of a Hebrew school, I nearly fell off my chair. Under the impression of that meeting, I spontaneously produced a long poem, 'Portrait of a Classmate', describing Olek from head to foot. The conclusion: not a thing had changed; then and now, pupils and teachers alike feared him.

Olek was a hoodlum who terrorized weaker classmates, skipped school, never studied – but, like Tolek, he had a good head on his shoulders. The same cannot be said of Salek Sperling (son of the Polrost Liquer Distillery). Salek's talents resided in his legs, which he inherited from his uncle Munio Sperling, the famed left wing of the Cracovia soccer team. We called him Munio in honor of his uncle, although his fraternity nickname, obviously based on his athletic looks, was 'Sis'. Not devoid of a sense of humor, Salek struggled from one class to the next, squeaked through his matriculation exam, and then emigrated to Palestine. He proved himself to be no great intellect, attaining the rank of sergeant as an artilleryman in the Palestine Brigade. Continuing in the Israeli army artillery, he ended up a major. Then came another surprise: entering civilian life, he opened a language school. I watched with my own eyes as he examined students enrolling in English courses – a sublimely delightful experience. Such surprises cheer one up, don't they?

When they were in school, parents played hooky, got under the skin of their teachers, sneaked off on dates instead of studying, smoked in the toilet and played the card game called 'nines' in off-limits dives. Unfortunately, they later forget about such glorious pasts and torment their children by denying them the very delights that they themselves once reveled in. What a shame. Experience teaches us that more than one straight-A student has turned out to be a run-of-the-mill mortal who can earn a living only with difficulty, worn down by life, living frugally – while former bullies, loafers, and screw-ups find success in politics, or even in science! When will parents ever learn anything from their own youth and that of their classmates?

To return to our fraternity bothers, there was one of them who let me – me, personally – down. This was Henek Goldman, or 'Vasco'. He had no taste for literature, and ended up transferring after various failures to the vocational school next door to our school. Nevertheless, I admired his talents as a handyman and expected him to end up as an inventor or construction specialist. In the end, having wandered through Siberia, he opened an auto repair shop. Presumably, it is a good shop. One way or another, therefore, his golden fingers are being put to the proper use. Another slow student was Brunuś Einhorn. 'Daft' nicknamed him 'Fountain' because streams of tears poured down his cheeks whenever he was called to the blackboard. Today, he is a foreman in a factory that makes television sets. He received 'vocational training' in the nightmarish coal mines of Vorkuta. His fraternity name was 'Flap' – Laurel and Hardy are known as 'Flip and Flap' in Poland, and Brunuś's round face brought Oliver Hardy to mind. He has not changed much. Yet another fraternity brother, the handsome Henek Zweig, 'Center', wandered into the Soviet Union and nothing more was ever heard of him.

Students from the provinces constituted a distinct element in our class. Some lived near Cracow in Krzeszowice or Swoszowice and commuted to school each day. At the end of lessons, they rushed out of the room to avoid missing the train home. Others lived in rented rooms or with relatives, and went home only at the end of the week. Most of them came from less-than-affluent families. Specific elements of their wardrobes made them easily identifiable: jackets handed down from their fathers or heavy boots (oh, that provincial mud!). They were talented and generally ambitious, although here, too, there were exceptions.

I recall Olek Rubin from Dzialoszyce, Dzidek (Izrael) Lewkowicz from Igolomia, and Fajgenblat from Wolbrom. Seweryn Kammerman came from Drohobycz, Zalman Sternberg commuted from Jordanow, and Kalman Grossmann-Weiss from Krzeszowice. Kalman survived the war in Russia and then returned to Poland with the Kościuszko Division. He rose to the rank of colonel in the Polish army. Then he emigrated to Israel in 1958. He remained in uniform for a time, and then entered civilian life. He continued in his military specialty and now holds a responsible position in the IBM computer firm. He could hardly take an active part in the social life of the class in the days when he had to race for the train after the final bell. Only here in Tel Aviv have we become close friends.

Another provincial with whom I had only loose ties at school was Szlomo Ehrlich. The only reason that he went by the nickname 'King Kong' was that 'Gorilla' was already reserved for Olek. Ehrlich looked so much like Fernandel that I dreamed of making a film in which he is mistaken for the French actor and goes on to a brilliant career … Szlomek came from Dąbrowa

Tarnowska and only joined our class in the final year. His father had died several years earlier, and his mother did whatever was required for him to be able to pass his matriculation exams and go on to university. The war left him in the Urals. After returning to Poland, he graduated from technical school and found a place for himself in the textile industry: he designed and manufactured material for coats, blankets, and so on. Other graduates of the same school addressed each other as 'Mr Engineer' and always included the abbreviation of academic degrees beside their signatures. Szlomek refrained from such pretentiousness. He emigrated to Israel in 1950. Unable to find a job in his own field, he went to work as an ordinary construction laborer. He was not ashamed of doing an honest day's work, and in any case had a wife and child to support. We had already been in touch back in Poland, and now found ourselves living in the same outlying district. I got to know him better, our wives became friends, and our children developed close bonds as they grew up together. Szlomo became a dear friend. I loved his wisdom, the Solomonic wisdom of the Jewish small town – the roots of the imposing tree of Jewish thought. Szlomek was wise for others, but came to me for advice on his own problems. Like all of us, he had difficulty getting started in Israel. By working hard and being reliable – how I valued that reliability and honesty of his! – he gave his son a musical education and sent him to study with the great violinist Shmuel Ashkenazy in Chicago. Szlomo himself sang beautifully in a warm baritone that he loved to show off, especially in liturgical songs. His wife Herta came from Bielsko in Poland. She played the piano; the whole family was musical. When things finally began going well for Szlomo after seven lean years, when his textiles began to be ordered by the best mills, he was suddenly involved, while driving his tiny car, in a collision with a tractor-trailer. And that was the end of his life. He loved people and people loved him.

Several of our classmates died soon after the war. Henryś Tislowitz, whose father had owned the Optima chocolate factory, died in Berlin as a lieutenant in the Polish army, just before the end of the war. Romek Blum studied shipbuilding in Glasgow and worked there as a naval engineer until he was consumed by disease. My friend Janek Zimmermann, a road engineer, died of chronic heart disease in 1982. We had two other engineers in our class: Zyga Ehrenhalt, employed in the chemical industry in Hajfa, and Romek Hirszprung, a mechanical engineer in the armaments industry. They had all been good at mathematics, and the latter three graduated from the Haifa polytechnic.

Most of my classmates who survived the war ended up in Israel. The only ones abroad are Milek Monderer, who has a thermos factory in Brussels; Lolek Helzel, son of the owner of the radio shop on Sienna Street who is a construction executive in the United States; and Izio Borgenicht, who is in textiles in London.

*

There were six of us, a group of friends who lived in the same neighborhood. We stuck together. After our matriculation examination, we went to Rosner's, the best photographer in Cracow, to pose for a group photo. The war broke up our pack. Julek Tigner's cousin, Tadeusz Szerer, starved to death in Russia – just like Julek's brother, Rysiek. Izio is in London and more or less keeps in touch, but never fails to 'report' when he visits Israel. Benek 'Pecio' Halberstadt, whose father had a currency exchange business in Cracow, took the long way to Israel, by way of Russia, and stayed in the army. He was always too good at bridge and soccer to accomplish much at school. Those talents stayed with him; he was the goalkeeper for his army unit and he still plays bridge – on what I might term the international level. Aside from this, he holds a responsible post as a warehouse manager in an armaments factory.

Wilek Nachhauser, today named Nahir, was a good pupil. Jews from Cracow will remember the firm of Nachhauser and Mond, Czech Jewelry, at the corner of Krakowska and Dietla Streets. The shop managed to get back on its feet after being wrecked by Haller's soldiers in 1919. The second-floor windows offered a good view of the Hebrew Secondary School Lag Ba'omer parade making its way to the Makkabi stadium. We were, and still are, close friends. The war separated our paths: I went to Warsaw to try my luck on Aryan papers, while Wilek went from the Cracow ghetto to the Plaszow concentration camp. Even then, we stayed in touch thanks to a certain Danuta Geller of Wieliczka, who indefatigably carried my letters to Wilek. He made it out of the camp alive, I survived my Aryan papers, and we met after the war in Cracow. Wilek later emigrated to France. All roads, however, lead to Jerusalem. Or to Tel Aviv. We are therefore together again and reminisce sentimentally over the old days. Wilek did not have an easy life in school, partly because of his reddish-gold hair. On top of that, he was a Don Juan. He had a girlfriend in the girls' class, which provoked his classmates to pranks that were in fact an expression of jealousy. The end result, however, is most important: Wilek married his old school sweetheart, Niusia Lis, after the war. His father's jewelry career may have influenced his present position; he is secretary of the Tel Aviv diamond market. After passing his matriculation exams before the war, he went to study in Grenoble but came home to Poland for summer vacation; the subsequent phases of his higher education included the ghetto and concentration camps. No one from his family – neither his talented younger brother Romek, nor his mother, nor his father – survived. Niusia followed the same road through hell. After the war, Wilek again studied in France. He expected to make something impressive of himself, at least a department chief in the Ministry of Industry and Trade. Yet who can say what guides our fates? Providence or dumb fate? Here in Israel, this haven of the shipwrecked, Wilek has not been spared further blows. His son Ilan, a charming boy the same age as my children, died defending his country. The Nahirs were left with only their daughter. All the friends of Wilek and Niusia go to Ilan's grave each year on the anniversary of his death. This is a wound that will never heal.

The war reduced our classmates' families to the minimum. Some survived but were left without parents and siblings. Others, like me, had more luck, and part of their families were rescued. Some survived but were separated by fate and never again saw those they loved. It may be that this 'winnowing out' of our families has encouraged closer links between us classmates who were not always close to each other in school.

Maurycy – or Moniek, Moshe, Marcel and, today, Majmon – Wasserman was one of the Bagatela crowd in school and kept company with Tolek Senft. Today, he is the soul of our alumni group (we have several such good souls). He used to live on Grzegorzecka Street in Cracow, which was out of the way for our band of six from Zielona, Jasna and Sebastiana Streets. His father was a wealthy garment factory owner who travelled to Vienna for premieres at the opera; the Depression wiped him out and left him

working as an impoverished salesman for the Kanold-Cosma-
Sarotti firm. Marcel transferred to our class from the Mizrachi
school with a certain amount of Judaistic baggage and a sharp
intellect. He also had a youthful preference for life's pleasures over
scholastic discipline. After our matriculation examinations, we
went together to the university to enroll in the law faculty. It may
be an understatement to say that we were shown the door by
National Democrat students who gave us to understand, with the
help of their knees and heavy clubs, that we were unwelcome
guests. It was a fine June day; I remember it well. We did not give
up. It may have been Marcel's intelligence that led us to write a
suitable letter of complaint to the rector of the Jagiellonian
University. We soon received an invitation to visit Professor
Dziurzyński, dean of the law faculty. He apologized to us for the
unpleasantness we had experienced, gave us his blessing, and
pointed out the way to the appropriate office where we were
given our student identity cards. Hitler did his best to prevent
Marcel and me from becoming lawyers. Marcel went to the ghetto
with his family. During the liquidation, he made his way through
the sewers to the 'Aryan side'. He spent several months on Aryan
papers, preparing to escape to Hungary. The plan, alas, came to
naught. Someone informed on the whole group before they could
take possession of the documents being prepared for them. Marcel
thus went to Montelupich prison instead of Hungary, and from
there to Plaszow. Miracles do happen, and Marcel is still alive after
Plaszow, Auschwitz and Flossenbürg. He returned to Cracow at
just that unfortunate moment in June when a ravenous crowd
almost beat him to death. He could see no point in waiting for
further miracles. He set out for Palestine with Rachelka, his
companion in the misery of the camps and former younger school
companion. Once here, he joined the army. He became secretary
to the Supreme Command of the Zahal, or Israeli army, with the
rank of lieutenant-colonel. Later, he was deputy to the general
director of the office of the minister of security, in the days of Ben
Gurion and Eshkol. As a civilian, he became the director of a large
industrial concern. As I write these words, he is manager of his
own firm, Sepen, which develops and backs international
programs. This in no way hinders him from backing the plans of
his old classmates and remaining in close, daily contact. Old school
ties matter … I feel good inside when I think about this.

114

*

Unless I am mistaken, Janek Zimmermann was the only student in our class who came from an intelligentsia family. His parents were university graduates. His father, Dr Juda Zimmermann, was a lawyer, Zionist activist, and member of Cracow City Council. His mother, Maria (née Salz), was an excellent pianist who had studied under Prof Leszetycki. Before marriage, she had given recitals and been a soloist with orchestras in Vienna and Switzerland. Afterwards, she was active in the Jewish Musicians' Union in Cracow and was repeatedly elected to its board. Janek's sister Anna, whom I describe elsewhere, graduated from the State Conservatory in Cracow with distinction. Janek was on the way to musical distinction as a pupil of Jan Hoffman, a Chopin specialist and distinguished teacher.

Janek's family thus had, in a certain sense, a higher social status. Yet I would not say, from the perspective of time, that this had any influence on Janek's position in our petty-bourgeois class, whose members were not badly off themselves. If there happened to be a tailor's son among these merchants' sons, it is a good bet that the tailor was of the elite sort. However, there were those who could not pay the tuition fees even though they received reductions. This sort of thing was not obvious, however. The school janitor did indeed come to the class at the beginning of each month with a list of pupils who had not paid their fees and who were therefore to be sent home. Quite a few of the pupils on this list, however, simply kept the money their parents had given them in their pockets and waited to be sent home so that they could avoid Latin or German class.

Yet take, for example, Lusiek Daniel. He indulged in such deception, although he was the son of a poor widow. He drew and wrote beautifully, was intelligent, belonged to Akiba – but he refused to study, and did so on principle (what good was a matriculation examination to a pioneer in Palestine?). And so, despite the fact that he was liked by the teachers, he did not pass from tenth to eleventh grade. He died of typhus in the Warsaw ghetto in 1941. I had been in correspondence with him and his death came as a blow: people were only beginning to die then …

To return, however, to Janek: he played not only the piano, but also bridge. His heart was sensitive to the younger girls at the school. He did not switch girlfriends often, but switch them he did. He danced, swam, went skiing in Zakopane in the winter and spent the summers at the seashore. He almost came to a tragic end a year before the war: he was shot on the beach by a friend who was carelessly playing with a gun. The bullet lodged in his throat and the doctors were afraid to try to remove it. Only 30 years later, in Israel, did he have it taken out.

Janek did not belong to any organization. The fact that his father was a Zionist was obviously enough. Besides, his serious approach to the piano, and the fact that he was a serious student, left him with no time for organizations. In general, the sons of the affluent Jewish bourgeoisie with whom he associated preferred sport, dancing, hanging out on the Planty and playing bridge to politics or pioneer training. I fell somewhere in the middle. I belonged to Akiba, but did not let it dominate my life; the meetings on Celna Street across the river in Podgorze were too far away. On the other hand, I was totally involved in my pack of friends, where Janek, Witek and Izio already had girlfriends and were starting to go dancing. I was a student life activist – following the spirit of the times, I organized dance evenings in the school auditorium. I could not avoid being inexorably drawn into the tango, although I never advanced to the foxtrot. Janek had a strong influence over me and my social life, particularly in the last years of school. I was a rather shy young man (although I did not let it show), and it was only Janek who introduced me into the world of girls. He 'set me up' with his girlfriend Renia, while he switched to Frania.

Later, during the war, I also inherited Frania from him in a certain sense. She began spending time in my garden. There was a boy who adored her at this time, a good boy, perhaps, but unintelligent and ugly. He seemed to have a great deal of money and was head over heels for Frania. Lord, how he suffered! She was not interested. When she went to the ghetto, I wrote a story about Janek for her. I wrote it purely out of longing, in an effort to recapture our happy years at school. Frania survived the hell of several concentration camps. She married Arie Reisman, who had been several classes ahead of her at school. Janek had already been in Palestine for a long time by then. Like a good Zionist, his father had sent him to the Haifa polytechnic immediately after he graduated. The father stayed in Cracow with the rest of the family. I saw them in the ghetto. That beautiful family was withering away as they struggled against fate. I cannot recall how Juda died. Janek's mother and sister died of exhaustion and typhus in Skarzysko, where they had to perform slave labor in chlorine and picric acid fumes.

Janek and I kept up a lively, warm correspondence as long as was possible, even after the Germans occupied Cracow. I managed to surprise him once by arranging for a bouquet of fresh flowers with my card on it to be delivered to his dormitory room on his birthday – as if I were in town. Then contact was broken off.

One of the first three letters that I wrote abroad after liberation was to Janek, at his address at the Haifa polytechnic. The letter lay in the post office for half a year, finally reaching Janek despite the fact that he had left the polytechnic long before. He had graduated and enlisted in the Palestine Brigade.

In our resumed correspondence, he informed me that he was getting married. Later, he sent a mass of romantic photographs from the wedding. I soon had the chance to meet his wife personally. Chawa, a pianist, was an energetic woman from a good family. For several years, she and Janek had been taking part each Saturday in *Musical Quiz*, a program on Israel radio. They were a 'musical couple' and regularly won all the prizes. Chawa was a sabra,[1] but she learned Polish – according to malicious acquaintances – in order to be able to eavesdrop on Janek, of whom she was said to be pathologically jealous. Then Oen was born. Today, he is an engineer and father of his own family.

Janek's marriage was not a happy one, and he decided after more than a dozen years to divorce Chawa. In our rather conservative little world, this was a shocking development. Shocking and painful, all the more so since Chawa had become a friend to us old friends of Janek's. Our wives, in particular, reacted in a sharply critical way. Soon afterwards, Janek married Zosia, who was several years younger than him. She was a widow and had a son, Adam, whom Janek adopted. As always, Janek was slightly troubled, but determined and uncompromising. When they moved into a new apartment immediately after their wedding (he always planned everything down to the smallest details), he did not inform us or invite any of us. He did not know how we would react. When I realized that he hadn't called me, I immediately telephoned him. I was perhaps the first of the pack to visit the newlyweds. I did not hesitate for a moment: my friend's decision was my decision. Soon, of course, the others followed suit and Zosia became 'one of the family'. Everyone loved her – a wife and mother, housekeeper and, for Janek, everything. Which is not to say that we turned our backs on Chawa; she, too, soon found a new husband.

As at school, so too in Israel, Janek was the pivotal figure in our social life, thanks to his personal charm, good taste, *savoir-vivre*, and a certain superiority resulting from his self-confidence. We all had our own lives and had started our own families after the war, yet we stuck together: Janek, Wilek, Marcel, Lolek, Kalman, Szlomek and Meniek … The group had peripheral attachments; we all had friends outside the school circle. But each member of the pack invited all the others to his birthday party. If he hadn't invited them, they would have come anyway.

In my first years in Israel – and very, very difficult years they were – I went to bed early one 16 November after a hard day's work. At ten o'clock at night I suddenly heard a hammering at the door and the Polish birthday song '*Sto lat, sto lat*'. My friends never forgot that I had been born. And so it became a tradition. Classmates' birthdays were the most important events in our social life, and a symbol of our friendship. As the main class rhymer, I had to come up with an appropriate poem for each birthday. And so it happened that first one, and then a second, volume of poetry arose from these poems, *What's Left of It All* and *Crumbs of Youth*, both published in Israel. I always wrote the poems at the last minute, on Friday afternoon (those birthday parties are invariably held on Friday evening, so that we can sleep in on Saturday). Each time, I swore that this would be the last one. I have not published the third volume, *Life Begins at Forty – or Maunderings on the Fortieth Anniversary of the Matriculation Exams*, and already have enough poems for two more volumes.

Every five years, all of us who were in the boys' and girls' classes organize a jubilee banquet, a reunion with established ceremonies. As class president, I am master of ceremonies. And I therefore have to write another new poem every five years. As each half-decade draws to a close, we all, and especially 'the girls', start discussing the issue: should we hold a reunion or not? In the end, we decide to avoid looking in the mirror and reluctantly agree: 'Alright, let's do it.' Then we all feel happy, excited and satisfied. For they are emotional meetings indeed. Within the realm of delusion ...

Janek, my dearest friend, was not present at our forty-fifth reunion. He had had an operation 12 years earlier, during which he was fitted with artificial heart valves. Those valves wore out before he managed to have them replaced. Only Zosia came to the reunion – one more faithful widow of a friend, like Szlomek's Herta. Brave Zosia: she survived the war as a child, sheltering in the ghettos and forests. Then she began burying those she loved. First, her original husband. Then her son: she had raised him to the point where he was about to graduate from secondary school, when he was killed by Japanese terrorists during the notorious attack on the airport at Lydda. He had gone there to wait for an aunt who was returning from abroad. Then Zosia's mother died in a car accident. Then her father. And now, Janek. Too many funerals for such a young woman. Yet life goes on: Janek's second son, Yoram, has graduated from the polytechnic in Haifa. The chain remains unbroken ...

NOTES

1   The *sabra* (or *cabar*) is a cactus fruit, thorny on the outside and sweet inside. These traits are attributed to children born in Israel, which is why the name is applied to them.

PART TWO

On a Narrow Footbridge

Motto: *All this world is but a narrow footbridge,*
and the most important thing is: Fear not!
(Rabbi Nachman of Bratzlav)

To my children and grandchildren:
To Jakov and Aliza
To Achi, Maoz, Peled, Eldad
To Shela and Hila
         and
To All People of Good Will,
and especially those who,
amid the tempests of the Second World
War,
reached out a hand to the hunted
and persecuted Jews –
I dedicate these recollections with love
         the Author

7. Everything Comes Tumbling Down

On the fifth day after the outbreak of war, I allowed myself to be swept up in the wave of refugees and joined, together with a group of acquaintances, the crowds heading eastward. My father and my younger brother Jozek had set out toward Lwow two days earlier, while I had decided to stay at home with mother, 16-year-old Klara, and 12-year-old Jerzyk. When I went to the recruiting office, they ordered me to wait for conscription orders. So I waited.

Father had not wanted to leave Cracow. He resisted as long as he could. Our apartment had been as crowded and noisy as a beehive from the first day of the war. The door never closed. Uncles came, aunts came, and children milled around everywhere. Discussion upon discussion. What would happen, how it would happen, what it was like in 1914, what the Germans were like, what they were capable of. And how long the war would last: probably not longer than two weeks or three, at the outside. We could hold out. The Germans might not reach Cracow. In the meantime, our quiet Zielona Street filled with crowds of refugees who had decided that there was no point hanging around, that the Germans meant business. Carts, fiacres, and here and there a car loaded with suitcases and jammed full of men, women and children snaking slowly forward among the onlookers, the groups of people engaged in passionate discussions while children clung to their legs. What was going to happen, what was going to happen?

A couple of German bombs had an effect. News about troop movements, paratroop landings, and about spies who had been apprehended and lynched by the crowds exploded every so often, causing an uproar that brought people out of their apartments and on to the streets. There were feverish preparations for leaving town.

The Steinmetzes, Grünbergs and Grosses, mother's family and father's family, sat around drinking coffee, debating, going out, coming in, urging, threatening, deciding yes and then deciding no. The formula 'They don't do anything to the women' was established. Men, however, risked repression, and it was better to stay out of the hands of the Germans.

Uncle Grünberg, a reserve officer, was a handsome man with a martial mien and bushy eyebrows. He spoke decisively in favor of leaving Cracow. Doing so was easy enough for him; he was a tea salesman and had no shop. But Gross, Jakub Gross, had two shops full of china and crystal, as well as a lovely apartment. And he was supposed to abandon all of that to the whims of fate? Home, shop, and everything he had earned in his life?

The giant Steinmetz perched on a small rococo chair in the living room and said not a word. Aunt Lana, mother's sister, could not stop talking. Patriotism and good intentions filled her blue eyes. It would be better if Josef left, because the Germans were looking for his sort. And he should take Guto along. With her command of German, she would get them out of any difficulties ...

Lame Rozia was there, and plump Tyla, and gloomy Mojsze, and rakish Henek ...

Mother, my wise mother, knew one thing: we should not split up, because there was no telling when we would see each other again. Either we all stay, or we all go. She had her experiences from the last war – yet she lost her self-assurance under the pressure of opinion and the general madness. Who could say what was best in such a situation?

I had no fixed opinion. I was inexperienced and hardly eager to take responsibility for anyone or anything. Pacifist in views and well-read on the subject of the horrors of war, I nevertheless felt no terror: 'The boil has been lanced', I told myself, 'and perhaps it is for the best.' An artificially maintained peace had led only to the voluntary surrender of Europe into the hands of that madman, Hitler ... But what should be done? I had no idea. I had fulfilled my civic duty and was now waiting to be called upon to bear arms.

Father did not want to go. On the third day, Uncle Grunberg waited downstairs with his whole family (his wife and three children) loaded on a horse and cart.

'I'm not going', father demurred. 'I'm not leaving Sala and the children.'

'Are you crazy, young man? You'll probably be the first hostage they take! You can't stay here!'

So father went. He wept as he said goodbye to us.

'You'll see each other again in two weeks,' said uncle, tugging at father's sleeve. 'There's no time to waste'.

Jozek went, too – the very one who had always been at loggerheads with father. But I stayed behind. I was waiting to be called up. However, those who were supposed to call me up left Cracow before I did, and so I, too, set out – two days after father. There was nothing to wait for, and the psychological pressure was growing by the hour: 'What? You're still here! What are you waiting for?' All the other men in the building had left. A group of acquaintances living nearby invited me to join them.

On the fifth day of the war, at dawn, I took up the backpack that mother had filled with provisions and clothing, and I started eastward. I walked with Henek, Kurt, Romek, and two other young men that I had never seen before. We were all loaded down with backpacks, sacks, suitcases, overcoats, and sweaters – and before long, we began discarding things along the roadside.

It was a beautiful, sweltering day, and the road was black with people, some on foot, some on horseback. Cars had been left along the way when they ran out of gas, although there was also a group of optimists pulling a car along in the hope that they would be able to buy a canister of gasoline somewhere at an inflated price. A lost child screamed as it looked for its parents; no one paid any attention. The last water in the thermoses was running out and the wells along the way had run dry, and our throats were dry with thirst and our eyes were filling with dust, so we drank water from a puddle – Brrr! Salvation was nowhere in sight. Stones found their way into our shoes and our legs fainted in exhaustion. We lost our way, then found it, or didn't find it, but new companions joined us. From time to time, there was an air raid. People left their belongings on the road and ran into the fields, disappearing, shouting: 'Children! Children!' The malicious birds with black crosses on them growled overhead, circling and sowing death.

I lay among cabbages. Ta-ta-ta-ta-ta-choo-choo-choo. Clods of earth squirted up all around me. I felt no fear. I was cut off, I was part of a great spectacle, of a film. I did not think: thinking would come later – but wasn't I lucky!

The air raid ended and the black lava flowed on. Not everyone – for there were wounded, there were dead; people would look after them, or perhaps not. Someone knew a shortcut to the nearest small town, so we cut through woods or a thicket where there was a little shade, thank heaven! At the edge of an enormous crater on the border of the woods lay the bloated carcass of a dead horse, and beside it, a soldier – a corpse with one leg blown off. A terrible stench and thousands of flies. The soldier's eyes were open in fixed mockery, and his blackened gaping mouth was twisted in pain, laughter or protest. People kept walking past. Some crossed themselves, others looked away, or held their noses, or pulled a child along – and they kept going, forward. It was my first encounter face-to-face with the horrors of war, with wartime death, wartime danger. 'A cavalryman falls in lovely war, his colleagues stop to grieve no more', the song goes. I was too tired to be frightened, or to say anything, but that image will stay with me as long as I live. A memento. A banal sight, isn't it?

We reached Bochnia and a good, caring family took us in for a moment. To wash, drink, drink, drink, and eat a bowl of warm soup. They were good people and I added them to my store of memories and even memorized their name – the Temans. And then onwards, toward Tarnow.

You learn things along the road: evil people with sour faces live in the roadside houses, and they offer neither food nor drink, and scream at you for being a vagrant and a beggar. Once you pass into the heart of a village, you find a different people there, who have feelings and care, who offer good advice, something to drink, and hospitality, and who let you sleep on the hay in their barn when the little room in the cottage is full. It's plain to see: the good will of those who live along the road gave out along with their supplies of water and food, with the thousands of strangers who called at their doorstep and trudged through their rooms without even asking, bringing in mud, stink and fear.

Sometimes, we slept in the fields. Despite all the fatigue and the emptiness of my mind, I could not resist the uncommon beauty of the sunsets. After the travails of the day I looked spellbound at its bloody red descent, wreathed in golden snowmen of cumulus clouds that turned into bears, mountainous landscapes, fuzzy heads, woolly sheep. My painter's imagination easily picked out those shapes. The skies were always red. They say it means a fair wind; they say it means a long, bloody war.

When we reached a train station, we all climbed on board a train that was supposed to carry us east, to Lwow. Instead of that, it attracted a hail of bombs and cannon shell, and we ended up beneath its wheels. Those airplanes pursued us the whole way, and the green German army surged eastward behind us. We were overtaken by news of bloodshed and glory, news of battles that either had taken place or hadn't. Reliable information from official sources reached us seldom. Faith that the front would be stabilized and that the Polish troops would stop the German deluge gave us comfort and strength. Otherwise, what was the point of fleeing? Where to? So we kept going forward, dirtier and dirtier, carrying less and less, more and more worried, but full of endurance. Farther, farther – don't surrender to the dictatorship of our fainting legs. We had come so far; we could keep going. How many kilometers to Lwow? Not far now. And once we got to Lwow, what? No one knew, no one even suspected, that the Soviets would occupy Lwow. That would come as a surprise. So: once we get to Lwow, what? Things will be fine.

And so it was that after six days of marching, dead beat, on our last legs, worried about those back home, worried about those who had set out before us, we found ourselves in the vicinity of Brzuchowice, outside Lwow. We wanted to reach that village of Brzuchowice before dark, so we followed someone's advice and took a shortcut through the woods. We got lost. We were not too worried; we would simply have to spend the night in the woods. In the morning, we licked ourselves into some sort of shape – there was even a brook nearby – and were preparing to continue our march, when we were suddenly surrounded by a group of Polish soldiers aiming their rifles at us. 'Hands up!' They took us for spies.

'Gentlemen, all joking aside. What kind of spies are we? We're fleeing from the Germans ...'

'And why aren't you in the army?'

'They never managed to call us up. We are traveling to find the army, to join up ...'

I tried to maintain a light air, but our uniformed fellow citizens did not evince any sense of humor. They wondered whether they should shoot us on the spot or take us to headquarters. We did not have particularly distinguished expressions on our faces as they blindfolded us. Was this supposed to be the end of our escapade, when we were almost there? They led us through the woods, jostling us with their rifle butts when we stumbled into tree trunks. Finally, we reached their commander's headquarters. Only then did they remove the blindfolds. A slender, rather elderly colonel looked at us grimly. Who were we? Where from? Going where? Why? Documents? Now what? There were spies everywhere, and we had been on military terrain. He advised us not to go wandering off the beaten track, and ordered us to be blindfolded again and led back to the main road.

Shortly afterwards, we heard that the Soviet army had entered Polish territory. I decided that instead of pushing on to Lwow, I would return home to mother, as my troubled conscience insisted. I counted on father's coming back as well. We were, after all, supposed to meet at home when the war ended. Our group broke up. Some of them decided to go on to Lwow, and others, like me, decided to return to the families they had left in Cracow. The retreat began. This time, there was no race against time and no rush, but it was still necessary to eat. The little money that I had brought from home was long gone, but since we were in a group, we managed somehow. This time, we wandered through the villages instead of sticking to the main road. Life seemed to be going back to normal. There was still no shortage of wanderers like us, but we sometimes caught rides on carts or even on motor vehicles. I was returning unenthusiastically towards the Germans; I had met the obligation that I had imposed on myself. When we heard that refugees were being stopped at the River Bug, I told myself: if they don't let me pass, I'm not going to make any special effort to get to Cracow. But no one stopped us. We crossed the bridge in Przemysl, and there I saw the Germans for the first time. It was an unpleasant feeling … I was not afraid, but my heart was afraid … I pretended to be brave, for my own sake and that of others. Perhaps they really weren't as bad as everyone said? I don't know how I came up with the chutzpa, or the naive unconsciousness, to ask a German soldier – a corporal? a sergeant? – for a ride. He was going to Tarnow by truck. From there I boarded a train that took forever to reach the outskirts of Cracow. My joy was mixed with uncertainty and worries about father. They had come to the apartment looking for him, and more than once. But in the meantime, there was my bed – my own soft bed! That was the most important thing. As to what came next, we would see …

On my return from that crazy expedition, I came down with an inflammation of the joints combined with an inflammation of the renal pelvis. Never before or since have I had anything similar. The pain! Especially when my good mother applied the unfailing remedy of a mustard plaster. The whole war seemed of secondary importance compared to that suffering. It all passed quickly, however, and my good humor came back. I decided to immortalize my Galician expedition in an essay on Polish village and small-town conveniences, under the Latin title *De srocibus Poloniae*. It was intended to be a chapter in a longer scientific work, my *Trattato della cloaca*. In this chapter, I systematized the various types of facilities: those without doors and those without back walls, without seats, without sideboards, with hearts carved in the door, with hearts carved in the seat, with boards over the gaping abyss and with ropes for support, and so on and so forth. Conceived as a doctoral dissertation, this work unfortunately has not survived (I do not know why Tuwim never wrote anything similar). This is a shame; all that architecture and that folklore will cease to exist someday …

In the meantime, the German authorities did their best to banish my good humor. New decrees appeared continually, limiting the freedom of movement and the freedom of thought of both the Polish and the Jewish population. For Jews, of course, it was more humiliating and discriminatory.

*

Just two days after their arrival, the Germans decreed that Jews must mark their businesses – shops and stores, cafés and restaurants – with the Star of David. Soon thereafter kosher meat slaughtering was abolished, and within a month forced labor (*Zwangsarbeit*) was imposed. The accounts of Jews in banks and savings institutions were confiscated, and the *Judenrat*, a Jewish government responsible for executing the Germans' orders, was created.

Starting on 1 December, Jews throughout the General Government were obligated to wear white armbands with a blue Star of David. Fear descended on the Jewish streets: the noose was tightening.

I tried to console myself with the thought that I would wear the national symbol with dignity. One way or another, it was the star of Zion … Why should I be ashamed of my Jewishness? Let them be ashamed! But this philosophy could help only to a degree. Winter arrived, and groups of Jews organized by the *Arbeitsamt* went out with shovels to clear the snow from the streets of Cracow. We began to understand the feelings of slaves or prisoners of war who must obey the commands of their victorious master. But why was I mocked by the rejects of Polish society, the dregs, the scum? Hadn't the Germans also showed them who was boss? Apparently not. However, the more intelligent part of the population and the more enlightened workers – simple, decent people – offered their solidarity, dread and sympathy (even if they did so in a passive way).

To tell the truth, I did not shovel much snow. Someone who needed money more than I did took my place. On the occasion or two when I went out, it was for the sake of solidarity and against the wishes of mother, who wanted to spare me such humiliation at any cost. Additionally, I was still recuperating from a very real illness.

The introduction of the Star was accompanied by a bloody two-day closing of the Jewish quarter. The aim was to plunder the Jews' jewelry and valuables, especially their gold and silver. We heard dire reports about the rapacious searches, accompanied by outbreaks of shooting and mistreatment of the residents of Kazimierz.

Soon afterwards, the thugs came knocking on our door. There was nothing for them to seize. Mother had made the effort to conceal any valuables well or to entrust them to Polish acquaintances. Three SS officers, with looks of rage on their faces and drawn pistols in their hands, roamed the apartment opening cupboards and emptying drawers.

'Here, here!' one of them called when he thought he had found something.

'Here, here … Here a dog is buried,' I inadvertently blurted in German with a pale grin.

I received an instantaneous and devastating 'smack in the chops' and found myself under the table without knowing how I had got there. It was such a skillful blow that I felt no pain! As I felt around for my glasses, I heard incomprehensible curses and threats. Only after they had left empty-handed did I realize I could not move my jaw. That, too, passed. I had got off lightly.

The gala victory parade, led by Himmler and Frank, took place right in front of Gross's. The occasion is immortalized in a photograph showing that bloodthirsty pair together with the Gross sign, at the shop on the corner of Szewska Street and the Main Square. Immediately afterwards, the shop was turned over to a *Treuhänder* (trustee), as were other large Jewish shops and firms. Most Jews managed to get along with these *Treuhänders*, who employed the Jewish owners as salesclerks in their own shops. Because the owners knew their businesses and the local market better, they came to arrangements with the commissars. They thus ensured themselves a living, and were able to look after their shops and prevent them from being stripped or run into the ground. They bustled diligently, counting on recovering their property someday. They could not foresee the approaching destruction ...

The *Treuhänder* of our shop did not seek any cooperation from my mother. He paid her a small monthly salary, but he did not want to see her in the shop. All the Christian employees continued to work there and stayed in touch with their former boss, informing her of the German commissar's various moves.

About a year before the war broke out, father had bought a small lamp factory from a craftsman named Gruszczynski. Father registered it in my name; I even spent some time running the place. Gruszczynski, a habitual drinker and braggart, continued working in the little factory and earned more than enough for his vodka. A few days after the Germans entered Cracow, he showed up drunk at our house, with a red nose, shining eyes and muddy boots. He was accompanied by a *Volksdeutsch* with a revolver. Gruszczynski demanded the keys to the factory from mother, and of course received them. I don't know whether he operated the workshop, or sold it again to someone else.

Those were days of various 'visits', mostly by German officers and clerks looking for lodgings and furniture. With papers from the *Quartieramt* (housing office), or even without any official documents, they rummaged through Jewish apartments, helping themselves to beds, mattresses, bedding, chairs and rugs of the better sort. They set themselves up in housekeeping. The *Quartieramt* commandeered rooms in the larger apartments and assigned them as the bureau saw fit. The Jews quickly realized that it would be better to find tenants themselves than to wait for the office to place any old thug in the apartment. They frequently offered rooms to their *Treuhänders* or their friends. Sometimes, the Jews recommended Germans to each other, or sent chance apartment-seekers or furniture-hunters to other Jews, just to get rid of them. 'Sir, why take a small room in my place? Go to the

Grosses at 12 Sarego Street. There you'll find exactly what you're looking for…' Thus our spacious apartment filled with all sorts of German tenants who were sent there or simply showed up. We began by finding a safe tenant for father's handsome, green office with its carved Baroque bookcases, deep velvet armchairs and a large self-portrait by Maurycy Gottlieb. All this became the domain of a modest train worker from Dortmund, who was recommended by our neighbor. Willy Althaus, a stout man in a dark-blue railway uniform, with a somewhat obtuse but reasonably pleasant face, felt uncomfortable at first in a room so inappropriate to his status, but then he got used to it. He behaved decently and allowed us to listen to the radio – when he was out, we tuned in to the Allied broadcasts from Toulouse. When he was preparing to go home for Christmas, he asked us for permission to take with him a pair of antique silver binoculars which I had received for my barmitzvah from my aunt, because he wanted to show them to his fiancée. Needless to say, he forgot to bring the binoculars back. Then, after the Jews had left Cracow, and when it was the turn of the Germans to leave too, he took the furniture with him to Germany – he had grown so accustomed to it …

Two other 'guests' settled in the formal dining room: Hans Gerst, an ascetic journalist from Hamburg with a wrinkled face, thin as a stick, but with a sense of humor; and the noisy, vulgar Alfred Rath, a small-time *Treuhänder*, a fat pig-faced type. Every morning, he used to walk to the bathroom half-naked through mother's bedroom, pausing at her bedside to tell her about the recent successes of the German army. These two, like our other 'subtenants', maintained relations with us that were decent, if not particularly friendly. Occasionally they brought us a chocolate bar, and occasionally they asked us to buy or sell something for them. They did not spend much time at home.

One morning, Rath entered mother's bedroom with a loud shout, waving the newspaper. In the paper was an article about Polish bandits who had shot a German near Warsaw. His friend Gerscht had gone to Warsaw the previous day.

'If it turns out that it's him, my friend Gerscht, I'll shoot you all like dogs!' Rath hollered, red with fury.

But Gerscht came back that evening, and everything returned to normal.

My sister Klara's pink room went to Dr Rudolf Rosenauer, a

serious, well-mannered businessman from Austria, who was head of the iron industry for the whole Cracow region. We did not fraternize with him much, especially since he spent most of his time outside the city.

The golden yellow Rococo living room, meanwhile, was occupied by Dr Johann Steinbeck from Vienna, a high official in the Gestapo, a handsome blond-haired man of 25. He maintained his distance, but promised that as long as he was with us, no one would touch a hair on our heads …

THE COFFEE POT

We were sitting down to dinner when a harsh buzz from the doorbell made us jump out of our seats. None of us had any doubt as to the identity of the person who had pressed the bell. In those days, two or three months after the Germans entered Cracow, people had already learned how to identify the person at the door by the sound of the bell.

Family members and regular visitors had agreed ways of ringing the bell, and even a visitor who was not initiated into these secret sounds made an effort to ring quietly, so as not to terrify the occupants. The buzz that shattered our peace that afternoon did not bode anything good.

'Darn it!' mother hissed. 'They can't even leave us in peace on a Sunday.'

A tension-filled silence descended over the room as we waited for another ring. And indeed, after a moment, there was another long, insistent ring, impatient and furious. Those in the room – my mother, Klara, Jerzyk and I – all felt the fear choking our throats. Tosia stopped working in the kitchen, but did not go to the door. Soon we would hear a loud knock or the thundering pounding of a fist … Our apartment wound in a circle around the entire second floor of our building, so that the doors of the last room (my father's office), which led out to the staircase, were located exactly across from the main entrance door, which led to the rooms we lived in. The electric doorbell and a sign with the name 'Jakob Gross' were affixed to the door of the office. Visitors not familiar with our apartment usually turned first to that door. Anyone who rang the bell was clearly visible through the peephole in the door opposite.

Intruders whose ring was not answered then turned to the door across the way, which bore no name or bell, without knowing that they were knocking on the doors of the Gross apartment again. On the one hand, this arrangement bought us some time to prepare for unwanted visitors. But on the other hand, it risked rousing the ire of German officers who would discover the trick when they came plundering for booty.

We cherished for a moment the delusion that they would go away without knocking on the main door. But the characteristic thumping was heard immediately after Tosia's frantic announcement: 'Two, in green uniforms!'

Klara grew pale and began shivering as if in a fever. Jerzyk clung to mother, and I sat at the table, frozen.

'Open the door!' my mother said to Tosia with a deep sigh. When one of our German tenants was home, visits by these unwanted guests were less dangerous, because the intruder, even if armed with a note from some *'amt'*, hesitated before transgressing the borders of legality. If he did not find what he wanted, he left without demanding a ransom, or turning the apartment upside down and inside out. But unfortunately, that afternoon none of our German tenants was home, which was one reason mother was more worried than usual. Another reason was that she had run out of money the day before and had had to part with the gold watch my father had given her on the occasion of the birth of their second son. She received barely 800 *zloty* for the watch, enough to buy food for a few days. She had changed her mind about hiding places in the apartment a hundred times, but none of them seemed secure enough to her. She finally concealed the money inside a porcelain coffee pot that stood on the top shelf of the glazed mahogany cupboard, alongside a tea pot, little milk jug, sugar bowl and 12 cups, all decorated with golden handles and a stripe of cobalt. These were our festive dishes, almost never used. My mother used them to hold receipts from the electricity company, the gas company, the cleaners and so on. Further down, on another shelf, stood a glassware set made by the world-famous Moser company, and in the lower part of the cupboard, not behind glass, stood a large china dinner set, and another set of crystal. Mother kept it all under lock and key.

Tosia opened the door, and two oafs in green uniforms pushed into the hallway. One was a colossus with silver epaulets on his uniform, an officer's cap and two stars decorating the lapels of his coat. The other was a head shorter, and a star lower in rank. My mother took a deep breath, and went to receive them.

'*Guten Tag!* May I inquire what you gentlemen would like?' she asked with an innocent face, as if they were the most ordinary of guests.

The colossus pushed her aside roughly but without malice, like a man removing an obstacle from his path, and entered the bedroom, which was next door to the dining room. His partner lagged behind, looking around. For a moment, they stood silently, assessing the cupboards and mirrors. Then the tall one pulled a note out from his pocket and asked, 'Is this Jakub Gross's apartment?'

'Ye-e-e-s?' mother answered questioningly, as if she wanted to ask: What's this all about?

'And where is Jakob Gross?'

Mother was always prepared for that question, in those circumstances.

'My husband left with the army and did not return. I think he is being held captive by the Russians, because if he were with the Germans, certainly he would have sent word by now.'

'Liar! Tell me immediately where your husband is hiding! Do you hear me?!'

It was always the same. They wanted to be sure that no man was in the apartment. In addition, they wanted to frighten their victims. My mother was used to this game, and explained calmly to the handsome officer that she wished her husband were at home, for who knew where the poor man was wandering and suffering in this cold.

'Shut your mouth!' the short one hollered.

The tall one, with the two stars, did not approve of his friend's crude outbreak, and said quietly, 'I've been sent here from the *Quartieramt* to obtain sheets, pillowcases and blanket covers.'

My mother dearly loved bed linen. She bought the most beautiful batiste and the best varieties of material. She did not even need to touch the material to assess its quality, and she had an unerring eye. She was always talking the wholesalers into ordering some sort of extraordinary new material. Then she would call in a seamstress and supervise the work herself. She loved everything to be finished to a t, with lace, embroidery and monograms. She could not stand inferior workmanship. It was a pleasure to gaze at the shelves full of gleaming white bed linen piled up evenly and tied with blue, pink and yellow ribbons depending on whom it was meant for: the adults, the children and the servants, separately.

At the very beginning of the occupation, in anticipation of the calamities to come, my mother began to clear the house of her valuables – jewelry, expensive paintings, crystal, china and bed linen – and turn them over to her Polish acquaintances. At home she kept only the most essential items, as well as a few decorative objects for appearances' sake. She had to act slowly, covertly, and systematically, to avoid arousing the suspicions of the neighbors and the German tenants. Bed linen was in great demand by the German officers setting up in housekeeping in the General Government. Therefore, my mother made every effort to clear her bed linen out expeditiously. She kept a cupboard full of nothing but sheets and pillowcases that were too old and worn out to use. Even this linen was arranged with unvarying fastidiousness, tied with ribbons and coquettish lace. When she opened the heavy walnut cupboard and said, 'Help yourself. It's all I have', the officers' eyes shone in delight. The booty looked enticing. They set about emptying the cupboard. The big oaf deftly untied the yellow ribbon that was decoratively wimpled on an elastic band. He pulled out the sheet that lay on top of the pile. It was heavily starched, stiff, and frayed around the edges. Aside from the darned places, it also revealed several gaping holes. The officer snorted and shuddered in revulsion. He threw the sheet to the floor and unfolded the next one. It was not in much better condition. At that moment the shorter one cursed juicily and began rummaging through the linen pillowcases. They had once been clouds of lace handiwork that revealed the pink liners. Over the years, the lace had worn away, grown tattered, fallen to shreds and turned yellow. The chipped buttons looked like an old man's teeth. Purplish, rusty and jaundiced stains attested to the many years of faithful service rendered ... The Germans were furious.

'*Donnerwetter!* You want to give us this? May you choke on it! Where do you keep the good linen?'

'You gentlemen must surely think that you are the first,' my mother replied stoically, though her face grew pale. 'I did have beautiful, white linen, the best ... Unfortunately, you gentlemen are late. Other officers have already been here. I am so sorry that there is nothing to suit your tastes.'

The short one fumed. He picked up a sheet off the floor, ripped it in one motion as if it were paper, and threw it over mother's head, erupting in laughter. The tall one chuckled, but was more restrained. Mother freed herself from the torn sheet, leveled a cold stare at her guests, and asked in the manner of a shopkeeper:

'What else can I do for you, gentlemen?'

The *Oberleutnant* gloomily surveyed the room, which now resembled a battlefield. Suddenly he noticed a black leather purse lying on the makeup table in the corner.

'Do you have money?'

'Money? I need some very badly. Unfortunately, my poor husband has left me with three children and not a *grosz* to my name. My shop has been confiscated by a *Treuhänder* who gives me nothing. Where would I get money?'

The *Oberleutnant* had meanwhile opened the purse, and emptied its contents. Out spilled scraps of paper, letters, tram tickets, a small mirror, a comb, and a handkerchief. Disappointed, he kicked the wallet like a ball, and honored the papers with another kick, scattering them all over the room.

'Where's the money hidden?' he roared.

'I already told you that I have no money. We simply have nothing to live on.'

The tall oaf was visibly disenchanted by the whole visit. He had no taste for going away empty-handed, but felt that he would not get anything here. Slowly, peering around, swallowing, he moved from the bedroom to the hallway, with his shorter friend trailing behind.

We three children had stood petrified at the bedroom door the whole time. Now we quickly made way and stood in the adjacent dining-room door.

As always in such circumstances, this was a moment of suspense and hope. Will they go or won't they? They're already in the hallway ... We want to gasp with relief – but not yet.

The Germans paused, hesitating. The short one pinned his questioning eyes on the tall one, who stood with his head lowered, as if considering whether he should say something in parting. Without lifting his head, he looked at us, the children, and then took a step in our direction. We parted like the Red Sea at Moses's prompting. The officer stood in the doorway, bracing himself with one hand against the jamb, and surveyed the room. He did so mechanically. We followed his glance from one piece of furniture to another: from the table bearing our unfinished dinner to the big black chest on the left side of the room, from the chest to the grandfather clock, from the clock to the piano where we stood frozen and then to the door of the next room with the *Quatieramt* requisition notice stuck to it, and finally to the glazed cabinet on the right. He yawned and made a movement as if he were ready to leave, and then he turned back and fixed his eyes on the large coffee pot that lorded it over the center of the glass-fronted cupboard. He walked over and pressed his nose against the glass. Mother entered then, with the other German behind her.

'Look, Hans, what a nice coffee service. I wonder what's inside that coffee pot there,' the tall one finally said. 'Could you please open the door?' he asked mother, his politeness tinged with irony.

At that moment, mother felt the end was near. It was not a matter of the coffee service or the money; she had lost larger sums in her life. But if the Germans were to discover the secret of the pot, and realize that my mother had lied to them when she said she had no money, they could kill her and us children on the spot. They could do anything! She sensed that she was standing at the edge of a precipice, and it all lasted less than a second.

'No. I will not open it,' she replied impassively, shaking her head.

'What?!!!' yelled Hans. 'You will not open it?!!'

'What do you mean, "I will not open it"? How am I to understand this?' the surprised *Oberleutnant* interjected. 'Open it immediately. I want to see what you are hiding in that pot!'

'I will not open it! You know very well, sir, that there is nothing there, and that it is not the pot that interests you, *Oberleutnant*. I noticed immediately that you have your eye on those Moser cups, but forgive me, sir, I really cannot give them to you. Believe me ...'

'What cups? Cups, for the sake of 10,000 devils!!!' Hans thundered. 'Open it, you old hag!! Open up immediately!'

But mother paid him no mind. All her attention was focused on the elegant *Oberleutnant*, who was temporarily dumbstruck.

'My dear sir, I see that you are an intelligent person who knows what the words 'Moser crystal' mean. Don't you?'

'Of course I know, but what's that got to do with it?'

You wouldn't by any chance come from the Sudetenland, would you, sir?'

'How do you know?' The German was surprised.

'I noticed the accent immediately. We did a lot of business with the Sudetenland – that's where all the greatest china and crystal factories are. We have a china and crystal shop, the biggest one in Cracow, in the Main Square. You must visit it, sir, a beautiful shop, you'll see for yourself. We've always dealt with the Sudetenland. I must show you something, sir, and then you will understand …'

Without pausing in her speech, she ran to the bedroom and took out of the closet a large, flowered candy box tied with a string. She untied it in one pull and began leafing through a sheaf of letters. As if hypnotized, the Germans followed her and studied her every movement. Finally, mother found the document she was after.

'Oh, there it is. A thank you note from Mr Moser himself. Do you understand, sir? For 20 years, we were his representatives for the whole of Poland … A nice letter, don't you think? What does he say? Here …' She helped the dumfounded German read. ''With the most profound gratitude and appreciation'' – now that's a firm for you! Are you, sir, from the Sudetenland, too?' She turned to the shorter one. 'Do you have a wife and children? Excuse me for asking, but I understand you gentlemen very well. It must be so sad for you …'

'Enough of this chattering! Open the cabinet immediately! Understand.'

Hans pushed mother brutally toward the dining room, and all of them stood in front of the glass-fronted cabinet again.

'Why have you suddenly become obsessed with my cups? What do you need cups for, sir?' mother continued in pleading tones. 'Please understand, this is a personal present from Mr Moser. For me, this memento is worth more than anything, and it's all I have left from those days … Anyway, I can give you much more beautiful ones!' In one swift motion, she opened the lower part of the cabinet and took out six beautiful cut crystal glasses.

'Do you see, sir? Much more beautiful! You can have them all, and I'll give you more wine glasses and cognac snifters, too.'

The *Oberleutnant* examined the glasses, then burst out, 'Damn it, why are you talking nonsense, you disgusting Jewess! Open up immediately! Immediately, understand? What have you got in those coffee cups?'

'Sir, my dear officer, sir, I will give you whatever you want, but I beg of you, please leave me those Moser cups. You know how sometimes a person becomes so attached to some object that ... that ... '

Mother was on the verge of fainting. Petrified with fear, I tried to say something. Klara broke out in tears. Hans ordered us children out of the room, and cocked his revolver. We set up an infernal screeching ... At that moment, mother dashed to the cabinet, opened the glass door, grabbed two of the three coffee cups, and placed them both on the table in a single violent movement. There was madness in her eyes.

'Here, take your cups! As you like!', she hollered, foam gathering on her lips as she removed from the cups and threw on the table old bills for gas and electricity, the stub of a pencil, buttons, hair pins, a packet of thumbtacks, a roll of thread, bills for the radio and telephone. 'Here's my treasure for you. Are you satisfied now?'

She was quivering with tension, and both Germans had gone pale.

'Calm down, please,' the one from the Sudetenland said soothingly. 'We're not going to do anything to you.'

They looked at each other not knowing what to do next. They had been thrown off the scent. Mother had won, but the game was not yet over. She now opened the chest of drawers in the other corner of the room, and began showing the Germans various types of china and glass, while urging them to visit her shop.

They left, taking some cups (but not the Moser ones) and some crystal.

For a long time, mother could not get over it. She lay on the couch breathing heavily. She felt better by evening, and began thinking of a better hiding place for the money.

PAPERS, PAPERS

I don't recall when or how I began collecting papers. Old school notebooks, summer camp diaries, illustrated periodicals and literary magazines, photographs, addresses, excerpts, clippings, brochures, concert programs with the autographs of great pianists and artistes, letters, letters and more letters – you name it, I saved it. And the postage stamps, of course. Guatemala, Costa Rica, Jamaica, and the Nyasaland triangular with the zebra on it. And

Anglas chocolate cards. Don't you remember Anglas chocolate bars? Made in Gdansk, ten *grosz* apiece, with colored wrappers. The milk chocolate was delicious, but the real treat was the surprise card inside. One series had the flags of all the states in the world. (Do you remember what the flag of Cochin China looked like? I do, although I never heard about that country again!) Or the peoples of the world (the Sioux Indians!), contemporary and antediluvian animals (the brontosaurus, the pterodactyl) … Many years have passed and I have seen a lot of different cards from chocolate bars, but I have never seen anything to match those color Anglas cards. And there were books, of course. Selected, collected and cherished. My life's dream was one more shelf, one more drawer. And a cupboard of my own? In the end, I even had a cupboard of my own.

Then the war broke out, the Second World War, with Hitler in the starring role. The papers had to make their sacrifice of fire and water.

First to be destroyed were the annual volumes of the satirical weekly publication *Pins*, full of caricatures of Hitler. Parting with them was regrettable. We decided to use them instead of toilet paper, and the annuals were transferred to the lavatory, which quickly became the merriest place in the apartment. Anyone who went in there forgot about coming out again … Some books and periodicals were burned in the stove, but a lot was left.

In the first months of the occupation, the book market was flooded with cheap German books. On the other hand, the second-hand book trade flourished. Money lost its value daily, but books did not become more expensive. In such circumstances my private library grew and grew. Its upper shelves contained about 100 poetry collections, and on the lower shelves stood the art books, led by Van Gogh and Cézanne in the beautiful Phaidon editions. The middle shelves were occupied by fiction, especially French literature. I was then passionately collecting Boy's translations, from Villon, Brantome and Rabelais right up to Proust. Nor, of course, was I without Maupassant, Zola, Anatol France, Rolland and Martin du Gard. As for Balzac, he was my favorite writer. Within a few months, I acquired almost a complete set of his novels in Polish translation.

Another area of interest was philosophy. This was not 'high' philosophy: the complete works of Plato, Nietzsche, Schopenhauer, Descartes, an accidental Lessing volume that shook me to the core, Tatarkiewicz's *History of Philosophy*, Emerson's essays, and other odds and ends.

My friends – and I had a lot of them – knew about my hobby. They gave me books as gifts. Before long, I had about a thousand of them. They began passing from hand to hand. Without movies, theatre or the radio, only books were left. And I never regarded books as completely private property. As far as I was concerned, a book did not even exist if its owner forbade you to pick it up for fear you would get it dirty. An unread book is a lifeless, superfluous stage prop. Collecting books to adorn bookshelves is snobbery. My books lived and acted. They opened people's eyes and brains. We discussed them at length and animatedly in the circle of friends who gathered around me.

Among and for my friends, I began translating the poems of Kästner, Rilke and Morgenstern. Why these particular poets – German, to boot? I do not know to this day if it was random, or a symptom. At that time, my friend Janek Zimmermann was in Haifa worrying about us. His sister Anka once brought me some of those poems and her translations of them. I did not like the renderings, and began doing them over from scratch. I got so carried away that I translated half of Kästner's *Lyrical Pharmacy*. Kästner's heros are shy little people, beaten and kicked around by fate, full of bourgeois complexes. 'Whoever knows himself will understand me,' Kästner says somewhere. I had the feeling that while reading his poems, I was conversing with myself. Reading Rilke, I fled from reality. Morgenstern added to my sadness the golden hue of a setting sun.

Anka and I translated some poems together, and we did others separately. I felt the joy of creativity. I got to know the poems, with their external construction and their internal structure, by translating them. I stopped being myself and turned into the poet whose work I was translating. I reworked each verse a hundred times until it conveyed the original as precisely and faithfully as possible. I did not even know then that a translation is like a woman – if it's faithful, then it's usually not beautiful, and if it's beautiful, then it's usually not faithful. Mine, I suppose, were too faithful … It is a fact, however, that I put a great deal of passion into that faithfulness. I loved those translations of mine. Eventually, there were several notebooks that I kept in a treasure chest with my dearest keepsakes.

The ghetto was set up. People were leaving for the villages and small towns. They wrote letters. The stack of papers grew.

Our family stayed in Cracow until the ghetto was sealed off. Only then did we decide to leave town. We rented a room in Czyzyny, on the outskirts of Cracow.

This was a period of panic, general chaos, and desperate efforts to get identity cards and passes. There was an exodus from Cracow. Some people moved to the ghetto, while others left the city because they could not – or did not want to – get permits to reside in the ghetto. A small group of skilled workers managed to stay in Cracow, waiting for the authorities to issue transfers to the ghetto or deportation orders. Among these was Emil Kornblüth, a tailor who lived on the ground floor of our building, a man of the utmost decency. He was related to mother, and we maintained close relations with him. When we decided that the time had come for our own exodus, mother packed her most valuable possessions, her best clothes, most priceless objects and dearest mementos – photograph albums and boxes of letters – into one suitcase. Not wanting to risk it in the uncertain traveling conditions of those times, she took it to Kornblüth.

'You don't have a deportation order yet,' she told him, 'so it's better if the suitcase stays with you for a few days, until things calm down a bit. Then I'll send a trustworthy *goy* to pick it up.'

Kornblüth agreed without hesitating. I decided to follow my mother's example and packed up my most precious mementos: papers, letters, photographs with emotional dedications (memories from my first love, my second and third), my most beloved art books, and the manuscripts of my own poetic inspiration. I carried all this to the honest tailor. He promised solemnly that, in case of any sudden deportation, he would take care of my things just as he would take care of his own.

Our evacuation from Cracow was organized in two steps. Mother and I left at night, taking the absolute minimum of clothing and essential housewares. My brother, sister and aunt were to come the next day with the furniture and the rest of our belongings.

This was February 1941 and there was a sharp frost. Mother and I spent our first night in Czyzyny on a dirty floor in a shabby house typical of the outskirts. We did not sleep a wink. There was no electricity. It poured down rain all night, and time seemed to last an eternity. Finally, dawn broke. We expected my brother and sister around noon. They were supposed to get a travel permit, without which it was impossible to move around. We knew that it was sometimes impossible to transport things even with those permits, and so we were very nervous. By around nine, my mother could no longer bear the suspense.

'You know what,' she said, 'I'm so upset, why don't you go to the mill and call Kornblüth on the phone and remind him that I absolutely forbid him to send my suitcase with the children. Please.'

Lord, how I dreaded going to the mill!

Numb with cold and hunger, I was overwhelmed with inertia and a distaste for going on living. Sticky black mud covered the lane, which did not even have a sidewalk. I was supposed to walk there – all the way to the mill! The huge steam-powered mill was no more than half a kilometer away, but it was under German administration. Would they allow me to use the telephone? Or would they give me a kick in the pants and throw me out on my face? I set off. The mud was clinging to my shoes, the rain and the wind were lashing my eyes mercilessly, and I felt, as the saying goes, 'as if someone had spit into my soul'. I had no trouble getting permission to use the telephone. I called Kornblüth: 'Mother asks me to remind you to hold onto the suitcase … And could you please keep my books and my box, too? … We'll collect them tomorrow or the next day … Thank you very much … We're fine, thanks. It's very nice here, except that it's pouring … Thank you once more … ' I returned home frozen, but feeling upbeat. What a fine feeling – to overcome your own laziness!

In the meantime, mother was making a fire in the iron stove, preparing breakfast, and beginning to unpack the things we had brought. We looked out the window every few minutes to check whether they were coming.

They did not arrive until the evening. It turned out their journey had not been free of obstacles. They had been stopped at the city limits, and even though they had all the required permits, they were searched. They had had to fight for each item they were carrying. Luckily, only a few things were confiscated – a few illustrated books, no more than one suitcase. I listened to this story in trepidation. Illustrated books? What books? What suitcase? No one knew for sure. 'Thank God we got through it!' they said. 'What an experience!'

'Wait a minute,' I said. 'Start over. When did you set out?'

'At 11 o'clock in the morning.'

'We thought we'd never get here,' Klara sighed.

'Sure. Listen to this! At the last minute, after we had loaded everything and the cart was already rolling, he appeared and threw another suitcase and some packages on the cart. He said that they were mother's, and he did not want to hold on to them because no one could say what tomorrow would bring.'

My mother and I, our hearts heavy with dark premonitions, ran to the cart and began searching furiously.

The suitcase and my package of keepsakes were gone.

This was a staggering blow for me. It was the first time in my life I had lost anything so precious as these apparently valueless objects that were priceless to me. I could get over the loss of my favorite books and photographs, but the manuscripts were what really hurt. What a fool I had been – as I've silently repeated a thousand times in my life. How could I have left those things there instead of taking them myself? I had lost what I had created so joyfully, my children who had stirred my emotions so. The only consolation was that I had overcome my inertia that morning and gone to phone Kornblüth. Another genius – he just couldn't stop himself from giving in to the universal psychosis. How fortunate that I had called. Otherwise, I would have felt guilty to the end of my life about disobeying mother.

But in the end, what did all this mean when set against the crimes flooding the world? What are a few books and papers? I tried to mollify myself with logical arguments, but it was not easy. The Germans had been in Cracow for a year and a half, and more than one misfortune had fallen about our heads: our family had been broken up and the Germans had taken the shop, the house, our belongings. Literally and figuratively, I had fallen in the course of one night from the top floor to the cellar, yet my heart had not skipped a beat over it. I had simply realized what the general situation was – and this made my own predicament seem unimportant and had helped me to escape into the realms of poetry, art and photography. That had been my treasure – too humble to tempt anyone else, but priceless for me because it was unique and personal. Since then, I have often lost my papers and souvenirs, but I have never felt such pain and such heartache as on that day.

I began to be a fatalist: those papers must not have been worth saving, which is why they had been lost. Good, I told myself, they only shielded you from reality. You held on to them like a drowning man with a piece of straw. Now you're free. The past is gone. Time to start over.

And I started over.

*

Times had come when you had to choose between forced labor and forced unemployment. My youngest brother, age 13, was a forced laborer by turns at clearing the ground for the Czyzyny airport, in the municipal gardens, and in a rubber factory. I was somehow passed over for conscript labor. So I sat at home reading or writing, and only rarely going outside.

Thus the stack of paper began to grow again.

My friends and acquaintances were scattered around the towns of the General Government. Some had gone to the ghetto. We kept up a lively correspondence, and I had no less than 30 correspondents. In those days, we wrote letters by the kilometer. People needed to confess, to unload the burdens weighing on their hearts. They looked for a kindred spirit, for contact on purpose with someone far away, like mountain climbers who, when an abyss gapes open beneath them, reach instinctively for any protruding root, just to have something to hang on to.

I did not have the patience to wait for the mail to be delivered. Each morning I ran to the post office to collect my letters, and then I would hole up in my room and read them slowly, word for word, time and again. Then I would immediately begin writing a response.

Some days, I would concentrate my correspondence with my friends in the ghetto into one joint letter for all, which I titled 'A Letter to Friends'. The letter would stretch over 30 double-size pages, and would become a sort of newsletter to pass from hand to hand. The main 'article', usually a philosophical essay, was followed by various 'columns' and even a section of puzzles and quizzes. The 'letter' was based on notes from my reading. At this time, I was beginning to make extensive, systematic notes about the books I read, a habit that I pursued with a passion throughout the occupation. I could not read without a pencil in my hand. I never interrupted my reading to write anything down. When I liked a particular sentence or hit upon an idea that stimulated my imagination, I put a check mark in the margin and went on reading. When I finished the book, I went back to the check marks and, after a further selection, copied them into a notebook and gave them numbers. Only then did I consider them seriously. And what did I discover? That out of 50 quotations about love from various books, at least 40 were nothing but clever plays on words or associations – false but glittering stones that crumbled into nothing at the first analysis. And the rest? Truisms, for the most part. Sometimes, however, there was a stunning phrase, a keyhole affording a glimpse of a treasure, a window on a new horizon, an air shaft to eternity. I was not bothered by the fact that I had to sift through so many tons of uranium ore to find a gram of radon. It was interesting and absorbing work, all the more so because I could share it with others.

In those days, my concept of happiness was a full life. I was happy among these papers and letters, filled-up notebooks, essays and articles. I did not notice that my happiness was contained in a tiny room on the outskirts of town. You can be happy under any circumstances, I proclaimed. We are the masters of our fate. Fate itself cannot be changed, but the perception of it can be controlled: it can be accepted with love and understanding (and then a person is happy) or with hatred (leading to lifelong misery). This theory came, I think, from Maeterlinck, whom I became acquainted with in those days.

My attitude evoked protests from Anka and other friends behind the walls of the ghetto. Their slavelike existence shaped their consciousness differently. They were trapped, whereas I had yet to experience the dangerous Nazi monsters directly. They sat there crowded together, locked up, classified; they performed slave labor or died of hunger and poverty. I was still breathing in the air and the space of the countryside, and only seldom did I see a German uniform.

Where did I get books? The apartment across from our house in Czyzyny was rented by Adolf Abraham Gumplowicz, owner of a well-known lending library in Cracow. As soon as I began to read books, I became a subscriber at his library, in Grodzka Street. Mr Gumplowicz came from a family that had contributed significantly to Polish culture. He was a short man with a proud, noble face and an expression that announced: 'Keep your distance'. He seemed like a statue, not of this age. He was conscious of his superiority to his young readers. He could presumably have found shelter with a Polish family, but a certain Jewish pride suddenly overcame him, and he did not want to ask anyone for charity or aid. He therefore lived in our neighborhood with his cook, Karolcia, and Plimpek the puppy, whom he would take out for a walk twice a day. He made friends with no one, although he did maintain active contact with me, a longtime customer and someone who might pass for an intellectual. To me and to me alone did he lend the books he had brought from Cracow. He never wore the armband with the Star of David. He sneered at the barbarous Germans. But once, when he had to pay a call at an office, he put on the armband. The village woman who brought him his milk in the morning looked at him goggle-eyed: 'Are you a Jewboy, sir?'

'No, woman, I am not a Jewboy. A Jewboy is a little boy with a dirty shirttail hanging out. Whereas I am a Jew! A big Jew with a black beard and sidecurls. Ha-ha-ha!' He underlined his energetic words with an appropriate gesture, and the terrified peasant woman scurried around the corner of the house, pursued by Gumplowicz's satanic laughter.

When the time came to leave Czyzyny, we decided to move to Grebalow. Gumplowicz chose Cracow. He came to bid us farewell, and that was the first time I had seen him emotional and depressed. Did he sense that we would never see each other again? As a memento, he left me Klaczko's *Florentine Evenings* and Taine's *Philosophy of Art*, my favorite books.

'Don't hide your light under a bushel' – I could not delight in the books alone. Joy must be shared. And so, in this new place, a new group of friends gathered around me, girls and boys who had stumbled into Czyzyny by chance, and again we sat together, read, argued, enjoyed each other's company – and escaped from reality.

Dolek Liebeskind often visited with his wife Wusia, with whom I had been in school. Dolek came to see his parents and his sister Miriam – Minka – whom I count among my dearest friends. We spent lovely Saturday afternoons together. I had been active for a time before the war in Akiba, the Zionist pioneer organization of which Dolek was now the leader. Akiba had always been the most powerful Jewish youth organization in Cracow. Far from ceasing to operate after the outbreak of the war, Akiba was now expanding its

148

activities and making contact with branches in other localities. After the June deportations, Akiba had changed into a clandestine self-defense organization.

Minka was a courier for the movement. She shared her dramatic adventures with me. She had the beautiful Jewish face of an intense young freedom-fighter. Her burning eyes and small but hooked nose were enough to give her away immediately. She loved listening to Leśmian's poetry. We spent long hours reading poetry with Genia, an orphan whom mother had taken in, along with Minka's cousins Wisia and Gizia Vogler, the Lerfelds, Henio Kudler, and other young people staying nearby. Minka simply worshiped her beloved brother, and accepted his philosophy of death. Dolek prophesied with absolute certainty that none of us would survive the war, that Hitler would destroy all the Jews and that we should know how to die with honor. Minka told me about everything, although she never tried to convince me or recruit me into the movement. I was grateful to her for this. Not that I feared death – I thought about it too much to fear it. However, I was not seeking death. I did not believe that we were all going to die, even though the pessimism around us was increasing. If they had tried to draw me in … but no, no one was calling me. Like Voltaire's Candide, I fortified myself in my intellectual garden and tended to my flowers 'despite the storm raging all around us'. Was I an egoist? It never seemed to me that people regarded me as egoistic. After all, the doors of my garden were open to all! Everyone was welcome in that garden that 'flowered at twilight, where miracles grew amidst danger and lawlessness'. I grew them out of nothingness by the flickering light in my eyes. That was my land of make-believe. Minka loved to sit in that garden – as did others – but afterwards, she was distant. She came sometimes, but her thoughts were elsewhere; I felt that the charms no longer had any effect on her, although she yearned for them.

Before the big 'operation' in Cracow at the end of May, the Germans decided to clear the outskirts of Jews. Some of the Jews, including Minka and her parents, along with her cousins Gizia and Wisia, moved to the ghetto. We decided to remain at large, and began looking for a place in the Mogila or Miechow area, until we found a room in the rundown village of Grebalow.

In those days, we received news of father's death.

FATHER'S DEATH

Father and Jozek ended up in Lwow as refugees, unprepared for winter, without clothing or money. Their situation was no worse than that of dozens of other refugees there, and perhaps even better, because father had a friend in Lwow, a china merchant by the name of Mr Awin, who had a shop in the Mikolasz Arcade. I had heard his name at home before the war; he must have been a client of the Gross firm. Mr and Mrs Awin were kind, optimistic people. They invited father and Jozek to stay with them, along with one more man, a Mr Rosner.

MY BROTHER JOZEK'S STORY

The cheerful Mr Awin gave us many proofs of his friendship and generosity. Father always promised to repay him after the war. 'Gross wird sein wieder Gross' ('Gross will be big again'), my father would say, playing on his name. And perhaps he believed it. Mr Awin had no doubt that 'Gross war gross' (that 'Gross had been big'). But as for the future, who could tell? Mrs Awin, who was adored by her husband, always appeared just like him, with a smile on her lips, and believed that all would be well. Or perhaps it was the sight of father's cares that prompted them to pretend they had no worries. Thus they hoped to keep Mr Gross's spirits up.

At first, father did not know what to do with himself. He helped out a bit in Mr Awin's shop. Once, when he was waiting on a Soviet officer, he addressed him as 'tovarishch' ('comrade'). The Red Army man snorted: 'I'm no comrade of yours!' This comment caused father a great deal of consternation.

The winter of 1939–40 came early. It battered us mercilessly. Father found work as a manager in a lumberyard. He had to stand outside on the cold days and guard the expensive heating material. His salary was small, but he needed every penny he could get. He had neither money nor valuables. He had long sold his beautiful solid-gold, 18-jewel pre-war Schaffhausen pocket watch. I was no help to him. On the contrary. I did find work in the evenings at a movie theater, but the pay was negligible. We were talking about father, however. It had broken his heart to part in such tragic circumstances from the family he loved. Whenever he remembered his past and those he had left behind in Cracow, he broke

150

down and cried. He grew older and lost weight by the day. All his considerable pre-war corpulence was gone. He simply shrank and withered. His tailor-made clothes, sewn by Kornblüth before the war, no longer fit. They hung on his body like something from a flea market. Mrs Awin tried to help him and to adjust the clothes to his new dimensions. Buying new clothes was out of the question. Everything was too expensive for us now. Uncle Steinmetz was doing much better. He traded in jewelry and foreign currency, and always had money in his pockets. Sometimes he had so much that, in order to be on the safe side, he left gold dollars in father's care.

Winter, the unyielding, flexible winter, the eternal enemy of the poor, gripped the land in its claws until the middle of April. In the end, the sun gained the upper hand. After the thaw, it looked as if something like normal life would resume. Then the walls were suddenly plastered with proclamations on the subject of refugees: The municipal administration invited people from outside the borders of the Soviet Union to register to make it possible for them to return home. Those who did not register would be regarded as having expressed their allegiance, and would be required to apply for 'Soviet passports'. This last part was understood by the refugees as being synonymous with accepting Soviet citizenship. We understood, of course, that such a step would have far-ranging consequences. What to do? Finding ourselves between the fire and the frying pan, we decided to register to return home. And we waited.

When waiting, people begin spinning colorful visions, living for the newest rumors, and praying to God. Especially during such cheerful holidays as Passover, the commemoration of the exodus from Egypt. A vast crowd gathered in the Lwow Reform synagogue. Everyone had so much to tell God, so many requests to raise before his altar, and so many cares to confess. Father, too, was among those good souls. Unfortunately, there were also evil souls there – pickpockets! Father had forgotten about Jozef Steinmetz's gold dollars. He had put them into his change-purse, had stuffed the change-purse in his hip pocket, and had completely forgotten about such earthly trifles as he hastened to pray at the synagogue. Such minor carelessness provides pickpockets with a decent living. Forty dollars in gold was a considerable sum in those days. Father was tormented by the loss of another's money, but Jozef Steinmetz, it must be said, took the news of his loss like a man of honor: he did not even murmur. He made a nervous gesture with his hand and took it in his stride. Indeed, it was a trifle compared to what awaited us all in the coming weeks.

My brother Jozek, who had a generous heart and a humanitarian world view, was – before he matured and settled down – 'nuts'. I have already sketched a partial portrait of him in these pages. When he had finished working in the 'lumber trade' (in other words chopping down trees in the vicinity of Rybinsk on the Volga), he crossed half of Russia on foot in order to sign up with General Anders's military formation. When he got out of the Soviet Union and volunteered as a paratrooper in the British Army, he wrote in the first letter we obtained from him after the war, 'Whenever I jump out of an airplane, I repeat mother's words: "Jozek, don't be crazy."' Perhaps he survived because he was crazy. And could that be why father didn't survive? Or why we did? It is eminently human to suffer over such questions. So, Jozek was 'nuts'. More: Jozek was like the proverbial Gypsy who lets himself be hanged for the sake of going along with his friends.

MY BROTHER JOZEK'S STORY

Who will ever understand the thinking of Uncle Joe Stalin? Who will ever prove the logic of his actions? Without a doubt, it was a personal order from Stalin to capture all those who had registered to return home. This was at the beginning of the month of May.

Early in the morning we awoke to the sound of blows emanating from the lower floors of the building. Mr Awin's apartment, in which we lived, was on the third floor. We knew the meaning of the noise perfectly well. We collected our clothes and quickly left the apartment, sneaking down the back stairs. Miracle of miracles: No one was guarding this exit! Quietly we crossed the entryway and went out into the street. No one stopped us.

Returning to Mr Awin's home was no longer possible, so we headed for the Grunbergs'. When we arrived at the building where they lived, we saw a military truck with an armed Red Army soldier standing guard. Half of Grunberg's family was already inside the open truck: Aunt Mala, her recently born baby girl in her arms, and two more of her four children. The rest were being loaded on at that very moment. Jozef Grunberg signalled to us to stay away, because he knew how dangerous things were. And too bad! Perhaps, if we had joined them ... Who can tell? Fate, fate ... man is born man.

We spent most of the day looking for a place to stay. Father finally found shelter for himself, while I was supposed to get a place in an art school where I was studying at the time. Therefore, we parted in the evening, and arranged to meet the next day. I was sure I would sleep at the school, and so was my cousin Gustek Steinmetz, who was with me. But in the end we both stayed out in the street. This is what happened: Gustek heard from someone that in a small shop somewhere he could get information about a quiet place to sleep. We arrived at the shop, located in a basement. Gustek went in, and I waited outside. He had barely managed to open his mouth when a Ukrainian secret police officer asked him for his 'passport'. Gustek had no passport whatsoever, so he was taken by the officer from the store and led toward the police station. While passing me, he managed to whisper, 'Don't leave me alone!'

So I asked the officer, 'Where are you taking him, sir?' For some reason, the officer forgot to ask to see my passport … He answered politely and gave me the address of the police station. Off they went. I had thus evaded the police, but I could not forget the sight of Gustek's face. My conscience gnawed at me. Out of compassion rather than intelligence, I ran to the apartment where my father was supposed to be. Unfortunately, I did not find him (or was this destiny?). I just grabbed the suitcase, the one my mother had bought herself in Paris in 1938. In my hurry and excitement, I did not even stop to see what was inside. Thus I deprived father of some important items of clothing, and more significantly, his reading glasses. With the suitcase in my hand, I ran to the police station and turned myself in as a refugee with no passport. The next day we were transferred to a military barracks that had been turned into a jail.

Two weeks later, when we were being taken to the train station for the 'transports', my father was standing near the gate of the jail. He called out to me. I could not understand what he said, but shouted in reply that he should not worry and that I would manage. Perhaps he wanted his glasses. Later, when I was in Sielo Pelniewo in the Rybinsk oblast *as a prisoner, I received a letter from him in which he mentioned the glasses and asked me to send them to him. For some reason, I did not fulfill his request. Only many years later, when my own eyes grew weak and I could not read without glasses, did I understand his hardship …*

*

No, my father was not thinking of the glasses when he saw his son Jozek being led away to the transport. He called out: 'Jozek, take care of yourself and write to let me know where you are!'

What did my father think about, what did he feel, when he came home discouraged and found – instead of his son – a few words of parting from him? Jozek's imprisonment, about which he might not have known any details, broke his spirit. He decided to volunteer to leave. But then something happened that to this day I still cannot understand: those in charge of the transports refused to accept father. Did he, perhaps, seem too old? They needed strong young people to chop trees in the forest. Father registered again, and then registered a third time after receiving word from Jozek in Rybinsk. But they did not want to take him.

I often think, choking back the sobs, about the loneliness of my father, who was so attached to his family and who cared about nothing else except family life.

Then the war between the Germans and the Russians broke out. Did my father flee from the Germans, or did he think he could return to Cracow and join us? That's probably all he thought about. For a long time there was no word from him. Then news began to arrive in a roundabout way, from Rohatyn. Letters full of longing and hope. Why from there? We had no idea, just like we had no idea why he later abandoned Rohatyn and went to live in Sarny, in Volhynia, with the Gruszko family.

We wrote to that address, but rarely received a reply. We got the impression father was planning to return to Cracow – but again contact was broken. For a long time we had no news and began to worry, although we knew that letters arrived only rarely. We were living in Czyzyny; it was June 1942. There had been deportations from Cracow, but our turn to move had not yet arrived. We had to find a flat in a region where Jews were still allowed to live. A few families, including the Voglers, the elder Grünbergs, and Dolek Liebeskind's family, had moved to the ghetto. We had no intention of moving to the ghetto. Some of our neighbors had managed to rent something in nearby Bienczyce, but we had to flee further, to Grebalow. There were several days left before moving day. Mother was worried about what would happen when father's next letter came, and how he could be notified about our new address. And then one of the bolder and rather thick-skinned neighbors, an unfeeling man, said: 'There won't be any letter coming, Mrs Gross, because your husband is dead.'

My mother grew pale – I was with her – but did not lose her composure. 'What are you talking about? Why are you saying such a thing to me?'

'Your husband is dead. Everyone knows ... They killed him. It's better for you to know.'

Everyone knew and we didn't know. They knew, but could not say where it had happened, or how, or when. We sat at the table, depressed, with tears streaming from our eyes. No one spoke. Around us lay baskets and suitcases – we had been in the midst of packing.

'Poor father,' my mother sighed, conquering her tears. 'He wanted to be with us so badly. He never wanted to leave home. I can't believe it ...'

Two days later, a letter from father arrived. It was brought by a Ukrainian named Bialas, together with a personal greeting from father. Father was preparing for the journey, and Bialas was helping him. However, it was no simple matter. The border was well-guarded. And the hunt for Jews was still going on. But everything would be fine. In two weeks, we would see father!

After the great shock, our happiness was somewhat restrained. It was a relief. We held in our hands the proof that the rumors about father's death had been groundless. How did people get such things into their heads? All it took was for one person to say something, and everyone repeated it. But who was that one?

Bialas ate, drank, took a little money, and left. With light hearts, we transported our belongings to Gerbil two days later. Two months after that, we were expelled to Wieliczka. We heard no more about father. We deluded ourselves that we would see him again, that he was searching for us in that maelstrom that drove us from place to place.

But he was no longer alive.

How did he die?

There are several survivors in Israel from the town of Sarny. At every opportunity, I question them. Gruszko? Yes, there was such a family. They all died. In the Sarny Memorial Book of Sarny, the list of victims of August 27–28 1942 includes members of the Gruszko family: grandmother Pesia (67), her son Aron (48), his wife Lea whose maiden name was Zingerman (48), their sons Jona (19) and Icchak (17), brother Baruch Gruszko (45), his wife Sara and their children: Lea (22), Aron (20), and Icchak (18). Father apparently lived with this family. Did he die with them? Or was he killed by a German bullet while trying to reach us? Perhaps he had been killed by that same Ukrainian, that Bialas, who had been

supposed to lead him to the General Government, to Cracow …
Such cases were not infrequent. Or had he died during an *Aktion*?
Perhaps he had been preparing to set out but had not managed to
leave the ghetto?

THE ACCOUNT OF ICCHAK GELLER, A
SURVIVOR OF THE LIQUIDATION OF THE JEWS
OF SARNY

*We learned of the terrible slaughter of the Jews of Rowne from a refugee
who managed to flee from there and make it to Sarny. He told us in detail
about the atrocious destruction of 30,000 Jews in the Sasanki forest, two
kilometers from Rowne. No one doubted that such a fate awaited us too.
On 25 August, a ring of Ukrainian police officers surrounded the ghetto.
No one was allowed to go out to work, and from the Polish population we
learned that in the forest nearby, four long deep trenches had been dug. We
understood that the end of the Jews of Sarny was drawing near.*

*… A group of underground activists prepared for a planned operation,
but it was thwarted by Neuman, a Judenrat man. He summoned the
young rebels – and with screams, threats and claims that they would bring
disaster upon thousands of women and children and the entire Jewish
public, and that they would be responsible for the killing of innocent
people.*

*I will never forget the night which preceded the murder. Many victims
fell. Many who tried to flee were shot on the spot. Many committed
suicide. Others put on shrouds, mumbled verses from the Book of Psalms,
and waited for death.*

*At 5 o'clock in the morning, the Gestapo men began running people
toward the ghetto gate at Topolowa Street. With German precision, they
began calling Jews in alphabetical order, and in groups of 200 people
they led them to a central point. The concentration camp had been
prepared in front of the municipal offices, in a large square surrounded by
a fence composed of three rows of barbed wire. In the square stood three
long sheds, left over from the Russian occupation. When we were brought
to the square, we suddenly encountered, to our surprise, the Jewish
residents of Dabrowice, Klosowa and Rokitna, who had been brought by
train. The Jews from Bereznice were forced to run to Sarny. Half of them
fell on the way, and those who were dragged to the place were covered in
cuts and blood.*

The people who had come before us had filled the sheds, so the residents of Sarny stayed in the square with only the sky for cover. The square was crammed with bodies of old people and children. To this day a vision hovers before me of the body of a six-year-old boy, punctured with bullet holes: A Ukrainian police officer had decided to test his automatic machine gun on him. This is how the Nazi criminals prepared for war against starving, exhausted, helpless women and children.

August 27 was a hot day. The sun burned hot and bothered the people, who had been standing in the square from the early morning hours, hungry and thirsty. Children fainted from thirst. Near the fence was a ditch in which foul water flowed. A small glass of water cost a five-ruble gold coin, a gold watch or some other piece of jewelry. Hair-raising scenes took place near the ditch. People who had no money to buy water attacked the fortunate ones who had managed to obtain a bit of the muddy liquid, and tried to steal the treasure from them. The result repeated itself over and over again: a few more dead, killed by the bullets of Ukrainians who 'intervened'.

The big slaughter began at exactly 2 o'clock in the afternoon.

Representatives of the Judenrat *were called to appear before the commander, and immediately afterwards, 500 people were led to the open trenches. In a short time we heard the first shots. They were accompanied by the screams and wails of those miserable ones. Next in line after the first group were the other groups from Rokitna, and then Klosowa.*

And then suddenly, rebellion broke out in the square. One Jew, named Mendel, had brought shears for cutting steel, and another Jew, Tendler, pulled out an ax from somewhere. The two began cutting the wire. When people saw this, they broke out in a run toward the fence. Before Mendel managed to cut the second row of barbed wire, the fence collapsed under the pressure of the crowd. The Germans began firing machine guns and throwing grenades at the fleeing crowd. At the same time they set fire to the sheds, where hundreds of people were crowded.

I was among those who fled. I prayed that a bullet would find me, so that I would not see the death of my wife and children. The rush of the crowd knocked me to the ground, and within a few seconds I was covered by a mountain of murdered, shot, strangled people ... I was ready to die and accepted my fate, but still some inner force pushed me to extricate myself from under the pile of corpses and run forward. I was saved against my own wishes.

On that horrible day, between 14,000 and 15,000 Jews were murdered in Sarny. Four deep graves swallowed the victims. Three in the forest, near

157

the offices of the local council, and a fourth not far from there, near a former tar factory.

Is that my father's grave? Was he in that camp along with the residents of Sarny? Did he try to escape with the others through the breach in the fence, and was he perhaps trampled during the escape? Or did a bullet catch him as he struggled with the barbed wire? God knows.

Questions for which there is no answer keep coming back. What if …?

If my father had stayed in Cracow, he would have shared, most likely, the fate of the rest of the first hostages, who were shot or sent to concentration camps in Germany. If he had been transported deep into the Soviet Union, would he have returned alive? Jozek Grünberg, full of energy and younger, perished … A proverb says that Poles are wise when it's too late. No one is wise, even in hindsight. People interpret incidents from someone's past, from someone's experience, in order to prove to themselves how wise they are. 'Didn't I warn you … ?' 'If it had been me …'

The fates of the masses are stereotypical in certain historical situations. They can be classified according to type. But the fates of the individuals who make up those masses are varied, and the road to the same grave follows the most roundabout routes, different for each family and person.

I can remember father's terrified expression when I nearly fell under the wheels of a train. It was late August 1939. He and I were on our way home from Rabka. I do not recall whether my brothers and sister had left earlier. Could they have taken an earlier train? I remember only the crowded train station, and the train that did not stop at that summer resort for more than a minute. In that minute, somehow, the whole crowd managed to pack into the train. Father went in first, and I was handing the suitcases to him through the window. As I was passing the last one to him, the train began moving. I tried to jump on to the steps, but they were very high, designed for higher platforms, and I slipped. The train was speeding up, and I tried again and then one more time. Father had raced to the door, opened it, and was shouting at me to stay there instead of jumping. But I wouldn't listen. I got hold of the handle and the rush of air nearly blew me under the wheels; I caught father's outstretched hand, and was saved. Poor father, white as a sheet, was too upset to speak. I tried to soothe him. I felt terribly bad about having upset him so. When we arrived safely in Cracow, he donated 500 *zloty* to charity.

The terrified face of the father who loved us so rose before my eyes as I rode the cart to Grebalow …

8. Pages from a Diary, 1942

At the same time that the blood-soaked *Aktion* was raging in Sarny, we in Grebalow prepared for another deportation. Two months had passed since we had been transferred there from Czyzyny, two more months of fresh air and 'normal' life. But rumors about the June deportation in the Cracow ghetto had already reached us. We were horrified, but tended to believe that the people deported from the ghetto had been sent to camps in Ukraine. Nonetheless, foreboding gnawed at us.

After the big operation in Cracow, the Germans began liquidating the small Jewish communities scattered throughout the villages. They crowded the Jews into the truncated ghetto or concentrated them in towns. At the end of August, the time came for Mogila, Bienczyce, Grebalow and the nearby villages and towns. We were ordered to pack and order a cart for the next morning. The farmer with whom we lived had an acceptable cart, so that problem was solved.

In the morning we were awakened by gunfire. Actually, we were not really awakened, because we had not shut an eye the entire night. We were packed and ready to go. The morning gunfire surprised us a little, and scared us a little. We almost never saw Germans in our village, and even the Polish policemen came our way only rarely. We were on good terms with the farmers, our landlords and the main suppliers of our food. The neighbors in the area were all quiet people. So why suddenly the shots? We soon understood. A drunken Polish policeman broke into our apartment accompanied by a teenager named Wojtek. Screaming, they ordered us outside. The landlord had not managed to hitch the horses to the cart. What was the hurry? The question infuriated the police officer. 'Who gave you permission to speak?! No questions! Out! Everybody – now!' He pushed us with the barrel of his gun, one after another.

Mother tried to calm him down. 'Wojtek, please tell the police officer we were already on our way out,' she said, pushing a banknote into his hand.

Wojtek broke into a stupid smile, tugged at his nose, and tapped the police officer on the shoulder. 'Mr Joziu, let's go. We have a lot to do and time is running out!'

'I'm not going to let this son-of-a-bitch go! He laughed in my face!' screamed the policeman, pushing my little brother Jerzyk to the wall. 'Put your hands up, you little stinker. I'll teach you to laugh. Move it, march! To the field!'

'I did not laugh, sir,' mumbled Jerzyk, as white as the plaster on the wall.

'Mr Joziu, leave the boy.' Wojtek tried to calm the police officer.

His coaxing was to no avail, and Jerzyk was pushed outside by the gun barrel.

Klara broke down in sobs. Wojtek tried to calm my mother. 'He won't do anything to him, Mrs Gross, he won't do anything to him, he's just kidding.' He nipped out of the room.

It is hard to describe the feelings that swept over me. It was all happening so suddenly and so unexpectedly. I felt paralyzed.

And then suddenly we heard the sound of a harmonica. We had no doubts: it was our Jerzyk, playing a well-known folk tune on the little harmonica that was always in his pocket: 'Aren't you sad, mountaineer, to leave your homeland?' A shot was heard, followed by another, but the tune continued.

A moment later, the policeman threw Jerzyk into the room and swore heartily: 'Don't you ever laugh at me again, you son-of-a-bitch, because you won't get away with it again!' And he left with Wojtek to prepare the other Jews for the journey.

It turned out that the policeman had led Jerzyk behind the barn, vowing solemnly to shoot him like a dog, but Wojtek somehow managed to inform him that Jerzyk was known in the village for playing the harmonica, and it was worth listening to the way he played ...

And thus, almost miraculously, Jerzyk saved his own life by playing his harmonica.

A long time passed before we started on our journey. The drunken police officer roughed up several Jews as an example, but luckily not enough to cause serious injury. Money helped. Around ten, the convoy of some 20 carts was ready to depart.

We still had a slight problem with our dog, Dina. Our landlord wanted to keep her, and for a minute we thought it would be best for her. He locked her in the house, to make the parting easier for her and for us, but Dina got out – no one knew how – and when we were already sitting in the cart, she appeared, jumping and barking. That did it. We could not bear the way she looked at us. It seemed full of resentment: is this the way to leave a friend? Jerzyk jumped down and helped Dina climb aboard. We departed.

With us on the cart were the Lerfeld family: Mrs Lerfeld, a kindly woman about 40 years old, her daughter Hela, a sensible and pleasant-looking woman of 20, her brother Wilek, 16, and their stepfather Mr Pineles, who was Mrs Lerfeld's second husband. I sat, silent and motionless on a suitcase stuffed with the books and papers I had managed to accumulate during our year in Czyzyny. I had begged the suitcase from mother; seeing how attached I was to my scraps of paper, she had agreed to part with some winter clothing. I guarded the treasure, resolved never to part with it.

The caravan crept along as the August sun beat down with increasing ferocity. The handful of policemen escorting us had little work aside from harrying the people who got down from the carts to stretch their legs. The ride along the potholed road was no pleasure. What pleasure could there have been? We trembled, chewing the delicious sandwiches that my mother had prepared and that she now forced on us. The tea in the thermos ran out quickly. Dina, always so merry, ignored the opportunity to move around freely. She lay sadly, curled up between the bundles.

The young Lerfelds argued constantly with their stepfather, Mr Pineles. They disliked the stuttering fellow whose cunning face was scarred from smallpox. It was difficult to understand what Mrs Lerfeld saw in him. He plainly had money. The widow probably wanted to provide for her growing children. How could she support them herself in such hard times? The Lerfelds had been our neighbors in Czyzyny, too. Young Wilek was in love with my cousin Nata Steinmetz, a student at the Fine Arts Academy. Nata taught him to draw. He clung to me, too: he drank up knowledge and he was maturing quickly. He treated me as some sort of a source from which he could draw encouragement, good advice, and good books. Nata and her mother had left Czyzyny several months earlier, while we stayed behind with the Lerfelds. Their quarrels with Pineles ceased only when he was away from home. Now, as they sat on the cart, they did not stop digging at each other for a single moment. Sunk in my melancholy thoughts, I paid them no heed.

162

We passed Bienczyce, Czyzyny and Rakowice. On both sides of the road, people stood and looked at us silently. The closer we got to Cracow, the more people there were in the gates of houses, in windows, on balconies and sidewalks. Occasionally someone would run up to one of the carts: a meeting between acquaintances. Short exchanges: What? Where to? Why? A policeman pushed away the more eager questioners. Someone tossed a food parcel, a bottle of water, on to a wagon. The caravan rolled on, slowly, never pausing.

The sun beat down more fiercely. It was an oppressive atmosphere, and it was getting worse. The tension grew as we approached the city. People moved from one cart to another, looking for friends. They wanted to be together. They analyzed the situation. Nothing good could come of this. Concentrating people ... Of course, they were concentrating them together so that they could liquidate them more easily. Just like in the ghetto two months earlier. So many taken away, no one knew where. There were those who knew. Others did not want to know. The name 'Belzec' kept coming up. Belzec – that was where the people in the transport had last been heard from. The anxiety was growing. Every so often, someone slipped away from the procession and disappeared among the ever-more-numerous onlookers.

Wilek Lerfeld sat down beside me.

'Look', he said, 'Poldek's disappeared. Imagine – he left his mother with his little brother and made a run for it. What a swine! How could he?'

'Don't judge Poldek. You don't know what you might do ...'

But Wilek would not calm down. 'Never in my life would I do that. Leave my old mother to save my skin. Could you?'

When we were passing the Cracow ghetto, I suddenly felt as if we had come to a funeral. A black, silent crowd clung to the barbed wire. The silence was terrible, and so was the clatter of the cart wheels on the cobblestones. The street was empty – and all those people behind the barbed wire. Suddenly, as we were passing one of the gates of the ghetto, my classmate Jasio Kremsdorf shot out of the crowd as if he had been catapulted, and clung to our cart. We had not been close at school. We called him 'Freckles', and all I knew about him was that he lived in Podgorze and his father owned a candy factory. 'Freckles' always had a pocket full of candy. He studied hard but displayed no great intelligence. A forgettable, ugly carrot top – next to him, a red squirrel was blond.

Jasio tumbled into the cart. 'Natek, save yourself. Run! They're going to finish you all off.'

'Where am I supposed to escape to?' I blurted out hoarsely.

'Come with me. I'll arrange everything. Save yourself!'

'I'm really grateful, Jasio, but I can't ... I'm with my mother, brother and sister. What happens to them will happen to me.'

'I'm begging you, save yourself!' Tears came to his eyes. 'Escape, Natek!'

'Freckles' started crying. I will never forget it as long as I live. He did not want to let go of our cart, not until one of the police officers grabbed him by the collar and called him to order.

The procession passed the ghetto and again we were surrounded by fields. Now almost everyone began to panic. Wilek, who was running around and jumping from cart to cart, came back and sat by my side again.

'Natek, don't condemn me. I want to say goodbye to you. I have to get away ... If I don't do it now, it may be too late. You don't know how hard this is.'

'Go on, run, save yourself, if you can ...'

'See, I can't help them! If there were some way I could help them ... I want to live ... So tell me, is there anything I can do here to help?'

'Go on, go already. God be with you! Take care of yourself. You won't be able to help anyone.'

He jumped into the weeds alongside the road and I never saw him again.

At about 4 o'clock, we arrived in Wieliczka.

*

We were housed temporarily in a local school, in the hope that a better place would be found for us the next day. Despite the exhaustion, we went into town to look for friends, luck, and lodgings fit for humans.

The center of Wieliczka was busy and bustling with refugees who had arrived from nearby villages that day and the day before. Everyone, like us, was looking for some apartment or arrangement. Everyone was asking everyone else: What next? The optimists – these are never lacking in hard times – believed that everything would be fine, that everything would somehow work out. The pessimists – of whom there are usually more – saw a black future. The war would not finish soon. And if it didn't finish soon, then they'd finish us off. How long could we endure?

Suddenly I ran into Rysio Apte, a friend from school, a few years younger than me. We had once worked together on a school play. After not seeing him for three years, I wouldn't have recognized him – he was the one who came up to me in the street. He had grown and changed. In his clean, blue overalls, he looked like a mechanic out of a French movie. We greeted each other heartily and embarked on a long conversation which lasted until the small hours of the night, and which even continued the next day. We said little about our predicament.

When he showed me his translations of Kästner (strange that he had also translated Kästner), I immediately realized how immature my own work was. Then he pulled out a portfolio of graphic works in a style reminiscent of George Grosz. I was speechless. Until then, I had known Rysio as a talented pianist and musician. Now I discovered a new Ryszard Apte! This was a great experience.

I too pulled some of my papers out and we examined each other, like two puppies, barking joyously. I showed Rysio letters, including some from our adored teacher Juliusz Feldhorn. I had sent him my translations of Rilke, and he had reciprocated with an entire essay on the technique of translation, on disintegration and reintegration of a poem. We spent several hours poring over that letter.

I had found a kindred spirit, a person who worshipped papers and books like me, who knew how to find in them another world, better and more beautiful than that in which he was destined to live, who knew how to escape to this other world, to enclose himself in it and become better through the very awareness of intellectual superiority.

Rysio was then 17, and was aware of what was going on around him. He had a feeling that he would not survive the war and, as he said, it did not matter to him. He only wanted to save his work from destruction. He transferred several copies of his poems to his friends, but as for his art – and especially the beautiful watercolors and the masterful miniatures – he was quite concerned. In two or three days the deportation would surely begin. Perhaps he should give them to the landlord for safekeeping? They're honest people, but can one really rely on them?

His father, a well-known Cracow lawyer and an excellent violinist, took faithful care of his paraplegic wife, who was wheelchair-bound. Her fate was sealed!

That night I slept at Rysio's. The next day, I left my suitcase at his house, and the two of us went to look for my family.

The town was in an uproar. The tension had reached its zenith. We looked in at the school where yesterday's refugees had been housed, but no one from my family was there. No one knew what tomorrow would bring, but one thing was clear: all the roads had been blocked off. No one could get out of Wieliczka. Jerzyk was working at the airport – a key job – and we expected to be able to go to the Cracow ghetto thanks to him. But for now there was no one to talk to. No one was honoring any certificates or passes and permits were being issued. The anxiety grew and thickened. Mother was surely racing from office to office looking for protection, friends, and understanding.

And I? I sat at Rysio's with my suitcase.

We roamed the streets of Wieliczka for a long time. We were somewhat upset, but not enough to prevent us from revelling in the floods of morning sunlight. Suddenly we were caught up in a commotion. Everyone was running in the same direction.

'What's going on?' I asked a passerby.

'A truck has arrived from the airport!'

We were happy to hear that there was some movement, that some contact had been made with the outside world. We ran. I saw mother in the truck. She was desperate because she did not know where to find me. Jerzyk had found Klara in the bath house. When she heard that a truck had arrived from the airport, she had pulled on her dress without even drying herself off, and she ran like a madwoman, wet hair and all, toward salvation. The large truck was almost full. Only those holding permits from the airport were allowed to climb in. We had such a permit.

'Hurry! Hurry!'

'And my suitcase? I have to get my suitcase. I'm not leaving without it! Besides, I have no permit on me!'

'Are you crazy? Hurry up and get in! I'll fetch your suitcase!'

Rysio ran home to get my papers, and I could not concentrate my thoughts. I prayed that the driver would refuse to take me. Jerzyk reached out a hand to me and somehow pulled me into the vehicle, which by now was completely packed. There wasn't room for a pin. Suddenly people realized that our dog was among the crowd and began to protest in anger. Someone caught Dina by the scruff of the neck and threw her on to the cobblestones. My heart broke at the sight of the poor dog standing near the truck, holding her head in a mute question: Are you going to leave me here? The tussle, which I described earlier, began. I finally concealed the dog. Jerzyk jumped into the truck, which took off with great speed. At that instant Rysio appeared with the suitcase. I managed only to yell: 'Rysio! The papers!'

The papers were in loyal hands, I tried to console myself. I could rely on Rysio. Whatever he did with his own papers, he'd do with mine ...

Two days later, the Jews were deported from Wieliczka. Rysio's paralyzed mother was shot immediately, his father was sent to Belzec, and my friend ended up in the labor camp in Stalowa Wola. He attempted to escape two months later, but was recognized at the train station and shot on the spot.

This was the second time I had lost my precious papers. I did not feel that same piercing pain I had felt before, in Czyzyny. The papers were really not worth preserving. To this day, however, I cannot get over the loss of Ryszard, a friend whom I had barely begun to get to know.

After a wild 15-minute drive, we landed at Zgoda Square in the ghetto. The truck was empty a moment later and immediately drove off. The group of lucky refugees scattered in all directions, so as not to be caught by the *Ordnungsdienst*. None of us had identity cards. We were in the ghetto illegally, and we knew it. I took Klara to Anka Zimmermann's, while mother and Jerzyk found Kornblüth's address. With them settled, I began thinking about whom I could drop in on, without terrifying them, when suddenly 'Freckles' was standing there before me ... my providence, my destiny.

*

I had friends and acquaintances in the ghetto, true dear friends for whom I would have done anything should they have needed help. There were Wilek and Lolek, Anka, Franka, Niusia, Titka, Dolek and Minka. We had been in constant touch when I lived outside of Cracow. I had written long, juicy letters to them. I did not doubt for a moment that any of them would have received me warmly and done everything to help make my life in the ghetto easier. But despite my belief in their friendship, I did not want to put them to the test. I do not know what I feared more: that they would let me down, or that I would place them in an uncomfortable situation. I was ready to stand by my friends to the end, but I never became dependent on mutual ties.

Standing in the ghetto, at the intersection of Jozefinska and Krakusa streets, I was in no hurry to decide whom to call upon.

And then Freckles appeared.

He did not ask where I had come from and where I was staying. He led me to a hideout in the cellar of a building next to the ghetto wall. Darkness had fallen, but I had the impression there were no windows there. A carbide lamp spread a dull light. Clouds of cigarette smoke filled the long room. Various types of men, some in the caps of the *Ordnungsdienst*, sat, walked around, came in, went out, argued, laughed, and whispered in the corners. I was dead tired and hadn't slept, so I neither quibbled nor made a big deal of it when Freckles made up a bed – probably his own – for me in a dark corner. He brought me something to eat and drink, and rigged a sort of screen out of a blanket. He was hovering over me like a mother or a devoted nurse, asking me if I was comfortable or if I needed anything. I was grateful to him from the depths of my heart. Could any of my friends have done more?

I stayed with Freckles for several days. He established contact with mother and the rest of my family, so that we all knew where everybody was. Without asking, I quickly came to understand that this cellar was a center for smuggling goods into the ghetto, and for all the other dubious business this entailed. The only people I knew there were Freckles and a Henryk Hacker, who had been in our class for a short time. I could not tell whether or not the people in the cellar were happy about the arrival of an outsider like me, but they gave no hint of their feelings. On the contrary, they treated me with a certain respect. My patron was obviously someone whose opinions counted. Freckles soon arranged identity cards for me and my family, so that I could move freely about the ghetto.

Freckles! I had never thought that he had it in him!

After the wide open spaces, greenery, birds, and noisy frogs of the village, the ghetto oppressed me. I felt like I was in prison. The crowding, the anguish and the tired faces of the friends I loved were an unbearable weight upon my soul. I, who not so long ago had so much in common with these people, now did not know what to talk to them about. They were exhausted by oppressive work of which there was no end in sight, while I continued to inhabit a private reality that existed only in me and nowhere else. So I went back to my books.

The four of us, with the dog, crowded into a big apartment on Krakusa Street, where three other families already lived. We tried as well as we could to avoid forced labor until the time when we could arrange a place to live in Cracow and begin existing on Aryan papers. This was not easy. Trucks and German soldiers came to the ghetto all the time, rounding up unemployed residents of the Jewish district for occasional work. I spent most of my time in the cellar, reading in turn Burckhardt's *The Culture of the Renaissance in Italy* and Durant's *Lives of the Philosophers*. I fled deep into my alternative reality and hardly gave a thought to what was happening around me. 'They're rounding people up!' shouted someone – and without raising my eyes from the page, I scurried to a different cellar and went on reading.

*

I was 'unlucky' when it came to forced labor. I cannot say why, but it always passed me by. I cannot even say that I particularly tried to avoid it. Things just turned out that way. I might have gone to work shoveling snow once or twice during the first winter of the occupation – perhaps.

A *Judenrat* had been organized in Czyzyny, and a Mr Krakauer, a very kindly person, was put in charge of the *Arbeitsamt*. My turn came. I was assigned to the Hans und Richter construction firm in Cracow. Through some sort of mixup, I never obtained a train pass. So it was impossible for me to report to the construction site. Without any sense of urgency, I informed the authorities that I could not travel to the city without a pass. It took another three or four weeks to arrange for the pass, and when I finally received it – again, without any sense of urgency – I used it to run errands in town rather than to report to work. I knew that I could not go on like this forever, but I did not intend to act until someone forced me to. Finally, in order not to overdo things, I reported to the firm. And

169

then the whole mystery was solved: it turned out that my name did not even appear on the list of workers! So – that was how it was. I promised the clerk that I would clear things up with the *Arbeitsamt*. I continued to use the pass on my trips to town.

I was walking along Basztowa Street in Cracow one lovely morning when an SS man stopped me: 'Identity card!'

I showed him my identity card and my pass. *'Wos mochst du denn in Stadt?'* – he asked me, in Berlin dialect, what I was doing in town.

I explained that I was employed by the Hans und Richter firm, and was just on my way to work.

'That means you don't work at all,' he said, looking suspiciously at me. Then, to my amazement, he tore up my pass. *'Komm mit!'*

Somewhat worried, I tried verbosely to explain myself as we walked along, until he snapped, 'Shut up!'

I did not know what to think of it. He led me into a courtyard, opened a wooden cellar door with a key, ordered me inside, and locked the door.

Through a crack, I could see a large, empty courtyard full of sunshine and surrounded by whitewashed buildings. Should I scream or not? Would anyone hear? Would they want to help? I decided to remain watchful and see how things turned out.

My tormenter returned a moment later. 'Go downstairs', he snapped.

I had no idea what he wanted from me or what he intended to do. I decided to be ready for anything, but to stay calm and avoid provoking him. It felt unpleasant to walk down the dark cellar steps.

'Hands up!' He had drawn his pistol.

I raised my hands in silence. The SS-man began feeling my pockets. He tossed a dirty handkerchief to the floor in disgust. Then, with a yelp of triumph, he pulled out my wallet. It contained a total of four *zloty* for a train ticket.

'Is that all?' He was visibly disappointed. 'And what's this? Aha!'

He had found the notebook where I had written the names of my Polish acquaintances in Cracow. He turned over the pages and then pocketed it. Finally, he pointed the revolver at me and shouted, 'Now let's see how fast you can run!'

Was he going to shoot me? I hesitated for a moment considering the possibilities. 'Get a move on!', he screamed.

I dashed up the stairs and outside. A moment later, I was on the street. Now I was in a foolish predicament. I had no pass, I had no identity card, and I was broke. I directed my steps towards a Polish friend's apartment. I was perplexed: should I mention the notebook or not? Who knew what that German would do with the addresses? He might try to blackmail my acquaintances. It would be better if they knew. With a heavy heart, I recounted my misadventure, describing the gloomy SS-man and recommending that they warn the others. They gave me a few *zloty* for a ticket and cursed me up and down. They were right, of course. I was ashamed enough to eat my own filthy handkerchief, except that it was lying back there in that unfortunate basement!

So, once again, I was left without a pass or papers. And, therefore, I did not go to work. I somehow managed to keep goldbricking that way until the deportation …

I had never been athletic, and I had always had weak hands that were unacquainted with hard work. I was not afraid of work – but I did not go around looking for it. What sort of merit was there in working for the Germans, anyway? No one held it against me that I was idle. They might have been a little jealous at the way that hard work passed me by, but they also wondered how I managed it. And in fact, I did nothing to avoid work. I never made payments, gave bribes, or hid. Yet my conscience pricked me. Something was wrong. My younger brother Jerzyk worked hard, first at the tire factory and then at the airport. People who were older than me worked, while I lived comfortably like a favorite of the gods, among my books and papers.

It happened about a week after I entered the ghetto. I had just walked out into the street when I witnessed a 'roundup'.

It was a cold October morning, but the clear sky promised a warm day. A large truck stood by the sidewalk, and two German soldiers were 'recruiting' people for work outside the ghetto. I could easily have slipped away into a back alley, but at the sight of the elderly Siegel, our neighbor from Grebalow, boarding the truck, my troubled conscience again raised its voice. I allowed myself to be caught. The truck filled up swiftly. We drove through town to a railroad siding in, if I recall, the Bonarka district. They gave us shovels and ordered us to unload coal from train cars to trucks parked next to them.

I had not the vaguest notion about this sort of work. My hands were better suited to a piano than to a shovel. Besides, one has to know how to work, and I didn't! Every time I tried to lift a few clumps of coal with the shovel, they scattered in all directions, even before I managed to raise my arm and toss them into the back of the truck. My clumsiness attracted the attention of the German overseer, even though I tried not to stand out among the group of 40 people swinging their shovels with great energy. He leaped toward me, grabbed the shovel from my hands, cursed me in German, added some kicks – and began to teach me how to hold the shovel and heave the coal. I was more than a little tired and wet with perspiration, although the work had just begun, and I was happy to be able to rest for a brief moment. I followed the smooth movements of the German with great interest – he knew how to work! – and when the shovel was given back to me, I tried very hard to perform my work as well as possible. But the result was pathetic. I received a few more kicks and another demonstration. After that I had the impression the *Sturmführer* was giving up on me. The air was scorching, streams of sweat poured off me, my hands threatened to break under the strain and came out in blisters. I was dying of thirst, and my heart was filled with feelings of shame and degradation, with contempt for the Germans and anger at myself, for needlessly ending up in this unfortunate situation. It was a miracle I managed to endure until lunchtime. I tried to convince him that not everyone is suited for physical labor, and that, to my great regret, I was among those who have weak hands … Therefore I had gone to the university to study law, and not to a vocational school. It turned out the officer was also a jurist. I steered the conversation toward German culture. We discussed Goethe and Kant. It seemed to me that I had won him over.

When I started back to work after the half-hour break, I felt that my hands would no longer obey me. My *Sturmführer* quickly forgot our conversation. He screamed, flew into a rage, and slapped and kicked me. Old Siegel tried to help, but I was too tired and beaten to understand what was said to me. Finally, the *Sturmführer* vowed that I would not get out of there alive. I couldn't even summon up the strength to be frightened. In the evening, when the work was over and we began boarding the truck, my tormenter pulled me brutally aside and told me that he was going to shoot me like a dog. I thought of poor mother, who did not even know where I had disappeared to. What would happen when everyone except me returned home? I was too tired to care. Yet an unpleasant feeling overcame me when my last companions in misfortune climbed into the truck and the tailgate closed behind them.

'Herr *Sturmführer'*, I said dispassionately, 'enough of this game. It's getting late.'

He raised his fist, but at the last minute changed his mind and decided to treat me to one more kick, while ordering me to run after the truck, which had already started on its way. The people in the truck yelled and the driver stopped. Only with great difficulty did they manage to pull me up; I would not have been able to climb in myself.

We pulled up in front of Montelupich prison. They ordered us to strip and made us run, naked and blackened with soot, to the showers. We were given pieces of soap – God knows what it was made of, but sand was certainly one of the ingredients. Then we went under the cold showers. Our bruised bodies burned terribly, but I was happy to be alive. We pulled our sooty clothes on over our wet bodies. It was autumn and the nights were chilly. We trembled with cold as they loaded us back into the truck.

We returned to the ghetto at ten at night. The curfew had started at eight, and the empty streets yawned before us. But fearful eyes peeked out of windows and doorways. Forty families, who had not known what had become of their loved ones, now sighed with relief. After some roundups, similar groups never returned to the ghetto and nothing more was ever heard of them.

Dina was the first who came running to greet me. In her first barks, I sensed some sort of reproach. Then she jumped on me and began licking and whining. Mother was waiting at the door. My poor mother. What a horrible day she had had! Klara bawled, as Klara would. Jerzyk was pale and only nodded: 'Come on, come on! All we need is for some policeman to grab us for being out after curfew.'

It was a good thing that it ended the way it did.

I swore that never again would I go willingly to forced labor, and that I would not let myself be caught on the street. My conscience would henceforth be less troubled.

*

We had prepared Aryan identity cards long ago. Before the June

Aktion, Uncle Szulim brought the unlikely sounding news that Jews were being choked to death with gas in Chelmno. We began to consider the possibility of spending the rest of the war on Polish identity cards. We were not the only ones. After the horrifying news that reached us from the *Aktion* in the Cracow ghetto, people began equipping themselves with Aryan papers. People kept these things secret, to prevent anyone who should not know from finding out, but everyone knew everything anyway, and if someone wanted to obtain a false identification card, they always managed to find their way to a 'broker'. So would our beloved mother fail to do so? Our intermediary was Adek S., who had a classmate who worked as a municipal clerk in the outlying hamlet of Swoszowice. Four sets of identity papers for us and another set for Uncle Szulim were to cost 10,000 *zloty* – big money!

We decided to sell *Self-Portrait in Oriental Dress*, a large, lovely oil painting by Maurycy Gottlieb. It was surely worth more, but Mr and Mrs Sroka, who had helped us a great deal by buying our china, crystal and silver, were not willing to pay more. A painting by a Jewish artist might be worth something someday, but at present it could not even be hung. It had to be taken out of its frame, rolled up, and hidden in the hallway, where it waited for better times. The Srokas were merchants, and commerce was in their blood. The good relations that had existed between us before the war survived – despite the fact that their assets continually increased, while we ceased to be human beings and became Jews, with whom all contact was forbidden. The Srokas believed that they were helping us by occasionally buying something at a bargain price. And they were indeed helping. But they could not overcome their nature and pay a little more, even when they were aware of our situation. We had no income, and were eating and depleting the property amassed during the 20-year existence of the Jakub Gross company. A bargain is a bargain and business is business: you have to know how to buy cheaply. This is not to say that, after the deal was concluded, Mrs Sroka did not slip mother a package of salami or fruit 'for the children'. This good Polish woman, a devout Catholic, believed that good deeds were recorded and would not be forgotten at the moment of the Final Reckoning …

We sold the Gottlieb and paid the price. In exchange, we were to obtain real identity cards, duplicates of existing documents, as well as authentic birth certificates. We provided our ages and professions, along with photographs. We waited a long time, with worry gnawing at our hearts: what if the man took the money and never gave us the documents? What could we do then? Finally, Adek informed us that the certificates were ready and that we would have to go in person to the Swoszowice municipal offices to collect them. This was a dangerous escapade. The official, however, did us a favor and came to us with a briefcase full of falsified documents and a stamp pad. We placed our fingerprints on the identity papers and on forms which the clerk took back with him. Only after he was gone did we look at the documents we had received. Suddenly, everything looked black.

My new name was Franciszek Grymek – what a name! Not that I have any class prejudices, but did this village name suit my face? The document shook my stoic calm, all the more so when it became clear that the other documents the clerk had brought also seemed maliciously prepared, making them almost impossible to use. According to her identity papers, my sister Klara – like me – was ten years older. In addition, her name was Janina Birkenfeldowicz. A Jewish name! Furthermore, she was a widow! It required a profound lack of conscience to take 2,000 *zloty* apiece for identity papers and set us up that way! Mother was awarded the name Maria Murdzenska (née Murdzia), and uncle was now Zygmunt Durakowski. Far from beautiful, but at least it ended in '-ski'. Jerzyk came out best, as Marian Wisniewski. It would not be easy to get used to calling him 'Manius'. And how we had begged for him to get papers with the name 'Jerzy' on them. At first glance, then, things looked ghastly. In the usual way, however, we tried to delude ourselves that maybe it was all for the best – after all, anyone with a blatant name like Birkenfeldowicz would have to be a super-Christian to live among the Poles!

In any case, we had other things to worry about. We packed the identity papers into a secret hiding place at the Srokas' apartment. They stayed there for five months. Then the time came.

From our first day in the ghetto, we knew we would have to leave sooner or later on Aryan papers. Better sooner than later. As soon as we had settled in, mother began going into town to look for an apartment. Thanks to Dolek, she had no trouble getting a pass. At first the task of obtaining an apartment for four 'Aryan' tenants – and of different sexes yet – seemed absolutely hopeless, but one day, in Sroka's shop, my mother met a certain Edward

Bujacz, a young, elegant man. He remembered mother well, he said, from the shop. Mother remembered him only vaguely, but the fact that she met him at the Srokas' apartment made her trust him enough to explain our situation to him. Mr Bujacz then offered to place us with his relatives in a house on the edge of a village in the middle of nowhere. A few days later, I had a chance to meet Mr Bujacz. To tell the truth, he did not inspire my confidence. He seemed to be hiding something. He was a little too smooth and sure of himself. But, for the time being, we had no choice. He did not ask for money. On the contrary, he offered to help by keeping property, paintings and other valuables for us. So we agreed that, when the situation became life-threatening and we decided it was time to escape, we would go to his sister-in-law Joasia's apartment. From there, Bujacz would take us to the village by car. We were in no hurry to implement our plan, though life in the ghetto was no idyll. We had to prepare, mentally and physically, for the change in identity. Besides, we were still not sure if we would take advantage of Bujacz's offer. Perhaps something better would come along.

But nothing better came along, and meanwhile that black day in the month of October arrived, that day of mourning in the history of the Cracow ghetto. Rumors started circulating in the morning that something bad was afoot, but life continued as usual. In the afternoon, the rumors became more upsetting. I ran over to Dolek's, and just in case, got permits for all of us to leave the ghetto. Yet we could not make up our minds to flee. Everyone knew that Förster collaborated with the Gestapo, but he also did good deeds for people. He was saying that there was no question of any deportation, but this only made things more confused and nerve-wracking.

We were living in the 'Small Ghetto', which was separated from the 'Big Ghetto' by Lwowska Street, where a tram line ran. We were afflicted by the general panic and ran like mad from one ghetto to the other with the exit permits in our pockets. Mother tried to reach Förster, but dozens of people were crowded at the entrance to his building and it was impossible to talk to him. Besides, there was no reason to. We ran from one 'knowledgeable' acquaintance to another looking for advice, until one of them blurted out of the side of his mouth, after hesitating a long time, 'Save yourself if you can.'

But it was too late. Groups of workers were still returning to the ghetto from work outside. No one was being allowed out, even with passes. We ran from one gate to another, in vain.

Darkness had fallen; it was six in the evening. The four of us stood at the gate between the Small and Big Ghettos, trying to bribe the policeman there. He did not react when Jerzyk offered him 50 *zloty*. He was afraid. In the meantime, mad, crazy rumors were coming one on top of another. Some people said that the ghetto was about to be surrounded, that an SS column was on the way, and then others claimed that we were already surrounded. Some people were still clinging to their illusions. We kept standing there, and the policeman kept telling us to go away, but he was not very forceful. Then another policeman came along and they began chatting. Suddenly, a tram came along. Without thinking, we ran behind it, along the fence down the middle of the street, keeping our heads down. Our act inspired a woman to run along with us. We were running down Lwowska Street in the dark with our dog Dina beside us. Flashlights were directed at us, there were shouts, and there were yelps of surprise and applause. In a moment, we were outside the ghetto area. We saw some suspicious-looking characters loafing on a street corner. They seemed to be watching us. We tried to act like unconcerned passers-by, but it wasn't really necessary. It turned out that no one was taking any interest in us. As soon as we were sure that we were not being followed, we turned into Dabrowki Street, where our acquaintance Colonel Dmysiewicz lived.

He was an unusual acquaintance. Mr Dmysiewicz had appeared at our apartment on Sarego Street in October 1939, on the recommendation of Prince Stefan Lubomirski, whom we knew well. Dmysiewicz had managed to escape from the front lines near Lwow, where he had been a garrison commander, or something of the sort. He was looking for a hiding place and for contacts, and feared falling into the hands of the Germans. We began talking and it turned out that he had been the officer to whom I had been led blindfolded near Brzuchowice when I had been trying to get to Lwow. As I have mentioned, he had given me a dressing down and told me to hit the road along with my companions and to go back where I had come from. So I had returned to Cracow. Two weeks later, he walked into my courtyard. Talk about a small world! We had, of course, helped Dmysiewicz and his wife and daughter to find contacts and a place to live. They had visited us subsequently several times. But on this October night, we were calling on them for the first time. They greeted us cordially, but in terror.

Spending the night there was out of the question. The building was too close to the ghetto, and it was reasonable to suspect that during an *Aktion*, the buildings in the neighborhood would be searched for fugitive Jews. We could leave the dog. We decided that Colonel Dmysiewicz would accompany mother and Klara to Bujacz's sister-in-law Joasia on Rajska Street, while Jerzyk and I would go to Plaszow, where Rudek Birnbaum, a cousin of mother's, worked at a camp operated by the Klug firm. Dmysiewicz told us how to get there, and made it sound as if it was 'just around the corner'. It turned out to be more difficult to find.

We were lost for a long time, and asked the few passers-by for directions, until we finally managed to make out the lights of the camp. But when we approached the barbed-wire fence, we saw by the address that this was not the camp we were after. We were ready to drop and did not know what to do next. Fortunately, someone appeared and showed us the way to the Klug camp, where we easily found Rudek, who hid us in an empty barrack.

In the meantime, the ghetto had already been cordoned off.

We spent two days in a corner of the barrack and did not stick our noses outside. Rudek brought us some potatoes, so that we would not starve. As soon as we heard that the *Aktion* was over, we returned to the ghetto with a work detail. We could see that a horrible pogrom had taken place there. The Small Ghetto, where we had been living, had been liquidated. People walked around in shock, looking for or trying to find out about relatives, friends and acquaintances. There was not a family that had not been touched. I met my old teacher, Mr Waldman, on the street. With his bad leg, he had survived, but 12 members of his family had been taken in the transport.

Mother and Klara returned from the city soon afterwards. Despite some difficulties, they had found shelter at Joasia's. That was a good sign. Everything indicated that the two-day *Aktion* had been only a warm-up for the next one, and that we would soon have to make a decisive move.

In the meantime, Jozio Bau appeared on the horizon. He was a young artist who was also a bit of a poet, collector and homespun philosopher. Once again, it started. There are people who seem to attract books. Whenever I spent any length of time in a given place, books began appearing, I do not know how, where from, or when. In the ghetto, after the deportation, books were simply lying in the street. Jozio, like me, was a book-lover. We collected them in enormous quantities and chose the best and most interesting ones, even though we did not know what tomorrow would bring for the books or for us. In macabre merriment, we composed satirical songs and wrote a parody of the whole Passover *Haggadah.*

Jozio, as an artist, was employed by the *Judenrat* in writing proclamations and announcements for the *Arbeitsamt* and other official institutions. Once, out of curiosity, I accompanied him when he was asked to write and attach numbers to the cells in the *Ordnungsdienst* jail. Behind bars sat beautiful blond girls, arrested on the Aryan side, with Aryan papers – who would have ever thought they were Jewish? Yet they had been caught. To this day, I see those sad eyes peering out from behind the bars …

CRACOW DID NOT LET US DOWN

The ghetto was becoming more and more crowded. We were living on Krakusa Street in one big room with the remnants of several families who had been deported. Dolek Liebeskind lived in a building nearby. We heard a commotion one night. Only in the morning did we learn that several *Ordnungsdienst* officers had come to arrest Dolek. He dressed calmly and allowed himself to be led to *Ordnungsdienst* headquarters. When they were almost there, he pulled out a revolver, threatened the unarmed Jewish policemen, jumped the ghetto wall, and escaped. They came to arrest his wife Wusia in the morning. After this episode, most of the rest of the Jewish underground left the ghetto.

One day, the ghetto was divided into Ghetto A and Ghetto B – for workers and for non-workers. The situation looked serious. We searched for good work assignments, but with no success. We had neither money nor connections. Individual passes were eliminated, and only work details were allowed to leave the ghetto.

We tried in vain to join the group of workers quartered at the airport (anywhere, as long as it was outside the ghetto!). Next, we decided to leave on 10 December with a group of workers who always marched along Mogilska Street. We planned to sit out the day in the Szymczakowski liquor plant there, before making our way after dark to Bujacz's sister-in-law's.

Unfortunately, things went wrong from the start. The detail changed its route, and we had no choice but to sneak away in broad daylight – without transit permits, without identification cards, without even any armbands. We had to walk through the snow-covered city, hiding our noses in raincoats that fluttered in the wind. Our winter coats had been left behind somewhere in Wieliczka.

My mother, Klara and I sat in the back room of the Szymczakowski offices, while Jerzyk went to Dietlowska Street, to inform Mr Bujacz that we had left the ghetto. But Bujacz was not home. Joasia was not due home from work before five. So we had to wait. The time dragged and our anxiety grew. In the evening, Jerzyk went out again. An hour and a half later, he returned with Joasia, but our disappointment and despair swelled when Bujacz's sister-in-law informed us that we would not be able to stay the night with her. The answer was no, and that was final! She was simply afraid. All our arguments were in vain.

It was 6:30 in the evening. The curfew started at 8:00. Now what? Klara demanded that we return to the ghetto. Mother and Jerzyk refused, period. As usual, I was undecided. Time passed. Then mother remembered that Uncle Szulim had stayed a few nights with the R. family on Dluga Street. If they had put up Uncle Szulim, then certainly they would not throw us out. When Mr R. saw us and realized what was up, he refused categorically. His wife was ill and he was afraid she would get worse; we could not stay there for any price; we were to leave – now!

Ten minutes remained until the curfew. Patrols covered the city. Mother ordered Jerzyk and me to go to Mr and Mrs Sroka, who lived nearby on Pêdzichow Street. She and Klara would manage somehow.

The Srokas did not disappoint us. Mrs Sroka, who opened the door, could not invite us into the apartment, because she had guests. But being a resourceful woman, she didn't need to think twice. She took us down to the basement, and after a while brought us sandwiches. We were grateful to her, but our false modesty prevented us from asking for a vessel that we could use in lieu of a toilet. The unheated basement was a large chamber where the Srokas grew mushrooms. We wondered if they needed watering, but decided not to take the chance. The pressure on our bladders was unbearable. Luckily, we found an empty bottle tossed in the corner, and it saved us … We lay down on some sacks of potatoes, huddled together, and made it through the night.

Early in the morning, Mr Sroka let us out of our hiding place. We went to Dluga Street, to check what had happened to mother. We were told that she and Klara had stayed with the R. family, but had left at dawn without saying where they were going. It turned out that mother had remembered a good customer of hers, Mrs Skawinska, who lived on Pilsudski Street. At the time, Mrs Skawinska was in Krynica, a resort town where she managed a small inn. SS officers occupied part of her apartment, but her maid Jozia, who knew mother well, agreed to put us up in the spare room for a few days. Fortunately, the Germans had gone home for the holidays.

That same day, the director of the Cracow Tax Office, Dr Grabowski, agreed to allow me to stay in his apartment until I left for Warsaw – despite the fact that part of his apartment had been commandeered by a Romanian *Volksdeutsch* acting as Superintendent of Schools. The Romanian, too, had gone home for Christmas. The Grabowskis, lovely people, put at my disposal one of the side rooms in their spacious apartment. I came back to life. I washed, caught up on my sleep, ate delicious meals that Mrs Grabowski brought to my room – and began again to translate Kästner's *Lyrical Pharmacy*, which by chance I found in Dr Grabowski's library … When the superintendent returned from his holidays and began to take interest in me, the situation became tense. I was forced to say farewell to this hospitable abode and return to Sroka's basement.

During that same time, my mother managed to place Klara with some other acquaintances of hers, the Rosiek family, at 31 Dluga Street. Here, too, Christmas paid off: the Germans who occupied half of the Rosieks' apartment had gone home to their families. Mr Rosiek, a stout man who managed the Agricultural Bank, was a devout, practicing Catholic. Mrs Rosiek was not as religious as her husband, but went to church every Sunday with her daughter Asia. Klara became friends with this girl, who was her age, and spent those three weeks (when the Germans were on vacation) in a family atmosphere. Her hosts were scared to death, but didn't let it show.

My mother wandered around town with her head wrapped in a peasant scarf, but anyone who knew her would have easily recognized her. And people did recognize her, but luck was on her side and she encountered no informers. Once, she ran into Mr Benisch, representative of the Giesche porcelain factory from Silesia. She was very happy, but he was less so ... It turned out he was a *Volksdeutsch*. Who knows – he might even have been a German agent on Polish soil before the war. 'Please go away. I don't ever want to see you again,' was his greeting to my mother. But in her wanderings around the city, Mrs Gross met friends she didn't know she had. Thus she ran into an office worker named Irena S., who 'passed her on' to her sister, Stasia Gawron. Mother moved into her kitchen – which became her strategic headquarters, the family command post. Here, mother laid her plans, and from here she made forays into the city to visit her various acquaintances, trying to find the best possible accommodations for us. We maneuvered as best as we could, and kept returning to the Srokas' basement on Pêdzichow when there was no alternative. From there – it was back to mother ...

*

We always went back to mother, through all the days of the occupation. To be more precise, during the time we lived on Aryan papers, when we were living among Poles, as Poles and Christians. Until then, we were never apart from her for even one day. Not in all our wanderings through the small towns, and not in the Cracow ghetto. Now, the four of us – mother, Klara, Jerzyk and I – had to live separately, each in a different place.

Living together would have been very risky. Besides, who would be willing to house four Jews in their apartment? Everybody in Cracow knew mother, and mother knew everybody in Cracow, so she managed to find each of us some sort of shelter. However, in those days of intensified hunting for Jews who had fled the ghetto, we were never able to stay in one place more than a week or two. Something always happened, and this would cause our hosts to panic. Then 'the apartment came to an end'. Where to now? Of course, to mother. One time this would happen to me, another time to Klara, and yet again to Jerzyk – around and around in a circle. No matter how hard we strove, connived, and racked our brains to find shelter, we kept coming back to mother's apron strings in her provisional apartment. We would go to her with heavy hearts: we knew that we were endangering both her and ourselves. If we did not find a new hiding place as soon as possible, we would all be caught and there would be no one left to save us.

At that time, my mother was living with Stasia Gawron, a small woman full of energy. A great patriot, Stasia was endowed with considerable nerve. She received mother with full honors and a hint of satisfaction that she, a petty bureaucrat, was sheltering that Mrs Gross whom everyone in Cracow knew. By inviting mother to live with her – albeit for a limited time, until she could find a permanent apartment – Stasia aimed to demonstrate her bravery. She had a subtenant: a German soldier Heinz Oltman was chauffeur to a rich Nazi industrialist from Berlin who, as *Treuhander,* managed Jewish factories that had been confiscated by the General Government. Oltman occupied one room, and Stasia lived in the other. My mother, as I said, took over a tiny corner in the kitchen. In a pinch, she could be excused as a village relative who had come for a visit – but it would be better if no questions were asked and no explanations were necessary.

Thus my mother had barely found a quiet warm corner, a temporary base for spinning strategic plans, when the very next day Klara visited her with bad news: Her place with the Rosieks was coming to an end. Stasia Gawron had a heart of gold and understood the situation. No problem! If there's room for the mother, there'll be room for the daughter. True, the folding cot was narrow, but the ironing board could be set up. And so one more subtenant settled into Stasia's kitchen.

Meanwhile, our basement hiding place at the Srokas' also 'began to come to an end'. The neighbors noticed the rustling noises from the basement: mice, or something else? Mr Sroka preferred that we clear out and not endanger him. But where to go? Obviously, to mother. All roads led to mother. We made a good impression on Stasia and she agreed to house us temporarily, together with mother and Klara, in the kitchen.

A long corridor led from Oltman's room directly to our kitchen. At the end of the corridor near the kitchen was the entrance to the apartment. Every time someone rang the bell or knocked on the door, we held our breath and our hearts pounded as we waited for Stasia to finish her business with the milkman or the electrician. Or perhaps the neighbor, going out to shop, stopped to exchange gossip. But Stasia showed no inclination to invite her neighbors in, and conversations took place at the open door. Oltman, a tall, handsome blond with a protruding Adam's apple, was discreet and never peeked into the kitchen. Nevertheless, our hearts pounded when we heard his heavy footsteps echoing in the hall. Especially nerve-racking was his habit of hesitating by the door for a moment or two – for us it seemed like an eternity! – checking his notes on the day's business and trying to remember anything he may have forgotten. We were afraid that at any moment he would open the kitchen door and ask for – who knows – maybe a glass of water? But he did not hear the beating of our hearts, and never opened the door.

The short winter days passed one after the other. Every day, mother went out with the peasant scarf wrapped around her head, in an effort to find a better, more permanent hiding place. She would return with promises and hope, but we were forced to be patient, because obtaining an apartment was no easy task. There was no choice, therefore, but to sit in Stasia's kitchen like mice under the broom, listening to Oltman's heavy steps every time he came or went. To tell the truth, Oltman was home relatively rarely. Usually, he spent three or four days a week driving his boss somewhere out of town, and on the days he worked in Cracow, he would come home late at night. When he was about to go away, he would notify Stasia of his return date, despite the fact that he had his own key. On the days when Oltman toured the cities of the General Government, Jerzyk and I slept in his bed. The kitchen was small, and the narrow cot – even with the addition of the ironing board and two chairs – was too small for four tormented souls. Oltman's soft bed seemed like paradise, and we waited impatiently for his departure.

One day, Oltman told Stasia that he was leaving for five days, perhaps even a whole week. We seized the opportunity. What a luxurious feeling! Frost and snow outside, a warm, soothingly quiet room – good night! Despite such joys, I could not fall asleep. The machine in my head would not stop running. Jerzyk slept the sleep of the innocent until morning. At midnight of the third night after Oltman's departure, immersed in my glum thoughts, I heard the scratch of a key looking for the lock in the dark. A moment later I heard the creak of the unoiled hinges, then the door softly closing. Not for a second did I doubt that it was Oltman, returning unexpectedly. Feeling devastated, I listened to his heavy slow steps coming nearer. In another minute he would enter the room, turn on the light, and – Jerzyk was sound asleep – then what? As a precaution, I hid my head under the feather pillow. Each second passed like eternity. I heard the snap of the light switch, and a second later a wail of complaint that seemed to issue from the depths of the grave: '*Gott im Himmel!* I haven't slept for 40 hours, and now this!' It was the voice of a broken man.

At the same moment, the door flew open and Stasia Gawron, in her striped pajamas, rushed in like a typhoon. She grabbed Oltman by the sleeve of his green uniform and began dragging him to her room. Before the German had a chance to come to his senses and understand what was going on, she had whipped her own bedding off her couch and laid Oltman's bedclothes in their place (we did not sleep on his sheets, of course). The whole time, she explained to the befuddled chauffeur in her limping German that her cousin had arrived unexpectedly from the village and would be gone in the morning. Blabbering on as the words came to her, she helped him out of his boots and laid him on the couch like an infant (weighing 90 kilograms) – still in his trousers. The mortally fatigued subtenant uttered not a word. He muttered something, which no one understood, and instantly closed his eyes. Stasia waited until he was sound asleep, then took her blanket and pillow and went to sleep in the kitchen, where my frightened mother and sister awaited her, convulsed in terror.

The next day, Oltman slumbered peacefully on Stasia's couch until noon, but Jerzyk and I sneaked to the kitchen at dawn. It was a bit unpleasant, but we joked and laughed with Stasia at how cleverly she had deceived the dense German. What else could we do?

We understood that this apartment, too, was coming to an end. Where could we go? Outside the window there was snow and a bitter frost ...

*

On her way to seek advice from Mr and Mrs Sroka one day,

mother ran into a teacher named Mrs Kapias on Szewska Street. Mrs Kapias had been one of our installment-plan china customers. She was unable to refuse to take in someone from the Gross family, at least for a short time, even though her housing situation was less than ideal. The choice fell on Jerzyk and me. Mother and Klara could stay with Stasia a little longer. We took a fiacre that evening to Borek Falêcki on the outskirts of Cracow, where Mrs Kapias lived with her sister and children. As a precaution, we got out of the carriage early and made our way to the house on foot. We climbed the stairs quietly, so as not to attract the neighbors' attention: no easy task, since Mrs Kapias lived on the second floor of a building whose very walls had ears. Our hostess welcomed us and prepared a special hiding place behind a partition made of cardboard boxes, which she had erected in the middle of a side room. I don't know where the boxes came from or what they were for, but clearly they were a natural fixture in the house, or else they would have attracted the attention of neighbors and visitors.

Jerzyk and I therefore sat behind the divider reading books. By chance, I found Limanowski's *History of the Socialist Movement*, or something with a similar title, lying in the corner. This provided a welcome chance to learn something about a field I had previously taken little interest in. It proved compelling. We were visited occasionally by Mrs Kapias's little daughters, Bozena and Dobrotka, who knew that our presence in the apartment was top secret. Even though they were little girls, four and six years old, they were highly disciplined and Mrs Kapias relied on their discretion. Children understood that there were many secrets in those days. Mrs Kapias was a Catholic imbued with deep faith. Her husband was detained as a prisoner, and only with difficulty did she make ends meet. However, she had plenty of energy and faith that the Germans would be defeated. She had contacts with the Polish underground: she brought us the freshest news from London radio each day.

Jerzyk and I were 'good customers'. We were not capricious, and we tried to sit as quietly as possible, all the more so because Mrs Kapias had an abundance of visitors: her daughters' friends, neighbors who came to borrow an iron, old friends with gossip to share, and perhaps clients (connected with those boxes?). I don't know if Mrs Kapias did in fact teach school in those days …

She could not have hosted other tenants like us, but she

recommended Klara to a family she knew who were looking for a nanny. However, she did not mention that Klara was Jewish.

Klara was thrilled. The Z. family was very nice. Although Klara had no experience working with children, she was sure she would somehow manage with the boy and the girl. And one would assume she would have managed if she had had the chance, but the very next day she was recognized by an electricity-company worker who had come to read the meter. 'What's Miss Gross doing here?' he blurted out to the surprised housewife.

And that was the end of that.

Klara returned to mother and Stasia. A few days later, Klara brought her boyfriend Szymon there for a 'transition period': He had fled from the camp on Jerozolimska Street. Unfortunately, his head, like the heads of the other prisoners there, was shaven, and he had to wait until his hair grew a bit before he could travel to Warsaw, where Uncle Szulim and Aunt Lana had already settled.

It was clear we would not be able to stay with Mrs Kapias for long. Mother therefore continued roaming the streets of Cracow, straining her memory: Who else could help us?

My next haven was the home of the Turek family. The Cracow painter Franciszek Turek, a student of Wyspianski, Stanislawski and Wyczolkowski, married Dr Maria Grünwald, daughter of a rich Jewish merchant from Krakowska Street in Kazimierz. While studying medicine at the university, Miriam met Franciszek and fell in love, a love so great that she converted and pledged her marriage vows in a Catholic church. Grünwald lived through this in great pain, and erased his daughter from the family. But my mother, who had gone to school with Marysia, did not break off their friendship, and would meet with the Tureks often. I knew them too, perhaps because I was interested in art, and always greeted the kindly painter, who still followed the style of the Art Nouveau period, when I met him in the Main Square.

Staying with the Tureks was not the safest idea in those days, because German law considered Maria to be a kosher Jew. They had been married for something like 20 years and few people may have been aware of Mrs Turek's shameful origins, but anyone sufficiently malicious or foolish could have brought disaster upon the entire family. True, this did not happen, perhaps because Franciszek and Maria were loved by all for their goodness and generosity. Still, the fear lurked in every corner of their home. I remember the hospitable sixteenth-century house at 9 St John Street as a Dickensian adventure, a place that could have been haunted. The sun's rays did not find their way into the dark courtyard, and the heavy curtains covering the windows absorbed the remnants of whatever light tried to intrude. Or was it only me, hiding in one of the dark rooms, who perceived the house this way? In this dimness, Maria seemed even larger than she really was, and Franciszek, with his goatee that suggested the turn-of-the-century Green Balloon Cabaret, even smaller. Children ran around the house: Mieszek, who was to become a priest, Leszek, who in time became an associate professor at the Mining Academy, and the oldest, the eternally busy Zosia. They were all so good and delicate towards me. And they were so terrified.

In the evenings, by the light of the carbide lamp, Franciszek Turek would show me his paintings of the alleys of Jewish Kazimierz, which were hidden in the attic, and would tell me about his beloved Cracow, the exclusive subject of his watercolors. Few Cracovians knew their city like Franciszek Turek did. Cracow was his life. Only as a student did he stray from the city and take a trip toward eastern Poland, in search of the folkloric motifs that were the subject of his academic work. He took an interest then in the wooden synagogues in towns like Wolpa, Sopockinie or Ostropol, and immortalized 20 of them in watercolors. In general, Jewish folklore fascinated him.

One day, while rummaging through Turek's secret storage space, I came across a book that the Aryan owner of the house had hidden, plainly fearing that it could cause trouble. This was Kramsztyk's *Talmud*, a slender volume full of quotations brimming with Jewish wisdom. I read it several times. Some of the parables and aphorisms dazzled me: 'A craftsman busy at his work may stay seated even in the presence of a king.' I was delighted. Work was enshrined on the highest pedestal. 'To find a friend, take a step up. To find a wife, take a step down.' I marveled at the wisdom of that advice. Later, I forgot it, and then when I remembered it again, it was too late …

The problem of 'two in the desert', which dealt with a question of life and death, gave me the most to think about. Two people lose their way in the desert. One has a water bag with enough water for only one person. If he shares it with his friend, they will both die of thirst. If he drinks it alone, his friend will die, but the survivor

188

will always be tormented by the memory of his friend's slow death. What is one to do in this situation? One of the wise men believed that saving one's own life was the supreme duty. But another wise man had a different opinion. For the entire war, this problem stayed with me. I encountered it on a practical level every day. My own opinion was that the water had to be shared. And so I shared it, and survived.

I was also surprised to find in that book a phrase that threw a new light on my work as a translator. 'Whoever translates a verse literally is a fraud!' No, of course, this was not about translating poetry – it was about the heartless enforcing of the letter of the law, without taking account of logic or circumstances. But how splendidly that thought could be applied in practice, where too close a translation can kill the sense and the character of the original.

Thus I sat in the home of the Turek family. I don't recall where Jerzyk was at the time. Mother had found a new address. Professor Cholewinski of the Mining Academy had been sent to Auschwitz, and his wife, a wise, good-hearted woman, decided to put mother and Klara up until they managed to arrange an apartment for themselves in Warsaw. For Warsaw was our goal.

The war showed no intention of ending, despite our optimism and the fervent prayers of the believers. The miracle did not want to happen – miracles must be helped along. We kept shifting from one apartment to another: a few days with the Srokas, then back to Stasia's, to Mrs Kapias, and then to the Rosieks' or to Gumplowicz's housekeeper, Karolcia. We bounced around for four months. I counted 14 different apartments that we stayed in, in a city where any child, without the least ill will, could have betrayed us into the hands of our tormenters and put at risk the good people who stretched out a hand to help us.

The last place in Cracow where Jerzyk and I stayed was back at Mrs Kapias's. Although we tried to maintain all possible caution, a policeman who lived in her building – an exceptionally repulsive character – found out about us somehow and let Mrs Kapias know about it. He was a villain who lurked on the roads, robbing poor people. He brought two down comforters home one day. His wife hung them in the courtyard to air out. Four-year-old Bozenka and five-year-old Dobrotka were playing there, and they smeared the comforters with sticks that they had previously sunk into the manure pile. They befouled the bedding deliberately and at length. When the policeman's wife saw the result, she flew into a rage and directed a merciless tirade at Mrs Kapias. Our landlady burst out crying and rebuked the terrified children: 'How could you? How could you do this? I'm surprised at you. Both of you are old enough to know better!'

'But we thought the comforters belonged to those *Volksdeutsche* women on the third floor,' the girls answered.

After that, we could no longer stay in Borek Fałęcki.

9. The Extortion Game

Aunt Lana had been in Warsaw for a long time with Uncle Szulim and their daughter. We sent Szymek to join them at the beginning of March, and warned them continuously by letter to prepare a place for us to live, because we, too, were finally going to have to travel to Warsaw. Answers came seldom and inspired no great hopes.

On Sunday, 1 April 1943 – April Fool's Day – we said farewell in the morning to the hospitable Mrs Kapias. We finally intended to travel to the capital. First, we went to mother on Pedzichow to obtain her blessing and some money, but it turned out that she had no money. There was no point in returning to Borek. I ran to Mr Sroka, and he loaned me 500 *zloty*. Mother could only say: 'Go in the name of God'.

Mrs Cholewinska escorted us to the station and purchased our tickets. Our only possessions were that wartime banknote with the depiction of a mountaineer on it and the two addresses of our aunt on Bagatela Street and Mrs Sroka's relatives on Sykstuska Street. We did not, however, want to count on the help of our relatives. We had decided to make a go of it ourselves. People did not enjoy visits in these conditions. Neither Poles nor Jews. There were occasions when a visit from a Jew induced an attack of hysteria.

The train was like all trains: we quickly made the acquaintance of our fellow passengers. You helped put people's baggage up on the rack, addressed them in friendly tones, played with the children … Jerzyk entertained the travellers by playing the harmonica, while I engaged a young priest in a learned discussion of theological, political and secular issues. The priest maintained that the handshake, as a greeting, was devised and used as a secret signal by the first Christians, while I averred that the custom must date back to time immemorial, when people held out their hands to those they met, demonstrating their good intentions by showing that they were not holding a knife.

Not far from Radom, the whole compartment full of people began praying and exhibiting signs of great anxiety. It was a known fact that trains to Warsaw were sometimes emptied at

Radom, and the passengers sent to Majdanek or, in the best of cases, to forced labor in Prussia. Now, however, there was only a superficial search and checking of documents. I used my false identity card for the first time. Nothing happened, although we had a good deal of fear to contend with.

When we had left Radom behind, we made the acquaintance of three sisters, rather young black marketeers, one of whom was travelling with a year-and-a-half-old child in her arms 'for protection'. What kind of speculator was this? She was a poor woman whose husband spent most of his time avoiding the *Arbeitsamt*, while she traveled twice a week from Warsaw to the town of Tunel and back in order – at the risk of her freedom, merchandise and borrowed money – to fetch a bit of flour or a few potatoes to sell. In this way, she supported herself, her husband, and her child. The poor, innocent child had to bear the discomforts of the journey in order to serve as his mother's (not necessarily effective) shield against the Germans.

We consulted our fellow passengers about Sykstuska Street where, we told them, our aunt lived. They had all heard of the street, but none of them knew where it was. Could we find a street in Warsaw when we had only an hour's time (the train arrived at 6:30, or closer to 7:00, and 8:00 was the curfew)? We decided to spend the night in a hotel instead, and began inquiring about lodgings. We were warned against doing so, for various reasons. One of the three women invited us to her place for the night.

I can say with a clear conscience that I met no finer people in Warsaw, and few anywhere who were equally decent. The sisters were married. Two of the husbands were there, and the third, Genia Bloch's husband, was in Prussia. Genia lived with her son and her elderly mother. She must have been the oldest sister. The second oldest, Mrs Pietras, had a son and a daughter aged between eight and ten. We stayed with the third sister, Mrs Walerka, who had the year-and-a-half-old daughter. I have not named the women first in order to depreciate their husbands. Far from it – they were fine men. In working-class families during the war, however, it was generally the women who were the head of the household. And so we stayed in Kolo, on the outskirts of Warsaw. Our hosts occupied one small room, and they let us have a couch. We talked a lot about politics the first night. Jerzyk played splendidly on the harmonica. We made a good impression.

The next day, we said goodbye to our hosts and indicated that we would take advantage of their invitation should the need arise. We also gave them to understand that we would be very pleased to rent an apartment in Kolo. We set off for Bagatela Street and the address that our aunt had sent us. But it turned out that she did not live there. The terrified occupants knew no such person. They had never heard the name before in their lives! A fine fix we would have been in if we had counted on our relatives and gone to Bagatela Street the previous evening. However, we did not give up easily – after all, we had mailed letters to that address and received replies! In the end, after we pleaded, they sent us to the laundry on Nowogrodzka Street where the owner of the apartment, Mrs S., worked. At first, she too was unwilling to say anything. Finally, after much hesitation, she stated that our aunt had not lived there for a long time, but only stopped by occasionally to pick up her letters. We were furious. What were we to do? We wrote a letter informing our aunt that we were in Warsaw and would like to have her address. We announced that we would come to Bagatela Street each day – so could someone please meet us there? We also went to Red Cross Street, where an acquaintance of mine supposedly lived, but it turned out that he, too, only stopped by occasionally to get his mail. And furthermore, he had not been seen at all for a long time.

Time passed quickly. In the evening, we found ourselves on Zlota Street. We asked everywhere about Sykstuska Street. Everyone, of course, had heard of such a street, but no one knew exactly where it was. Wasn't it in Zoliborz? It was too late to go there. We began looking for a tram stop and asking people how to get to Kolo.

We were feeling fine in this strange city where no one knew us. But we were unaware of the danger hanging over us. That very evening, we received a lesson in caution.

We finally found the right tram stop and were waiting there when I suddenly felt a heavy hand on my shoulder. I looked slowly around. Behind us stood two men. One was short and stout, with bushy brows above his dark, penetrating eyes. The other was blond and tall.

'Please allow us.' We said nothing and permitted them to lead us into a dark doorway. It was a partially destroyed building where no one was living. Our first slip-up – a terrible feeling. No one in Cracow would even know how we had died! Oh God, Oh God, what could we do? A dog's life. Too bad. We went upstairs.

'You're Jews!'

'Us? What do you mean?'

They took our identity cards. One read them out in a halting undertone. The other took out a pair of handcuffs and attempted to slip them on my wrists, but I squirmed and maintained a half-joking, sarcastic tone throughout the conversation. The extortionists checked our Jewishness and all doubts were eliminated.

'So what now?' the fat one asked.

'Nothing,' I said. 'You gentlemen let us go and that's the end of it.'

The fat one sent the thin one to get a fiacre. 'We're going to the police station.'

I grabbed his arm to stop him. 'Cut out the stupid jokes! Just let us go. You can see we haven't got anything. We arrived in Warsaw today and this is the greeting we get.'

They searched our pockets and found the 500 *zloty*. 'Have you got any gold?'

We had nothing else except our good fortune. Our extortionists asked us what we intended to do in Warsaw and then decided to let us go. 'But don't hang around town too much, because if we catch you a second time, you won't get away so cheap. OK. Go already. Go.'

'Just a minute,' I said. I don't know how I summoned up so much nerve. 'Do you intend to leave us completely broke? We haven't even got a *grosz* for the tram!'

They looked at each other and – this is incredible! – left us 200 *zloty*. A hundred a head … Never again did I come across such magnanimous extortionists. They went on to give us advice on how to act on the street. They told us we should comb our hair differently and grow mustaches – and then they left.

That first lesson had come relatively cheap.

Unable to find Sykstuska Street (it later turned out that there was no such street in Warsaw, only in Lwow), we had to stay in Kolo, this time at Genia Bloch's.

*

The situation was unbearable. We had spent ten days in Warsaw, without a *grosz* to our name, without the address of any relatives

194

or acquaintances, unable to obtain even temporary residence permits in the city housing bureau. The good people who were looking after us had nothing against our staying longer and eating their bread. I tried to pay for the corner that they let us use in their small apartment by giving lessons to their children, and hoped that I would be able to repay our debts in full once we had money. But no money came to us. The 200 *zloty* that the extortionists left us gradually melted away on our trips downtown by tram in search of our relatives and acquaintances. They had come to Warsaw before us and had managed to set themselves up as Christians, among Christians. Aside from the address of Aunt Lana, alias Dobrecka, we had several others. For instance, there was our uncle, 'Zygmunt Durakowski'. There were our friends, 'Janek Sarnecki' and 'Kazimierz Kurek'. It turned out, however, that they did not live at the addresses they had given us. People did not know them, or did not want to betray the whereabouts of a Jew whom they allowed to use their address for correspondence. We had no choice but to write one apparently mundane letter after another, informing them that we had arrived and were waiting for news, for contact. Waiting.

The days flew past, and no answer came. Our hosts grew slightly concerned that we had still not registered as subtenants. This was of little importance to them, for they were only tenants themselves, but the owners of the building, the Wisniewski brothers – both of whom had carrot-red hair – began getting curious about us. We promised to arrange things in the next few days; we were simply waiting for our old residence permit slips to arrive from Cracow. We needed these to register in Warsaw. The slips that we needed did not arrive (because no one ever sent them), and the tension grew. On the surface, nothing was wrong – we exchanged smiles, jokes and news from the front. Yet the red-headed brothers could see what the situation was. They were prepared to arrange our registration for a mere 1000 *zloty*. That was hardly an excessive sum. We would have agreed willingly, but where could we get 1,000 *zloty*? If only we could find Uncle Zygmunt, or some other relative, or even an acquaintance … We pretended not to be interested in the offer, since in any case we would be receiving the needed papers any day now …

Time was passing, and our depression was growing.

We went to the family of a certain socialist member of

parliament whose address had been given to us by Edzio Birn, a dear friend of mine who now went by the name of Kazimierz Kurek. We knew that he was living in Warsaw with his mother, and expected to find him at the member's apartment. As in the previous cases, this turned out to be only a 'correspondence point'. Without any great hopes, therefore, we left a letter for him. He would certainly get the letter, but would there be a reply? And if there were, would we still be at our present address? We felt the ground shifting under our feet.

The combination of despair and indignation produced a straightforward idea: Why not find the address of the person we were looking for in the city housing bureau? We did not decide immediately to do so, because hanging around offices was dangerous. We knew that agents and extortionists waited in public places for customers like us. We decided, nevertheless, to take the chance. There must have been 64 citizens named Kazimierz Kurek in the registry book. From among them, we chose 16 who were more or less the same age as Edek. One way or another, we had nothing better to do. We would go from house to house until we found him ... But which Kurek should we call on first? We wrote all the addresses down on separate pieces of paper, threw them into a hat, and drew a winner.

What happened next was incredible.

When we went to the first address that we had drawn from the hat, the door was opened by none other than Mrs Birn. We knew her well, and she knew us. She went white as canvas. If she had been able, she would have slammed the door in our faces, but it was too late. We had slipped inside without waiting for an invitation. Only when she had locked the door and drawn the chain did the expected question come: 'Who gave you the address?'

Her tone left no doubt as to how infuriated she was with that informant. I could do nothing but tell her how we had managed to find the address of Kazimierz Kurek. Edzio's mother had an attack of hysteria. 'Oh my God, my God, we're done for! How dare you? The Gestapo will be here any minute. You should be ashamed of yourselves. Nobody does such things! Lord, what will become of us? What can we do now, what can we do?'

Poor Edek emerged from the other room. He did not know whether to rejoice at seeing us alive and well in Warsaw, or to calm his mother down. We tried to convince her that there was nothing to fear. 'We saw dozens of people looking for addresses at City Hall. Besides, are they going to hunt down all 64 Kazimierz Kureks? Why?'

Nothing we said could calm Mrs Birn. She would have to find a new apartment immediately. This one was 'blown', thanks to us!

We felt very bad. Given the circumstances, we did not even mention our own difficult predicament or the fact that we had intended to ask for a loan. That would only have made her more upset. We simply left our address and promised never to come back, even though Edek begged us to ignore his mother's hysteria and to visit him whenever we could. With exaggerated caution, we left the apartment separately and returned to our neighborhood.

'Anything from Cracow?' we asked our hospitable landlady.

No letter had come. Instead, one of the Wisniewski brothers had come to see Genia and had questioned her in detail about us. He told her that we would have to leave if we had not registered within two days, because no one ever knew how such matters could turn out.

The situation looked hopeless. We started wondering whether it might not be better to return to Cracow, even though we had left such a step as the last resort, if all else failed. We had run out of addresses; that is, we had left letters everywhere we could, and we were waiting for an answer. Someone should act. But no one answered. Our misadventure with Mrs Kurek-Birn had dampened our eagerness to return to the municipal offices and look for such a common name as Dobrecka. We did not feel that we could go on much longer without money and without residence papers. It was easy to envisage how this game of cat-and-mouse would end. Yet where could we go?

The next day was Sunday. A quiet, peaceful day. We decided that Monday would be decisive. I would go downtown in the morning to check whether there was any news from Aunt Dobrecka or Uncle Zygmunt, and if not …

Monday morning was gray, with drizzle falling from a sky full of clouds. I left home with no great enthusiasm. My thin raincoat offered little protection, especially when gusts of wind blew at it. The Kolo tram station was marked by a post standing in an open field, exposed on all sides. People stamped their feet and rubbed their hands together, trying to warm themselves up, as they waited in small groups. I was standing off to the side, some distance from the others, wrapped in my gloomy thoughts, when I suddenly felt a hand on my shoulder. 'Oy, young man, young man, why so sad?'

I turned my head. Behind me stood an old railroad man in work clothes. He was smiling from beneath his mustache.

'What have I got to be happy about?' I replied. 'These are hard times. We've all got worries and troubles …'

'Keep your head up, young man! You've got to have hope! Things will turn out alright – you'll see.'

'Who knows what will happen before they turn out alright?'

'Oy, young man, young man, don't give in! Were you in church yesterday? Remember yesterday's Gospel?' Without waiting for me to answer, he went on, 'St Peter was sitting in the boat on Genazareth Lake fishing, and suddenly the Lord Jesus appeared before him, walking on the waves just like I walk along the tracks here. Peter couldn't believe his eyes. The Lord Jesus stopped a few meters from the boat and said, "Come to me".' Peter looked to the left and the right – water all around. And the Lord Jesus said, "Come to me!" Peter stood up, and when he heard the call for the third time, he stepped from the boat right into the waves. And as soon as he stepped out, a great wind arose, Peter hesitated, and he began to sink. He thought his time had come. And then the Lord reached out his hand and pulled him up, saying …'

I knew that story from the New Testament, so I finished the railroad man's sentence for him: '… "Oh ye of little faith, why have ye doubted?"'

At that moment, the tram rattled up and stopped right in front of me with a terrible screech. I jumped on ahead of everyone else. Then the others got on. I looked around for the old railroad man, but could not see him. A good feeling came over me. My inborn optimism and hopeful spirit, which had seen me through more than one difficulty and obstacle in these hard times, returned. I repeated silently, 'Oh ye of little faith, why have ye doubted?'

I jumped off the tram and looked both ways, trying to decide which way to go. And there, right before my eyes, was my dear friend, holding out his hand. This was unbelievable. Szymek – now Janek Sarnecki – whom I had been looking for over the last ten days!

At certain points in my life, there have been proverbs, fables or anecdotes that have cast a bright light on the road ahead. The heavens have opened before me like a window on eternity.

198

The story of the miracle on the waters of Genazareth (Lake Kineret in the land of Israel) so distant and yet so close to my heart, was one such signpost. More than once or twice since then, in the hard times that I have not been spared, I have repeated in the depths of my heart, 'Oh ye of little faith, why have you doubted?'

The figure of Jesus had begun to interest me long before the war. It was not so much the Gospels that attracted me as the literary Talmud that had grown up around them. I read Renan, Ludwig, Merezkowski and Mauriac. I was fascinated by the figure of the great Teacher who had not been understood by his contemporaries or their descendants. I had always wondered why the great teachers of humanity like Buddha, Socrates and Christ had left no written words behind, wielding instead the spoken word that never died. Perhaps they did not write out of a fear that their writings would be misunderstood, that deceivers would translate them to suit their interests? They sowed the seed of faith and love directly into the soil, into the hearts and minds of their pupils, and they knew how that seed would sprout fervent love, a love that would endure over the centuries.

Could that word come again into my heart by means of papers, magazines and books? It takes more than flint and tinder to make fire; there must also be a person who strikes the spark, who starts the fire. A teacher who has been blessed with grace. I had such a teacher: Juliusz Feldhorn, a writer and a poet. With that same power of love that he had absorbed from his own teachers, he inspired love in me, opened the door, endowed the written word with the magic of the spoken word ...

When I was thinking so much about Christ, about the Teacher, I never dreamed that the ideas and knowledge I had gained that way would soon prove useful in the battle for my life, or that the magic of the word that had fascinated me would become a source of living waters, from which I would draw faith and strength during the war – the faith in man. I had been prepared in a very important way. I took that faith into the war. Many lost that faith when they looked into the eye of the Age of the Furnaces. Not I. Perhaps this was because my wartime experiences did not involve physical suffering that could have broken even me, but instead required me to stand up to prejudice, blind hatred, stupidity and naïvety. I do not know. But the faith that had been inculcated in me by a humanistic education was sufficient throughout the course of that struggle.

*

We moved in with Janek out of necessity.

Aware that we could not hold out for more than a few days in our lodgings in Kolo, we decided to visit Janek – even though we knew that doing so might expose him to unpleasantness.

Janek told us a little bit about his landlady. I was cheered at the news that she was relatively young and had an artistic soul: she painted and sang. Unfortunately, Janek has no judgement when it comes to people. I learned then that if he says this or that about someone, then it is safe to assume that the opposite is true. Janek was a good, well-liked, honest boy, but his strong point was uncommon handsomeness, which had an effect on women. Marysia introduced herself to me as 'the widow of my fortunate late husband'. She was a tall, sloppy, long-necked person with a horsey face and horsey teeth. She spoke in the outmoded urban jargon of Warsaw, and enlivened our first visit with the Schubert song *Der Lindenbaum*, in an acceptable Polish translation. Marysia, of course, did not know who the composer was. When she began by thundering, 'Over the spri-i-i-ing the landen grows, and under the landen's pleasant shade', I feared I would burst out laughing. I recited several Romantic lyrics as recompense for the song, and these were such a hit with the landlady that she would not let us leave; Jerzyk and I stayed for dinner. It was an extremely modest dinner; Marysia was not prospering, and Janek was nearly broke. I skillfully brought up the fact that we needed a place to live.

Dear children, God forbid that you ever find yourselves without a roof over your head. Should this occur, however, remember that there is not a woman in Poland who will not find an apartment for anyone to whom she has taken even the slightest liking. Marysia found one. She sent us to a relative of hers in the Praga district.

You who survived the war on Aryan papers know the routine for renting an apartment. You know how necessary it is to avoid the mere hint of urgency, even if you are in danger of being thrown on to the street that day or the next. You know the suspicious glances, the probing questions, the demand for references. We had no references. Marysia, with whom we had spoken once, was our sole reference. We had no money and no *Arbeitskart*, and we were rather shabbily dressed.

'Where do you gentlemen work?'

'At Beer's tire factory on Bracka Street. Except we haven't started yet; he's just hired us. You see, sir, Mr Beer has just left on a business trip, and asked us to wait for a week ... You know how things are ...'

We finally struck a deal. We were to come back the next day at six in the evening. We breathed a sigh of relief. In our situation, an apartment was the most important thing of all. Many of our acquaintances had developed an apartment neurosis. Such a neurotic receives no visitors, let alone anyone who might want to stay for the night. A decent person turns into a swine. Those who have been without an apartment understand this perfectly.

And yet we had an apartment. Or so we thought. Carrying a small suitcase, I met Jerzyk at six in the evening on Kawêczynska Street, at the door of (so we thought) our new landlord. Yet he behaved as if he had no idea what we were talking about. He finally declared that his cousin was coming to Warsaw and he was unable to rent us the room.

'But please let us stay for at least this one night, because we'll never make it back to Kolo before the curfew!'

He was not moved. We wasted more time on vain recriminations and supplication. We finally went away. To Janek's. For one night. No more. At the most, two nights. And as usually happens in such cases – we stayed.

We spent our days running to the housing office for addresses, and then we wandered various districts and streets in the foreknowledge that we would find nothing. And in the meantime, we stayed on at Janek's.

Janek occupied the room belonging to Zofia, who travelled to Warsaw three times a month, did her shopping, and returned to her village. During those two or three nights a month, we were supposed to sleep in Marysia's room, and the rest of the time in Janek's room. And, of course, it was all kept secret from Zosia.

Few people have ever heard of Ciasna Street, a dead-end off Swiêtojerska. When fate drove us there, that little street, which had once been part of the Jewish district, had not yet been taken over by new residents. A few people sheltered in number five, the last property at the end of the street. Through a hole in the fence, you entered a long courtyard leading to the ruins of a bombed-out house. On each side of the courtyard was a two-story tenement. We lived on the ground floor of one of these, across the way from the doorkeepers. Initially, Janek attempted to use the curtains to conceal this fact from the doorkeeper. Just as Lessing said that Raphael 'would have been the greatest of painters even if he had had no hands', so it could be said of our doorkeeper that, even if he had been deaf and blind, he would still have sensed the presence of a villager.[1] Deciding on a change in tactics, I risked trying to strike up a friendship with the doorkeeper. I succeeded splendidly. We made new friends in Mr Kowalski and his wife – especially once they learned the truth about us.

When we first went to visit Janek, Kowalski watched us suspiciously and trotted after us to eavesdrop on our conversations. Once we moved in, I got to know him better. He was a very decent man who, despite appearances, had no ill intentions toward us. As we eventually discovered, he was concealing and feeding 11 villagers, just like us, in his basement. Unfortunately, they became the victims to their own recklessness and impatience. They fell for the Hotel Polski trap, a sham opportunity to emigrate to America, staged by the Gestapo.

Kowalski was a simple man. A soothsayer had foretold that he would not live out the war, which troubled him deeply. I was an eyewitness when a woman learned in the Kabala predicted just the opposite. This, however, failed to console him. 'For five *zloty*, she could hardly tell me anything different,' he confided. 'That other one took 100. I understand how things are. He wanted to show me my dearly departed father in a dark room, but I ran away. So you explain to me, Franek, how could she ever tell me the truth for five stupid *zloty*?'

When he got to know us better, his misgivings evaporated. I knew the Gospels better than any of the neighbors and could toss off quotations at will. That covered my traces. Jerzyk had what they called 'very good looks', and Janek's weren't bad. The worst thing was that we were unemployed.

We cooked for ourselves. Those dinners were interesting! But they tasted good, as did the rationed bread and coffee – sometimes with saccharine – that we had for breakfast. We received a little money from the relatives we located, but we had no idea how we would be able to pay for our residence permits. Our landlady began to pressure us lightly, and the doorkeeper made it clear, although he was not insistent, that we should take care of this matter. We played for time and won. An acquaintance loaned us 1,000 *zloty* on our word of honor. We obtained the necessary permits and registered ourselves.

We slowly got to know all our neighbors. There was Helenka (strangely enough, she, too, had horsey teeth), a good woman on the second floor who occasionally received visits from her two brothers. There was Mrs Sanecka; I shall tell her story separately, but it bears stating that she looked as Jewish as it is possible to look. There was another similar poor woman who sold matches on the street corner. There was Maniek, a bullish young man who was excellent at dancing the polka. There was Piotr, a *Volksdeutsch* who worked for the Todt Organization – and there was Leonard Winiarek, a hairdresser.

Edward was Marysia's first cousin. Her affectionate nicknames for him included Dasi, Edas, and Edziula. Both of their parents looked askance on their love and forbade them to marry. I gained the impression that Edas was not terribly eager to become a husband; intimate relations with his cousin, even without benefit of clergy, were sufficient for him …

I had always wondered what two people talk about when neither of them has anything to say. I had assumed that such people find it impossible to be together. Looking at Edas and Marysia, I understood that nature, in her bounty, offered the two lovebirds a range of absorbing diversions, among which jealousy was the sweetest, followed by arguing on even the silliest pretext and trading insults, and ending with smashing something, at the very least a mirror. Then came discussions of acquaintances, fashion, hygiene and love. Such variety in courtship is very pleasant. Discomforts seem trivial when compared to the miraculous moment of apology. Petty quarrels and abuse are charming episodes, and jealousy is a sign of deep, authentic love. The disappearance of jealousy means: 'You don't love me any more.'

Edas was a specialist at spicing up their romance. We sometimes listened to epic quarrels through the wall. In company, Edas made only quiet scenes. Very quiet. Silence was of the essence. He would come in, sit down, and remain as silent as the grave. At first no one paid any attention, and our landlady went on having a grand time. At a certain moment, however, her sensitive heart warned her that all was not right. 'Why don't you say something?'

Edas sat in silence.

'Come on, speak up!'

Edas sat in silence.

'Have something to eat.'

From Edas – nothing.

This would begin to get on Marysia's nerves, and she would use stronger and stronger language. Edas sat in silence. More and more upset, Marysia would begin to cry, to curse him in the hope that he would respond and tell her what was the matter. The atmosphere in the room would grow unpleasant. Finally, Edas would get up and walk slowly outside. Marysia followed. After some time, they would return reconciled.

Edas also knew more effective methods. A party goes on late into the night. The phonograph rasps away – the records were too ancient for the words to be comprehensible. At a certain moment, someone notices that Edas is gone. Nothing to worry about. He must have stepped outside for a moment. The moment turns into an hour. Marysia becomes upset. She starts searching all the corners of the room. There is no point searching a room furnished with only a bed, a sofa, a table and four chairs. Marysia runs to the outhouse with an oil lamp.

'He must have drowned. What misfortunes I have with that boy!'

The outdoor toilet, however, displays no marks of tragedy. That outhouse would drive the thought of suicide out of the mind of the worst pessimist, just as the greatest optimist would despair of using it for its intended purpose. They search the whole building and the courtyard, waking up the neighbors. It is almost one in the morning. Finally, Edas returns. He wanted to go home (for he lives elsewhere), but has decided to offer 'one last' proof of his good will … This is hardly the only time that Edas has disappeared. The incident was repeated three times during our brief stay on Ciasna Street. It always ended emotionally, with hugs, apologies, 'never again', etc.

Once, the apologies were so tender ('you sweet scoundrel, you angelic stallion') that Marysia outdid herself. 'Bite me, Edas, bite me!'

There was silence … and then, a moment later, an inhuman scream. Edas had nearly bitten Marysia's lip off. The blood streamed out. Now the sweet scoundrel had turned into a rotten old scoundrel, and the angelic stallion into a horse's ass. If only I had the talent to describe such scenes. Zegadlowicz, rise from your grave! But 'love forgives everything' and the night heals all wounds. Everything was fine the next day and the loving couple again delighted the residents of 5 Ciasna Street with duets of *The Lindenbaum* and *A Sleighride for Two*. Edas had a voice that was quite pretty, but small.

After we moved in, Marysia began receiving visits from Piotr Slowik, a *Volksdeutsch* who was on medical leave. His father, old Slowik, had been in the business of producing children. He taught them to play the xylophone as soon as they were old enough. In order to create the desired comic effect, a child xylophonist should be no older than seven. Pops Slowik therefore tried to time his production in such a way that a replacement was ready and trained by the time each performer was seven or eight. When we met him, the old man was 60. His thirteenth child, Krysta, was the same age as one of his grandchildren. Before the war, Slowik had traveled around Poland with his family, accompanying the xylophonist on clarinet in second-rate cabarets and cinema-revues. Under the Germans – having become a *Volksdeutsch* – he accompanied Krysta in German canteens.

And his son Piotr worked in the Todt Organization (German work battalions). His wife was a Polish woman he had met while working in Germany. In his day, he too had played the xylophone in many a movie house and cabaret, and he thus knew lots of films. That was the only subject on which I could ever talk to him – and he regarded himself as an educated man of social graces. When he was going on and on one day about his knowledge of films, I asked him if he had ever seen *Rembrandt*.

'What was the title? Ah, yes, I remember. *Robert and Bertrand*. Of course I've seen it.'

I knew Mrs Sanecka's story partly from her own accounts, and partly from those of the doorkeeper and the tenants. As I mentioned earlier, Mrs Sanecka's appearance was such as to leave no doubts about her origins in the mind of any person of ill will. She was thus subject to constant extortion. She had been one of the first tenants on Ciasna Street. Back then, she had a job at Wedel's or some other candy factory. She worked all day along with a female friend who lived with her, and who walked home with her in the evenings.

This did not prevent her from drawing the attention of two tram drivers who also lived here. Warsaw tram drivers showed great patriotism, devotion to the resistance movement, and loyalty to Jews who were in hiding. These two, however, were exceptional knaves. They entered Sanecka's apartment one evening and demanded a large sum of cash. They also blackmailed Sanecka's friend, who had nothing to do with Judaism. The women refused to be intimidated. As a result, the abject tram drivers went to the police. Mrs Sanecka and her friend were jailed, but so were the two bloodsuckers, since Sanecka accused them of extortion. They spent more than half a year in the slammer and supposedly received a good beating (probably because they had tried to go into business on their own, without splitting the profits with the professional extortionists). After release, the two tram drivers moved out of Ciasna Street; they could not bear the contempt with which the other tenants treated them. Mrs Sanecka's friend was set free after a few days, but Sanecka spent several weeks behind bars. Her freedom was won in large part thanks to the doorkeeper Mrs Kowalska, who attested to Sanecka's Aryan status and claimed to have known her before the war. By the time Sanecka returned home, she had lost her job. She lived in poverty until she met her sad end (like many others, she fell for the Hotel Polski ruse). By the time we moved to Ciasna Street, the tram drivers were long gone. Mrs Sanecka, however, was a regular guest at Marysia's.

Life on Ciasna Street did not lack for variety. There was always a party, someone's birthday, and from time to time a quarrel like something out of Wiech. Every celebration was a gala affair, although horse meat was often served. The phonograph played old waltzes, Jerzyk tweedled along on the harmonica, and I sang Jurandot songs – and we had fun! At least it looked that way. In fact, we disliked these parties. They exposed us to the gaze of strangers, and provided an occasion for speculation and curiosity. We had a choice between shunning popularity, or being very popular. I chose the second option, knowing that once we had won the hearts of these simple folk, we would not be betrayed even if the truth about our origins came out. Besides, good humor is always appreciated. I believed that we could only be harmed by someone who had a grudge against us, or by a stranger. I therefore tried to act natural and to treat these people as equals.

We went outside for fresh air on the beautiful May evenings. As we sat on chairs in the courtyard, I pointed out to my neighbors how some stars were red, others yellow, and still others blue. They observed this phenomenon, which they had never noticed before, with wonder and delight. I went on to tell them about the distances between the planets, and about Mars and the moon. They listened intently. Nevertheless, one of these astronomical evenings concluded with a question that was posed to me in all seriousness: 'Is it true that Mr Twardowski is on the moon?' This led to a discussion of Twardowski, folk beliefs in spirits, and so on. On another occasion, I told them about ancient Greece and Rome – in a fragmentary way, of course, and on a popularized level. I won respect for myself and for my knowledge. I understood that simple people are hungry for knowledge and beauty, but only feel this hunger once someone has opened their eyes for them. And the only kind of person who can do this is the kind who will not burst out laughing when asked about Twardowski on the moon. Laughter would be offensive and off-putting. So I told them things in an honest, serious way.

We could never feel at ease, despite the general affection we enjoyed. Above all, we feared that our landlady would quarrel with her neighbors. In fact, we feared all quarrels. When there's an argument, you have to take sides. If you support X, then you make an enemy of Y, and vice-versa. We tried to avoid expressing judgements, but what could we do if our landlady was one of the parties in a quarrel?

Mr Leonard Winiarek began calling on Marysia in regard to her new sub-tenants. That is, in regard to us. He wanted to check, just to make sure. I cannot recall a single occasion when he was sober. By trade a hairdresser, he was half-Polish and half-Italian. His mama, Mrs Crucinelli, had a macaroni factory. I jokingly referred to him as Leonardo de Winiarek; he described himself as 'an intelligent sort of s.o.b.' He was indeed an intelligent cheat, borrower, practical joker, and a generally dark character (matched by his black shirts and black, crinkly hair). The 'intelligent s.o.b.' earned a good living, but never brought any money home – he stopped along the way to drink with pals of a similar disposition. His wife and child literally went hungry, and there were occasions when Mrs Winiarek had to ask her neighbors for a few potatoes. Marysia was too tender-hearted to refrain from commenting aloud on this. Little did she think, of course, that we could be the ones who suffered because of her remarks. Mr Winiarek began by delicately hinting that he knew who was bad-mouthing him. Then he threatened that his enemies would end up where the stiffs are, but he remained obsequious and polite towards Marysia: 'I bow as low as your mother's shoes.'

The showdown came after Winiarek's skirmish with Mr Kowalski the doorkeeper, who maintained friendly relations with Marysia.

Leonard returned from downtown at about ten o'clock that evening, and he was feeling no pain. Even after the eight o'clock curfew, policeman and Germans crossed to the other side of the street at the sight of a drunk. Kowalski went to unlock the front gate, and received a *zloty* for his trouble from the teetering hairdresser. 'There you are, Mr Kowalski, and don't you ever forget that you're dealing with a respectable man.' Instead of going to his apartment, he waited until Kowalski had locked up again. 'I really am respectable, isn't that right?' he asked, revelling in his own generosity. 'Admit it. Nobody else tips you like me.'

Kowalski had not been a doorkeeper before the war. He lost his temper. 'A dog wouldn't lick your face! Take your *zloty* and go to hell!' Saying this, he flung the coin at Leonardo and turned away to go back to bed.

Leonardo felt insulted. He caught hold of the doorkeeper's coat. 'I treated you like a human being and gave you my hard-earned money!'

'You piece of filth. You can take your money and ...'

When such discussions occurred in the courtyard, every window flew open, and everyone who was not yet undressed ran out to observe how the interlocutors turned into wrestlers. The most fervid *kibitzers* were quarrelling husbands, who raced to take an active part in the brawl. The scene begs for the pen of a Wiech. There was too much darkness and confusion for me to describe anything, but the results were an enormous bruise on Winiarek's head and a torn coat for the doorkeeper. Both sides swore that this was not the end of the affair and they would show who was who. From that night, Winiarek stopped visiting us. Only once, seemingly by accident, did he stop by to inform Marysia what he thought of people who did not know how to mind their own business.

*

Easter was approaching. That year, it fell a few days after Passover. We did not have any idea how we were supposed to celebrate. Fortunately, our meeting with Janek had been followed by contact with other acquaintances and relatives, including Aunt Lana and Uncle Szulim-Zygmunt. Thanks to them, we made new Polish acquaintances who managed to fill us in on Easter customs. Not that Catholic customs were completely foreign to me – our maid, Tosia, had observed the traditional ceremonies for 15 years. She had taught me Christmas carols when I was a child, and I remember that she made Easter eggs by boiling them in onion broth and then etching designs on the brown eggshells with a needle. I also remembered how she sang the archaic song *A Joyful Day Has Dawned Today*, but I could not recall the melody. When I asked my new Polish friends to teach me the song, they shrugged and said, 'Just sing along with the others.' They had too many other things on their minds before the holiday to give singing lessons, so I ended up not mastering the difficult tune and learning only the opening verses:

> A joyful day has dawned today,
> For which we all did clamor and pray.
> Christ is risen from the dead this day,
> Alleluia, Alleluia!

We went to church on Holy Saturday to have our eggs blessed. I felt that the whole courtyard was watching. I sent Jerzyk ahead to reconnoiter and see what we would have to do, and in the meantime I waited in the line of parishioners with the basket in my hand and a heavy heart. Mother had arrived in Warsaw with Klara two days earlier. They had installed themselves for the time being with acquaintances, but I could not sleep nights worrying about them. I had reckoned on their coming later, but they had been unable to remain in Cracow over the holidays, because their hosts had wanted to spend the holiday as it should be spent, with guests, and they did not want to risk having two dangerous women in the apartment. Everyone in Warsaw was also caught up in the holiday. It was hardly the right time to go apartment-hunting. Jerzyk and I were existing in our room like two mice waiting for the broom. So I stood there in line, wrapped in my gloomy thoughts. The scraps of conversation that reached my ear were not always cheering. Then Jerzyk returned from his scouting mission and said, 'There's nothing to it.' He was right. The priest sprinkled water on the eggs and we went home.

At this time, everyone had begun saying that something was happening in the ghetto. No one knew exactly what. Shots could be heard, and occasionally a larger explosion. Presumably it was a deportation action. We knew all too well what that meant.

The next day, there was definite news from the other side of the wall: The Jews were fighting. The Jews were defending themselves! It was a sensation, the main subject of conversation.[1] The rumors came one after another, and turned out to be true. The Germans set up an artillery piece on Krasinski Square, not far from our lane. Every few minutes, it fired a shell over the wall. The ghetto began to burn.

Only then did I connect the Ghetto Uprising[1] with an incident I had witnessed several days earlier. It must have occurred on the evening of 20 April. A powerful explosion shook the air, and then there were gun shots, a series from an automatic rifle, and individual pistol shots. A moment later, three men dropped into our courtyard from the ruins on the Nowiniarska Street side. One was limping. He might have been wounded. The other two carefully concealed something, perhaps weapons, under their coats. Their passage through the courtyard left its denizens stunned. In a blink of the eye, the young men were gone. Everyone said it must be some sort of resistance operation, either sabotage or an armed reprisal, but no one associated it with the ghetto. Nevertheless, we had felt that something was about to happen …

We were invited for Easter dinner by our neighbors, who laid a table for the whole courtyard. The main dish was horse cutlets in a thick brown sauce. That was the first time we had ever eaten horse meat – and it turned out that one can eat horse meat.

After dinner, we all went to Krasinski Square. A holiday fair was being held there. Swings and a carousel had been set up in the middle of the open space. A crowd of colorfully-dressed people had come to have fun, as they had done each year from time immemorial. A joyful day had dawned, and so adults and children rode up and down on the carousel to the tune of carnival music, while the ghetto burned in the background. Young couples soared upwards on the swings. I will not try to match the descriptions of this scene by Andrzejewski or Milosz, who wrote, in *Campo di Fiori*:

> At times wind from the burning
> Would drift dark kites along
> And riders on the carousel
> Caught petals in midair.
> That same hot wind
> Blew open the skirts of the girls
> And the crowds were laughing
> On that beautiful Warsaw Sunday.

(translated by Czeslaw Milosz)

With my own eyes I saw it, and my heart overflowed.

Each day that dawned was more unbearable. Those good people, our neighbors, made it clear that we should bundle up our belongings and go elsewhere, while there was still time. We redoubled our efforts to find a new apartment. We became the customers of two real-estate offices, and ran around the city from morning to night – Jerzyk and I separately. Who would get lucky first? Yet before we went our separate ways each morning, we stood for a long moment at the wall of the ghetto, staring into the clouds of smoke that billowed from the windows of the burning buildings near Swiętojerski and Nowiniarska Streets. Wherever dense smoke did not cover it, the sky was red. We could not fight back the tears. The stone resting upon our hearts was crushing us – we could not sustain that stone, and we could not rid ourselves of it. Once, we saw a man jump suddenly from a window. He flashed like a meteor in the morning sun and disappeared behind the wall separating us.

German soldiers carried out grotesque maneuvers on Krasinski Square. They crawled along the cobblestones while amused crowds of onlookers watched from the sidewalk, hurling caustic remarks. We did not stay long. We did not want to attract the attention of a chance bounty-hunter, and in any case we were in a hurry. We set off in our separate directions.

Our chase was exhausting, both physically and spiritually. Poisoned arrows pierced our ears from all sides: 'It's a good thing Hitler's doing the job for us.' However, there were also voices of warning: 'Today them, tomorrow us.' Some people lamented the conflagration of the buildings – a part of Warsaw was burning! Still others openly admired the heroes of the ghetto: 'Look at those Jews! Who would have thought that they'd be able to take up arms and fight!' The Getto uprising evoked widespread echoes in the underground Polish press. Everyone knew about it and everyone was talking about it.

For the Jews living in Warsaw on Aryan papers, those were days of blood and glory, days of terror and despair. Day by day, the hunting of those fleeing to the Aryan side grew more intense. Day in and day out, dozens of Jews were caught and taken to the Gestapo. Others fell victim to the extortionists and common criminals who preyed on fugitives. One day, I found myself in the hands of a group of hoodlums who were hunting Jews. I was on my way home, tired and discouraged after a fruitless search for an apartment. It must have been my weary eyes, full of smoke and dust, that gave me away. I'll be home in a few minutes, I thought with relief, when a ragged, dirty boy blocked my path. 'Mister, he says – 'he pointed at a bigger delinquent, who had been walking right behind me – 'that you're a Yid.'

I was clear-minded enough to growl, 'Out of my way! Scram!'

At that moment, another one stepped from the shadows and grabbed the sleeve of my coat. 'Mister, if you don't give me money, he's going to call for a policeman!'

'Shut up, scum, and get out of my sight!'

I hastened my steps, but another and yet another of them rose up out of nowhere to block my way. I pushed them aside and began running down the street. They were right behind me. That was when I spotted young Slowik, the *Volksdeutsch*, in the gateway of our building. A red armband with a big swastika on it circled the sleeve of his brown Todt Organization shirt.

'Piotr', I said as I raced up to him, 'look who's bothering me. Why don't you tell them a thing or two?'

He was somewhat surprised, but he stepped into the street and let out a screeching roar that almost burst my eardrums.

The gang turned tail and disappeared around the corner. I was safe.

Jerzyk was already waiting in our room with his impressions from an eventful day. Not far from where we had split up that morning, a manhole cover had lifted and a young woman climbed out. Before she even realized where she was, a policeman came up to her. 'You're a Jewess, aren't you?' he said. 'Show me your papers!'

A crowd of various sorts of onlookers gathered instantly. Taking her time, the woman opened her handbag. She pretended to be looking for her identity card. The policeman watched her with an ironic smirk on his face. Then she suddenly pulled out a little bottle and squirted something right in his eyes. Blinded, he let out a scream as the woman darted quickly through the dumbstruck crowd and disappeared down a side street.

We had not even finished recounting our stories when our good neighbors showed up offering us cups of *ersatz* coffee. Once again, they gave us to understand that there were informers living in the building, and that it would be better for us to go away. No one could tell what would happen the next day.

But we had nowhere else to live. We simply had nowhere to go.

*

In particular cases, proverbs can lose their meaning. Take the Polish saying: 'Where two fight, a third gains'. In our situation, it would be more accurate to say: 'Where two fight, a third loses' – especially if that third one is a Jew in hiding. We were the third party. The two who fought were Marysia and Napiorkowska, a seamstress who lived on the other side of the courtyard. It is not clear where the roots of their discord lay. The immediate cause was Marysia's friendship with Mr and Mrs Kowalksi, the doorkeepers, to whom Napiorkowska never spoke. That enmity, in turn, had roots of its own, but there is no space to recount all the details here.

Suffice it to say that Napiorkowska never visited Marysia, which is the reason that we did not know her except to see her. I should add at this point that I had poor eyesight. Napiorkowska, on the other hand, had sharp eyes. She saw instantly just who I was. After the fight with Mr Kowalski, Winiarek became friends with Napiorkowska and her husband. That couple encouraged his animosity toward Marysia and sent him as a spy to check on our ethnic background.

The frosty relations between Marysia and Napiorkowska grew even worse. Non-specific soliloquies were enunciated in the courtyard about certain people who stuck their noses in where they weren't wanted. These orations developed into more personal remarks on such themes as the filthiness of the lower portion of the underwear of one lady or another. The concluding remarks, of course, were always biting commentaries on the subject of Jews. As the allusions grew increasingly unambiguous, we could tell that things were going to end badly. We bent over backwards to find a new apartment. Tension hung in the air. The commandant of the building, Karol, issued an unveiled prognostication on the approaching end of our careers. He alluded openly to the fact that there were Jews living there. It was no business of his, but he thought that they should move out immediately unless they wanted to be caught. I pulled an ignorant face and said that, if there really were Jews there, then people should warn them and help them to find a new apartment. I mentioned, as an aside, that I was also looking for an apartment and hoped to find one in a day or two. But a day passed, and then another, and there was no sign of any new apartment.

About six o'clock one lovely May evening, we were returning from apartment-hunting. Jerzyk took a detour to the shop to buy some potatoes for the potato soup that would be dinner, while I headed home. I was carrying a bundle of wood kindling for the stove. I was exhausted and mildly discouraged, but I felt no evil foreboding. Then, I suddenly had the wind knocked out of me. Three young men were walking from the doorkeeper's apartment towards our room, with Mrs Kowalska trailing behind them. I had no doubts that it was finally happening. Thoughts ran through my mind like lightning: Make a run for it! But where? Janek must be at home. He'll never manage. They'll take him. He's finished. The apartment's blown – where to spend the night? Krysta, the little sister of Piotr the *Volksdeutsch*, scurried past. I hurriedly, but distinctly, told her, 'Wait here a minute. When Jerzyk comes, tell him to come back in half an hour. Understand?'

I walked toward the apartment. Let it happen.

In our room, Janek stood against the wall, white as a sheet. A grim character with a revolver stood facing him. The other two immediately aimed their guns at me. 'Hands up!'

214

'Calm down, gentlemen,' I said. 'What's the meaning of this? I'll put my hands up in a moment. Just let me put this firewood in the corner.' I calmly placed the kindling next to the stove, while mentally sketching a defense plan.

I had had more than one brush with extortionists since arriving in Warsaw. I had even developed certain methods of behaving and pretending that I was not frightened. I had ways of getting out of the trap. This, however, was the first time I had faced three armed characters. They might be ordinary extortionists, and then on the other hand they might be police agents. Extortionists wouldn't risk carrying guns – that could earn them a bullet in the back of the head.

Before I even finished stacking the kindling, they were all over me, searching my pockets: a potato, my identity card.

I smiled half-mockingly, but my spirits were sinking. Lower and lower.

'How much did you pay for this identity card?' one of them asked.

I did not answer.

They showed Mrs Kowalska, the doorkeeper, out of the room. 'When you gentlemen leave, please stop at my apartment,' she said on the way out.

Now they got down to brass tacks. It was hard to conceal the fact that we were Jews. For men, the situation is clear-cut. The best thing to do is to put your cards on the table. I nevertheless tried a little trick that had worked once – a matter of hypnosis, of suggestion, of proving that black is white. It didn't work. So we knew where we stood. Janek, fortunately, kept his mouth shut. All he could accomplish in such situations was to dig himself in deeper.

The thugs ordered us to get dressed and come with them.

I lay down comfortably on the sofa and declared that I had no intention of moving from the spot.

They started grabbing, cursing, and trying with all their might to pull me off the couch.

'Slow down, gentlemen. Let me ask you something.' I squirmed out of their hands. 'How much do you get for taking a Jew in? 500? Take my coat. It's sure to fetch 2,000. So you're 1,500 ahead of the game and the deal's done.'

They were outraged – was I trying to bribe them? We'll teach you a lesson, kike! Come on, move it!

They dug their shoes into the floor and took a firm hold of the edges of the sofa.

'I'm not going,' I said. 'Do what you want. Shoot me on the spot if you want. I'm as good as dead anyway. I know it's all over. But please tell me something.' I tried one more time. 'I'm something of a psychologist, and I'm very interested in what sort of pleasure you get out of sending a perfect stranger to his death. Just to kill him, for no good reason at all. It must be pleasurable. Otherwise, you wouldn't do it. Please don't tell me it's on account of that lousy 500 *zloty*! Or because of idealism. There must be a particular pleasure in sending people to their deaths.'

One of the hoodlums was boiling over with rage and looked ready to hit me. Another one took hold of my sleeve: 'Come on, let's go. You all have to die because the whole world suffers because of you.'

'Because of who? Me? Do I look like such a force that I can make the whole world suffer? At the moment I can see and feel that I'm the one who's suffering, and that the world finds me insufferable.'

They laughed. I had broken the tension for a moment. There was a spark of hope – but only for a moment. 'Alright, cut the chatter. That's enough.'

I wiped the cold sweat off my forehead. I glanced over at Janek, who had been leaning against the wall like a plank the whole time, and hadn't said a word. I went back to trying to persuade the thugs. I looked calm, but I wanted to scream.

'Well, then, we'll go. But first, please answer my question.' I showed off my wisdom. 'You're getting ready to turn a man in, just like Judas betraying Christ for a few pieces of silver. Do you know who I am? I may never have harmed anyone in my life. I may even have helped someone ... Doesn't that matter to you? Can you stand having someone's life on your conscience? You look like a person who thinks. So think about what you're doing. I don't know if you believe in God. Probably not. You see, I believe. I believe that a wrong done to an innocent man is never forgotten. God is still in His heaven. Think about it. Take what you want and leave us alone!'

I was in fact addressing just one of them, who was obviously the boss. He had a gray, gloomy face and a dull expression in his glassy eyes. The other two must have been his helpers. They hesitated and whispered to each other, shrugging their shoulders at the intractability of the third. He was as immovable as a boulder. He just kept saying no, and no again.

I could tell that my nerves were ready to snap. In a moment, I would commit some act of desperation that would lead to a horrible explosion. I quickly took a gulp of air and steeled myself for the final assault. I had been laying out the most relevant, but also the most banal of arguments. Now I was past the point of speculating. I was not playing a game, no matter how pleasant it would be today to say that I was pretending. My life was at stake. You are free to regard it as a cheap melodrama if you wish.

'Sir, you have a mother. If she's dead, then I apologize for hurting your feelings, but I swear on the memory of your mother: Think about what you are doing. You see, my mother happens to be alive. She worked like a slave all her life so that she could raise me to be a human being. She worked her fingers to the bone to get me an education. I am sure that your mother wanted no less for you. Does she know what you do for a living? Would she be happy if she knew that her son earned his living by sending people to their graves?'

I had won! I had found the human spot in the monster's heart.

My beloved teacher in the Hebrew school had taught me that man is good by nature and that in even the most evil man in the world, in Macbeth (we did not yet know that there could be someone who was much more evil), some human instinct lies hidden. I looked for it in my persecutors throughout the war, and I always found it. That is why I walked out of that hell alive. I swear to this by all that is holy, and always repeat it: I was saved by my faith in people and by the fact that I had no money …

The battle had gone on for more than half an hour. After paying me the gracious compliment that I was 'quite a talker', they set about searching our apartment – even though there was nothing to look for except grinding poverty. They took the 200 *zloty* that Janek had just brought home as his week's pay from the factory, my overcoat and my brother's, and the coat from Janek's new suit. He was wearing the trousers. There was nothing to pack it all in. I wanted to get rid of our guests as soon as possible, so I ripped the faded, mended rag – which Zosia proudly referred to as a bedspread – off the bed and wrapped the loot in it. That bedspread later cost us 800 *zloty*, which it took me a long time to repay.

One of the extortionists left with the bundle, but the other two stayed for ten more minutes. They gave me some useful advice as to shaving or growing a mustache, and combing my hair with a part or without. At the end, they said that we could safely remain in that apartment. And then, finally, they left.

Only then did my hands begin to shake feverishly. I could not control it. I was exhausted. It took me a long time to be able to force a single word out through my throat.

The courtyard had been empty the whole time. Although it was May, all the windows were shut. As soon as the silhouettes of the hoodlums disappeared through the gate, the whole building came to life. Heads were sticking out everywhere, and everyone was asking, What did they want?

'Nothing,' I said. 'Someone informed on us. Said we were Jews. They came, checked, turned the apartment inside out for the sake of routine, and left. That's all.'

Now, everyone was our friend and rejoiced at the way things had turned out. They suggested that it was Napiorkowska who had informed. She sat across the way in her window, preening like a brood hen. She watched all the guests making their way to our apartment, until there were so many of them that she could not resist running over.

'They say I sent those agents. That's not true,' she claimed. 'I wouldn't hurt a fly, much less a fellow human being.'

'You know, Mrs Napiorkowska, I don't think I could hurt a human being, either.'

I did not say another word. She blabbered on for a while, and then left glumly.

That was when Jerzyk came in. It turned out that little Krysta had warned him in time. He had climbed up on the roof overlooking the passageway out of the courtyard and had armed himself with a big stone, ready for action in case the blackmailers managed to lead us out of the apartment.

Marysia and the doorkeeper, Mrs Kowalska, wanted to take revenge on Napiorkowska. They knew a German who could 'teach her what it means to cause trouble'. This would not have done us any good, aside from the fact that using a German in such a case seemed somewhat immoral. We could have taken our revenge 'on our own', through the resistance organization. However, we did not do so.

Kowalska was a wise, good woman. She came to us the next day and simply told us: 'If you're villagers, then there's no sense going to the Germans, because that would only make things worse for you. We can take care of that Napiorkowska some other way. If you're not villagers, we'll turn that German on her.'

I did not have to fear anything with Mrs Kowalska. From that moment on, our relations with her and her husband were even more heartfelt. Mr Kowalski was a decent man. But his wife, simple to the point of naïvety, was the guiding spirit. Her brother was a priest and had told her various tall tales that she accepted at face value – such as that Jesus had turned a Jewish woman into a pig, which was why Jews were not allowed to eat pork. Yet her true wisdom showed itself in everyday life, in relation to other people, and not in words but in deeds, in the straightforwardness with which she met human obligations. A readiness to help everyone who needs help is true wisdom and goodness. Love of one's neighbor is true wisdom. It solves all problems unambiguously.

We soon learned how matters stood with us from Mrs Sanecka: Napiorkowska had gone to the police and reported that there were Jews living with Marysia. She was not prepared for the answer she received: 'So what? They're people, too. Go report them to the Gestapo on Szucha Boulevard.'

Napiorkowska had not gone to the Gestapo. But the district police chief had sent the agents. He may have been trying to cover himself, or he may have been motivated by greed. We knew for sure that they had been agents and not freelance extortionists: Mrs Kowalska had insisted on seeing their identity cards.

We lived on Ciasna Street for a few more weeks. This was unforgivable recklessness on our part. Once extortionists picked up the trail of a Jew, they would usually keep coming back and harassing him until he breathed his last. By some miracle, we finally found an apartment on the other side of town and said goodbye to our neighbors. It was a touching farewell.

Mrs Kowalska said warmly, 'If you ever need a place to stay, or if you get into trouble, come to us. You'll always find a bed and a bowl of soup here'.

NOTES

1. In the slang of occupied Warsaw, 'villager' meant Jew – people going to sell things in the ghetto called it 'the village'.
2. The Warsaw Ghetto Uprising broke out on 19 April 1943.

10. Like Hunted Animals

Mother and Klara were the last of the family to come to Warsaw. Uncle Szulim, alias Zygmunt Durakowski, had been the first to leave Cracow. The Lubomirski family gave him the first roof over his head, and he somehow took care of himself afterwards. The next one to take her chances in the Aryan world was Aunt Lana, as Danuta Dobrecka, along with her grown daughter Nata, or Malgorzata. Before the war, Nata had had a Polish boyfriend. He had been head over heels in love with her. Now he was in a prisoner-of-war camp. He sent letters to his mother, who lived in Warsaw, asking her to look after Malgorzata. Aunt Lana and Nata therefore 'had an address' when they set out for the capital. They were soon joined – as soon as the hair that had been shaved off in the camp grew back – by Szymek, a.k.a. Janek Sarnecki. I, Franciszek Grymek, arrived at the beginning of April, accompanied by Jerzyk. Although his identity card bore the name Marian Wiśniewski, he went on calling himself Jerzy, or 'Jurek', to use the normal diminutive. And then, just before Easter, mother ('Maria Murdzenska') and Klara landed on the Warsaw cobblestones. Klara's false first name was Janina, or Janka, but the surname in her papers was, unfortunately, Birkenfeldowicz. This led to a whole string of close calls and blackmail threats, let alone causing Klara to feel terrible – and that was always the beginning of trouble. Klara and mother tried to stay in Cracow as long as possible. For various reasons, however, they exhausted their last opportunities for lodging with noble-minded people who had offered shelter to these persecuted women without asking, in most cases, for any compensation. They finally had to set out on the sea of fate.

Word of the Ghetto Uprising had reached them by the time they took their places, with their hearts in their throats, in the overcrowded compartment of a passenger train bound for the occupied capital of Poland. The news hardly improved their mood. Anxiety tore at them, even though they believed that they had an address for the first night.

Klara's 'looks' were so-so, not necessarily Jewish but then again, not necessarily non-Jewish. She had dark hair; it was not curly, but it was too short to wear in a braid. Her nose was short and rather wide: non-Jewish. Her lips, on the other hand, were full and sensuous, the kind of lips that Jews are said to have. She had bright brown eyes with a tinge of green. In those days, when they were increasingly filled with terror, those eyes grew larger; the greenish hue dominated the brown. It was nothing you couldn't live with, especially if you were a woman. Women's Jewishness couldn't be proven by 'outpatient clinic' methods. The combination of not-entirely Slavic 'looks' and that dreadful surname so carelessly imposed upon her by an official nevertheless cast a shadow of suspicion. We sometimes thought about changing that identity card, but we never had the money to do so.

KLARA'S STORY

Mama and I counted on living with our acquaintances, Mr and Mrs D., but I also acquired one more address, just to be on the safe side.

A 15-year-old girl called Ela had been a visitor at the friend's house where I spent my last days in Cracow. Ela must have realized that I was Jewish. When I told her that I would be traveling to Warsaw and needed a place to stay, she gave me her uncle's address without even stopping to think. I did not write it down, but committed it to memory so that I could go there if the need arose. The next day, apparently having thought things over and realized the danger involved, Ela began trying to steer me away from the idea of going to her uncle's. She said that he was coming to Cracow for Easter, that she didn't like him anyway because he favored her sister Ziuta, and that it would be a bad idea, in general, to go there. She said he would probably turn me away. I tried to allay her fears by repeating that I already had a place to stay in Warsaw ...

Neither Jerzyk nor I had ever met this Ela, so we were taken somewhat aback by a letter from Klara containing this request: 'Stop in at the Rozyckis' at 10 Marszalkowska Street, convey greetings from Ela and Ziuta, and ask whether or not they've received the letter from Ela and whether I can spend the night at their place. Please arrange this one way or another.' Such missions are not particularly pleasant. Yet we were already well aware of

221

what it meant to be without a place to stay, and how important each acquaintance and stopping-point is for people coming to Warsaw for the first time.

We stood for a long time outside the Rozyckis' door before we could bring ourselves to ring the doorbell.

'Who's there?'

Try explaining through a closed door who you are and what you want.

'We're from Cracow, from acquaintances of yours ...'

They invited us into a normal, middle-class living room.

'Ela asked us to stop by. Well, not exactly Ela, because we left Cracow three months ago. But we just got a letter from a friend of Ela's who wanted us to check whether Ela had warned you that she was coming. Could she stay here the first night?'

Of course, the Rozyckis knew nothing about all this. They had not had a letter from Cracow for a long time (that postal service!), but yes, why not, let her come. And by the way, how are Ela and Ziuta? What's new with them?

It is not easy to convey the latest news about someone you have never laid eyes on, but we managed somehow. Of course, I had to tell them about my job (Jerzyk, obviously, was in school) – and we took our leave.

You breathe a deep sigh of relief when that sort of conversation is over.

The train arrived at the main Warsaw station at 4:30 in the afternoon. A red sky and billows of smoke from the burning ghetto greeted the two counterfeit Aryan women. Mother and Klara went immediately to Dr Drochocki's on Koszykowa Street. He was a converted Jew who had held a high official post before the war and was a long-time friend of the family. His mother, Mrs Deiches, came from a respected Cracow family. She had been with us in Czyzyny and had died there before resettlement in the ghetto. She had been a very old lady, and mother had cared for her until the end. Her son had never answered the letters that mother sent to him before her trip to Warsaw, but there was no reason to doubt that he would help her in a time of need.

Drochocki went white when he saw the two familiar women on his doorstep. This heretofore decent man practically became hysterical when he learned that they intended to spend the night at his home. Two days earlier, the police had arrested his lodger –

who had turned out to be Jewish. We must understand that, given the circumstances, this was no laughing matter. His wife ruefully supported his arguments. And so mother and Klara found themselves on the street at six o'clock in the evening. At least the Drochockis permitted them to leave their suitcases there.

After thinking things over, mother decided to go to Odolanska Street, where her sister Lana and her niece were living with a Mr Gasiorek. Klara decided to try her luck with the Rozyckis.

KLARA'S STORY

I rang the doorbell with a trembling heart. But everything went unexpectedly well. When I introduced myself as a friend of Ziuta's and said that I had come to Warsaw for a few days, they greeted me effusively. I was finally able to wash and have a rest. After supper, my hosts took me out on the balcony to show me 'the Jews being fried'. They had a splendid view of the glow from the burning ghetto. My heart was constricted and hammers were beating in my brain. I said, 'Poor people'. Mr Rozycki laughed and said there was no reason to feel sorry for them. Tears came to my eyes. Fortunately, it was completely dark out there. Yet I felt somewhat calmer, since they obviously did not suspect me. I spent two days with the Rozyckis. Two days in a normal apartment, speaking in a normal tone of voice, sitting down at the table to eat – and such delicacies, which I had not tasted for a long time! I have to admit that they were hospitable. Rozycki had a good sense of humor and was very self-confident. It is true that he could not refrain from joking about the Jewish sound of the name 'Birkenfeldowicz'. Nevertheless, he promised to find me a job in the company he worked for after I observed that I would like to settle in Warsaw.

Klara came to see us on Ciasna Street the day after her arrival. We introduced her to Marysia as our cousin and Janek's girlfriend. I decided to go to Odolanska Street with Klara in order to see mother and try to figure out what to do next.

We waited for a long time at the tram stop on Marszalkowska Street, but no tram came. It was still early, and it was a beautiful day, one of those early spring days when life smiles at you and you smile back. We therefore decided to walk. By the time we reached Zbawiciela Square, we could tell that we were being followed. Maintaining a merry demeanor, I imparted this grim information to Klara. A young hoodlum kept rushing forward to look at my face or grab at me, while calling 'Jozek!' I supposed that he must have come here from the streets of Cracow, where he had met my brother. Now he took me for Jozek. Similar mistakes had been made when I was in school. Klara and I walked into a druggist's. Perhaps he would leave me alone. But he didn't. He watched us through the window. Worse, there was now someone older with him. We bought toothpaste and looked at various sorts of powders before deciding to leave.

We had barely stepped outside and he was back. 'Mister, that guy over there says you're a Jew.'

'Tell him to kiss my a**,' I retorted.

'But he wants money.'

'If you don't leave me alone, I'll fix you up so that your own parents won't recognize you!' It was amazing how these dialogues repeated themselves. All these young extortionists used the same method.

There was a break for a moment, and then the conversation resumed. We were walking all the time. 'Mister, that other guy's going to call a policeman,' he said, grabbing my sleeve.

'So let him, if he feels like going to jail,' I said impetuously as I pulled free.

At that moment, a tram pulled to a stop where we were walking. It was a number 10. We jumped on to the first car. Our persecutors jumped into the second car.

We sprang off at Rakowiecka Street. Since that was a busy stop, we could not be sure whether the extortionists were behind us. We thought we glimpsed them on a street corner. Going into various shops and getting on and off trams, we kept fearing that we were being followed. We dreaded the possibility that they would discover the apartment on Odolanska Street. When we finally arrived there, we did not tell anyone what had happened.

KLARA'S STORY

After that first lesson in caution, I returned to the Rozyckis' in something less than a good mood, but without any sense of foreboding. Mrs Rozycka let me in and immediately told me the wonderful news: 'You'll be so happy. Ziuta's coming this evening! She should be here by suppertime!'

I thought I would faint. Supper was already on the table. The tasty food just wouldn't go down. I tried to maintain my composure and pretend to be thrilled at Ziuta's impending arrival. The doorbell finally rang. Their son ran to the door and I heard his delighted cry 'Ziuta!' a moment later. I shivered, but only for a fraction of a second. An instant later I was in the foyer with my arms around the neck of a girl I had never seen before. I kissed her and wondered out loud how she could fail to recognize me, when she herself had given me her uncle's address. I finally managed to get her into the bathroom so that she could wash her hands. As soon as we had this moment alone, I explained what I was doing there and made her swear not to give me away. She promised solemnly and she kept her word, but her uncle was not as naïve as we were. He immediately understood what was going on. And yet, despite his glee at the way the Jews were being fried, he did not turn me over to the Gestapo. Instead, he ordered me to leave their home at dawn and to thank God for the fact that he allowed me to go. My knees quaked as I walked down the stairs.

When Klara went back to the Rozyckis' some time later to sell something (at their son's request), old Mrs Rozycka ordered her out of the apartment in the loudest and most vulgar of ways, despite the protests of her embarrassed husband and son.

*

After arriving in Warsaw, Klara changed apartments five times in three weeks. Nevertheless, she found herself out in the street on 12 May. The last place she had stayed was with us. She had shared a bed with our landlady Marysia, who was hardly thrilled with the arrangement. Marysia much preferred sleeping with her Edas. Yet it would have been unthinkable for Klara to sleep with us – with three boys. Even in such mad times, there were things that could not be justified. Klara, too, was hardly thrilled about sleeping with Marysia – the latter may have washed at some point, but there were no outward signs of this. To make things worse, Klara felt very badly at that time. She had a fever and dizzy spells, and there were moments when she had trouble staying on her feet. Although she was discouraged and terribly exhausted, the vital instinct maintained the upper hand over her despair and fever.

But what was she to do when she had to leave the apartment, when she had nowhere to go? We felt helpless. Should she rejoin mother, once again? There was hardly enough space for three Jewish women to take shelter there. Klara opted for a hotel. To this day, I cannot imagine how we ever allowed her to go there.

We said goodbye to her at around five in the afternoon. Our hearts were breaking as she set off to rent a room in a hotel on Zlota Street. The first question she was asked at the desk was, 'You're not Jewish by any chance, are you?'

'Me? Of course not!'

'It's all the same to me whether you are or not, but I just thought I'd warn you that the Gestapo come here every night and take the Jews away, just in case ...'

Klara was praying for a miracle as she climbed into the clean hotel bed. And a miracle occurred.

The air-raid sirens went off at around ten o'clock. An air raid?! There hadn't been an air-raid alarm for years. But Soviet planes had arrived in support of the fighting ghetto – too late, as it turned out.

No one ran with such pleasure to the shelter, and no one listened with such a light heart to the bombs exploding nearby, as the formerly cowardly Klara. In normal circumstances, such an event would have driven her mad with fear.

We, too, sighed with relief and stood joyously in the courtyard to watch how the sky was lit up like a Christmas tree. It nearly ended tragically for us when a shell fragment tore into the eave spout next to where we were standing.

The all-clear sounded two hours later. The Gestapo did not visit the hotel that night. Zlota Street was burning. The bombing did a lot of damage, but most importantly, it pushed ethnic matters off center stage for a certain time.

The next day, however, Klara's recent anxieties took on new dimensions. Klara went to the Drohockis', but they did everything they could to prevent her from staying there and practically threw the sick girl down the stairs. They advised her to see a doctor, and even gave her an address on the condition that she never reveal who had given it to her. And so Klara went to see Dr Niedzielski.

KLARA'S STORY

The noble Dr Niedzielski may still be alive somewhere in Poland. Mama and I went to his office. As soon as he saw us standing in the doorway, he pronounced: 'Hepatitis'. Without even asking, he said, 'I'm sure you don't have anywhere that you could go for treatment, so I'm sending you straight to the hospital.'

And he wrote out an admission order. He did not want to take any payment for the consultation. We walked downstairs with tears in our eyes. In general, two feelings are engraved in my memory from that period. The first is a hoarseness and the throat accompanied by tears, caused by my feelings of gratitude for the goodness shown to me. The second is a trembling in the knees, combined with what someone has quite accurately described as the feeling of 'swallowing your own heart'. This was caused by fear, mortal fear. We felt something close to joy as we left Dr Niedzielski's. I would be given a bed and a roof over my head. Today, when I am a mother myself, I understand what my poor Mama experienced as she fought for the lives of her three children. We reached the hospital: quiet, perfect cleanliness, and that bed. Mama could feel at peace in regard to me as she left. I slept like a rock. I spent a month in the hospital. To my misfortune, I grew healthier by the day, despite the fact that I secretly did everything I could to prolong the illness. Far from sticking to the recommended diet, I ate things that were downright harmful. Dr Niedzielski came to examine his patients every day. Although I looked disgustingly healthy after sleeping for a few days and nights and receiving decent food, the doctor kept extending my hospitalization.

Klara's life in the hospital was pleasant and merry. Before long, she had made the acquaintance of all the other patients in the big ward, and her good humor and love of singing never left her. Everyone liked her. They jokingly referred to her as 'the little Jewish girl' (which was hardly something that made her happy), but she laughed it off and sang all the louder during their daily Maytide liturgies in honor of the Blessed Virgin Mary. She learned the words on the spot.

By this time, the three of us – Jerzyk, Janek and I – had survived the big extortion adventure that had cost us our coats. When we went to visit Klara in the hospital on Sundays, we were the only visitors in shirtsleeves. Klara scolded us, because it was still chilly outside. And in general, who went around without a coat on a Sunday? We could have told her the whole story, but what was the point of spoiling her good mood?

We went on joking and talking about this and that. At one moment, we heard the sound of a glass breaking as it fell to the floor. After a brief pause, someone said, '*Mazel tov!*'

Then we heard several people break out chortling. Janka-Klara was obviously not the only little Jewish girl in the ward.

One lovely afternoon – May 1943, was a beautiful, sunny month – there was shouting and calling in the hospital courtyard. A moment later, a modestly dressed woman went walking quickly down the corridor to an examination room, where she sat in an armchair. There were no doctors around. A pair of German soldiers came trotting along an instant later, accompanied by two hoodlums off the street.

'*Wo ist die Judin?*'

'She's got to be hiding around here somewhere', said the boys as they began opening doors. 'Oh, there she is, the Jewess!'

The Germans burst into the examination room like mad dogs. They started trying to drag their victim out by the hair, kicking, spitting and manhandling her ruthlessly. The woman tried to say something, but they would not let her speak. Her eyes, mad with fear, pleaded for mercy. Smiles broke out on the faces of the stupid boys from the street.

The patients lay there frozen. Then there was a gunshot. That was the end.

One of the Germans wiped the sweat off his forehead as he ordered the nurses to attend to the corpse. It was clear from what he said that the hoodlums had gone up to the woman on the street and attempted to blackmail her. She had run into the hospital courtyard, thinking that she could hide there. But the boys had grabbed hold of the first soldiers they saw: 'Oh, a Jew! There, there!' The pursuit had begun.

After that incident, Klara begged to be discharged from the hospital. Dr Niedzielski agreed that she had been there long enough. But she had nowhere to live. So he kept her there another week.

*

At eight o'clock one June morning, a week after being released from the hospital, Klara set out to visit mother on Odolanska Street. She had no sooner stepped out the front door of her temporary lodgings than she was stopped by a Ukrainian policeman who demanded her documents. Before she could even take out the horrible identity card, the policeman had made up his mind. 'You're a Jew in any case, so there's no point looking at your papers. Come with me.'

Klara denied it and flew into a rage, but this only made him more determined to haul her in. The Ukrainian took her to the police station on Szpitalna Street and turned her over to the desk sergeant. As ill luck would have it, this was exactly the moment when the Germans arrived with the Jews they had caught during their night-time sweep through the hotels. The noise was indescribable: cursing, crying and the stamping of boots.

The sergeant decided to hold her fate in abeyance for the moment. He shoved Klara into a toilet and said, 'Wait here until I come for you.'

The cries and the pleading grew louder. Pale with fear and still considerably weakened after her illness, Klara was nevertheless unable to restrain her feminine curiosity. She put her eye to the keyhole. A melancholy procession was passing: six Germans with rifles, and the nine Jews they had caught. Among them was Klara's classmate from school, Lusia. The girl walked along, pale, with her head hanging down. Her lips were slightly parted, and her expression reflected the fear seen in animals that have just been put in a cage.

When the Germans had gone, the sergeant pulled Klara out of her hiding place. 'Don't even try to explain! Have you got friends or relatives here with money?'

'Yes, I have.'

'Have you got their phone number?'

'Yes.'

'Then call them, so they can bail you out. Tell them to bring 10,000 *zloty*.'

Although doing so was highly dangerous, Klara called Uncle Zygmunt. Could anyone have done otherwise?

Upset, uncle ran to mother with the tragic news. Mother wrung her hands, but kept her wits about her. Such a sum – but she would have to raise the money. Time was passing. She ran from one acquaintance to another. This one was broke, that one had just spent everything he had, a third one had had the money the day before, and a fourth one might have it the next day. The clock was running. Until that moment, it had been crawling, and now it was ticking at a breakneck tempo. By 12, she had managed to raise the ridiculous total of 2,000 *zloty* by pawning possessions that no one would want to buy anyway. Now, who could take that money to the police? None of her Aryan friends was ready to accept the mission. They were afraid. Could they be arrested for going there? The clock was running. Mother was going crazy. Save my child! Aunt Lana was sympathetic, Uncle Zygmunt was hopeful, but it was Jerzyk who decided to go, in spite of mother's protests. She could not bear the thought that one more of her children would be at risk. Yet Jerzyk was sure of himself. With his goyish looks, no one would suspect him.

He went to the police station and explained to the desk sergeant that he had had a telephone call from a Miss Birkenfeldowicz, with whom he had business dealings and to whom he owed money. He had come to give her the 2,000 *zloty* he owed her.

'So the pathetic Jews were afraid to come themselves, and they sent some little snot instead,' the policeman commented.

The desk sergeant still insisted on 10,000, but the family could not come up with any more. Two thousand would have to suffice. It simply had to. And it did. After ten hours of suspense, Klara was released at six o'clock in the evening.

KLARA'S STORY

Jerzy and I were back on the street, with pounding hearts, trying to act like a couple of strangers. We could not afford to put each other in jeopardy. Streets, more streets, addresses acquired by miracle, the burning ghetto and the terrible news from there, our hearts breaking for those we loved and some sort of instinct that forced us to keep clinging to life. Streets ... addresses ... Marszalkowska Street: three nights with a doorkeeper. Pulawska Street: smoking cigarettes and cursing Hitler all night with a woman named Hanka. She gave me a relative's address. Odolanska Street ... Filtrowa Street ... Where would it end?

Klara had plainly not run out of luck, for she was hired a few days later as nanny for a four-year-old. She again had a roof over her head and a bit of bread. On the negative side, she was expected to take the child out for walks. But on the positive side, the child offered her a sort of protection.

One Sunday, Klara went for a walk with Janek (who had the day off) along the Vistula. She had her little girl with her. Not far from the Kierbiedzia bridge, a group of thugs came up to them. At first, they limited themselves to remarks. 'Look, Felek, they've got a baby as camouflage.'

'They think the baby will help when everybody can see that they're Jews.'

Janek picked up the child and started walking faster. The hoodlums did not give up. As they passed a street photographer, Janek told them, 'Why don't we pose for a picture together? Then we can all have a souvenir.'

The extortionists hesitated for a few moments, but then surrounded Janek and Klara again. The whole group walked along in funereal silence. This was finally broken by one of the gang, who went back to the old formula: 'Mister, there's a guy over there that knows you from Cracow.'

'So let him come up to me. Where is he?'

'He's around the corner there.'

'So go get him.'

Someone ran off to fetch the supposed acquaintance. Ten paces further on, a German gendarme stood on the bridge. Seeing that there was no way out, Janek handed the little girl to Klara. 'Make a run for it! I'll see you at home.'

With the child in her arms, Klara jumped on to a passing tram.

In the meantime, the 'acquaintance' appeared. 'Give us your trousers! We've already got the coat, and we've been looking for the trousers. That's what gave you away!'

As I mentioned above, the extortionists had left Janek in his trousers when they took his suit coat. It was a loud suit in a rare brick color. Little wonder that the owners of the coat recognized the matching trousers.

'Take off your trousers! We're going to the police!'

'What for? There's a German policeman on the bridge. Why don't you go to him?'

The whole time, Janek kept hinting that he was not alone, that he had friends from the 'underground' nearby and felt safe. Seeing that they were not going to get anything out of him, the hoodlums demanded enough money to buy a bottle of vodka. However, Janek had only 30 *zloty* in his pocket. Without taking this paltry sum, they left him in peace.

When Janek went to set Klara's mind at ease, she pleaded with him never to wear those cursed trousers again. As soon as she made enough money, she would buy him a new pair!

'Thank God it's over!'

She did not know, poor thing, that it was just beginning ....

*

People with so-called 'bad looks' lived in an atmosphere of unrelieved danger. They could be blackmailed by their landlords, neighbors and acquaintances; they could be blackmailed on the street and in trams. The loss of self-confidence that grew worse by the day led to indecisive movements, a worried look in the eyes, and finally the complete abandonment of self-control. It ended in disaster.

Experienced 'paper Aryans' regarded it as unsafe to live at the same address for more than three months, even if there was no apparent danger. This was a theoretical concern, for it was very difficult to find a place to live at all. A solitary person could get by. A family made things worse. In practice, we all accepted the correctness of the tactic of the biblical Jacob. Having received a flock of sheep as dowry, he divided it into three groups. If one part of the flock came down with disease, he reasoned, he would still have the other two parts. Yet no matter how well we understood this principle, it was difficult to put it into practice. First, there were material difficulties and the cost of renting several different quarters. Furthermore, it always turned out that, just when you had settled into a new place, a relative or acquaintance would end up homeless and need somewhere to sleep. That was usually the beginning of a landlord's suspicions of the lodger. Landlords had to be accustomed gradually to various odd visits and to the fact that strangers stayed overnight more and more often. Finally came the moment when, with an uneasy heart and a terrible feeling inside, it was necessary to tell a lie about someone who had just arrived from Cracow and had not yet been able to find a place to live. It was necessary to maintain a poker face while reminding the landlord of the benefits (especially monetary ones) of providing lodgings. Once this matter had been negotiated successfully, it was time to begin thinking about putting up yet one more member of the family, who would inevitably have compromised their Aryan credentials at the place where they were living. In this way, we all ended up together at certain moments. That was always a no-exit situation. It was just this sort of bottleneck that formed in Mr Gasiorek's apartment on Odolanska Street.

Gasiorek had been a secret-police agent before the war. During the German occupation, he went to work for a photographer and maintained close relations with the Gestapo. Lana and Nata moved in with him in March 1943. Aunt Lana cooked his dinners and paid him 200 *zloty* for their lodging. Uncle Zygmunt also came there for dinners; he played cards with Gasiorek and sometimes stayed overnight. When mother arrived in Warsaw, she stayed with Aunt Lana because she had nowhere else to go. They said that mother had formerly been a cook in a certain aristocratic manor house, and would be in Warsaw for six weeks. That was the recommendation that Uncle Zygmunt supplied her with. In order to forestall unnecessary conversations with the inquisitive Gasiorek, he said that Mrs Murdzenska was an excellent cook, but as deaf as a log. From that moment on, mother took over the function of cook. Nata went to live with acquaintances at this period. We sometimes came to Gasiorek's door like beggars, and mother would give us sandwiches she had prepared for our dinner.

Then Klara arrived in July, after carrying her cross through all the adventures and torments of blackmail and sickness. After her most recent misadventure, she gave up her job as a nanny and returned to mother. Nata-Malgorzata returned at the same time. She had fallen seriously ill and had been in the hospital. She had to leave when someone recognized her as a Jew.

And thus there were four Jewish women living on Odolanska Street in July 1943: mother, Klara, Aunt Lana and her daughter, Nata. This was a situation that could not go on for long without attracting someone's notice. That is exactly what happened, and before any preventive steps could be taken.

Three men knocked at Gasiorek's door one morning. Malgorzata opened the door.

'Does Dobrecka live here? Or Birkenfeldowicz?' Without waiting for an answer, they pushed their way inside.

Mother was in the kitchen, dressed like the maid. That is what the extortionists took her for. They did nothing to stop her; seeing what was going on, she simply left.

Every Jew's dream was a backup apartment. At the slightest slip-up or suspicion, you could go straight to your back-up apartment – if you had one.

We, too, had dreamed of such a place. The actor Kazimierz Szubert, from Cracow, once offered mother a beautiful apartment in the Warsaw suburb of Sluzewie. The price was low, only 1,500 per month. Low or not, we were unable to afford it. Now, mother recalled that address. She had left all her papers back in the kitchen. Dressed as a serving-woman, with a scarf on her head, she made her way on foot to Sluzewie. After a long march, she found the place and rang the doorbell. The door was opened by a policeman! 'Who are you?' he asked the peasant woman he saw standing there.

'Is this where the l-l-laundry woman lives?' At such moments, mother also pretended to stutter, in order to gain time to think.

'Let me see your documents!'

'W-W-What?'

'Your identity card!'

'Y-Y-Yes, I'm absolutely sure.' Her pockets were completely empty.

'Damn it, woman, it's bad enough that you stutter, and you're deaf, too!' The policeman called for the maid who was employed in that apartment and asked, her, in reference to mother, 'Do you know this woman?'

'Never seen her in my life.'

That was a fortunate answer, for in fact she knew mother well.

'Well, then, get out of here, and fast!' said the policeman, closing the door in her face.

As we later learned, the apartment in Sluzewie was being searched for Jews, even though none had lived there for a long time. If we had had the money, that would have been our backup haven. This just goes to show how people were sometimes saved precisely by the fact that they had no money or backup apartment.

On Odolanska Street, in the meantime, the three women were under heavy assault from the extortionists. While refraining from admitting to their Jewish origins, they failed to adopt a suitably determined attitude. The extortionists threatened them with the Gestapo on Szucha Boulevard, then acted out the usual comedy (what a comedy!), before finally demanding 70,000 *zloty*!

Malgorzata and Klara attempted to win sympathy by telling about their recent stays in the hospital. Malgosia coquettishly showed off her fresh stitches and attempted to unload a gold watch on the extortionists, who did not want to take it. While searching the apartment, they found mother's identity card. On the photograph, mother looked like a typical Jewish woman. Only now did the thugs realize that they had allowed the bird to fly the cage, and they were furious.

This was no laughing matter. The women had no cash, and could not even dream of raising such a vast sum in a short time, even if they sold everything they owned. Nevertheless, they agreed to give the blackmailers 35,000 that afternoon, and the rest the following day. The hoodlums took each woman's identity card (except for Aunt Lana's, so that she could go out to raise money), and said that the money should be delivered to them at Unia Lubelska Square. Then they left.

Before the extortionists had departed, Uncle Zygmunt came for dinner, as was his custom. He was stopped at the door by a neighbor who had realized what was going on. Only thanks to her did he avoid falling into the trap.

Such money, of course, could not be obtained on demand. By the appointed hour, they had raised only 3,000. Aunt Lana went to the meeting with that sum. She returned feeling much better, for she had handled the situation well: she had negotiated a much lower payment, to be delivered in installments at three-day intervals. The blackmailers had also given her Malgorzata's identity card and promised to return one more document each time a payment was made.

Gasiorek came home for lunch that day much later than usual. Apparently he had learned about the whole incident from a neighbor. Confident that the matter had been settled, the three women naïvely slept on Odolanska Street that evening.

The next morning, Gasiorek did not go to work. Three completely new agents arrived at around nine o'clock. They stated that the previous day's blackmailers had been police agents who had been under orders to arrest the women. Because they had failed to do so, they had themselves been arrested. These new agents did not seem well oriented in the question of who was supposed to be the Jew here, but the lack of identity papers seemed to offer irrefutable proof.

'Get dressed to go.'

As the women prepared to leave, Gasiorek assured them that he would get them out and that nothing would happen to them. Klara tried again to solve the problem. 'Can't this be taken care of somehow?' she asked. 'It has nothing to do with me because I'm not Jewish and I'll be released immediately, but wouldn't it be better for you gentlemen if you had a chance to make a little money?'

'Well, alright, but there would have to be an immediate payment of 20,000,' was the reply.

'But that's impossible. If these women went to Aryan acquaintances, of course, they could borrow the money. I can stay here as a guarantee.'

The agents agreed, but insisted on accompanying their victims. 'What?' Klara exclaimed. 'Do you think that anyone would open their door to these women, let alone lend them money, if they were accompanied by police agents? Look, I'll stay here. If the sum is not paid, you can take me in.'

After conferring among themselves, they agreed. Three o'clock was set as the deadline for payment. Aunt Lana and Malgorzata left, while Klara stayed with Gasiorek and the extortionists. Gasiorek sat himself down to play solitaire, while Klara tried to amuse the gangsters. Three o'clock approached. Klara kept smiling, but anxiety was filling her soul. Three o'clock passed, and they waited, but there was no sign of either the money or the two women.

'Well, let's get ready to go. You'll come with us, Miss.'

'If you like,' said Klara nonchalantly. 'But I'm sure they'll bail me out. They must not have the money yet. Let's wait a while longer.'

The agents decided to leave Klara under Gasiorek's supervision. They came back at five. Nothing changed. The tension grew. Finally, at seven, a neighbor knocked at the door. There was a telephone call for Klara.

When my sister came back, she said that there was only 7,000, and it could be left with Gasiorek's aunt. The rest would be paid the next day. The extortionists agreed to leave Klara with Gasiorek, having first extracted her word of honor that she would not run away. Klara stayed for the night, feeling safe there – as if she had anywhere else to go. However, while Gasiorek was still asleep the next morning, she packed her things, borrowed Gasiorek's tram pass which was lying on the table (she did not have a *grosz* to her name), and disappeared.

One cannot always keep one's word of honor …

11. *Niemcewicza Street From the Front, and Asnyka From the Rear*

A RACE WITH TIME

In mid-May, Janek, Jerzyk and I were still sitting in our old apartment. Klara was in the hospital then, but could not stay indefinitely. Mother was living temporarily with Aunt Lana. Uncle Zygmunt was looking for a place. We had put our names down at the housing exchanges on Krucza and Wilcza Streets. There was a general belief, certainly not baseless, that these exchange offices cooperated with the Gestapo. We were taking a risk, but we had no choice. Long experience had convinced us that the offices functioned according to the following principle: new clients were given addresses that were either no longer current, or whose owners had no intention of taking new lodgers, or that did not exist at all. Only after a month of using the bureau's services could one count on obtaining genuine offers.

Our pursuit of an apartment permitted us to meet people and to become experienced at talking with them and avoiding tricky questions. People were generally afraid to rent apartments to young men like us. Young men seldom had work assignments, there was a risk that they could belong to the resistance movement, and in general it was impossible to say what sort of trouble they could cause. There were some landlords, like the one on Kawêczynska Street who was described earlier, who would agree to rent an apartment and then back out at the last moment.

Our biggest problem was our lack of references. We always claimed to be able to provide them, and made liberal use of names and titles like 'professor' and 'engineer', before acknowledging regretfully that our references lived in Cracow.

'Why have you come to Warsaw?' was a standard question.

'Do you know what it's like in Cracow?' we would answer. 'It's simply impossible to live there; it's stifling.'

We tried to avoid saying anything concrete.

After a month of running up and down staircases and from one building, street or district to another, we stumbled on Mrs Ewa Ebert, who had a room to rent. It was on Czerniakowska Street, in a building inhabited exclusively by Germans. Mr Ebert, as we learned later, was a *Volksdeutsch*. The kindly landlady smothered us from the beginning in effusive generosity. She had indeed been planning to rent the room to only one man, and rather an older one, but she promised to talk things over with her husband. She wanted to keep our hopes up, and invited us to come back at two o'clock the following morning. The ground was burning under our feet, but too bad. We had to wait. The next day, she still did not have an answer for us.

'Would it be too much trouble if I asked you to come back at six o'clock in the evening?'

What could we do? We came back. It turned out that Mrs Ebert was holding a small party that evening. She invited us into the dining room, and we spent an hour in pleasant company, sipping liqueur and consuming delicious hors d'oeuvres and cake. There was, of course, no mention of the room for rent. On the other hand, there was immediate, and extensive, mention of the burning ghetto and the Jews. One of Mrs Ebert's guests was her cousin. This latter woman made no secret of her great aversion to Jews and communists. As I always did on such occasions, I took up the cause of my brothers. I served up my opinions in a relatively thick sauce of humor in order to avoid offending my possible future landlady. For her part, Mrs Ebert took a reasonable and conciliatory standpoint. Across from me sat a handsome, well-groomed blond young man named Krzepicki. He took almost no part in the discussion. When he did say anything, it was along the lines of 'those Jews have tried our patience long enough'. I was suspicious of the way he kept out of the discussion about Jews. When we left, I told Jerzyk that Krzepicki must be 'a Jacek' (our code-name for Jews).

'With those looks?' my brother retorted. 'He's nothing but a lousy antisemite.'

The question of the rental was postponed to the next day. Then, everything indicated that we were about to find a place for ourselves. At a certain moment, the conversation shifted to questions of the *Arbeitsamt*, residence permits, and so on. Mrs Ebert asked to see our identity cards. Jerzyk showed her his.

She turned to me. 'And yours?'

How could I show her a document asserting that I was a 33-

year-old journeyman cobbler? That would automatically undercut all the trust that I had built up during the cultured conversations with Mrs Ebert. Should I take the risk? What a shame about the apartment ... I decided to save it – if not for us, then for Uncle Zygmunt, who was also facing eviction at that point.

'Excuse me', I said, as if I had just experienced a flash of dazzling illumination, 'but you were right in the first place, Mrs Ebert. This apartment is not right for us.' Jerzyk looked at me as if I had lost my mind. 'However, I have an older acquaintance, Dr Durakowski. He would certainly take this room.'

'Really? What sort of man is he?'

'Oh, he's a very cultured gentleman. A close friend of the Lubomirski princes. You'll see what he's like when you meet him.'

And so it was Uncle Zygmunt who rented the room in the Eberts' apartment, just across the corridor from Krzepicki.

And we remained without a place to live. Mother wrote to Cracow, asking for the address of Zosia Kucz, a clerk whom she knew. The address came. Zosia turned out to be in no position to rent us an apartment, but she introduced us to a friend of hers, a Mrs Janiczek, who lived on Filtrowa Street. For the time being, Mrs Janiczek had no room for us. Three Jews were living there, although two were expected to move out soon. At least this was a new place where we could meet mother in safety.

One day, Jerzyk was on his way to Zosia's when, in the gateway of a building on Asnyka Street, he saw a sign reading 'Room for Rent'. We decided to go there. Even though we had only recently met her, Mrs Janiczek promised to back us and give us a reference. We made our way to the apartment in question. It was part of the enormous complex belonging to the ZUS insurance company, at the corner of Asnyk and Niemcewicz Streets. We rode the elevator to the fifth floor in a state of anxiety.

When I saw the plebeian-sounding name Alicja Scislo on the card affixed to the door, I told Jerzyk, 'This is where we'll live. If she can be Scislo, then I won't have any complexes about being Grymek.'

The landlady invited us in. She was a beautiful, well-cared-for woman of around 40, the widow of a lawyer. Like everyone, of course, she intended to take in only one lodger, preferably an older gentleman.

'Only one of us?' I said. 'No problem. Let it be one.' I put Jerzyk forward as the candidate. 'The boy's studying and he needs peace and quiet. I'll drop in on him from time to time, because I have to help him get ready for his examinations. In any case, I've just gotten over an inflammation of the joints, so an apartment on the fifth floor wouldn't be very suitable for me.'

'Where do you work?', she asked me.

'At the power plant,' I said, because I was supposed to obtain papers from there. 'I haven't started working yet. I start in two weeks, because I haven't got the strength yet ...' Illness excused a lack of employment.

'And references?'

'There's Doctor Durakowski' – we provided references for Uncle Zygmunt, and he provided them for us – 'and then there's Mrs Janiczek. She lives nearby, on Filtrowa Street.'

I talked a bit more with the attorney's widow about painting and poetry, while praising her taste, her beautiful pictures, and so on. When we left, we were convinced that Jerzyk would have a place to live for 400 *zloty* per month.

Half an hour later, the widow turned up at Mrs Janiczek's. Mrs Janiczek persuaded her to let both of us live there. 'Add another 100 to the rent and let them live together.'

The great thing about all this was that Mrs Janiczek did not even know the 'Aryan' name that I was using. When the widow questioned her, she said, 'I don't know that Franek so well, but Jerzyk comes from a very well-known Cracow family, very decent people. You won't be disappointed!'

*

We moved in two days later. It was the very last moment. Marysia could no longer keep us on Ciasna Street. Edas supposedly knew nothing about our close call with the extortionists, but he flew into jealous rages over us. Only Janek remained on Ciasna Street. He lived there for another month and a half, until he had no choice but to start living at the factory where he worked.

The attorney's widow, Mrs Scislo, had two interconnected rooms to rent, a larger one and a smaller one. Both were in need of remodelling, and the furniture was less than modest and in a lamentable state. We took the larger one. It was very gloomy, because its window faced north and opened on to the courtyard. For two people, however, it was more comfortable. There was no wardrobe. One leg of the table was wobbly, but the table was large. The two chairs looked so rickety that we preferred from the very beginning to sit on the daybed. That most important piece of furniture in the room was the image of poverty and despair. Some of the springs were ready to poke through the top, and others had already poked through the bottom, forming hills and valleys. An abundance of bedbugs lived in it. One of the conditions set by the landlady when she rented us the room was that we have the bed fixed. We had the best of intentions. When we learned, however, that the job would cost 800 *zloty*, we realized it would have to wait until our financial outlook was brighter. The attorney's widow was not insistent. Not more than once a month did she ask when we intended to have the bed fixed, and we gave evasive answers or joked about it. Usually, we were 'waiting for an upholsterer from Otwock' who was supposedly going to come to Warsaw and do the job cheap.

If that bed could have talked, it would certainly have been an antisemite. It would tell how many Jews had taken advantage of it during the war without showing the slightest consideration for the state of its springs. Since it was the only piece of furniture in the room that anyone could sit on, and since we had a lot of guests, both Jewish and Aryan, the bed was subject to terrible exploitation.

In the evenings, Jerzyk gave concerts on the harmonica. These attracted the neighbors and the widow's large family. Jerzyk loved taking risks and playing games. He often played Jewish melodies like *Ma oz Tzur* (a Hanukka song) or the national anthem *Hatikva*. He confided to his listeners that the first was an American foxtrot, while the second was the Czech polka that Smetana had used as the basis for his symphonic poem *Vltava*. This drove me mad.

'Quit playing those songs, you idiot! Every Jew in the whole apartment complex will know about us!' My admonitions had no effect.

The widow's son Bolek was a handsome beanpole with one stiff leg. He played the violin. Menuhin he wasn't. His repertoire consisted of two pieces, Beethoven's *Romance in F-sharp* and Vivaldi's *First Violin Concerto*. I do not know if he was taking lessons in those days or only practicing to keep from getting rusty. In any case, he devoted a great deal of time to that difficult instrument, to his mother's satisfaction. As to the neighbors, they had to get used to it. Bolek was slightly uncouth; like all tall people, he tended to look down on others. He was satisfied with himself and with his intelligence, which he exercised from time to time in conversations with me. He did not lack dynamism. He spoke loudly and laughed loudly, although his sense of humor was rather limited.

The widow was an extremely delicate person. 'Sleeping Beauty' fit her perfectly, and it seems to me that that is what we called her. She slept late, and she spent a lot of time in front of the mirror when she was not asleep. She liked herself very much; she was fascinated with herself. This suited us fine, for it meant that she took little notice of what was happening around her – and a great many things were happening that anyone else would have noticed. She was very distinguished and had a mannered way of speaking. This was no affectation. It was the way she talked. The thing was that she spoke little. Although she seldom went out, she did not flit about the apartment and we were hardly aware of her presence. She was a very convenient sort of landlady. As we got to know her better, we began taking advantage of the way she refrained from interfering in our lives. These were stormy and, in a certain sense, quite noisy lives – not to speak of the fact that, when we had no choice, we violated certain canons of domestic safety …

I cannot specify the degree to which the widow's mental laziness contributed to her ignorance of our obnoxious origins. For a long time, in any case, we never spoke with her about Jews. She, by the same token, never intimated that she suspected us of Jewishness. I had come to regard it as a rule that, after spending about two weeks with us, people caught on. Perhaps she was only testing me when she chose me, of all people, to stand as her witness when she applied for a new identity card. This was hardly a pleasurable experience. Refusing would have been out of the question, and I did not attempt to do so. My heart was pounding as I handed my terribly unconvincing identity card to the clerk, but he noticed nothing strange about it. He did not even glance at me. He copied down the information, with '*Schustergeselle*' at the top, and handed it back to me. The widow was shortsighted, and she did not try to read my *kenkart*. Why would she want to? The whole procedure seemed natural, but I complained about what an unusually hot summer we were having as I wiped the sweat from my forehead.

Marysia Scislo was 18, but seemed younger. She was pretty, graceful, and good-hearted, but she seemed immature for her age and for the war years. She began to mature when we lived there. This must have been partly under the influence of our brisk social life, in which she took part. That social life included people she knew, and then acquaintances of people she knew, but also our Jewish friends who often visited us because they had nowhere to go. Marysia loved to sit in our room listening to the verses of Leśmian, Tuwim, and Zegadlowicz, or of Hemar and Jurandot. Then there were Jerzyk's concerts. He never took much persuading before picking up his harmonica. Later, when Klara began visiting, we organized spiritualist seances. We regarded them as harmless fun, but they drove Marysia into a state of wild excitement.

I knew a very rich repertoire of poetry by heart. I had never deliberately memorized Leśmian's texts, and cannot say how or when they stuck in my mind. I especially liked his 'maimed verses', beginning with the gimpy 'Cobbler' who made shoes to fit the feet of God, through the 'Soldier' who returned from the campaigns insane and so strange that he could not move but by hopping, to the out-of-control 'Hand', with a mind of its own, that grew and grew. This poem may have had some influence on the way I behaved in church:

> When I cross myself, what a sign of the cross,
> It's enormous because I can't stop the momentum;
> When I get in reach of some fresh blades of grass,
> One swipe – to eternity I've sent them!
> My Hand, my excessive Hand,
> I try to make a prayerful fist!
> This hand is something I can't stand,
> Ten times bigger than my wrist!

That was my litany. I crossed myself with an exaggerated sign of the cross, or brought my hands together in prayer and rocked to the rhythm of the verse until Marysia could not help bursting out – this was in the later period when, surely encouraged by the remarks of neighbors or guests, it began to dawn on her that I might be a villager – 'Hey, Franciszek, you rock back and forth like a Jew in church!'

I might have had an answer, but it stuck in my throat. I would only make a mock-mysterious face and point toward heaven. This might have meant something, or might mean something, but it explained nothing.

I had long been convinced that what saved me was my deep faith in people and my lack of money (I had nothing to lose). As I write these words, I also begin to feel that I was saved by Leśmian – by poetry in general, but especially by Leśmian. His poems were an escape from reality into a world of fantasy and uncanny beauty, of an immortal mythology into which I escaped along with my listeners. How could they ever turn me in after I had given them the great gift of 'The Two Maciejs'?

For us 'Aryans', a job was almost as pressing a problem as an apartment. In the first place, a person needs something to live on; furthermore, even if money is no problem, he must appear in the eyes of his landlord to be employed. In no case is there a rational explanation for sitting at home all day. Our acquaintances told their landlords that they had jobs. They came to us in the mornings, sat there as long as they could, then went off to visit other acquaintances before returning home in the late afternoon or evening. I have mentioned that we initially told the widow Scislo that Jerzyk was studying at the clandestine secondary school, and that I was preparing him for his exams while recovering from an inflammation of the joints and preparing to start work at the city power plant in two or three weeks' time. I was determined to find a job in that period, especially since we really did need money to live on. The mother of 'Kazik' – Edzio Birn – had contacts with the underground Bund. At around that time, she arranged 'salaries' for us of 500 *zloty* per head. That paid our rent and helped mother, who had moved in with Mrs Janiczek (following the extortion on Odolanska Street) for 1,500 per month. So the rent was paid. I decided to begin giving English lessons. I had started learning that language six weeks before the war. Despite the interruption of those lessons, something had remained. When a copy of McCalum's excellent textbook fell into my hands by chance, I realized that I could give lessons to beginners. I knew a few songs, like *It's a Long Way to Tipperary, My Bonnie is Over the Ocean*, and a few numbers from *Snow White*. This, too, was teaching material. I prepared my lessons in the morning and my pupils came in the afternoon; sometimes, I went to them. They all lived in the big ZUS housing complex. No one suspected that I had a very, very poor knowledge of English. The only one who knew was Uncle Zygmunt. He visited occasionally and sometimes helped me prepare my lessons. He knew English quite well and used to say, 'Have you no fear of God? After all, you are crippling your students for life!'

The students, however, were highly satisfied and recommended me to their friends as an excellent teacher. I had pedagogical talent.

At this time, we discovered a new source of income: ceramics. Jerzyk used to go shopping at Narutowicza Square. He came home one day with a few clay vases, ashtrays and bowls, thinking that we might be able to paint them and sell them for a profit. I remembered the patterns on Viennese ceramics and knew how to hold a paintbrush. So I bought a small set of ordinary school water colors and set eagerly to work. We then poured a layer of clear varnish over the painted 'ceramics'. They looked beautiful. Jerzyk took the merchandise to Narutowicza Square with the intention of standing there and selling it. However, he showed them first to the owner of a shop and mentioned the modest price of 20 *zloty* a piece. The shop owner took everything, paid, and asked for more. We were thrilled; within a few days, we had prepared a beautiful collection. We realized that our price was too low, so we calculated what we could earn, re-organized the way we worked (one painted the background and the other the design), and thought that we had solved two problems: our income and my sitting at home. Imagine our disappointment when Jerzyk went to the shop and came back carrying everything we had produced! To put it mildly, he had been received in an unfriendly way. It turned out that when water was poured into the vases, it soaked through the porous material and produced blisters and pimples on the painted side. Horrible!

All our work had come to naught!

However, we did not despair. We began varnishing the vases inside and out, and in any case we informed the shop that the vases were not meant to hold water. In our search for new clients, we stumbled across Manfred Milke's, one of the biggest German shops on Krakowskie Przedmiescie Street. Our hand-painted wares were so popular that the manager promised to buy all we could produce, on condition that we make him our exclusive distributor. We agreed readily. Milke gave us an affidavit stating that we were working for him – for a German firm – and we doubled our production. Our friends helped us to fabricate these 'Viennese ceramics'. They had nothing to do and hung out at our place anyway, and this gave them a chance to earn a few *grosz*. By the way, I never laid eyes on the Manfred Milke shop – and vice-versa. I sat at home painting, while Jerzyk attended to the marketing end. This went on for two or three months. Then, when more and more people were being rounded up on the street, it became hazardous to go to town with large packages. We were forced to cut back our production.

*

As I have mentioned, the 'Room for Rent' sign that saved us had concerned two rooms. After we rented one, the second stood empty. We knew that it would eventually be rented by a Jew: only a Jew in hiding could pay such rent for such a room. We prayed that it would be someone with 'good looks'. Only after the war did we learn that one of the people who had contemplated renting that very room was a pretty blond girl from my class at school, Irka H. When she caught a glimpse of me and Jerzyk, she hurriedly withdrew.

Our landlady, the attorney's widow, was out one day. In her absence, a shy young lady came to the door and asked me a series of silly questions. I asked her to return later. Then I turned to my brother and said, 'Jerzyk, that was our new neighbor. She even has fairly good looks …'

Cesia did indeed rent the room. The way she had rented the room was one sign of her being Jewish. Another was the fact that she was willing to pay so much for such a gloomy room. Yet another sign was the company she kept: one girl who looked 100 per cent Aryan but was painfully shy, and a second, Zosia, who looked as Jewish as could be, and was extremely cheeky. Cesia worked in an aircraft factory and had Saturdays off. That struck us as funny and we joked that she must be very observant if she did not work Saturdays. Cesia was completely disoriented and assumed that my brother and I must be a pair of dangerous National Democrats.

Around this time, Jerzyk brought a tiny kitten home. He was in the habit of springing such surprises in a carefree way that knocked me off balance. 'What do you think you're doing?' I objected. 'The widow will throw us out on our noses along with that kitten! As if we didn't have enough to worry about.'

'Leave it to me. Everything will be fine,' my younger brother assured me. Then he went off to see the widow Scislo.

By the way, let me observe that we seldom ventured into her part of the apartment. The widow liked Jerzyk very much – who didn't? – and was delighted with his visit. 'How are things, Jerzy?' she asked. 'How's business? Selling many vases?'

'Thank you, not bad, except for those roundups on the street! I almost fell into an ambush near Zbawiciela Square, and managed to duck into a doorway at the last moment. And can you imagine, Mrs Scislo, a guy was standing there and he started trying to sell me a kitten. A tiny, sweet little kitten …'

'Oh, Jerzy! What a shame you didn't buy it!'

'Well, in fact, I did buy it.'

And so there was one more of us. The training, feeding and sanitary care of the kitten fell to me, of course. The kitten took a liking to me and began sitting all day long on my shoulder, after which people began calling me 'the sorcerer's son'. It was a wise kitten. It understood everything except what was going on when I opened a book. Then it would jump down off my shoulder and curl up luxuriantly on the smooth pages. Try explaining books to a cat.

As soon as Cesia had rented the adjoining room and a bed had been placed there, she quickly managed to create a cozy, feminine atmosphere. Our kitten began going there uninvited. The room was sunny, even in the autumn, and there was a bed there. In Cesia's absence, the kitten would lie on her bed, soaking up the sunshine. Cesia came home exhausted from work one day, washed, and climbed straight into bed. A moment later, we heard a scream. Cesia didn't like cats, and the uninvited guest in her bed infuriated her. We had too much on our minds to worry continually about where the kitten was, but Cesia was convinced that we had deliberately put it in her bed to irritate her because she was Jewish. Talk about malicious antisemites! In order to demonstrate her Aryan self-confidence, she strode off to complain to the widow. Our landlady decided that we should give the kitten to someone who had more space. We felt bad about losing our little friend. Jerzyk left the antisemitic cat with acquaintances in Sluzewie.

We were somewhat irritated with Cesia and even let her know it. Then we decided to be more supportive, and peace reigned among us. Cesia finally figured out who her neighbors were. She revealed that she was in fact a physician. This surprised me; the 'manual laborer' from the aircraft factory hardly seemed like a university graduate.

Cesia's predicament in the 'Brunswerke' factory was quite difficult in those days when she revealed herself to us. Nine of the dozen or so Jews (on Aryan papers) working there had been arrested in the preceding week. Someone was obviously informing on them. Cesia was convinced that this informant was a young female worker who had approached her outside the factory once and started a provocative conversation. Sure that the police would come for her soon, Cesia wanted to stop going to work. She sometimes slept downtown at the apartment of an old, socialist working-class woman who could tip her off as to upcoming raids on factories. She would stop at home for only a moment, to check whether the Gestapo or employment police had come looking for her. I hardly need add that we, too, found this situation highly uncomfortable. Nothing happened, fortunately. Cesia was lucky: an acquaintance in the employment office managed to arrange for her to quit her job.

Cesia was a fugitive from the Warsaw ghetto, where she had worked in the hospital. She told us about the unbelievable conditions there. There had been no food, and patients had starved to death. This had enabled the doctors to gather data for a unique study. Using the ghetto population as an experimental sample, the physicians had definitively established the stages of starvation.

Polish acquaintances had extracted Cesia and her mother from the ghetto and had produced Aryan papers for her. Some early episodes of extortion and accidental exposure had cost her everything she owned, but the situation had subsequently stabilized. Cesia went to work in the factory and her mother found a job.

Cesia's mother, however, had bad luck with employment. She first worked for someone in a village outside Warsaw. A Jew who had been starving in the woods turned up one day, asking for water. The farmer called the police, who shot the Jew on the spot. This had so outraged the village that the offender had to flee to

Warsaw in fear of reprisal. Cesia's mother found other employers, but they were soon arrested as Jews. Her next employers had nothing to eat themselves, and required inhuman labor from the old woman.

Between one job and the next, the old lady stayed with her daughter, who explained her as a visiting aunt.

These women faced desperate poverty. After leaving the aircraft factory, Cesia had nothing to live on. She received some aid from acquaintances, but she could not, and did not, want to count on them in the long term. Without even telling her, we asked Adam (whom I shall describe elsewhere) to grant her 500 *zloty* aid per month. It then came out that someone else, a certain N., had arranged similar support for her months earlier – and had been keeping it all for himself. N. was a suspicious character in any case, and Cesia had not pressed him for the money. N. presented himself as a sort of liaison man between the Home Army resistance movement and the communists, but was basically a disreputable figure.

Cesia had only one extortionist. This was someone who may have remembered her from her time at the university before the war. She encountered him in Warsaw several times; on each occasion, he put her through hell. He pulled her into doorways or strange apartments and extorted her last *grosz* while spinning visions of the gallows. Cesia once stood on the sill of a fourth-floor window, threatening to jump. The hoodlum ran out, but waited below, twenty paces away. Cesia managed to escape and to hop into a passing rickshaw. 'Go fast, I don't care where!' The rickshaw driver understood what was happening and they managed to flee. He refused to take more than 20 *zloty* for the fare.

On another occasion, Cesia was crossing Grzybowski Square when she saw her extortionist a hundred paces away. He spotted her, as well, and walked towards her. Fortunately, a tram was passing just then. As it slowed for a curve, Cesia jumped on and tried to disappear into the crowd. As usual, however, the tram was too tightly packed for this to be possible. Her extortionist broke into a run and jumped on to the steps of the tram. Cesia could think of nothing to do except to tell the conductor, 'Sir, that man is an extortionist and he's persecuting me.'

Without hesitating, the conductor went over to the intruder and slapped him twice across the face. In the confusion, Cesia squeezed her way to the back platform and jumped off while the tram was running at full speed.

After each of these encounters, she returned home desperate enough to commit suicide. It took her a long time to calm down. It was a good thing that we were there: she had someone to share her tragic experiences with.

THE IRREPLACEABLE NINA

Nina lived on the ground floor. She came to visit the widow's daughter, Marysia. She loved to tell about how she had lived in Paris before the war. She had no hatred of 'villagers', but no affection for them, either.

'That problem doesn't exist in France,' she said. 'You can't tell a Jew from a non-Jew there. They have so many different races. Once, I was sitting in a café in Paris with a very nice man from Poland. In the Polish way, I began complaining about the Jews. Imagine the look on my face when he stood up and told me that he was one himself! Two weeks later, I met another young man and – can you believe my bad luck? – the same thing happened! I thought I would die of shame. So I learned to watch myself!'

She said all this as she walked along a street on the edge of town with Jerzyk and me. I felt like saying, 'You're a really unlucky girl, because I'm another one!' However, we had not known each other long enough for that. As a little child, Nina had sat on Roman Dmowski's knee. The far-right politician Wladyslaw Seyda was the dearest friend of her father, a virulent National Democrat with an estate near Poznan. Yet fate decreed that Nina would spend most of her time among people with democratic views. She cooperated with the socialist wing of the Home Army. Like a great many Poles, she was in the habit of boasting that she could 'sniff out a Jew a kilometer away'. The fact that she was harmless made her attitude charming. She sometimes imitated 'an old Jewish woman', twisting her somewhat ratlike features in an amusing way. The most fortunate thing for us was that Nina herself looked like a typical Jewish woman. She had taken up her lodgings on Asnyka Street after escaping from Majdanek; with the Gestapo on her trail, she was unable to obtain a residence permit immediately. The doorkeeper had shouted to the apartment owner, loud enough for the whole courtyard to hear, 'I've been wondering when that Jewess is going to register!'

People were afraid to rent her a room because they took her for a Jew. It was typical, however, that she was never bothered by extortionists despite spending whole days running around the city with underground literature. If you did not feel yourself to be a Jew, then no one would try to blackmail you, no matter how 'bad' you looked.

I benefitted from Nina's 'semitic features'. Whenever the doorkeeper made any remarks about concealed Jews in reference to me, I could shrug it off: 'So what? He thinks everybody's Jewish.'

In Nina's eyes, I was not a Jew. And so who was I? A man of the underground!

'That Franciszek is deep, very deep, in the conspiracy. You can't get a word out of him!' she would say in awe.

'You'll never find anything out because I don't know anything,' I would tell her jocularly.

An answer like that was 100 per cent proof that I was in the underground. And when Nina found out about something, she made sure that the whole building found out.

When we moved into the widow Scislo's apartment, Nina found out the same day. Nina was interested in men. Although Mr and Mrs Scislo came from Poznan, Nina was not a close friend. Marysia was too young, too inexperienced, and too much of a silly goose to be much company for Nina. Free and free-thinking, with her European sophistication, Nina rather spent time with university students. The fact that she was experienced, on top of her attractiveness and feminine charm, meant that she was surrounded by boys seeking female warmth – but not necessarily lifelong love.

Only when we appeared on the horizon did Nina become fast friends with Marysia. After about two weeks, she invited us to her name-day party. We then became very close and affectionate, although there was nothing sexual. I wrote her a silly verse for the occasion, punning somewhat awkwardly on her name and spinning out a conceit about how, if we ever played a Chopin concerto for four hands, the music would continue even after we left the keyboard. Nina liked it, and so did her guests. I achieved a new status in the eyes of the neighbors and the numerous young guests at her party.

Nina then began supplying me with the underground press. She delivered the main *Information Bulletin*, as well as papers printed by the various political parties, from the far right to the socialists. Only then did I become fully informed about the international situation and developments on the front lines.

Nina is one of the people for whom I have maintained the greatest gratitude and respect. Unconscious of doing so, she helped us – my family and friends – more than anyone else. To put it in a simple way, she was a human being. You could count on her when you needed any kind of help. She never refused and she never stood there with a helpless look on her face when it was necessary to do something. It is true that she did not like Jews very much. Nevertheless, when I learned of a case where an extortionist had to be eliminated, I turned to Nina rather than to people who seemed to be better disposed to Jews than she was.

Nina was a straightforward patriot. She understood her duties as an underground soldier in a practical way, without philosophizing.

*

Once we had installed ourselves in our new room, I dreamed of having a rest from extortionists, chance accusations and disasters. I wanted to settle into the new place, form lines of defense, and calmly work out a strategic plan for the whole family so that we would not have to improvise our escape and rescue plans at the last minute. Yet reality never granted any breathing room. We were under stress all the time. We were all existing on thin ice that could crack at any moment, under any one of us. Whenever you reached out a hand to save someone who was drowning, you were pulled in, too. Others had to come to help, and they managed to save the day somehow, but then everything returned to the same perilous situation as before. We trudged along, stumbling, slipping, falling on one leg and then the other into air pockets under the surface of the ice. And we still could not see the shore …

Jerzyk and I had barely caught our breath on Asnyka Street when the all-too-predictable thunderbolt from an overcast sky fell on the part of the family living on Odolanska Street. Mother and Klara managed to leap to shelter at Mrs Janiczek's on Filtrowa Street. Aunt Lana began haunting the trains from Warsaw to Cracow and back.

252

However, her daughter Malgorzata, who had just escaped from the hospital with the incision from her operation not yet healed, was in no shape to ride the trains. So she came to our place.

After we had been there for only four weeks, we did not expect the widow Scislo to look kindly on our having such a fiery brunette stay overnight.

I went to ask Nina for advice. I told her that Malgorzata had escaped from Pawiak Prison, was wounded, and had nowhere to live. She needed help. Nina was incapable of remaining indifferent. First of all, she took Malgorzata to stay in her room. By a lucky coincidence, her brother Andrzej came from the country to visit her the next day. He was a partisan with the National Combat Forces in the countryside, and was under orders to return immediately to his base. Nina turned Malgorzata over to him. He escorted her to his aunt's estate in the Lublin district. There, Malgorzata was under the care of two good souls. In particular, there was a Mrs Grabowska who, in spite of having a very troublesome daughter of her own, 'adopted' Malgorzata as her second child. She lacked for nothing there. Under the care of Mrs Grabowska, Malgorzata soon recovered her strength and the full bloom of her exuberant beauty.

A Jewish labor camp attached to an ammunition factory or some similar enterprise – Malgorzata never learned exactly what – was located in the woods a few kilometers from that estate. The manor house supplied the camp with vegetables, and it was usually Andrzej who delivered them. When Malgorzata was feeling better, she asked Andrzej if she could accompany him. He agreed readily. Mrs Grabowska always gave Malgorzata a few bundles of food 'for the poor Jews' behind barbed wire. Andrzej looked disparagingly on such practices, but did not protest. He limited himself to a few biting remarks; he had a great aversion to Jews.

'One day', Malgorzata told me later, 'we drove a whole cart full of sacks of carrots to that camp. Andrzej tried to make a deal with the young Jew who was guarding the gate. Andrzej gave him to understand that he should mark the receipt in such a way that there would be one sack of carrots left for the black market. Then they could split the profit. The young Jew replied in no uncertain terms: "You offspring of filthiness! Do you expect me to cheat my own brothers? Not on your life" – and he spat in disgust. Andrzej went white as chalk and answered not a word. Only on the way back home did he say through gritted teeth, half laughing and half in fury, "That damned Jew!" Seldom in those hard times', Malgorzata concluded, 'did I feel as light-hearted as then.'

Andrzej had a deadly hatred of Jews and communists; indeed, Jews and communists were the same thing for him. He was famous throughout the district for his views. One winter day, Nina told me, he was taken prisoner in the forest by leftist guerillas, who may well have been Jewish. They kept him lying face-down in the snow for 12 hours while debating over what to do with him. Just when Andrzej had resigned himself to dying there, they released him. What became of him afterwards, I cannot say.

*

Malgorzata had not yet returned to Warsaw from her convalescence, when new problems landed on our daybed.

Uncle Zygmunt knocked at the door one day. He was not alone. He had a guest. I did not recognize him at first, but then I realized that it was the blond-haired man we had met at Mrs Ebert's party while arranging Uncle Zygmunt's apartment. I deduced from Uncle Zygmunt's shaken expression that another extortion scam was afoot. Could that young dandy be so abject? However, Krzepicki had not come to us as an antisemite. He came as a hunted Jew.

Here is what had happened. As I mentioned earlier, Waclaw Krzepicki (his real name was Marek Margulies) had excellent looks – an authentic *goy*. He had bleached his red hair golden blond. His hound's tooth suit was immaculate and pressed razor-sharp, his suede shoes brushed, and his tie perfect. As if he had stepped out of a magazine. No one would have dreamed that he was a Jew. He had only one weak point: he was a Warsaw native. A great many Poles, including his classmates from school and people from the street, knew him. Living in Warsaw was unsafe for such people. But Marek had been so sure of himself that he took the risk. When Uncle Zygmunt moved to Czerniakowska Street, Marek had been living there for several months as Waclaw Krzepicki. The two sub-tenants struck up neighborly relations that never went beyond the accepted norms of politeness and mutual favors. They did not suspect each other – or at least Uncle Zygmunt did not suspect Krzepicki of being Jewish. Until the day when his doorbell rang. Zygmunt opened the door and three men pushed their way

254

inside. They had come for Krzepicki, but Uncle Zygmunt assumed in his ignorance that he was the object of their attentions. After a few sentences had been exchanged, the assailants realized that Zygmunt, too, was a villager. Two birds with one stone! There was no way out. Having tied a string around the suitcase containing their wardrobes, Mr Krzepicki and Mr Durakowski allowed themselves to be escorted to the fiacre waiting at the front door. Several onlookers were already standing around. Thinking that this was a case of everyday extortion, the helpful doorkeeper had summoned a pair of passing German gendarmes to check the papers of the three men who seemed to be common blackmailers. It turned out that they were Gestapo agents. The fiacre set off toward Gestapo headquarters on Szucha Boulevard. Uncle Zygmunt and Marek tried negotiating with their captors, but to no avail. Neither persuasion nor an offer to ransom themselves with the valuables in their possession had any result. They rode along through the center of Warsaw until a young passerby stopped the fiacre at a busy intersection. 'Marek!' he cried. 'What are you doing here? Where are you going?'

It turned out that this was a Pole, a classmate of Krzepicki's from school. He may also have known the Gestapo agents; upon learning what was happening, he quickly brokered an agreement. Having paid the appropriate ransom – in other words, having given the extortionists everything they owned: a gold watch, a diamond tie-pin, a few gold coins, and two men's suits – they were released. Obviously, they did not return home. They came to us instead.

What could we do? They could spend one or two nights here. The widow was hardly elated. Persons who were not registered as living in a given apartment were not allowed to sleep there. And what if, God forbid, there were to be a surprise search of the whole building? So what could we do? We went to Nina. Nina always found a way out.

I did not tell Nina that Wacek was looking for an apartment. I simply introduced them. Wacek was an intelligent, cynical young man. When his sort has a touch of elegance and self-confidence, they attract the opposite sex, rather than repelling them. I could tell that Nina liked Wacek. He could not, of course, inform her immediately that he was homeless. First things first. In the meantime, the two men spent two nights with us. Sleeping four people on one daybed need not be uncomfortable, providing that chairs are placed where they can support the legs of the sleepers.

Wacek moved out after two nights. Having learned earlier how to do so, he decided to spend a couple of nights in the German gambling casino. He spoke German well, and he spent the whole night wandering from table to table, watching the gamblers, before returning to our place, exhausted and yawning, at dawn. He lay on the daybed for a while and then helped us paint vases.

Uncle Zygmunt was our 'valet' somewhat longer. He was suffering from sciatica and bladder trouble in those days, which meant that he had to get up to relieve himself several times each night. This did not escape the notice of the widow. At first she said nothing, but she called me on the carpet several days later: everything had its limits, we were taking advantage of her good will, we were putting the whole building at risk, and if we decided to entertain overnight guests, we should at least ask her permission. What was I supposed to say? She was right. I admitted as much, apologized for our incorrect behavior, told her a tale about Mr Durakowski and how he had to come to Warsaw for some time, and asked her to allow him to stay two or three more nights. The widow allowed herself to be mollified. At heart, she was a good woman. I took no pleasure in abusing her indifferent tolerance and violating the residence laws – but we had no choice. Helping people in need came first. That was our principle.

Uncle Zygmunt returned to Czerniakowska Street several days later on the express wishes of his landlords there, who had been questioned only in regard to Krzepicki. Nothing at all had been said about Zygmunt.

Within a week, Krzepicki had become sufficiently acquainted with Nina to inform her that he had had to leave his apartment. Why? – in the world of the underground, it was bad form to ask such questions. If he had to, then he had to. Nina therefore informed her landlady that her cousin from Lublin would be visiting her and staying with her until he found a place of his own. Wacek landed at Nina's and slept there for a month, until he found a place of his own. Or perhaps Nina found it for him. I do not recall.

*

Our social life flourished as we made the acquaintance of more of our fellow residents in the ZUS apartment complex, but most of all thanks to Nina. Once she understood that she was dealing with an underground intellectual, she made every effort to introduce me to her friends and acquaintances from academic and creative circles. I thus made the acquaintance of a certain publisher who was giving writers commissions for books that he would publish after the war. He told me how he had just purchased the memoirs of Cejnar, a notorious Warsaw confidence man who had sold the Copernicus Memorial and the Kierbedzia bridge to gullible hayseeds.

I offered the publisher a book on 'Folk Elements in Polish Painting', since I was interested in this subject at the time. We agreed that I would submit a sample chapter and an outline of the whole book. Having learned about this, Nina 'loaned' me a likeable student from the Fine Arts Academy (or perhaps the art history institute). He was called Jurek. As reference material, he brought me transcripts of lectures by Professor Marian Lalewicz, whom he referred to affectionately as 'Lalunio'. Along with two of his friends, Jurek had set up a puppet theatre. They rented a room on Marszalkowska Street for their performances. They were looking for texts. At that time, I had been planning to work on Mirek Jelusich's *Don Juan*. Since I was interested in the Don Juan theme, I offered to write the libretto for a puppet opera. Jurek reacted enthusiastically and invited me to come see one of their performances. This did not strike me as such a good idea and I tried to weasel out of it, putting him off one day at a time until I finally had no choice but to go.

It was a cold, rainy night in late October, and I still had nothing to wear except the paltry old wind-lashed overcoat that I had brought from Cracow. I left home only reluctantly. *Noblesse oblige*, however. Five of us set off for the theatre: Wacek, Jerzyk, Marysia, Nina and I. We were good and wet by the time we reached the small auditorium on the fourth floor of a large public building. We took our seats. To this day, I remember the circular staircase with its wide stairs and columns, and the crowded corridors – but I cannot recall the address, or which building it was, or which corner it stood on. I did not know Warsaw well enough.

The lights went out and left us sitting in that pleasant theatrical half-light. In those days, I always preferred half-light. To tell the truth, I felt anxious. I was uncomfortable sitting there in my shabby, out-of-season attire – that was not my style for attending the theatre. This shows how neurotic I was; after all, people accepted me as I was and, in any case, my dress suited the fashion of my proletarian–intellectual identity. Yet I could not accustom myself, and it always seemed that inquisitive eyes were focused on me and my miserable wardrobe.

I was sitting with Jerzyk and Marysia; Wacek and Nina were two rows in front of us. The auditorium was almost empty. I tried to follow the performance once it began, but there was a guy nosing around near Wacek. First he sat in front of him, then he moved behind him, then he disappeared. I felt instinctively that something was going on. And, indeed, Wacek soon came to me and whispered, 'Take Nina and Marysia and clear out. I'll take care of myself.'

I sighed regretfully. Damn it, I had been in the mood for the theatre! I was angry at myself, at Wacek, at the whole world. There was no time to lose. I went up to Nina, who had failed to notice anything, and said quietly in a tone that brooked no contradiction: 'Come on!'

She started objecting: 'What do you mean? Why?'

'Don't ask why. Wacek ordered me to clear out, and that's enough. He knows what he's talking about.'

We slunk out of the auditorium. It was dark: rain, fog, and one umbrella for all of us. As the Russians say, 'Sad, boring, and nobody to punch in the face.' Numerous patrols were checking people's papers on the street. That was all we needed. We somehow managed to slip through the German net by loitering and sneaking through gateways and corridors, until we caught a tram. By the time we got home, we were soaked to the skin.

It turned out to have been yet another of Wacek's acquaintances from school, who may have been harmless but was certainly reckless. I swore that I would never again go to any sort of performance.

*

Wacek had a very self-centered philosophy. He had his principles and, as he liked to say, he knew what suited him intellectually and what didn't. He did not talk about Jews. If others brought up the subject, he assumed the stance of a moderate antisemite: while hardly defending, God forbid, the Nazi crimes against the Jewish people, he acknowledged the rationale for 'the economic struggle, of course'. That was the Wacek I had met during our first encounter at Mrs Ebert's. He had known immediately who I was, because I spoke sympathetically of the Jews. So he told me later. His tactic may have been appropriate. For me, however, it was more important what people would say about me when they discovered that I was Jewish. I had decided irrevocably that I would always take the side of the Jews and defend them. I wanted to have clean hands and a clean conscience in regard to the people whom I befriended and whose confidence I gained. That was why I could look everyone in the eye after the war and say, 'Yes, it's true I'm a Jew, but I'm the same person you knew. I have not changed my skin, only my name.' I discussed this subject often with Wacek. He was four years younger than me. While I did not like his cynicism and arrogance, he struck me as a bright, experienced person – the sort who knows what he wants. And then he revealed himself to me one day as a scoundrel and an irresponsible snot.

He came to see us in the afternoon, which was not his usual custom. He had taken Nina to the hospital that morning. It turned out that he had got her pregnant, and she had gone to get rid of it. No – I wasn't shocked. I knew that it was not the first such procedure for Nina. She had many friends. It wasn't such a big deal for her; in any case, she didn't make it into a problem. I felt bad that this had happened with Wacek, but I did not see it as a misfortune. At most, it was a lack of fortune. 'Nina's been around,' I told him. 'She'll be alright.'

'That's the point', he replied, 'she's experienced, but I'm not. Advise me. She wants me to pay the hospital bill. It might not be a lot of money, but I have no intention of paying, on principle. When you come down to it', he continued, 'she's the one who raped me. I'm innocent. I went there because I had nowhere else to live. I had no such intentions, while she …'

I felt angry enough to punch him in the face. 'What do you want me to say? Is this the way a gentleman talks? You're a scoundrel and a little s**t, understand? Of course you're supposed to pay! Some day, we'll all pay for your recklessness!'

Wacek was not convinced, but he promised to think it over. He was used to arguing with me. We held different views on many matters, but my opinion still counted with him. He left highly irritated, but I was convinced that he would pay the bill, as he should. And yet …

Wacek spent the whole day wandering around with money in his pocket and a head full of conundrums, until he fell into the hands of extortionists again. They had been watching where he lived and were waiting on the street corner. They cleaned him out of everything that he had left after the last extortion incident, right down to the last *grosz*. He had no means of paying the hospital bill, if he had ever intended to. If I had had any money, I would have loaned him what he needed, but we were living through hard times then after getting out of the ceramics business because of all the street roundups.

Wacek did not pay for the procedure and Nina was very angry. She never wanted to see him again. Her relations with us did not change at all. We went on being friends and benefitting from her ability to help us and our acquaintants, right up to the outbreak of the Warsaw Uprising.

After the end of the war, I revealed my Jewish origins to my Polish acquaintances. I could no longer stand my assumed name. As soon as I was back in Cracow, I wrote to all my Warsaw acquaintances whose addresses I knew. They were scattered throughout Poland, since Warsaw had been burned to the ground. Nina was the only person to whom I did not reveal myself. I deliberately refrained from looking for her, and do not know to this day where she is. And yet she had done more for us than anyone else. I wanted to explain to her what and who I was, to thank her for everything, and to say, 'I am a Jew'. Except that I dreaded one question: 'And what about Krzepicki?'

Or perhaps I am mistaken.

This matter weighed very, very heavily on my conscience. Like it or not, I had introduced Nina to the reckless boy, and I was therefore the one who bore the responsibility for his actions.

MISTER MOELLER – TWO ARKADIUSZES – KORCZAK FROM CRACOW

When we moved to Asnyka Street, the apartment across the corridor was vacant. A Jewish man and his family had been living there; they received just enough warning to escape an hour before the Gestapo arrived. The apartment was soon taken over by Mr Moeller, the commandant of the building. He had previously lived in a different apartment in the ZUS housing complex. Some people said that he was a *Volksdeutsch* while others denied this. In any case, his arrogance and incredible cheekiness, combined with an explosive temper, ensured his general unpopularity.

It would have been unthinkable for the commandant to fail to learn that an underground activist named Franciszek Grymek had moved into the building. He was anxious to meet me as soon as possible. This took little conniving, since we ran into each other in the elevator. Barely had we introduced ourselves when he went on the attack: 'Do you play bridge?'

'A little …'

'Great. We need a fourth player! Can you come at eight this evening?'

I could. I found the invitation highly gratifying, since making friends with the commandant of the building meant a great deal to someone like me. I rang the doorbell across the corridor at eight o'clock sharp. Mr Moeller had a mouthful of food when he opened the door and led me into the living room. Asking me to wait until he and his wife finished supper, he casually threw a typescript on the table in front of me. 'I'm sure you've already read this …'

I nodded and made a gesture to indicate that he should not trouble himself on my account. When he had left the room, I inspected the clandestine publication. It was *S*, the daily bulletin of the underground. Nina had never given me a copy. She brought me the monthlies and weeklies, like *The Information Bulletin, Poland, State Thought*, the socialist *Freedom, The Sword and the Plow*, and even the National Combat Forces' *The Struggle*.

The Moellers soon finished supper and the third player appeared (I was the fourth). He was a smallish young man named Arkadiusz Dobrowolski.

Moeller was a robust, handsome man with a thick brush mustache under his ample nose. He spoke loudly, adding emphasis with his hands and spraying saliva to the left and right. He was no great bridge player – nor was I – but his lovely young wife was a complete zero. Her husband castigated her with insults and vulgar epithets whenever she made a mistake. I cannot recall her name, for her husband never referred to her in any other way than as 'you sweet little bitch'. It later turned out that he was madly jealous – without reason, as far as I could tell – and smacked her on the face or wherever else he could reach. The woman's imploring screams carried into our apartment. She sometimes complained to me. I felt very sorry for her, but there was little I could do to help, except to try to influence her husband by jesting about his over-excitability.

The bridge evenings brought us very close together. When Moeller was preparing for the baptism of his infant son – whom he referred to affectionately as 'the filthy little beggar' – he invited me to act as godfather. I tried to excuse myself on the grounds that I did not own a decent suit, but Moeller had a snobbish preference for just such shabby-genteel intellectuals as me. I obviously looked the way a man of the underground was supposed to look. When it was time for me to be entered in the parish register, I pulled out my unfortunate *kenkart* and felt somewhat out of place. However, the priest did not even look at the document, and only asked for my name and occupation. I hesitated. Mr Moeller understood readily. Although he had not seen what was written in Franciszek Grymek's papers, he said, 'Give your true occupation.'

I winked at him and said, 'Painter'.

Three gentlemen came calling on Moeller in his absence one autumn day. Since no one answered, they rang our doorbell. Jerzyk went. 'Who's there?'

'The police. Open up, please.'

We both blanched and looked at each other, trying to decide what to do. Jerzyk finally opened the door. When we realized that they were looking for Moeller, we sighed with relief. In the meantime, the door on the other side of the corridor opened – the terrified maid had heard our voices. The three men entered, followed by Jerzyk and the widow's daughter. They presented their police identity cards and then began looking in the wardrobes. They did not take anything. They asked a few questions about Moeller's daily habits, and then left.

We were upset and telephoned Moeller's shop immediately. He and his wife arrived a few moments later. After listening as we and his maid recounted the details of the visit, he brought his entire fortune to our room. This consisted of a few ten-dollar bills, a couple of rings, his watch, and so on, along with his papers. He asked us to conceal them. I learned from these

262

documents that he had been a Polish maritime officer and had served on practically every freight and passenger ship that flew the Polish flag. There were also a British driver's license issued in Palestine, an affidavit that he was an Argentinian citizen, and four passports.

Later, he sometimes talked about his visits, while boasting of his amorous conquests – not particularly to his wife's delight.

'I've had women with names from every letter of the alphabet,' he said, and then listed the fiery brunettes and passionate blondes from various exotic countries.

'Have you had anybody with Y?' I insisted.

'What a question! No less than two! Yvonne and Yvette! Ah, those French women …!'

Moeller cherished a wild hatred of Jews. He called them 'those filthy beggars', although, as I have noted, this was also his pet name for his infant son. In fact, it was only European Jews who were filthy beggars. He would willingly have exterminated the lot of them (he had belonged to a fraternity in his home town of Poznan), except that Hitler had beaten him to it. On the other hand, he raved about the Palestinian Jews, to whom no amount of praise could do justice. His excess of temperament came out in the exalted way he told a story, like a typical sailor.

'Francesco', he said, using his private nickname for me, 'you would not believe what splendid people they are. Boys as solid as oak trees, sun-tanned to a deep bronze, and hospitable! God, I loved those kibbutzes. You've never seen anything like it. And Tel Aviv! Talk about a fantastic city!'

He could never have guessed how pleasant it was for me to listen to his tales of Palestine.

My friendship with Moeller served as excellent camouflage from the doorkeeper, who had an exceptionally well-developed olfactory sense. I far preferred for the doorkeeper to think of me as a political conspirator, rather than as a Jew. I was therefore not concerned in the least when Moeller would spot me in the courtyard and cry out, 'Francesco! Francesco – come here on the double. What's the news? What have you heard?'

I would look in the direction of the little room, put on a worried expression, and indicate the doorkeeper with a gesture. Moeller would shrug and put me at ease by saying, 'It's alright. You can talk. He's one of us.'

Moeller was the sort of gossip that one finds only among sailors. This habit became more and more dangerous. With no ill intentions, he would talk to the doorkeeper about acquaintances of his who were sheltering Jews, giving the exact addresses and noting that he hoped those Jews survived. Once, within earshot of a judicial official, he said, 'Francesco, that woman who rents a room at your place is a Jewess!'

When I denied it, he said what I had heard so often over the last few years: 'I know them. I can spot a Jew a kilometer away.'

To which the court official rejoined, 'Well if that's true, you ought to try to get her to move out immediately. Otherwise, she'll put the whole building in danger.'

Moeller placed unlimited trust in me and left me the key to his apartment when he left for vacation in May. He asked me to sleep there and keep an eye on the place.

Just then, I found myself in immediate need of places for several acquaintances to sleep. I did not want to abuse Moeller's trust. However, I could not say no to my friends.

As Janek-Szymek and I lay sleeping in my neighbor's apartment early one morning, we heard a key in the lock. Fortunately, I had also put the chain on. I was determined not to open the door if there were to be an apartment-by-apartment search. Now, however, I crept to the door in my pajamas and saw Moeller's mother and uncle attempting to get in. I took off the chain and ran back to the bedroom, locking the door. We dressed quickly. I sneaked Janek out, and then I left. My maneuver must have been noticed, however. Moeller came to Warsaw the next day and asked me to give the key to his mother. He said that she was going to move in. This unpleasant incident did nothing to undercut our friendship. Moeller consistently believed that I had been sheltering another member of the underground in his apartment.

Moeller had many enemies. He was by nature a good man, but incredibly quick-tempered. This led to many faux-pas. He was the sort of person who could turn into a model citizen if he were a character in a novel – but not in real life. He had offended too many people and spread too many wildly exaggerated rumors.

I tried to locate him after the war. A common acquaintance informed me of the sad end of Moeller's tempestuous life. Shortly after the war, he had been named to an official position near Gdansk or Szczecin. The vicinity of the sea attracted him. He acquired a motor vehicle of some sort and drove northward, toward happiness. Along the way, he ran over a mine and was blown to bits. He left behind his 'sweet little bitch' and small son – I hope they have found a peaceful haven somewhere.

*

I met young Arkadiusz Dobrowolski during that first game of bridge at the Moellers'. When I saw him in the dentist's waiting room several days later, I had difficulty recognizing him. He spoke to me first and I could tell that we would be friends. We later met during those bridge games at the the Moellers'. When I realized that Arkadiusz brought clandestine newspapers to my neighbor, I also began bringing mine. In this way, I initiated an exchange of newspapers and became the local liaison between two different underground structures that had been unaware of each other's existence.

Then I met Arkadiusz's family. He and his father had the same first name. Arkadiusz Senior, a distinguished elderly man with a flourishing old-fashioned mustache, was an extraordinarily magnanimous and helpful person. A socialist, he had taken part in the Russian Revolution. His apartment was a distribution point for the weekly socialist press and the daily *S* bulletin.

Once, when we had known each other for several months, Arkadiusz Junior called on me in an agitated state. There had been an arrest within the distribution system, and he feared that someone might inform on the whole network. Perhaps they already had the addresses of all the distribution points. Could I take over the distribution of 50 copies of the newspaper, on a temporary basis? I agreed without hesitation. I was pleased that I had grown from a casual liaison between Nina and Arkadiusz into an active conspirator.

From then on, a pleasant female courier came to see me every morning, carrying 50 copies of the *S* radio bulletin rolled up in a bundle. Two days after I happened to mention to Nina that I was now distributing the underground press, she brought me a new piece of furniture: a graceful desk with a secret drawer, where I kept back copies and various documents. I made most of my deliveries within our massive housing complex. Sometimes, I also had to carry parcels downtown, where I arranged various items of business, made appointments, and so on. With my not-so-good looks, this was somewhat troubling, but I never refused a request.

Cesia had contacts with the Polish Workers' Party. In early 1944, she began bringing me *The Voice of Warsaw* and other communist publications. In return, I gave her bulletins and periodicals that I obtained. Such wide-ranging activity only reinforced my standing in the building. I felt very good about it all. Arkadiusz Senior liked me very much. I began visiting him on a daily basis. During those evenings at his apartment, I frequently encountered a middle-aged man who, I was sure, was Jewish. I felt that he had no doubts about me from the very beginning. Initially, Arkadiusz Senior told me nothing about 'the doctor'. Only when I noted the latter's absence one day did I learn that he had been blackmailed and had had to flee to Grodzisko. He turned out to be an associate professor of veterinary medicine at Warsaw University. I cannot recall his name. He liked me very much and, as Arkadiusz Senior told me, became worried and asked about me whenever I failed to turn up.

Arkadiusz Dobrowolski Senior was a philosemite. He had worked in the construction industry, and had a high regard for the work of Jewish craftsmen. He always defended the Jews in general conversations. He spoke about the honesty, conscientiousness and realistic calculations of the Jewish craftsman, who could set a modest price, use the best materials, do his work well, and still support his family in abundance. Long experience, on the other hand, had shown Arkadiusz Senior that Polish craftsmen took large down payments which they then drank, so that they then could not afford materials. They did their work shoddily or left it unfinished. I tried to tell him that things were perhaps not always so bad, but he defended his opinion. He regretted that the Polish workman could not calculate properly; he saw this as the beginning of all the trouble. The root cause, he averred, lay in the low level of education and the lack of vocational schools.

At the Dobrowolskis' I often heard talk of a priest, of whom I had also been informed elsewhere, who sheltered Jews. Yet even this respected clergyman could not escape extortion. Some of his friends laid a trap for him. Fortunately, the priest found out about the informers; by the time the Gestapo arrived, the Jews were nowhere to be found. The senior Gestapo officer, an urbane Viennese, supposedly told the priest, 'I don't understand you Poles. What kind of people are you? You never give us a moment's rest. It's nothing but informers' denunciations, all day and all night. Nowhere else is it like that, only in Poland.'

Arkadiusz Senior sometimes complained about the antisemitism in the Home Army resistance organization. 'An old comrade-in-arms of mine from the last war, a Jew, contacted me', he said, 'and told me that he wanted to do his patriotic duty. He asked me to put him in touch with the partisans. I relayed the request to a commander I know. He was a decent man, but he castigated me: 'You know very well that I'm no antisemite and I hate to turn you down, but you have to understand that the boys would get upset. They won't take orders from a Jew. I have two Jewish officers, and I have to invent the most fantastic assignments so that they have as little contact with the boys as possible. I'm sorry, but that's the way it is. Try your luck elsewhere.''

What I loved to listen to best of all were Arkadiusz Senior's stories of his adventures during the Russian Revolution. One of them has stuck in my mind. During the fighting between the Reds and the Whites, there were all sorts of situations: local cease-fires, small-scale agreements, truces. Arkadiusz took part in one such meeting between the hostile forces. The negotiations were held in a luxurious first-class saloon car that happened to be sitting at the local train station. When they concluded their discussions and signed the agreement, one big oaf who had been taking part in the talks got up, took hold of the window curtains, and ripped them down off the rod. Immediately, another one did the same with the curtains at the door. Then the others threw themselves on the velvet upholstery, and in an instant the car had been stripped of everything that could be carried away. They all disappeared, leaving Arkadiusz Senior alone with an old Bolshevik. He regretfully surveyed the desolation, heaved a deep sigh, and shrugged. 'See, Comrade', he told Dobrowolski, 'what a whorish nation it is! What can you say?' The old Bolshevik waved his hand dejectedly, picked up a bench from which all the upholstery had been stripped away, and trudged off into the evening gloom.

The Dobrowolskis were a patriarchal household of the old school. They cultivated their family life fastidiously. All the relatives gathered for every holiday and domestic observance. I took part in some of these gatherings as the only non-relative

(Jerzyk was then at school in Otwock). They treated me better than a son.

I have no doubt that Arkadiusz knew exactly who I was.

*

As he hurried around town with the ceramics, Jerzyk happened to meet a friend from Cracow. This young man was also named Jerzy, and was the son of a prominent dentist. When he supplied himself with Aryan papers in the Cracow ghetto, he assumed the name Korczak. Did he know that this was the name of the director of a Jewish orphanage?[1] In any case, our Korczak was to supply us with many Jewish occupants of our daybed, and he himself would use it more than once. He had 'good looks' and deported himself like a typical tough kid off the streets of Cracow. He was, in fact, a dangerous little snot who put as at risk more than once through his irresponsible ideas and thoughtless exploitation of our apartment and good will.

When he sailed into view, he was still living in the dormitory in Sluzewie run by the RGO charitable organization, making mistakes while leading morning prayers, conspiring with the other boys, and defending the youngest orphan there, a boy named Bolek whose ineradicable mark of Jewish descent made him a plaything in the hands of the older boys, especially in the showers. With all this, Korczak was happy.

And then the Gestapo came to the dormitory one night and arrested several boys as members of a Polish underground organization. Korczak and several of his friends fled, even though no one was looking for them. If the shoe fits, wear it. He had the brilliant idea of coming to our place with his friends. So there we were: three Jews and three Aryans. Nights were not very comfortable, even though it was warm. The boys, and especially the ones who were not in on our secret, made themselves so at home that the widow couldn't help but notice. She may well have been a very discreet woman who never intruded on us in the evening, but the boys got so noisy that even she could not help noticing that we had company. She was very unhappy.

The next day, she invited me to her room. 'Franciszek, two people stayed overnight with you again.' There had in fact been four. 'I am telling you for the last time that I do not want anyone in this apartment who does not have a residence permit. I want you to swear that it will not happen again.'

'I can't swear,' I answered. 'If someone comes and tells me he has nowhere to sleep, I am not going to turn him out. If you do not want more than two people sleeping in our room, then I can sleep in the attic. I will not invite anyone, but if someone comes and says he has nowhere to go … Would you be able to turn anyone away in such circumstances?'

We had such conversations quite often.

One winter afternoon, Korczak brought us a new client. This was Jan L., from Cracow. By coincidence, Jan, his mother, and his brother had been lodging with the widow Scislo's cousin. Of course, we did not know this until Korczak brought him to our room. This happened for the following reason: Jan's brother Stefan was in the Home Army. He was a 16-year-old boy, reckless and bold. This Stefan had returned home one November afternoon and found a search in progress. The police were not interested in his family, but rather in another lodger. Stefan could have gone to his room or walked away. Instead, with his pockets full of underground publications, he began obstreperously asking the police what they were doing there. At first, the police ignored the boy, but one of them finally decided to search him. It takes little imagination to tell what happened next. They took the boy to Gestapo headquarters on Sucha Boulevard, and he never returned. Janek and his mother left that apartment in a hurry, afraid that they would be suspected of being Jewish. Their landlady later reported that there had been no such suspicion, but Jan nevertheless went to a trusted doctor and submitted to an 'Aryanization' operation. He was in tremendous pain and despair when Korczak brought him to our room.

Those were the times when I was frequently going to the Moellers' to play bridge. I asked Jan if he played. He replied in the affirmative. Thinking that it would be good to keep him out of the widow's sight, I suggested that we visit my neighbor. It was a macabre evening. Jan turned out to be a very poor player. Furthermore, he was in excruciating pain and a very bad mood, and the cards are always lousy when you're in a bad mood. Jan lost more than 100 *zloty* to Moeller, even though we played for very low stakes. An enormous sum. It was all very depressing. We left at two in the morning and all four of us – Jerzyk, Korczak, Jan and I – slept on the daybed.

A week later, Mrs L. found an apartment. Three weeks later, the whole family left for Hungary. They survived the war there.

*

Aside from his 'normal' adventures, the carefree and energetic Jerzy Korczak also had amorous adventures, of course. He had a girlfriend named Anka Bogucka. He met her by chance; she was the daughter of a teacher from Warsaw. At Mrs Bogucka's, Korczak met her lodger, a certain Adam. Adam had highly inappropriate 'looks', but a great deal of self-assurance. He pretended to be Hungarian, and may even have had Hungarian papers, which were very popular just then. Adam arranged welfare payments, documents, and so on for Jews. Korczak introduced my brother Jerzyk to him. He was not aware at that time of all Adam's activities, but only of the fact that he had contacts with the underground. Even though the boys entertained suspicions as to Adam's being a villager, they clung to him because he impressed them with his knowledge, generosity and general character. Adam, in his turn, readily spent time with the boys, never suspecting them of being Jewish (those good looks again!). He regretted the fact that they were not in school and decided to have them educated at the cost of the underground Polish state. This was during the winter, in the first months of 1944. The boys had finished all but the last two years of secondary school. Adam took them to Swider, where he probably had to go in any case for security reasons. Soon, however, he managed to draw attention to himself in those new surroundings by going out for walks when it was not necessary to do so. The police called one day. Jerzyk and Korczak were at home, but managed to slip away. The visit must have been quite expensive for Adam, but he was left in peace afterwards – except that he had to go back to living at Mrs Bogucka's in Warsaw, and did not so much as stick his nose out the door. In the meantime, he had managed to enroll Jerzyk and Korczak in the next-to-last year of a clandestine secondary school in Otwock. They had until the end of March to make up all the material they had missed. Adam paid for their tuition, room and board at the RGO[1] cafeteria.

Adam liked to surround himself with young Aryans. Some of his young associates made friends with Korczak and his girlfriend Anka. Adam helped them all without exception, with money, in their studies, or in falsifying documents without charge. He enjoyed enormous respect, and all the more so because his underground activity was known.

One of these young people who came to the Bogucka apartment was a plump, overgrown fireman and former secondary school pupil from Poznan named Duda. Duda fell head-over-heels in love with Anka Bogucka, even though everyone knew that Anka was Korczak's unofficial fiancée. Duda began trying to undermine his rival. Dull-witted as he was, he set about it systematically. He asked a friend who was going to Cracow to sniff around and find something out about these Korczaks. It turned out that Korczak was a popular name not only among Poles, but also among Jews. Duda's friend returned with the sensational news that Korczak came from a Jewish family who had converted to Catholicism before the war, and had a shop in Cracow selling herring. Duda was quick to inform Anka of this – and Korczak had told her that his father, a captain in the Polish army, was in a prisoner-of-war camp.

When Korczak paid his next visit at the Boguckas', he did not know what happened. They all had odd expressions on their faces and Anka was crying. When she began declaring that she loved him no matter what, Korczak understood that someone had spilled the beans. He pretended not to understand anything, although he did not ask too many questions. Despite his consternation, he still felt safe. Then Adam filled Korczak in on what Duda had said. Korczak was just regaining his balance when Duda appeared. Korczak attacked him with great nerve, heaping him with abuse and making him into a laughing stock. This was one thing he was good at. From that day on, Mrs Bogucka would never open her door to Duda. Korczak was again in the ascendancy.

In view of the danger that events might take a dangerous turn, the boys decided to tell Adam the whole truth. Jerzyk, in particular, insisted. He was therefore left to handle the unpleasant business. The boys were on extremely close terms with Adam, who had even explained that if they were too embarrassed to speak about anything, they could write their questions on a piece of paper, and he would hand the paper back to them with the answer written on it. Jerzyk now proposed exactly such an exchange. He and Adam sat down on opposite sides of the table.

Jerzyk wrote: 'Fake'.

Adam wrote: 'What's fake?'

Jerzyk: 'I'm fake, you're fake'.

Adam: 'I don't understand'.

Jerzyk: 'You're pretending'.

Adam: 'I don't understand'.

Jerzyk: 'You're just the same as me'.

Adam: 'What does that mean?'

Jerzyk: 'A villager'.

Adam: 'I don't understand'.

Jerzyk: 'A Jew'.

To which Adam replied aloud, 'Me, a Jew? Are you crazy? What could make you say that?'

Jerzy was embarrassed, but tried not to show it. 'Are you trying to make a fool out of me? You look as Jewish as Jewish can be, and still you deny it. I thought you'd feel less absurd if I admitted it to you first.'

Adam went back to the beginning and denied it all again, but then he lowered his voice and said, 'My mother did in fact have Jewish ancestors, but that was five generations ago. But you? You have excellent looks …' He reflected for a moment, and then said, 'Korczak too?'

'Yes.'

When Korczak entered the room a moment later, Adam greeted him triumphantly. 'Well, well. Now I understand everything. In fact, I had an idea earlier. Remember when we were walking in Swider and someone shouted "Moses" at you?'

From then on, Adam made sure that the boys observed every possible safety measure when they visited him. He kept aiding them, and even extended that aid to many other Jews by arranging for them to obtain monthly subsidies of 500 *zloty*. In time, Adam admitted his own Jewishness and told them his real name. He turned out to be a well-known Warsaw teacher.

Mrs Bogucka knew the truth. One of the most dramatic moments in our contacts with Adam came during the great roundup in the Praga district in the spring of 1944. German gendarmes were going from apartment to apartment, carrying out a thorough search and checking documents. Adam did not want to expose his landlady and her family to danger. He decided to go out on the street. This was a terrible moment for Mrs Bogucka. She realized that Adam would not have a chance outside, and yet she agreed with his decision. Adam took his farewell among tears. In the end, however, Anka broke down and refused to let him go. She kept him there against her mother's will. By some miracle, their apartment was not searched.

I recorded my recollections of Adam and many others for the archives of the Jewish Historical Commission in Cracow in 1945. Today, looking back at them, I have suddenly realized that 'Adam' was the pseudonym used by Dr Adolf Berman, chairman of the Jewish National Committee and a member of the Council for Aid to the Jews in Warsaw. I am convinced that Berman was that guardian angel who looked after Jerzyk and Korczak. Never before had I even considered such a possibility. Unfortunately, Dr Berman,whom I knew well, died some years ago. His wife died long before he did. Now, there is no one left with whom I can check this supposition.

*

After Adam had arranged for Jerzyk and Korczak to move to Otwock, the room seemed very big and quiet. Korczak had been especially noisy, surrounded as he always was by new friends who matched him in spinning unlikely yarns. And Jerzyk? I used to say back then that he was the only person in the world who could upset me with his reckless behavior, unexpected ideas and unpunctuality. He showed up late when we arranged to meet somewhere, and left me hanging in suspense when he did not return home on time. Had he been caught in a roundup, or fallen into the hands of extortionists? Could he be at the police station? Would he return home accompanied by blackmailers? And yet Jerzyk always came home – half an hour late, and with a good excuse. He had run into someone, he had had to show someone how to get somewhere, he had been unable to return home by the normal route. He always got home just before the curfew.

Once he left for Otwock, I lived in luxurious conditions. I spent a lot of time reading and making notes. I translated a little, doubled the number of English lessons I gave, and visited Arkadiusz and

Nina more often. After the unpleasant episode with Krzepicki, Nina dropped in on Marysia less frequently.

In general, the winters were more calm. The summers were dangerous. Everything bad happened in the spring or summer. Extortion was less frequent in winter, when people went around wrapped in heavy overcoats. The scarves that covered half of people's faces made it easier to conceal the Jewish secret from the eyes of the extortionists. While external risk diminished, there was more prying and insistence at home. Now, as I sat in my room, I had more frequent visits from the widow, her daughter Marysia, and her son Bolek. They came to chat, to catch up on the latest political news and commentaries, to keep up to date on family matters. Had I heard from Jerzyk? How was he doing in school? When was he coming to visit? These were not always pleasant discussions. There was a greater tendency to touch on themes that had previously been left undisturbed, at least as far as open, direct questions went.

When I look back on my conversations with people in those days, I see that I was usually the one who set the agenda. That is why the subject of villagers either did not come up at all, or came up suddenly, inappropriately, in an unlikely way.

For instance, there was an occasion when the widow interrupted one of my literary divagations: 'Ah, these Jews, Franek ...'

'What about the Jews, Mrs Scislo?'

'They're terrible!'

'Terrible? I don't think so. One's worse, one's better. One's a thief and one's honest, the same as with Poles or the French. In my class at school, there were some that were very popular and decent, even though they were Jews.'

'Well, people don't talk about that sort.'

'Precisely. People don't talk about that sort. Why?'

'Those Jews in the traditional long coats dominated commerce and paralyzed the economy. Look at how the Poles buy and sell now that the Jews are gone!'

'Well, there's nothing to worry about. Those Jews in the traditional long coats – which are nothing but a survival of the old bourgeois way of dressing – won't ever return to Poland, if they offended your sense of style. As for the market stalls on Zelazna Brama Square, you can also be sure that the Jews will never return there. They won't want to. Polish commerce, which has benefitted so greatly from the German occupation' – I was being sarcastic now – 'will survive.'

She made a helpless gesture. 'Why were things the way they were before the war? The engineers – all Jews. The physicians – all Jews. The lawyers ...'

'Don't exaggerate,' I said, trying to calm her down. 'Your late husband was no Jew, so don't say "all Jews". In any case, this is a curious and interesting thing. The universities were practically closed to them. If they were admitted at all, they were only a handful. They were ostracized, combatted by all legitimate and non-legitimate means, and still there were "so many of them". It seems to me that if Polish students had spent less time worrying about the Jews and more time worrying about their own education, then they would not have had to worry about the competition from the Jews. And by the way, look at all the prominent Jewish specialists that have won fame for the good name of Poland abroad. Our own weak economy willingly took the credit for their achievements, without ever indicating that those "Poles" were in fact "Jews". Not that I see anything wrong in this.'

'Perhaps. But they kept so much to themselves that they had nothing in common with us.'

'I'm afraid you're mistaken, Mrs Scislo. If the Poles had only allowed it, the Jews would have assimilated long ago and no one would even know who they are. Does history lack for Jews who were heroes in the Polish insurrections, who were writers, who loved their country? Orzeszkowa had a lot to say about that, and she knew what she was talking about. And Mickiewicz? Yet Poles were always worrying about who had a Jewish grandmother. They wouldn't even allow people who changed their religion to melt into the community. The most important public issue was ritual slaughtering, while the nation sank into worse and worse backwardness. And the only ones who have any interest in keeping society backwards are those who don't believe in their own honesty.'

The widow was unable to hold her own in arguments with me. Basically a good woman, she had no opinions of her own. She accepted uncritically whatever she heard, and then repeated it. She could say one thing today and something entirely different tomorrow. All the more, I wanted to inculcate my principles in her. I knew that she respected me and paid heed to what I said.

When you live with a secret, you can find it difficult to avoid reacting directly or indirectly when someone touches on that secret. This is a matter of your prestige, and of preventing people from thinking that they are so superior that they can look right through you.

I was not angry with Marysia when she flirtatiously called me by a Jewish name or said that I 'rock back and forth like a Jew in church'. It was her desire not to seem naïve that made her ask my guests (the ones she knew well) whether they knew anything about my Jewish background. Most of them were Jewish ... Bolek also gave me to understand from the first that he knew everything. I could see that he was bursting to say it straight out.

When I revealed my secret in a letter to him after the war, he replied: 'I knew that you were a Jew almost from the moment you moved in with us, but I did not want to indicate that I knew.' The sort of efforts he made are indicated by the following episode.

As I was sitting peacefully in my room one day, there was a sharp ring at the doorbell, followed by hammering on the door. My heart leapt to my throat. Should I open the door or not?

'Who's there?'

'*Gestapo. Aufmachen.*'

I was quaking. Too bad. I waited a moment, gathering my courage. There were curses and pounding at the door. I slowly slid back the chain and opened it. Bolek was standing there with a devilish grin. 'I had you fooled!'

The blood was hammering in my brain, but I replied with melancholy calm, 'You can joke around with me, but I wouldn't advise pulling that number on anyone else.'

Bolek was a good boy. His childish jokes were mixed with a seriousness that was rare in people his age. Our long and truly friendly conversations left me in an optimistic mood.

On several occasions, someone asked me directly about my background. I did not always have to lie. There were times when I confirmed their suspicions and others when I had to throw up a smokescreen. I had a complex on this point. It seemed to me that everyone knew who I was and asked only out of boredom or to check my honesty and see whether or not I trusted them.

Bolek once asked me without warning, 'Are you a Christian, Franek?'

I answered his question with a question. 'Does baptism make a man a Christian?'

He did not relent. 'Do you believe in the Five Commandments of the Church?'

This was the first time in my life I had heard of five commandments. I answered directly: 'No'.

'Why not?'

'I'm a pantheist. I do not need any intermediaries in my contacts with God. As for all sorts of commandments, I think they exist for the sake of people who are unable to form their own ethics. People who know themselves are capable of forming their own moral codes sanctioned by their own internal needs and discipline, rather than by the dictates of a higher Being'.

The conversation turned to questions of faith and religion.

What I liked best about Bolek was a rare quality: he could be convinced by a correct argument.

My brother and I were so sensitive that we knew exactly what people were saying and whispering about us. A gesture, a grimace, a word, ill humor, an unreturned smile and a thousand other petty details could have great significance for our moods. With Marysia, especially, I could tell when her suspicions built up to a dangerous level.

Some three weeks before Christmas, I could tell that something was eating at Marysia. I did nothing to make it easier for her. Then, one evening, she began: 'You know, Franciszek, there's something I want to tell you.'

I could see that I was not going to avoid this conversation. I knew exactly what she wanted to say, but I asked her, 'Yes, what is it? What's on your mind?'

She was silent. We were sitting there alone, across a table in the dim light of a carbide lamp. The room was chilly. 'I don't know how to say it.'

'Well, you don't have to say anything,' I joked. 'It'll pass. You can tell me some other time.'

'No, I have to tell you today.'

'Go ahead. I'm listening.'

'Well, you know, Franciszek', she began reluctantly, in an uncertain tone of voice, 'it seems to me that you and your brother are going to have to move out.'

'Is that all. I thought it was something serious. Don't worry, we'll come to visit you. We've been intending to change apartments. This one is too expensive for us.'

I wanted to distract her by being garrulous and maintaining a good mood, but Marysia kept going sadly back to the subject: 'Do you know why you're going to have to move out?'

'Are people talking about us?'

'No, of course not. Nobody's saying anything. Really. Nobody. That's not why.' I felt relieved. Marysia plowed ahead. 'I don't know how to put it ...'

'It doesn't matter.' I wanted to throw her off track. 'One way or another, we'll be moving out. I don't know whether your mother's got other plans for this room, or if she's renting it to us too cheap, or if your brothers are coming to Warsaw. It doesn't matter to us.'

'Still', she went on, 'I wanted to ask you something ...'

'OK. Try to ask.'

Listen ...' Her voice dropped to a whisper. 'Are you Polish?'

I chuckled. 'Is that what's bothering you? After living with me all this time, seeing what sort of work I do, can you doubt that I'm Polish? People do say that I've got something Ukrainian in my looks, because my father comes from Stanislawow, but you can be sure that I am not Ukrainian! I'm amazed that you could have any doubts.'

'The thing is, you see', she said, choosing her words carefully and avoiding looking me in the eye, 'that if you and Jerzyk were not Polish, then you would have to move out.'

'Well, look, this is a pointless discussion because we're going to be moving out one way or another. I was going to tell your mother tomorrow. Nothing to worry about.' I changed the subject.

Outside it was December: snow, frost and no prospects of another apartment. Too bad. Six months in one place was a long time. Some would say it was too long. We should have thought of it earlier.

Marysia, in the meantime, was chattering away again, satisfied that she had said what was bothering her. Still, she had to deliver the rest of her prepared oration: 'So many Jews are around now that you never can tell. For instance, there were four lodgers here before you moved in, one after the other. And they were all Jews.'

'I'm not surprised. The only people that could pay such money for a room like this are Jews – or people like Jerzyk and me, who have our own reasons for wanting to live precisely in this district.'

278

We talked on and on. I explained to Marysia how the Polish underground looked after Jews, that there were special funds for them, that Jews were people, too, and that there was no reason to fear them. Instead, one should help them.

BELLA

Korczak was in the habit of telling about his flourishing emotional life. He existed in a state of permanent infatuation. Only the objects of his feelings changed. He had very good looks and wandered around Warsaw without fearing extortion on the street. One day when he came to see me, he was beaming more broadly than usual. 'This time, she's really special! You've never seen anyone like her. She's beautiful and intelligent. I'm telling you, Franuœ, it's a pleasure just to talk to her.'

'What's her name?'

'Bella Rapowska.'

Shalom, Bella, I thought to myself.

'From Warsaw.'

'No, from Lwow.'

It all fit. Dr Gross delivered a snap diagnosis: 'Her real name wouldn't by any chance be Bayla Rappaport?'

'Are you crazy?'

'Don't say I didn't warn you.'

'What makes you think so?'

'If she's so beautiful and intelligent but still hangs around with someone like you, that's reason enough. Besides, no self-respecting Aryan has a name like that.'

'You're talking nonsense.'

'Let's wait and see.'

In those days, Korczak was taking his meals at the RGO cafeteria at 6 Sierpnia Street. That was where he met Bella. Jerzyk met her soon afterward and was similarly impressed. Bella readily agreed to meet with the boys. 'Poor thing', I said, half-mockingly, half out of genuine concern, 'she feels safer in "Aryan" company.'

Jerzyk did not like the 'Bayla Rappaport' hypothesis, and took a wait-and-see attitude.

When Bella visited us the first time, any doubts I may have had were dispelled. I was struck by the modest – far too modest – behavior of the 19-year-old girl. She was a tall, well-built blonde with wavy hair that fell loose to her shoulders. She had wide, doe-like eyes that betrayed a spark of merriment, but now seemed frightened and wary. She must have been intimidated and a little embarrassed among the noisy crowd in our room that afternoon. I appraised Bella with an expert eye. One racial trait could give her away: her full, sensuous lips. She, too, may well have sensed that there was something funny about me, but the piles of newspapers and the numerous Aryan guests (some of whom were Jews with 'good looks') threw her off the scent.

When the boys left Warsaw that winter, I lost contact with Bella. Somewhere around April 1944, she unexpectedly came looking for the boys. They weren't there.

'Do they write?' she asked me.

'They write.'

'When are they coming to Warsaw?'

'They'll be here Sunday.'

'This Sunday?'

'Yes.'

'Well, say hello to them from me.'

'Thanks. I will.'

'Well, I guess I'll be going …'

'Wait, what's the hurry? Why don't you stay for a while?'

She stayed. Afterwards, she came back frequently. I soon began giving her English lessons and saw her several times a week. We talked about different interesting things. I could sense that there was something continually left unsaid, but I did not try to get her to say it. And then, one day, we were talking about Ernst Kretschmer's *People of Genius*. I remarked that genius results from the mixing of the races, and Bella blurted out that she, too, was of mixed race.

'And so perhaps you'll turn out to be a genius,' I told her, making light of her remark and changing the subject.

We continued to maintain the distance between teacher and pupil.

I was giving a great many English lessons in those days. I taught rather to meet people than to make money, although I was not exactly overflowing with cash. There were many people whom I taught for free, like Bella's friend Ela. There was a big roundup in the Zoliborz district in May or June 1944. Bella did not come for her lesson the next day. Ela showed up two days later to tell me that Bella's uncle, the person she loved most of all, had been arrested. I supposed that the man was in fact her father. She had often spoken of that uncle with great affection and wished that I could meet him. She had shown me his photograph: there was a close resemblance between them.

Bella came the next day. She was broken-hearted. 'Why', she said. 'Why? So many rotten people will survive this war. And they took him away! Such a wonderful man. Our landlord made him leave the apartment and hide in the attic. That was what doomed him.'

I consoled her, without any great conviction. What could I say? That was when I first referred to myself as a Jew. Bella was shocked and amazed. 'Aren't you afraid to admit that you're a Jew? How can you be sure that I'm not with the Gestapo? You're all the same and this is why you're always getting arrested. How can you all be so naïve?'

Now it was my turn to be shocked. 'I didn't think you were in any doubt as to my origins.'

'I wonder exactly what it is that you think of me. You probably think that I'm Jewish, don't you?'

I had no idea what to say.

'Well, that's the way it always is,' she went on. 'Wherever I go. As soon as I meet someone with a little bit of heart or intelligence, they turn out to be a Jew. I'm under some sort of curse!'

Now I've really stuck my foot in my mouth, I thought. How am I going to get out of this?

In the meantime, Bella took a picture from her handbag. It showed a young man in a German uniform. 'This is my cousin,' she said. There was a tender dedication on the back of the photograph. 'He's on the front lines in Holland, and he wants to marry me after the war.' There was a touch of irony in her voice. 'He's a decent boy. My aunt is a *Reichsdeutsch*. She lives in Lwow.'

We were both silent for a long moment.

'You know,' she said, lowering her voice, 'that wasn't my uncle. It was my father.'

'I know.'

'How do you know?'

'I know a lot of things.'

'He was a Jew by descent. My mother's an Aryan. Czech. The whole rest of the family is German. And there's nothing I can do for him. Nothing.'

Bella was pursued by her father's Jewishness. The professors at the Warsaw conservatory she attended had been impressed by her. Aren't you perhaps Jewish? they asked. Only a Jew could play that way. Bella was the best student. Her friends said: She's as intelligent as a Jew. She had no luck in her attempt to win her father's release from Pawiak Prison. Two weeks later, her aunt got a letter from a released prisoner who had been in the same cell. Bella's father had found himself assigned to interrogation by an officer with whom he had served in the same regiment back in Austrian times. That old colleague had pledged to do what he could. But all he could do was ship him to the front lines in the next group sent there.

In those times, so difficult for Bella, we got on a first-name basis. She poured out all the resentment and pain caused by her ambiguous identity. She felt alien when she was among Aryans; she feared them. She did not know anything about Jewry. She liked Jews because of her father, and because of their heart, intelligence and subtlety. She suffered from an alienation complex.

One day, we went for a walk in the Zoliborz district. This was an exception for me; I did not like leaving my own neighborhood. We walked back to Krasinski Square, where we waited for a tram. One finally pulled up at the tram stop. I was already on the step when someone caught at my sleeve and pulled me back. My heart leaped to my throat. Damn! I had not been blackmailed for a long time. I turned around – it was Mr Kowalski, the doorkeeper from Ciasna Street. He was overjoyed to see me alive. Why didn't I ever visit? What about my brother? I looked around. Bella had vanished. The poor thing had thought that it was beginning, and she had pushed deep into the crowd inside the tram car. I only saw her again when she got off.

*

Bella's father was not the only victim of the springtime roundups from among our acquaintances. Mrs Birn, the mother of Edzio – Kazimierz Kurek – came to visit one day with grievous news. Her only son, the apple of her eye whom she had so jealously guarded, had been caught in a roundup on the street. He had landed in Pawiak Prison. I was shaken by the news. Edek was one of my closest friends. Although his cautious mother had forbidden him ever to visit us, we had stayed in touch and each knew what the other was doing.

I had not known him before the war. We were the same age and came from the same city, but had never met. Then Mrs Luba Birn came to see my mother about something in the fall of 1939 and brought her son along. Mrs Birn was a tall, energetic, superior sort of woman. Her pride and joy was her brother, Fensterblau, a well-known builder in the town of Gorlice. It was Fensterblau who had put her in contact with the Polish socialist party.

Mrs Birn left Edzio with me while she closeted herself with my mother for a secret conversation. Being a good host, I showed my guest my library. When he took an interest in the little volume of Leśmian lying open on the table, I knew that we would be friends. Edzio thus joined the group of people who came to visit me in those days. I had met each of them in an accidental way. They all brought friends of their own. Edzio was tall and slender, with an elongated face and big, sad, anxious dark-brown eyes. He turned out to be a valuable addition to our group. With his knowledge of literature and his liking for poetry, he was something of a bohemian. He read verse beautifully and had excellent rhythm. Brunon Jasienski's folk rhythms and Leśmian's mysticism were his specialty. I learned a great deal from him during the poetry evenings that we held with our friends. After several weeks, once he had become one of the group, he brought his friend Jas Grodecki. This was the first and only *goy* in our crowd. With curly blond hair and misty blue eyes, he had brains and was no fool – although he was not particularly wise, seeking out Jewish company in those days. He drove the Jewish girls crazy.

Mrs Birn and her son did not go to the ghetto. They used their socialist contacts to obtain Aryan papers and went to Warsaw. When we were living in Czyzyny, I received letters from Edzio and sent the answers to relatives of the prominent socialist Daszynski. I have recounted in an earlier chapter how it was that I found Kazio Kurek in Warsaw.

Mrs Birn blamed herself for what happened. She had kept her son at home all winter so that he would not catch cold. She was a bossy woman, and Edzio was an obedient child. In any case, he felt good at home with the books that his mama brought him from the public library. When spring came, she decided that he should go out to get some fresh air. As she said, she forced him out on to the street so that he could catch some sun. A pale face could give a Jew away. So he went out – and never returned.

As usually happened in such cases, Mrs Birn could not accept the truth. A woman like her, familiar with the rules of the game, should have known what every Jew had learned from the experience of others: once a circumcised man crossed the threshold of the Gestapo, he never came back. At the very best, if they did not kill him on the spot, they would send him to Auschwitz. Yet Mrs Birn persisted in the belief that she could save her only child. It cost her a fortune. She ran from intermediaries to the intermediaries of intermediaries. Each of them made promises, each of them took her money, and none of them did a thing, because nothing could be done.

The day after the arrest, she obtained a message smuggled out from Edzio. He said that he had acknowledged that his mother was Jewish while claiming that his father was Polish, in the hope that *mischling* status would be better than that of a normal Jew. The last thing she learned, after four weeks of frenzied investigation, was that Edzio had been sent to Auschwitz. Nothing more was ever heard of him.

Mrs Birn never forgave herself as long as she lived. She died alone in an old people's home in Israel, in spiritual and physical torment.

JANEK AND JANINA GO TO JADZINY

Once Jerzyk had gone to Otwock, it seemed that our long-time dream would be realized at last: each of us would have a separate apartment.

Only Klara and mother were still living together at Mrs Janiczek's. From time to time, Klara managed to find a job as a babysitter. Mother was comfortable on Filtrowa Street. The fact that she did not have to conceal her identity from her landlady was a great psychological advantage. Besides, neighbors and uninvited guests seldom called at the apartment, since Mrs Janiczek was frequently away on 'smuggling' expeditions. She brought kielbasa, butter, cheese and other peasant specialties to Warsaw from the village. Then she traded these goods to the

Germans for coffee, tea or chocolate. Her business thrived. Mrs Janiczek was away from home three or four days a week, but she made a good income. She plowed her earnings into her daughter Lili's hope chest, buying her a fur coat, material for dresses and suits, silverware, crystal and rugs, in addition to a supply of gold and dollars. There was enough to last out this war and the next one, but there was never enough. She loved her daughter very much. Mother's presence was convenient: she cooked dinner for the girl and kept an eye on her to make sure that she did not run wild. At 18, Lili was a pretty blonde with dark-blue eyes. She was graceful but not particularly energetic, even a bit on the lazy side, and she liked her mirror. In short, she was simply a girl with no outstanding good or bad sides. She liked mother very much and appreciated her advice. Lili had friends her age, mostly boys, presumably connected with underground organizations. She always had the latest news, although she did not always know what it meant. Mother did not go out any more than she had to, only showing herself on the staircase from time to time 'for hygiene's sake' as she went out for light shopping.

Mother never came to our room. We visited her, but not very often. We did not want to attract unnecessary attention from the neighbors. Uncle Zygmunt, on the other hand, was a frequent caller on 'Maria Murdzenska', for mother had miraculously recovered her *kenkart* and went on using that name. She had been promised a new one, but the 'fake document factory' was swamped with work, and she had to wait. Uncle Zygmunt continued living in the German house on Czerniakowska Street. He made friends with Aurea Jäger, a German woman who lived one floor above him and who worked in a German pharmacy. She was an old maid – but then again, not all that old. A kindly, cultured older gentleman who spoke excellent German could hardly fail to arouse her interest. He charmed her, I have no doubt, with his personal magnetism and worldliness. Furthermore, the fact that he suffered from sciatica and had his other ailments could only make him all the more attractive in the eyes of a pharmacist. Miss Jäger surrounded Uncle Zygmunt with concern and brought him medicine that even Germans needed special permission to obtain. Uncle told us repeatedly of her devotion and generosity. He trusted her, but not enough to share his secret. He even wanted us to meet Aurea, but we never did. Not at that stage of things ...

Klara and Janek frequently visited us on Asnyka Street, but separately, as if they did not know each other. Working in the factory, Janek could only come on Sundays in any case. The two of them were just faces among our many guests, and did nothing to attract special attention. Klara's visits were all the more useful now that the room was less crowded. She brought me dinners from mother – saying that they came from the RGO, where she told people she worked.

The question of our dinners was resolved in different ways at different times. There was a period when we cooked potatoes and pea soup for ourselves. During another period, we took dinners at a very good and cheap (12 *zloty*) canteen at 5 Piusa Street. That ended when a policeman checked our documents there, fortunately without complications. When mother came to Warsaw, we gradually accustomed her landlady to the fact that we sometimes came for dinner. Later, we stopped there for sandwiches wrapped in newspaper.

After moving to Asnyka Street, we began taking our dinners at an acquaintance's on Filtrowa Street, and later with a certain housewife who charged 30 *zloty* for very skimpy dinners. Subsequently, she even raised her price. In the long term, this was more than we could afford. We restricted ourselves to soup only, ordering a full dinner on Sundays. We started going back to mother's. One of us would take dinner for two. During the period of the round-ups, Klara used to bring me dinner. Jerzyk was in Otwock then, and came to Warsaw only once a week, on Sundays. Klara, therefore, visited me often. I introduced her to Marysia – without, of course, letting on that Klara was my sister. Marysia, however, was sharp and stated that Klara bore a striking resemblance to me. I tried to laugh it off, but it worried me. 'That Janka must be a relative of yours.'

I was helping Marysia with the dishes one afternoon when she suddenly asked, 'Tell me the truth. Isn't Janka your sister?'

'Yes!' I shot back.

'Ahhh, you see. And why did you always tell me that you haven't got a sister?'

'Because I haven't got one.'

'What? You just admitted it.'

'What am I supposed to say if you ask such stupid questions?'

'Now I don't know what to think. Have you got a sister or not?'

'Have I got one or not? Have I?' I mocked, trying to hypnotize her.

'Why are you making such a big deal out of it?'

'Why are you asking so many questions?' I went on the attack: 'Just suppose, Marysia, that Janka is my sister? You can tell that I'm trying to hide the fact, so why do you try to expose me? It's my private business in the end. Do I ask you about your private business? Have I ever asked you to tell me a single secret? This is a shameful indiscretion on your part!'

Marysia was embarrassed and explained that she had only asked out of friendly interest. Yet she just couldn't stop herself. 'Oh, alright', she said. 'But what's the story with Janka? Is she your sister?'

'You can answer that one for yourself,' I said in exasperation. 'You decide.'

She did not say anything more on the subject. But she found other occasions to drive me crazy.

After that incident, I decided that I should minimize Klara's visits to me. I began going to mother's more often.

In the meantime, there were new problems with Janek. The ground was beginning to burn under his feet at the factory. He lived on Elektoralna Street, and the daily walk to the Czerniakow district filled him with fear. He had 'acquaintances' along the way. He was once surrounded by more than a dozen hoodlums near Zelazna Brama Square. Not wanting to start a chase scene, which could always be dangerous, he stepped into a doorway with two big oafs wearing brass knuckles. They had already taken his *kenkart* and all his money, and were preparing for a more thorough examination of his person when a middle-aged man came along. He flashed a police agent's identity card and demanded that the boys show their documents. One of the thugs handed Janek's *kenkart* back to him awkwardly, and then began making conspiratorial faces to the agent. 'What are all of you up to?' the agent asked. 'Dirty business?'

'No, we're just talking,' Janek said.

One of the hoodlums couldn't keep his mouth shut. 'He's a Jew, sir.'

'So what if he's a Jew? Does that mean you have to lynch him? All of you, scram!'

Having said that, he walked away. As soon as he was gone,

however, the thugs picked up where they had left off. Janek was so desperate that he ran after the agent and asked him for protection. The agent chased the gang away, walked to the tram stop with Janek, and waited until he had got on safely, so that the hoodlums could not follow him. From that time on, Janek never took the shortcut through the square. It was worth taking the long way around, even if it meant leaving for work ten minutes earlier. But then he lost his job and lost his apartment. He had to think up something new. And, as so often before, it was Nina who came to the rescue.

When the Russian front drew near to Lublin, Nina's mother, Mrs Wiercinska, had to move to a tiny estate at Jadzin near Grodzisko and start from scratch. Nina asked me more than once whether I knew of a gardener and a serving-girl, because her mother could not run the place alone. This was heaven-sent at that particular moment, but I could not simply mix Nina, Klara and Janek up together all at once. It was necessary to wait a while, to work on them until 'they wanted it'.

First, I took care of Janek. He had no qualifications as a gardener, but he was handy and was not afraid of a hard day's work. But did he want the job? I attempted to convince him, but it would be best if Nina herself asked him. Janek did not take much persuading. He was a well-brought-up young man, and they were very happy with him on the farm, especially since there had been no men there at all, only ladies.

Once Janek had been there for two weeks, it was Klara's turn. I was afraid that someone else would take the job first, but there was a lot of work on that estate, more than one servant could do. I indicated to Nina that I might be able to put her in touch with Janka Szczubial, who sometimes came to visit me. She was not, to be sure, a professional maid, but I could vouch that she knew how to cook. The only question was whether she would agree or not. I did happen to know, because she had spoken to me about it several times, that she was dying to move from the city to the countryside. So perhaps it might be possible to persuade her.

And in the end, it was possible.

KLARA'S STORY

I remember that it was a beautiful day in May. After years in the city, in various rooms, cellars and spaces where it was impossible to go outside, I found myself in the genuine countryside. It's easy to imagine my delight in the flourishing plants or the eagerness with which I breathed the fresh air. The Germans were on the rampage in Warsaw, while here the silence was broken only by birdsong and the lowing of the cows. Janek and I walked slowly along the road to my 'position'.

A little house among the trees and bushes – it seemed like paradise on earth. The fact that I had no idea of housework was a different matter. The lady of the house was overjoyed that I had arrived. Finding servants was not easy in those days. She informed me at once about my obligations. Above all, I was supposed to milk the cow. My God, I nearly died of fright at the sight of a cow. Before the war, I had never dared approach within 20 meters of such a beast on the meadow in Cracow. Now I was to stand face to face with our cow. I was afraid to enter the barn. Janek explained that it was an exceptionally placid animal, and that cows in general never hurt anyone. I was glad that Janek was there. He explained the milking process, and I managed it somehow. Fortunately, there were no witnesses; otherwise, my reputation would have been ruined. It was worse with the chickens. Mrs Wiercinska instructed me to check whether they had laid eggs. To this day, I do not know how this is done. I found a long stick and chased all the hens outside. Then I searched the henhouse for eggs. I didn't find any.

There were six people at meals. They had to have something to eat, and I was supposed to cook it. But how? The first day, I was supposed to make tomato soup. I had never made tomato soup, or even eaten tomato soup, because I hate tomatoes. So I cleverly asked Mrs Wiercinska how she made tomato soup, because perhaps she liked hers different from what I made. I managed to extract a rough idea of what the soup was supposed to be like, and I set to work with enthusiasm. For the first three days, nobody ate a morsel of the dinners. But no one said anything, since they were terrified of losing their cook. On the fourth day, Mrs Wiercinska bought me a cookbook. That was how I began my career as maid of all work.

Mrs Wiercinska, the widow of a high-ranking officer, was head of the household. They had had a large estate near Poznan, but had been evicted by the Germans. The son had rented this little estate near Grodzisko so that his mother could continue playing country gentlewoman. Her sister, Countess Grabowska, whose husband was in a prisoner-of-war camp, lived there, too. Each woman had a daughter. Mrs Wiercinska's daughter Nina lived on her own in Warsaw, while the 16-year-old Danusia Grabowska lived with us.

Klara later told us many stories of this Danusia, whose boyfriend was a raftsman on the Vistula, and about the way all the girls used to chase after Janek.

The worst thing for Klara was that no one came to visit her. Everybody needs acquaintances and friends, if not family. And so the time came for me to visit Klara in her new job. And, of course, to visit Nina's mother, in the name of our friendship. I was invited repeatedly and the visit was announced several times. I kept making excuses, most of all in order to spare myself a journey by train. I finally decided to go one Sunday. Having completely lost the habit of travelling by train or tram, where one is exposed to the relentless stares of others, I felt terrible. Somehow, however, I made it to Grodzisko. I asked around until I located the estate, and was welcomed hospitably over the threshold at around five in the afternoon.

Nina's mother was a solidly built old lady who worked from morning to night and made everyone else work, too. And there was lots of work to do. That was part of the reason that I spent little time with Klara. In any case, it was Mrs Wiercinska that I was visiting.

She and I sat on the veranda once the sun had gone down, discussing current affairs. At a certain moment, with no prelude, she asked, 'And what are your views on the Jewish question?'

'There are no Jews, so there is no Jewish question,' I replied with a smile.

'Oh, there are lots of them left. There are supposedly 300,000 of them in Warsaw alone.'

'Nonsense, my dear lady. Do you mean to state that every third resident of Warsaw is a Jew? There cannot be more than 30,000 of them there, and the number is shrinking constantly. Officially, there are 80,000 left in the labor camps. Those can be saved only by a miracle or by the sudden end of the war. Fifty thousand Jews are in hiding. What kind of percentage is that, in a nation of 30 million? Is it even worth calling it a problem?'

'Well, they will return from abroad.' She was not about to concede defeat. 'Whole masses of them fled to Hungary, to America.'

'But who will return? What for? Did they have it so good here? Did we love them so much that they will want to return? Or do they have it so bad in America and elsewhere? Those who are left in Poland will attempt to emigrate to Palestine.' Whenever I said such things, I had the impression that Poles reacted with irritation rather than contentment. I felt a certain embarrassment on their part.

'Still, Hitler has done the right thing ...'

I stifled this chatter with the usual arguments about the responsibility borne by those who uttered such opinions. Then the discussion turned to Palestine and the issues connected with emigration – with which Mrs Wiercinska, of course, was totally unfamiliar (and I could hardly blame her). Nevertheless, she spoke with great self-assurance (which upset me mildly).

'What is the present attitude towards the Jews in Warsaw?' she enquired in conclusion.

'The intelligentsia', I replied, 'has already forgotten what the word antisemitism means. The persecutions that they themselves have suffered have awakened their human instincts and straightened out their way of thinking. People from those circles are very helpful to the Jews. But the venom of antisemitism, as spat out by Nazi propaganda, has not vanished without a trace. The lowest spheres, the dregs of society, have been infected with it, and their hatred is even worse than before the war. I am talking about those who serve the Germans and who profit by doing so. Intellectuals, true intellectuals, have purged themselves of all prejudice,' I assured her forcefully.

Not wanting to leave my hostess in an awkward situation, I shifted the conversation to a new subject.

The next day, Klara told me what Nina's mother thought of me. I was very nice, but I must have something to do with the Jews. Perhaps there was a grandmother about whom I knew nothing. There was certainly something there ...

NOTES

1. This director, who had himself borrowed his name from a character in Polish literature, Janusz Korczak, became one of the most celebrated Holocaust heroes.
2. RGO – Rada Główna Opiekuńcza – a Polish institution opened in wartime, in charge of needy people.

12. Why Maria Went to Auschwitz and Klara to Zakopane

The front began drawing closer to Warsaw in the spring of 1944. Hopes rose for a quick conclusion to the war, and tensions also grew. The hunt for hidden Jews went on without a break. Each day, I heard about someone being caught by the Gestapo or about the discovery of a group of Jews hidden in a 'bunker'. Such reports were sometimes true and sometimes false, but they exacerbated the anxiety felt by those in hiding and those concealing them. They also had an effect on the widow Scislo. On the other hand, our conditions were better than ever. The race with time had begun: would we trip up at the last moment? The end of our suffering seemed so near.

The courier went on delivering the rolled-up underground newspapers each morning at eight o'clock. Each day, I marked the progress of the Red Army on my map, along with the positions to which the Germans had withdrawn. The daily German newspapers aided me; they reported on German movements soon after the fact, although less precisely.

My predominant impressions from that period are of great confusion and the enormous clouds of dust raised by the tanks and armored vehicles that sometimes drove through Warsaw at very high speeds – running for their lives! This could hardly fail to have an effect on the population of the capital. On the one hand, there was demonstrative rejoicing at the German defeat, and on the other there was lawlessness and an infectious flight from discipline. People looted shops, supplying themselves with food at any cost. They counted on the Germans to give up Warsaw without a fight, and everything began drifting, as if no one was in charge.

I could not believe that the Germans would abandon Warsaw without resisting. Following the movements of the armies day by day, I knew that they put up fierce resistance at 'bridgeheads' at even the smallest rivers. Then, on the point of being surrounded, they withdrew to 'previously prepared positions'. Would they fail to defend the Vistula River, a great natural obstacle in the path of the Russians? I was aware, of course, that underground Poland was preparing an uprising intended to seize control of Warsaw before the Russians arrived. I also realized full well that the great army approaching from the east did not cover great distances each day. Rather, it moved forward in stages, gathering its forces, organizing its movements according to a plan and the opportunities for carrying it out. Even when news reached us that the Russians were near Warsaw, therefore, I hardly expected them to enter the city in a day or two. The atmosphere on the streets, however, suggested that the end was imminent, and that it would be painless.

In these conditions, my personal situation seemed less than enviable. I was, in fact, engaged to a certain degree in underground work, but strictly speaking, I had never enlisted (or perhaps I had been put down on a list without my knowledge). I did not belong to any cell or 'five', and I had no commander to assign me to any post or function once the uprising began. In the meantime, the whole building watched me as if I were General Bor-Komorowski himself. What should I do? Tell Nina the truth and ask her to put me in touch with someone? It would be better to turn to Arkadiusz – but after what he had told me about Jews in the Home Army, I felt that the best course would be to wait and undertake my own decision at the appropriate moment. Perhaps the best thing to do would be to simply leave home at some point and link up at random with a fighting unit.

The solution to my predicament came in an unexpected, undramatic way, but at the very last minute.

Jerzy Korczak knocked on my door on the afternoon of 31 July. He had come to Warsaw from Otwock for a few hours on an errand. With his characteristic verve, and without allowing me any chance to object, he insisted that I go to Otwock with him. He completely disregarded any doubts I may have had. 'Are you crazy? What are you going to do here?' he asked. 'Why would a healthy man want to jump into a sickbed? Hurry up, the train leaves at five.'

So I packed a few personal items into my briefcase, perhaps including a shirt to change into, and perhaps not, and I went off to say farewell to mother.

As I walked down the stairs (the elevator must have been out of order; I do not recall), I met a neighbor every few steps. When they saw me with my briefcase in my hand, they understood by some instinct that the time had come, that it was beginning, that I was going – where? They bade me farewell with tears in their eyes, and shook my hand. I was deeply moved, but also embarrassed. No one asked me anything, and I said nothing. At the foot of the stairs, Mrs Dabrowska threw her arms around my neck. There were tears in her eyes. A moment later, Mr Moeller was tugging at my sleeve. 'Francesco! Remember me!'

'I won't forget.'

That was how we said goodbye.

I found Uncle Zygmunt with my mother. The Janiczeks weren't at home. I stopped in to take my leave, as if I were leaving for a brief vacation. Mother was happy that I was going to be with Jerzyk. 'You have to keep an eye on him, so that he doesn't run completely wild!' We did not say much. I had a train to catch.

'I'll see you in a few days,' I called to her.

Did I say this thoughtlessly, or was it a wish? We separated for a few days, and I would not see her for nine months, by which time mother would have been through hell.

In my life – as, I think, in everyone's life – there have been several painful moments where I did something or failed to do something that I should have done, where my mistake caused a situation that I wish I could undo – even though it cannot be undone. Where I wish something had not happened, although it happened indeed. To reverse the irreversible. A feeling of regret like a wound in the heart. Sometimes this was a matter of stupidity that no one remembers, that no one even knew about – yet I remember it and think of it with rue. Just such a moment was this: leaving mother in Warsaw out of carelessness, recklessness, egoism or thoughtlessness, while I withdrew to a 'previously unprepared position'. I could have said, 'Mother, there's no reason to stay here. It will be safer on the other bank of the Vistula, and liberation will come more quickly – perhaps tomorrow. Come with me!' But I did not say it. I did not propose it. Of course, mother might have been unwilling to leave the apartment suddenly, in the absence of her landlady. Perhaps … and perhaps not. In any case, that wise son on whom mother relied, with whom she sometimes consulted the steps that needed to be taken in a given situation – that son now, pardon the expression, thought only of covering his own behind, saving his own skin. He left mother facing the Great Unknown. Never will I forgive myself, although I try to explain to myself that I did not treat that trip as an escape from the battle, but rather as an escape, at worst, from myself ... some sort of inertia, some immobility of the heart and mind ...

The trip from Warsaw to Otwock behind the 'samovar' steam locomotive lasted four hours. When we got there at nine in the evening, the Germans were gone, and the Russians had not yet arrived.

The Warsaw Uprising broke out the next day at five o'clock in the afternoon.

*

I saved my skin. Mother went from the Warsaw Uprising through the Pruszkow camp, and on to Auschwitz.

Although she was not young and strong, one really would have expected her to find a way to escape and avoid the camp. A sick woman with a head that was bald except for a few strands of gray hair curling against her temples, practically toothless – at Auschwitz, her kind went straight to the gas chambers, and then into the furnaces. I knew mother and believed in her continually active brain, with its ability to find a way out of every danger and every predicament, even the ones from which there was no way out. There was only one thing I was not fit to comprehend: how such a wise and resourceful woman could get herself mixed up in that kind of mess to begin with. Why didn't she escape? Why didn't she take a bold, courageous step – anything, rather than to go to Auschwitz! Crowds of people were herded from burning Warsaw to Pruszkow, and many, many of them were transported from there to Auschwitz, but many others, and especially the older people, were freed on the basis of intervention by their workplaces, their friends, or their relatives. Others sneaked away, escaped, disappeared ... When you come right down to it this was a far different matter from an 'operation in the ghetto' (although, God forbid, I do not wish to downplay the dangers of the evacuation). But anyone with a head on their shoulders should have been able to find a hole in the fencing around the improvised camp at Pruszkow. Only when I heard the story from mother's own lips did I understand.

295

MOTHER'S STORY

There were three of us in the apartment: Lili, Uncle Zygmunt and I. Zygmunt visited me often, especially just before the Uprising, when none of you was around. Where was the poor man to go? He was just as lonely as I was. On the morning of the outbreak of the Uprising, Mrs Janiczek went to Grodzisko to take delivery of her merchandise. She was supposed to return the following day. Of course, she never returned. Nor could Uncle Zygmunt return to Czerniakowska Street. Whether he wanted to or not, he stayed with me and Lili. This went on for approximately ten days, until the Germans began evicting everyone from our district. Since a shot had been fired from one of the windows of our building, we were all treated as political prisoners and put under special guard. The Germans announced that we were to take as much hand baggage as we could carry and line up in the street. I wrapped a few of my things in a bundle, like a village woman, so that they would be easier to carry. Besides, what possessions did I have left? A dress, a nightshirt, a few pieces of underwear. Zygmunt had nothing except his toothbrush. From the time when he was detained by the Gestapo at the beginning of the war, he had never gone anywhere without his toothbrush. He had no personal belongings; he had left everything behind on Czerniakowska Street, which was cut off from our district. To make things worse, there were only women living in Janiczek's apartment, so he could not even look for a shirt that might fit him. Both of us, then, were free of possessions and of worries about our possessions. Lili, on the other hand, was faced with leaving a home packed full of valuable dresses, coats, sweaters, bedding, pillowcases, tablecloths, lingerie, not to mention crystal, silverware, porcelain – the whole hope chest. What should she take and what should she leave behind? How could she carry it all? In what? She flitted like a madwoman from room to room, repeating, 'What will I tell mama?' How would she explain that her mother's beloved daughter had left this or that behind? But she did not have much time to think. She packed two suitcases and put on several dresses, one on top of the other, and then a fur coat – and one more fur coat over her arm – hers and her mother's.

'How are you going to carry it all?' I asked her pityingly.

But she did it, somehow. Her friends and neighbors helped. And poor Uncle Zygmunt with his sciatica also helped a bit. So we set out along the road.

Don't ask what the road was like. The city was burning behind us, and the sun was baking our faces. The miserable column moved slowly forward, accompanied by the hysteria of the women and the shouts of the police. Dust and smoke penetrated our eyes, noses and mouths, along with soot from the burning houses. I remembered the burning ghetto and what Poles had said then. Some had been shocked, while others had been happy that the Jewish problem was being solved. And there were those who said, 'Don't rejoice! Today the Jews, tomorrow us! When they finish off the Jews, our time will come.' Now, as we walked that trail of torment, I heard: 'It's divine retribution! God is punishing us for having rejoiced at the liquidation of the ghetto.' That is what they said.

We reached Pruszkow several hours later. We were crowded into a provisional camp on the grounds of the former locomotive repair shops. The enormous halls, resembling hangars, were scattered around the extensive terrain. People were terribly exhausted, too tired to stand on their swollen legs. Lili set her suitcases down on the concrete and stretched out as still as a stone. Zygmunt was terribly downcast. He worried only about me: was I alright, did I want something to eat? Of course, I was tired. But after I caught my breath for a moment, I set out on a reconnaissance of that enormous camp. I wanted to hear what people were saying and find out what chance there was of getting out of there. Crowds of people stood on either side of the main gate. Every so often, a name was called over the loudspeakers. Friends, relatives and acquaintances were trying to win the release of those who had someone to protect them, or who had important jobs, medical certificates or anything of the kind. I listened for a while, more out of curiosity than out of the hope that Mrs Janiczek would come to try to ransom us or at least to get her daughter out. I did not tarry there. I understood that, in all that confusion, there was little chance that anyone would want to talk to me about getting out.

When night began to fell, I set off for the other end of the camp. There, I was surprised to find a second gate, a sort of service entrance with a German soldier standing guard. He was not particularly young. I went up to him and began speaking to him in German. I pretended that I only wanted to pass the time, and I remarked that it must be hard for him to be in a strange place so far away from his family. I asked him where he came from, and so on. He did not respond at first, but then his tongue loosened, and I soon got down to brass tacks. I explained that I, an old woman, had been brought here by mistake, along with my ailing husband and our daughter, and that the great Third Reich would derive no benefit from our presence. My husband needed medicine that he could not get here, and although I was not rich, I would willingly give him a little money so that he could buy a present for his wife, a souvenir, if he would only let us out.

After all, no one would see or hear. I kept after him and after him, but he had a hard time making up his mind. In the end, hesitating and looking around in every direction, he greed to let the three of us out for the relatively small sum of 1,000 zloty. He set only one condition: no suitcases or parcels! He did not want to risk that. Anyone who saw us with suitcases would understand that we had escaped from the camp.

And he added: 'You have to hurry up, because I won't be on guard here for more than another hour!'

I was happy as I went back to find Zygmunt and Lili, to tell them the news as quickly as possible. It was not easy locating them among the thousands of people, although they had not moved. I imagined the joy they would feel at this unexpected liberation, and I was already planning how we would slip off to avoid attracting anyone's attention.

I was surprised to encounter a completely different reaction than I had expected. Zygmunt, of course, was overjoyed: 'I always said you had a ministerial mind,' he said, clapping his hands together.

Golden-haired Lili betrayed no signs of joy. She crinkled up her nose – and said nothing. When I began trying to hurry her up – come on, let's go, time's passing – she suddenly said, 'I'm not going anywhere.'

'What? What do you mean?'

'I'm not going without my suitcases.'

'Have you gone mad, girl? We have a chance to get out of here, and you're thinking about your suitcases?'

But she stood her ground.

'Mama worked so hard to buy me those things,' she said in a muffled voice. 'It's my whole dowry. The material for my wedding dress, that beautiful blue suit.' The tears began flowing down her cheeks. 'How could I ever explain to her that I left it all behind?'

'Look, you silly thing', I tried to persuade her, 'I've lost far more than that. Leave those rags here, and as soon as the war's over, I'll buy you far finer ones! You'll see! You'll look like a queen at your wedding. The most important thing is to get out of here healthy. The war won't last much longer. We'll all be rich and happy, and you won't lack a thing!'

But she kept repeating, over and over: No! She wanted Zygmunt and me to go. She would fend for herself without us.

Zygmunt tried to influence her. He had an unusual gift of persuasion, and Lili had often admired his wisdom and charm. But it was all in vain. This time, no charm had any effect. Then Zygmunt told me that it might be better to leave Lili there after all. Her situation, as a pure Aryan, was far better than ours in the final analysis. If they discovered who we were, which was quite likely, that would be the end of us. We would not be able to help either Lili or ourselves.

'That's all very fine and beautiful,' I answered. 'You're 100 percent correct. But what will I tell Mrs Janiczek when I see her? What will I say when she asks, "Where is my child? I put my life at risk to save you", she will say, "and you left my daughter at the mercy of fate and escaped, to save yourself." How will I ever look Mrs Janiczek in the eye?'

My heart was aching and I was furious. If I could only convince that blonde-tressed blockhead! To be so close to freedom, and so far. God, God, where could I find the strength to go on?

'No, I must stay with her,' I told Zygmunt. 'But you have no obligations. You owe nothing to anyone. Escape! Take advantage of this chance. Come on, let's go to the gate.'

But now he was the one who resisted. He did not want to leave me, his sister, to her fate. 'What would I do without you? You're the only person I have left. We need to stick together, to watch over each other.'

The hour passed, wasted in fruitless persuasion of Lili. I felt my insides twisting with regret and powerlessness. What an opportunity! I felt like tearing that silly doll to shreds with my fingernails. And she sat there on her suitcases sobbing quietly. I finally began stroking her golden hair. 'Quiet, now. Don't cry, now, don't cry. There might be another chance. God won't abandon us.'

I was overwhelmed by terrible fatigue. I suddenly felt that my legs would no longer carry me. Sleep, sleep – but sleep would not come.

And thus they packed us into the cattle cars and carried us to Auschwitz.

*

Klara's situation in Jadzin became vague and unbearable after the outbreak of the Uprising – and Janek's even more so. A young man, built like an oak tree, busying himself with gardening while Warsaw was fighting, and people were shedding their blood in a fight to the death. Then someone spread the rumor that Janek was the son of a minister in the Polish government-in-exile in London.

KLARA'S STORY

They said that Janek and I could not have known each other very well in

Cracow. How could I, the daughter of a driver (at Wawel castle, but a driver nevertheless) know Janek, the son of a pre-war minister – that was how the rumor went. Janek denied the tale and constantly told Nina that this was not the truth about his family, but no one believed him – even though there had been no minister named Sarnecki. The Wiercinska sisters formed the theory that, as the son of a minister, Janek had had to change his name and go into hiding. So he was a guest at Jadziny, while I was a servant. That was the arrangement that gradually evolved.

When the Uprising broke out, Nina returned immediately to Warsaw to join the fighting. She returned after three days; she had been raped by three soldiers from Vlasov's army. Ewa, the daughter of the owner of the estate, also went to fight. She soon came back without an arm and a leg. Janek, meanwhile 'waited for orders'. The situation grew more and more uncomfortable. People were looking at Janek with such aversion that we decided to set out for Cracow.

Mrs Wiercinska was angry at Janek not only because of his 'waiting for orders', but also because she had caught us kissing in the kitchen several days earlier. That threw her off balance because she had had her eye on Janek for Nina.

We told Mrs Wiercinska that evening that we were going to Warsaw. She had no objections to Janek's plans, but my departure meant that she was losing her servant – and a hard-working one who was satisfied with low wages, and did not talk back to her. It was all a great shock.

She tried to bring me to my senses. When that did not work, she flew into a fury: 'You silly girl, don't you know that rich boys catch girls with pretty words, just to take advantage of them? You don't think he's going to marry you, do you?'

'Maybe he will,' I answered.

We left Jadzin the next morning at dawn with bundles on our backs and the hope in our heart that the war would be over before we reached Cracow. As usual, we were in an optimistic mood as we opened a new chapter. The Warsaw Uprising had been underway for three weeks, I think. The most fantastic stories were being told. We saw refugees from Warsaw along the roads, so perhaps we were not at so much risk. Janek, of course, chose our route. I never had any sense of orientation. Janek could tell by the sun 'which direction Cracow was'. We walked through the forests almost all the time.

If I remember, we spent the first night in the loft at a peasant's. We reached his cottage at nightfall, and he received us hospitably and offered us supper. We sat down tired and hungry at the table and the farmer's wife carried in two dishes (dumplings in milk, just delicious!), a big one and a small one. We started eating immediately – I ate from the small dish and Janek from the bigger one. It turned out that the bigger dish had been for the farmer and his family, and the smaller one for the two of us. We felt terrible at having shown ourselves to be so unsophisticated.

Another time, we stopped at an estate where there were many refugees from Warsaw. The owners were not so hospitable; they barely permitted us to sleep on the hay. The next day, in a small town, an old Jewish woman who looked about 40 (in those days, that was 'old' for Jews) – we spotted her at once, and she probably knew who we were – asked where we were coming from and where we were going. We were already on our way when she came up to us with a parcel. We opened it later in the woods. I remember how touched we were: aside from food, it also contained a pocket knife.

After several days' march, we found ourselves on the Pilice River. We could not cross the bridge to the other side, because there were Germans on the bridge. We walked farther, until Janek spotted a boat on the opposite bank. Since he had swimming trunks with him, he changed into them, swam across, and towed the boat back. We crossed the river without any problems and disappeared again into the woods. Following the sun all the way, we came to a wild pear tree heavy with fruit. Since we did not have much food, we devoured the fruit. We had gone several kilometers farther when Janek remembered that he had left his swimming trunks under the tree. Without thinking, he started back to get them. I stayed where I was, picking blueberries. Time passed, and I grew aware that I was alone in the woods. I started worrying that something had happened to Janek, and in general I was filled with fear. When Janek returned, he told me that he had suddenly realized how foolish and thoughtless he had been to go back for those trunks. He was filled with panic when he realized that something might happen to me in the meantime.

I remember a village we wandered into on Sunday, as well as the cottages where we got something to eat or drink. I can still see a wonderful image: women in fabulously colorful costumes walking to church along the village road. I had seen such costumes in the theatre, but never dreamed that people actually wore them. That village remains in my mind as a place completely cut off from reality.

Reality was not colorful. I hurt my leg, which developed a bruise and then swelled up so badly that I could not think of continuing the march. We were near Opoczno, so we decided to try to get on a train. In the town, we experienced a shock when we realized that we were walking a street paved with gravestones from the Jewish cemetery.

I cannot recall how we got on the train, but I do remember how we were riding along at night, dozing off, when Germans suddenly got on at a station and began checking people's documents. All the other people in our car were elderly. The Germans demanded: Arbeitskarte! Janek showed them his, but I could not find mine. They were preparing to take me away when I found the document in my bundle. Since I had looked for it so long, the Germans did not believe that it was mine, and they shone a light in my face to compare me with the photograph. It was an Arbeitskart provided by the German who bought 'Viennese ceramics'. It might have saved my life, because they left me in peace. Once the Germans were gone, all the old women told us how they had been praying for our safety. Everything may have happened quickly, but it had seemed like a century to us. We reached Cracow without further adventure the next morning. The war was still on. We had to wait at the station for the curfew to end, although the station was hardly the safest place for us. I cannot remember the order in which we 'visited' the people who might possibly be able to provide us with a hiding place. In any case, I believe that we went to see Zinaida first. We found her barely alive. She had just been released from a concentration camp.

Zina Kolotowkina was the wife of the tailor Emil Kornbluth, a cousin of mother's who lived in our building. He had brought his wife back from Kiev, and they lived, madly in love, along with their daughter Galina. They were very sweet people and we liked them very much.

When the Jews had to leave Cracow, they decided that Emil would go to the ghetto while Zina and Galina, as Aryans, went to live on Dluga Street. Emil was taken from the ghetto to a camp in Czêstochowa, where he worked as a tailor. As far as I know, conditions were tolerable in that camp; in any case, nobody died there. Nor were people transported to worse camps. I think that it was a work camp, rather than a concentration camp. Emil sewed clothes for the Germans and was in a rather privileged position. The poor man made friends with his boss – so he thought – to such a degree that he asked if his wife could visit him. The German replied that she could not come to the camp, but a meeting could be arranged in town. Emil wrote to Zina and told her to come to Czêstochowa. Zina cooked a chicken and baked a cake, and appeared carrying a food basket on the designated day, at the specified place. The German came with Emil. When Emil indicated his wife, they were both arrested, before they could even approach each other. They were accused of being part of a communist conspiracy. Emil was shot in prison, and Zina was released many months later, when she was on the point of death. This all happened in September

1944. After hearing this tragic story, the only thing we could do was to say goodbye to her as quickly as possible.

We decided to go to Mrs Kapias. Along the way, on Jana Street, we ran into the German named Orwat who had lived in our apartment on Zielona Street. He was on a bicycle. When we saw him, our legs turned to putty. We had no doubt that he had recognized us. We walked stiffly on as he rode away; after a moment, we looked back, and he was looking back, too. That was all. That was a moment when we tried to swallow the hearts that had leapt into our throats.

Mrs Kapias was not in Cracow. We found only her sister there. She was terrified, because there had been arrests in the family. She fed us, although we could feel that she was only waiting for us to leave.

We had nothing to look for in Cracow. I suddenly thought that we should go to Zakopane – for no other reason than the fact that I liked that resort in the mountains. And I still had the presence of mind to remember that Mrs Cholewinska had a sister there. We hardly expected her to be eager to give us her sister's address if we told her that we were looking for a place to go into hiding, so we decided to pay her an innocuous visit and only mention by the way that we would be making an excursion to Zakopane. Perhaps she would reveal her sister's address and we would be able to stop there for a while. In films, such ploys always seem artificial, but in this case, it worked perfectly. Professor Cholewinska warned us at the outset that it would be dangerous for us to stay with her, but she invited us in for a cup of tea and asked us about our plans. I managed to remark casually that we were going to Zakopane, as if we were going there on vacation. She immediately asked if I could check on her sister, from whom she had had no news for two months. People did not write addresses down in those days, so I committed this one to memory: Villa 'Sunbeam', 9 Kasprusia Street. We had the address. It would turn out to be a lifesaver, even though we never even laid eyes on Professor Cholewinska's sister, then or later.

*

Mother, like every mother, was an exceptional woman. Have I mentioned that already? No matter. I am prepared to repeat it over and over. Not only exceptional, but wise and charismatic. Others – Jews and non-Jews alike – knew this. And there was something more: she was an honest, moral person. Which did not hinder her in developing her unusual commercial talents. There were few merchants in Cracow to equal Sara Gross. I only say this by the way, since commercial talent does not always go hand in hand with honesty. And is wisdom always accompanied by morality and honesty? Absolutely! And so I ask you: where was the wisdom, when a Jewish woman, the mother of four, hiding in Warsaw on Aryan papers, went to Auschwitz with a silly 18-year-old girl instead of guarding her own life and the life of her brother? She did it so that evil or stupid people on the streets of Warsaw would have no occasion to say that she had left a Christian child at the mercy of fate while saving her own Jewish life. And yet it was as plain as the nose on your face that her self-sacrifice could do nothing to help the girl! And so her self-sacrifice defied explanation – and that's where the deep wisdom lies. An honest heart and a conscience in good order.

However, let us listen to the next instalment of Maria Murdzenska's story:

MOTHER'S STORY

All along the way, I was thinking of how to get out of that trap, and coming up with various plans. I was furious with the lovely, foolish girl. She just sat there on her suitcases, but I was convinced that her eyes would be opened here in the cattle car, and she would no longer block our way. Zygmunt was motionless in depression; he shrank into the corner under the burden of his dark thoughts and said nothing. I still did not know what to do. When we got to Auschwitz, I realized that there was nothing I could do. We had gotten ourselves into a terrible predicament, into an abyss from which it was hard to escape. Nothing remained except to stay cool, despite the hysteria into which some women were falling. I tried to appeal to their reason, telling them they should maintain their dignity in the face of their persecutors. That helped. The men were soon separated from the women. I only managed to exchange a few words with Zygmunt. He was terribly sad. He had the feeling that we would never see each other again, that we were parting forever. He knew that I had a few valuables from home: a diamond watchband, a watch and earrings. He begged me to get rid of those things. If the Germans found them, they would shoot me on the spot.

'Be careful! You've got children waiting for you! They need you, so you're not allowed to risk your life! I believe that you'll survive this hell

and return home. I haven't got a chance. Sooner or later, they'll discover that I'm a Jew, and that will be enough to send me to the showers. But you'll survive. It's your obligation to the children. Don't put yourself at risk. Get rid of that jewelry because it'll be your downfall! Promise me, Sala!'

When he got excited, he threw caution to the winds and called me Sala, as if we were back home. He cried, the poor man. I, too, had tears standing in my throat, but I tried to calm him down and stiffen his spirit: 'Don't be afraid. We've gotten out of worse things, we'll get out of this, too. You have to survive so you can tell about all we've been through.'

And so we parted. When he was a long way off, he called, 'Be careful! Be careful!' Those words still ring in my ears.

*

They took Zygmunt to Oranienburg.

Mother and Lili remained for the time being in Auschwitz and went through all the known phases of admission to the camp. The Warsaw group received the red triangles of political prisoners. Lili's suitcases were taken to the warehouses, and that was the last she ever saw of them. They cut off her golden locks and shaved her pretty little head. Mother was around 50 when she reached Auschwitz. Her wispy gray hair and almost total lack of teeth, which she had lost during the war, made her look older than she was. Now, the differences between her and the other female prisoners were effaced to a degree; they covered their shaved heads with scarves, just as she covered her bald head. Most of them were young women, although a few were middle-aged. Mother was one of the oldest women in the barrack.

MOTHER'S STORY

I did not throw my jewelry away – and not only in view of its monetary worth. Could I throw away gifts from my husband? How could I dispose of the only mementos of our home? I thought that parting from that watchband would be like parting from home, and condemning myself never to return. Now I think that, just as I guarded those diamonds, so they also guarded me. They aroused my vigilance and served as my cameo. When we were led to the bath house, we all had to undress and we each received a piece of soap – it was more sand than soap. Naked, we had to walk single file and hold our arms up. Before we reached the bathhouse, we had to hop over a ditch that had been specially dug in front of the entrance. An SS-man stood there to check that the women were not concealing anything under their arms or between their legs. Holding my jewels under the piece of soap, I jumped the ditch with my arms raised and entered the bathhouse. Later that night, I broke the watchband into four pieces and concealed it in the wooden clogs I had been given. There I kept my mementos from home the whole time, until the end of the war.

It took me only a short while to determine the nature of the camp and of the dangers to women my age. I reconnoitered the terrain the next day and discovered Jewish women prisoners living on the far side of a barbed-wire fence. I asked one of them if there was anyone from Cracow there. Thus I made contact with Rutka S., who held the position of Kapo. She told me many things. There were times when I was able to help those poor women.

We women from Warsaw could receive packages from our relatives. I was the only one without relatives. But I remembered that Klara had corresponded with a friend named Sydzia Konis, who was now called Janina Ziolo. She had been taken as a Polish slave laborer to a farm in Gols, near Vienna. I was sure that she, too, would need someone to correspond with; everyone should have relatives. I cannot say what miracle it was that allowed me to remember Janina Ziolo's address. I sent her a postcard. She was very cheered to hear from me, and informed me that Klara was in Zakopane with Janek. Shortly afterwards, she sent me a parcel of peas, and continued to do so regularly. These parcels were a great help.

They were beginning to hold roll calls and selections. Young girls, including Lili, were sent off to Germany as laborers. The older ones were being kept at Auschwitz for the time being. I tried to keep everyone's spirits up. I told them that they should stick together and refuse to break down, which is what the Germans wanted. I reminded them that the end of the war was approaching and the German defeat was inevitable. I chastised them for their pessimism, and they feared me. They feared me and clung desperately to me. My words were a lifesaver for them. Some of them suspected me of being of a different faith, but they did not dare provoke me.

When I understood the danger I was exposed to at roll calls, I simply stopped showing up for those assemblies. I hid in the dark corner of a barrack and waited until the danger was past. I found a friend, a young doctor from the krankenstube, *or infirmary. I visited him frequently.*

That was a safe place. I never told him that I was Jewish, but he must have known. He enjoyed talking with me. He was perfectly aware of everything that was happening in the camp, warning me of selections and permitting me to hide in times of need in his office or on the ward.

One day, he said, 'Maria, there is a big selection coming up and women your age will go to the furnaces. There is no way of avoiding it. I will not be able to help you, because they will clear out the whole hospital. If you wish, I can put you down for a transport that is leaving today for another camp to the south of here. I think it's the only answer. I won't keep you here any longer.'

I followed his advice. He gave me a food parcel for the journey: bread and marmalade. After various adventures in a train that was bombed several times, we arrived at Ravensbrück.

*

KLARA'S STORY

Since we had very little money, I decided to visit the Grabowskis before we left for Zakopane. I knew that mama had left 'some things' with them. I hoped that they themselves would bring this up and give us some money to get rid of us. Mr and Mrs Grabowski greeted us cordially. I immediately indicated that we were preparing to leave for Zakopane, and I imagined that they received this news with great relief. In any case, we were treated to more tea and chat. Mr Grabowski was convinced that the war would be over soon and our parents would return. He asked if we had money and insisted that we take a few thousand that mama could repay when she returned. I kept repeating that we could not accept a loan, because I did not know when we would be able to repay it. I did not say a word about our property. Mrs Grabowska went off to see a doctor she knew and returned with a dressing for my injured leg. When we left, she gave me some warm underwear and a cake. The dressing helped; as for 'our things', Mr Grabowski returned everything to mama on her first day back in Cracow. He told me that he had not mentioned the deposit to me, because he had feared that I would sell it all and mama would have nothing when she returned. Very honorable people.

We traveled by train the next day. I cannot recall where we spent the night. We reached Zakopane in the afternoon and, naturally, went straight to 9 Kasprusie Street. It was August; the Warsaw Uprising was still underway. We went to Kaprusie Street and knocked and knocked, but nobody opened the door. A neighbor walked over and told us that the owner had gone to Rabka two months earlier. That sent us into despair. What could we do now? Mrs Cholewinska had assured us, when giving us her sister's address, that we could live there. We knew no one in Zakopane, we had come from the Uprising. When he saw that we knew the family, the neighbor tried to cheer us up. Naturally, he asked all about the Uprising. Then he finally revealed that he had the key to the apartment. We could spend the night there, and he would confer with his friends in the meantime to see what could be done to help us. So we had a roof over our heads for one night. Before evening fell, we peeked through the curtain at the beautiful mountains. Down below us, on the street, there were only Germans, but somehow we were not dying of fear.

The next morning, the neighbor came with several women. They advised us to go to the RGO, because they were aiding people from the Uprising there. At that time, few people from Warsaw had reached Zakopane. Later, thousands came, and they had so much money to spend that the natives of Zakopane hated them. While Warsaw was still burning, however, patriotic emotions prevailed. Leaving Janek 'at home', I went to the RGO with two of the women. Naturally, everyone there wanted to know all about the Uprising. I was introduced to Mrs Rosinska, who initially made a horrid impression. She was an old lady with an enormous wen, and looked just like Baba Yaga. She said that we could live in her loft, and she took me there. Along the way, I informed her that we had no money; she just snorted. She would never take money from Warsaw 'children'; doing so would tempt God's retribution. The only thing she worried about was whether we would find the accommodation acceptable. The Hideaway Villa, which was where she took me, stood next to a stream in a picturesque forest setting. It was in terrible shape. There had once been a boarding house there with many rooms. When we moved in, the rooms were occupied by refugees from all over Poland. No one paid anything, of course (I write 'of course' because I had had the good fortune of meeting Mrs Rosinska; I never met anyone else like her). Although the owner could barely hobble along, she carried soup from the RGO for her lodgers. And so, we were accepted into that 'family'. The poverty was shocking. Mrs Rosinska had a daughter, Marysia, who also greeted us with an open heart. Marysia was divorced. She worked at City Hall, so there would be no problems with our residence permits, although it was almost impossible to obtain permission for permanent residence in Zakopane.

For the first two days, nothing happened. We sat in the kitchen in the *evenings while the neighbors came in to hear our tales from Warsaw. We ate the soup and rough dark bread that Mrs Rosinska delivered. On the third day, I went out to look for a job. After half a day of wandering around, I had lost all hope of finding anything, and was on my way back to the Hideaway. Just before the bridge over the stream, there was a tiny food shop. I stopped there determined to spend all the money I had left (70 zloty) on horse meat kielbasa (ten dekagrams). As an afterthought, I asked if they might have any work for me. The woman running the shop shook her head and began telling me how they had nothing, and how in general there was no work to be found in Zakopane. But another customer spoke up: at the German Rebirth boarding house on the slops of Gubalowka, they were looking for someone to take care of children. Naturally, I went there immediately. As I climbed up and up the endless steps, I met a woman in a white smock. I assumed that she was a nurse and asked about the job. She told me to come back the next day and ask for Jozia. It turned out the next day that Jozia was a cook, not a nurse. She told me that there was no opening for me. I started crestfallen back down the steps, but when I was halfway down I realized that I ought to check in the office (and not with the cook). So I went back. I was received in the office by a woman named Zofia, who turned out to be from Poznan. I presented myself, and she looked me over from top to toe. I was wearing a pink, pre-war dress (although the weather in Zakopane was turning cold), daddy's smoking jacket, and wooden clogs. She said that there was an opening in the kitchen, but that it was hard work, not for me. I began reassuring her that I was not afraid of work, that I had been a maid and that a job would be salvation for me. She allowed herself to be convinced, or rather, she wanted to give me a chance (I was never sure if she might not be 'ex nostris'). She hired me to join the kitchen staff. I returned to the Hideaway on wings of joy, bearing my news. Marysia Rosinska, in the meantime, had arranged Janek a job digging ditches for the power company. It was only for a few days, but it paid well. There, Janek met someone from his schooldays – but everything went well; the acquaintance said nothing.*

I went to work in the kitchen. This meant that I was warm and had something to eat. The cook I had met earlier, however, was incensed that I had been hired after all. She gave me the worst job: I had to carry coal from the flooded basement to the fourth floor. In those days, however, it was good to have even that job. In any case, people have more luck than good sense. Two weeks later, when I was ready to drop from exhaustion, everything changed at the Villa Rebirth (its name in those days was Front-Kampfer-Dank). The German children were evacuated to

Czechoslovakia, and the place was turned into a convalescent home for lightly wounded soldiers. At first, this news terrified me. Later, however, it turned out to be a change for the better, because I was promoted to the post of cleaning woman and waitress. Furthermore, Jozia stopped persecuting me. I was assigned to the fourth floor, where there were fewer rooms – and less mud. When people came back from walks, they tended to leave the mud below on the lower floors. I had been pretending ever since I was hired that I did not speak German; I cleaned and said nothing. Things were generally quiet, even though there were 300 officers and soldiers living there at a time (for stays of two to three weeks). They roamed around Zakopane, coming back to the dining room at meal time. They had brought Russian girls, who had been serving their unit for a long time, with them. These Russians were experts and filled me in immediately on the way they worked. At each meal (and the Germans were fed sumptuously), we were given bread to slice, portions of butter in squares, jam to be divided into portions, and so on. They instructed me in slicing the bread very thin so that out of several loaves one whole one would be left over. They trimmed the edges off the pats of butter, and so on. For the Russian women, this was art for art's sake, since they did not lack for food in the workers' quarters where they lived. For the Hideaway, on the other hand, this was the beginning of the golden age. To make matters better, Janek was employed as a 'heizer'. He went around lighting the furnaces in several resort hotels that were now unoccupied but had to be kept in readiness in case the army needed them. Almost every evening, he came home with a sled loaded down with coal. You can imagine how happy everyone in the Hideaway was. Mrs Rosinska said that Janek and I were heaven-sent. It was a harsh winter; by October, the snow was already knee-deep.

*

KLARA'S STORY

One day, when I was waiting on tables, one of the Germans asked for another bowl of soup. I do not know why, but there was a regulation forbidding second portions. Zofia poured out the soup and we carried it to the tables. The guy who asked for a second portion had no teeth and could not eat bread. So I asked Zofia for a refill for him.

As I served him the soup, I heard, 'Janka, du bist Jude!'

I froze. My back was to those 300 soldiers who had heard his comment.

My heart was in my throat. I turned slowly around and shot an offended glance at the one who had made the remark.

I conferred with Janek that evening at the Hideaway. We realized that there was nowhere to escape to. I went to work as usual the next day. As I was mopping the corridor, the German from the day before came in sight.
'Guten Morgen', *he called heartily.*

When I did not answer, he asked why I was angry. I told him that I would not speak to him if he was going to call me a Jew. He burst out laughing and explained that he had watched how I wheedled that extra bowl of soup. He had asked his waitress for a second helping and had got nothing. And so, I must be a 'Jew' if I could manage to get that second helping of soup. A stone was lifted from my heart.

A second occasion when I had to swallow my heart occurred at the very end of the war (which, for us, was 28 January). According to my false papers, the birthday of Janina Szczubial (my birthday, in other words) fell on 1 January. The soldiers were so bored that, among other things, they went to the office and pestered Zofia to tell them the birthdays of the various members of the staff. I naturally knew nothing about this and, in addition, 1 January meant nothing to me. In any case, I was going about my cleaning on the fourth floor one day when I suddenly heard the voice of Kazia, a secretary in the office, calling me from the ground floor: 'Janka! zum Oberleutnant!'

I felt as if I had died. They had called one of the Russian women in exactly the same way a couple of weeks ago, and things had ended very badly. She had been fortunate to avoid being sent to prison, and they had literally pitched her out on the street. The cook had had his eye on her, and had reported on her for stealing butter when she refused to reciprocate his affections. I did not have butter on my conscience, but my brain seemed to have turned to butter. My legs trembled as I descended from the fourth floor. My whole life ran before my eyes. I had different ideas, but kept asking myself what I could do. At the bottom of the stairs, I asked Kazia why they had called me. She replied in German that instead of asking questions I should report immediately to the office. She said this in a very sharp tone.

I knocked at the door and heard a guttural 'Herein!'

I stood in the doorway and saw that the Oberleutnant *(a six-and-a-half-foot-tall German) was talking on the telephone. The minutes lasted centuries. All he did was keep repeating into the telephone* 'Ja, ja, jawohl'. *It lasted forever. My knees had turned to jelly, my heart was in my mouth, my head was spinning. He finally finished and rose in front of me (my eye level was somewhere below his chest). He looked at me carefully. 'Hmm, du bist Janina Szczubial?' he asked in his bass voice.*

I nodded, but could not produce a sound.

He suddenly cried out gleefully, 'Du hast Geburtstag habt, *gratuliere!' – and handed me a ration coupon for three meters of fabric as a birthday present.*

I left the office as if I had been shot out of a slingshot and let out a nervous squeal that I could not control. The girls knew that I had been summoned by the Oberleutnant *and thought I must have been caught in some major theft. A few curious soldiers had also gathered. When they learned what had happened, they surmised that the Poles must be even poorer than they had thought – give them three meters of fabric and they cry for joy.*

The cook was named Ernst. As he worked his way through the Russian women, he came to Rita. Rita was not a voluntary worker, like the others, but rather a slave laborer. She was an engineer. Her husband was a pilot. She knew nothing about his fate. We became fast friends, perhaps because we were somehow different from the others. As I have mentioned, she had no taste for a romance with the cook, who subsequently took his revenge on her. Now he came after me. When he tried to kiss me, I smacked him in the face without even stopping to think about it. I was slightly worried about my own quick temper, but I did not worry too much because he was forbidden to have anything to do with Polish women. I was right; he said nothing. But while we were serving the Sunday evening snacks at the end of the week, one of the girls whispered that Ernst had been in the room where we prepared portions and had taken my bag away. I immediately realized what had been in the bag. I was fortunate that on that particular day I had taken only a couple of slices of bread and a jar of boiled potatoes. I thought that wasn't so bad, so I headed straight for Ernst to make a scene about my bag. He shot back that all Poles were thieves, that he was going to take my bag to the Oberleutnant, *and that I would end up rotting in prison. Without thinking, I went off to find the* Oberleutnant. *It would be better if he heard it from me first. I said that Ernst had taken my bag, that I was supporting a family, and that my salary of 120* zloty *would buy me two loaves of bread a month. So I thought that if a slice of bread or a couple of potatoes were left over and I took them, it should hardly be considered theft. The* Oberleutnant *smiled and said that I should have come to him earlier. He promised to give me a pass allowing me to take leftovers home. The next day I could show this pass to the guards and did not have to worry about smuggling food past them any more.*

Afterwards, times were really good at the Hideaway as we ate butter and meat.

And Ernst left me in peace.

*

Winter in Zakopane and winter in Ravensbrück. Mother, who had always had weak kidneys, suffered in the cold. How did she survive in the unheated barrack, in a top bunk exposed to drafts? The answer must lie in the victory of the spirit over the weaknesses of the body. Cases are known from the concentration camps of illnesses that stopped getting worse or even vanished as a result of willpower, the will to survive no matter what the adversity. I assume that this is what occurred in mother's case. She never lost her spirit. From the moment she reached Ravensbrück, she began looking around for ways to survive and make her life more bearable. There was severe frost, and the food was miserable.

MOTHER'S STORY

I noticed that the people employed in the kitchen – some of them were Germans – had to supply their own fuel, and dragged tree trunks and branches from the nearby woods. I told them, 'Haven't you got enough to do in the kitchen? Aren't there any prisoners who can work? I'll organize a group for you and they'll bring chopped wood to the kitchen every day.' They liked my idea. I organized a 'Holzkolonne'. In exchange, I was allowed to go into the kitchen to warm up, and the women whom I recruited to help me were given an extra portion of warm soup. That was important. The feeling that they were needed was also a consolation for them. I became 'the leader' once again. I kept their spirits up, and they looked at me as if I were sitting on a rainbow. Their faith reinforced my self-confidence, in turn – and God only knows how lonely I was, how I was suffering, and how I struggled each day to stay alive.

My mother had a good deal of luck, but luck was part of her personality, her wisdom, and that rare intuition that was characteristic of her. She sometimes faced a sudden, unexpected threat that demanded an immediate response. There was always

313

only one response that was correct and that offered a way out. She always found that response immediately. How? Where?

One day, I heard my name being called over the loudspeaker: 'Maria Murdzenska report to the camp office!' That had never happened before. What could they want with me? I did not know what to think. Had someone informed on me? Full of foreboding and heavy at heart, I stood before the German officer. He looked at me for a long time, then asked me my name.

He repeated the question twice before saying, 'You've got a package from your sister.'

My shock was such that I reacted spontaneously, without thinking, 'From my sister? What sister?'

'What? You have no sister?' The officer sprang out of his chair.

There was no time to think, so I gulped and said gloomily, 'I have a sister, of course. But I do not speak to her, because she is a German. I want nothing to do with her!'

I cannot explain how that idea came into my mind. In any case, I realized that the only person who could send me a package would be Aurea Jäger, the pharmacist from Warsaw who was Zygmunt's friend. And I was right. After the Uprising, when Warsaw had fallen and been burned, she decided to find Zygmunt and did not rest until she had traced him to Oranienburg. Zygmunt, in turn, asked her to find his sister Maria Murdzenska, from whom he had been separated in Auschwitz. Aurea did not know me; she had never laid eyes on me. She looked for me in Auschwitz and found me in Ravensbrück. Along with the very good food parcel, she enclosed greetings from Zygmunt. She sent several more packages. I admired that woman, who had demonstrated such devotion, such willpower, and had taken on such a responsibility in those mad times. It is hard for me to express the gratitude that I felt towards her. I had always believed that we would survive the war, and I fought every day to make sure, but an incident like that gave me strength and redoubled my vigilance.

Some two months had passed when word suddenly ran through the camp that all the political prisoners were to be sent home to Warsaw. The news had come from the camp superintendent himself. The women who were my fellow prisoners went mad with delight. I alone refrained from greeting the rumor with joy.

'Are you crazy?' I asked them. 'You think they'll take you to Warsaw? To the Jugendlager is where they'll take you!'

Not far from the main camp was a smaller one, called the Jugendlager.

Those who went there never returned. They mistreated the prisoners ruthlessly there, worked them to death, and shot them like dogs. 'Maria's the one who's gone crazy,' said my companions in suffering. I warned them: 'There's nothing to be happy about. Think logically. Have the Germans ever done anything good for us? Why would they suddenly want to take us to Warsaw? Haven't they got anything else to worry about?'

But this time, mine was a voice crying in the wilderness. 'The war's ending, and we're going back to Warsaw!' they told me.

The next day, there was a big roll-call assembly. Polish female prisoners were ordered to take all their belongings. A German major, a tall, handsome man, gave a ceremonious speech: 'Your cares are over. The authorities have decided to send you back to Warsaw. I hope that you will remember that you have been treated well in this camp.'

When he finished, before the order had even been given to march off to the trucks that were waiting nearby, I stepped forward and approached that officer. He was surprised – everybody was surprised, because such chutzpa had not yet been seen in that camp. 'I have a request, major, sir,' I said loudly in German. 'I would like to request that I be allowed to remain in the camp. There is nothing for me to return to in Warsaw. My home has been burned down and I have no family. I've grown accustomed to the life here; I feel good here. Please permit me to stay.'

The major listened with his mouth hanging open, as if he could not understand what I was saying. He looked to the left and the right, at the officers standing around him, and then snapped, 'You want to stay? If you want to, then stay, stupid woman, stay!'

All the other women were soon loaded on to the trucks. Disconsolate, alone, orphaned, I went to warm myself in the kitchen.

So I stayed in the camp, and survived. All the other women were, of course, transferred to the Jugendlager. Only a few from among that Warsaw group survived.

*

Uncle Zygmunt did not live to see liberation. He died a martyr's death in Oranienburg three weeks before the Allies liberated the camp.

Along with Janek, to whom she was married by then, my sister Klara set out westward after the war thinking of reaching Palestine. As we know, the way to the Promised Land was blocked and the door of paradise was locked. And so the newlyweds stopped over, among various places, in Leipzig. Klara remembered that Aurea Jäger came from Duisburg, so she immediately placed an advertisement in the local newspaper.

KLARA'S STORY

Two days after we placed that advertisement, we received a letter from Aurea. It was the first knife in our hearts: she attached a death notice that she had had printed, announcing that Zygmunt Durakowski had died of typhus in the Oranienburg camp on 14 April 1945.

We corresponded with Aurea even after we had moved to Munich, where she visited us several times. The things she told me were so horrifying ... After long efforts, she had reached Oranienburg and saw Uncle Zygmunt through the fence. He was the mere shadow of a man, in prison rags, barely strong enough to stay on his feet. When he recognized her, he began calling out, 'Save me Aurea, save me!' Hearing this, several Germans attacked him, beating and kicking him until he lost consciousness. For years afterwards, I wondered if Uncle Zygmunt might not have survived if she hadn't gone there to see him.

Then I always remember how upset I was with Aurea during the Nuremberg Trial, when she would say how sorry she felt for the defendants, how terrible it was to see how their leaders were being humiliated, and so on. We argued about it and I thought I would scream with rage. Today I might be able to understand her point of view, but back then I felt only disgust.

I never informed mama about the meetings with Aurea, because I could not see the point of burdening her with a sorrow she would bear until the end of her life. Uncle Zygmunt had died, and that was already more than she could stand.

Throughout our eight months in Zakopane, we wondered if Mrs Rosinska knew about us. Whenever anyone said anything about the Jews, she attacked them and left them reeling. In general, she never said 'Jews'. Instead, she called them 'Israelites', and did not conceal her sympathy for the Jewish people. We therefore supposed that she had figured out who we were. She was so generous and loved us in such a genuine way, as well as a mother could, that we kept wondering whether or not to tell her. We finally concluded that it would be better not to. If she knew and didn't say so, that meant that she preferred to pretend that she didn't know. And if she didn't know, then why should we give her one more thing to worry about? We were sure that she would never throw us out. We did not tell her even after the Russians arrived, and we set out on foot for Cracow. Only several months later did we return to Zakopane. We decided then to put our cards on the table. Yet it is very difficult to suddenly tell someone with whom you have lived on the closest terms for months, 'I'm not me'. We had a hard time telling her. We started by revealing that Janek's real name was not Sarnecki, but Halbreich. Then we told her that I was not Szczubial, but Gross.

At that, Mrs Rosinska said, 'Ah, so they must surely have wanted to make Volksdeutsch of you'.

We didn't know what to say. We understood that she had never suspected a thing. We could not bring ourselves to say it, so we simply showed her our identity cards from the Jewish Committee. She looked at them and said, 'Well, isn't that a surprise! But it doesn't mean anything, does it? To me, you're Janek and Janka, and you're my children.'

And that was that.

We often visited her. We simply felt as if we were going home – first the two of us, and then with our daughter Jadwiga, whom Mrs Rosinska idolized and introduced to everyone as her granddaughter. She thought that Jadwiga was the most talented child in the world.

Right after the war, we bought Mrs Rosinska a radio (she always lamented that the Germans had confiscated hers). She took it to the hospital. Marysia informed her that her mother was ill, and we went to visit her. When we went into her ward, all the patients greeted us joyfully. Mrs Rosinska had talked about us all the time and had dreamed of seeing us one more time. The next week, we were on our way back to Zakopane. She had died in her sleep early in the morning. We could only help escort our Great Friend, with her Great Heart, to the cemetery. You don't meet people like her any more.

I suddenly saw mother standing out in the street. I picked her up in my arms like a feather and carried her up to my room on the fourth floor. She was so thin. I had never imagined that I would see her looking like this, because she had always been stout, robust, heavy. I was the one they called 'skinny as a rail'. But no one who remembers those days or has seen the photographs of the people rescued from the German camps will be surprised: this was how the people called 'Musselman' looked – skin and bones.

Mother returned on my birthday, 2 June 1945. It had taken her a month to walk the whole distance from Ravensbrück to Cracow.

Who could describe my joy and emotions? Until today, the tears come whenever I recall that moment.

Lili returned healthy and unharmed from slave labor and soon got married. Mrs Janiczek invited mother to the wedding. However, mother stubbornly blamed Lili for Uncle Zygmunt's death, and was so rueful that she did not want to see the girl. 'Anyway, she'd never be able to look me in the eye,' she always said.

Mother loved Cracow with a great love. She was born here, grew up here, raised her family here and lived many happy contented years here. She loved Cracow, and Cracow loved her. When she returned from the camp, she found nothing left of what she had left behind – the people she loved best, her fortune, her family that had been scattered to the four winds, her home where strangers now lived, her shop, which had already been nationalized. Yet even with all this, she did not want to leave Cracow. She opened a small shop on a downtown street. As before the war, she was in the habit of walking to the Noworolski café at four o'clock for a cup of coffee and a piece of pastry. Her children, Jerzyk, Klara and I, who had survived thanks to her, married, left Poland one by one, and started new homes of their own in Israel. The fourth, Jozek, settled in London. Yet mother stayed on in Cracow. She was bound to her Polish friends and to the few Jews who were left. In the end, however, she was overcome by her longing for her children and grandchildren, and by the sickness that finally flared up after all she had been through. Mother came to Israel as part of the 1958 emigration wave. Alas, she had little time left – no more than a year. The sickness that had been unable to defeat her in Auschwitz and Ravensbruck now proved stronger.

Surrounded by her children and grandchildren, Sara Gross died in Tel Aviv.

13. Habent Sua Fata Papieri

Having recorded the fates of mother and my sister, I shall now return to the moment when I parted from them, when I left for Otwock just before the Uprising broke out. The next day, or perhaps two days later, Red Army patrols entered Otwock. I could not wait. When I saw the first Soviet soldier on the street, I ran out to meet him. I wanted to greet him in his native tongue. I had been preparing for this moment for half a year. In Warsaw, I had bought *A Thousand Words in Russian*, a self-teaching book intended for German soldiers on the eastern front. Day by day, page by page, I had diligently taught myself to read and write. Now, I would try to say something aloud in Russian. I had learned by heart several poems of Pushkin and Lermontov, all in anticipation of that longed-for moment that was growing closer by the day. When I saw the young officer, I opened my mouth with a joyous '*Zdravstvuytie, tovarishch*'. I told him that I was a Jew and wanted to thank him for liberating me. He did not seem particularly delighted. He looked at me suspiciously, shook his head incredulously, and said in a cold, even hostile tone, 'You're a Jew and you're alive? Something funny must be going on here. We'll have to investigate this matter …'

That was my first encounter with freedom. From that time on, I got used to hearing that surprised, skeptical, 'You're alive?' Somehow, I got used to it. Nevertheless, the reaction of that Soviet officer was as painful as if he had stabbed me in the heart.

Shortly afterwards, however, local authorities of a sort were established. I went immediately to the town offices to report that I was a Jew and wanted to return to my real name. To my amazement, they advised me politely but firmly to hang on to my Aryan papers, because it was not yet safe to be a Jew. I did not understand what they meant. I was free, liberated from the Nazi nightmare – what else could threaten me? I did not know what they knew – that the struggle was still going on against the underground, which did not wish to submit to the new order. Many innocent Jews fell victim to the ruthless fighting between the underground and the security organs of the people's government – even some who had just been liberated from the concentration camps, or were among the waves of people being repatriated from the Soviet Union. Some were murdered as 'communists' (as the NSZ¹ saw it, all Jews were communists), and others were liquidated out of the fear that they would try to reclaim their property, which had passed into the hands of new owners.

I had no idea of what was going on as Poland emerged from under the Nazi yoke. I only took in what my eyes could see and my ears could hear – that is, what was happening close at hand. I knew about a group of Jews who had come out of hiding in Otwock. I first met them during Yom Kippur at an improvised prayer house. When units of the Kosciuszko Division, part of the Polish armed forces organized in the Soviet Union, passed through Otwock, I tried to spot soldiers among them whose looks reminded me of 'the old days'. When I approached one of them, he was happy. He informed me that the next day was Yom Kippur and invited me to a nearby Polish house for the *Kol Nidre* prayer.

There were still no newspapers, so I decided in a reflex of spontaneous enthusiasm to publish a mimeographed paper called *Voice of Mazovia* in Otwock. The first issue consisted of greetings to the liberators. I decided to do it, and I did it (someone may have helped me; I cannot recall). On Sunday, I stood selling (or giving away?) copies to people as they came out of church. I did not feel particularly at ease in this role. I was inhibited and embarrassed, but I wanted to overcome my 'bourgeois complexes'. My deed earned me a trip to the police post, where I was interrogated on suspicion of spreading defeatism. The newspaper looked superficially like an underground publication, but it contained not a word against the new authorities. In the end, I was released and even granted permission to publish, but only under official control. By then, my enthusiasm was gone.

In Otwock, I stayed with the kindly and generous Kuczynski family, where Jerzyk had lived for more than a year while attending clandestine school. I met his teachers and made new friends among them. Both Jerzyk and I were completely broke, but we had a roof over our heads and something to eat thanks to the Kuczynski family.

In order to get a better idea of what was going on, I set off, walking and hitching rides on military vehicles and farmers' carts, to Lublin, the provisional capital of People's Poland. I had little trouble making contacts at the highest levels, that is, with Wincenty Rzymowski, the minister of culture and art. He offered me a uniform, a high rank, and a role in the cultural and educational branches of the Polish army. I had never had any enthusiasm for uniforms or the army. Therefore, I returned to Otwock in order to continue intense 'private' volunteer work. I was waiting for the moment when I could return to Cracow. Jerzyk and Korczak joined the army. Jerzyk returned from Berlin as a lieutenant, and Korczak climbed higher.

The whole time, we could see the glow of the fires on the far bank of the Vistula. It was visible even in Otwock. A great tragedy was unfolding there. All of us, civilians and soldiers stationed in Otwock, lived through that. I had left my mother and other relatives there on that far bank of the Vistula. My manuscripts were there, too ...

*

Only in the winter did the Soviet army break through and enter Warsaw. I went there shortly afterwards. It was one great heap of rubble. I spent half a day climbing over the ruins and the barricaded or stone-clogged streets in the effort to reach my manuscripts on Niemcewicza Street. I went around in circles and lost my way, unable to find my bearings in this haunted city that stank of ashes and decomposing bodies. Finally, I reached my goal. The five-story building still stood there. The bottom floors were blackened with fire, but the upper windows seemed not to have burned – although their dark, vacant appearance boded nothing good. There was still hope in my heart. My papers were on the fifth floor. I quickly climbed the half-smashed, half-burned skeleton of the staircase. I pushed my way into the apartment. It was not difficult to enter, for the door had simply ceased to exist. I stood in the doorframe for a moment, collecting my strength and thinking: could it be? Perhaps it will all be just as I left it.

The illusion lasted only a moment. Charred papers lay everywhere, the furniture was gone, and only the broken table, with one leg missing, knelt in the middle of the room like the ox in the manger scene.

Surveying the destruction with an aching heart, I thought of Carlyle. When the historian finished the years of scholarly labor on his immortal *History of the French Revolution*, his servant had thrown the one manuscript into the fire, thinking Carlyle had left it out to be discarded. The author returned two minutes later – too late. The next day, he began rewriting his work from scratch. That story had always moved me and inspired my admiration. I would have gone crazy had I been in Carlyle's shoes, I thought more than once. I would have roared like a wounded lion. Over those ashes in Warsaw, I felt like Carlyle. I decided to start from scratch.

Freed from the nightmare of the war, I once again began accumulating papers. I believed that the end of the war also marked the end of that strange fate that seemed to hang like the sword of Damocles over my books, papers and works. Now, I could assemble them in peace. What threatened them now?

I began to live – and my papers began to live. They began to serve others; they stopped being a world in which I sought a refuge from reality. On the contrary, their new role was to serve the present moment, rather than eternity.

I returned to Cracow. It would be hard to say that nothing had changed. The city had been prettied up and made cleaner, sadder, more boring and more provincial – even though it had been the capital of the General Government only a month before. It was Cracow without the Jews. I know many people who never went back to their native cities and small towns because they were repulsed by the idea of encountering the ruins of the past, the shades of those who had been murdered, the emptiness that is the emptiness of the heart. I returned.

I yoked myself to the work of the Jewish Historical Commission and began recording my own memoirs and those of others. I made no attempt to endow them with a literary form. I wanted to collect them as raw material, as testimony. I worked madly, as if I intended to make up for those lost five years, and the pile of papers grew.

I lived alone for a long time before I tracked down the surviving members of my family, who were scattered around the world. I was free, but I had no one to talk to. I wanted to share my joy with someone, but there was not a single address in the world that I could mail a letter to. Then, I remembered the International

League of Young Friendship in Boston. On request, the League put young people from all over the world in contact with penpals.

I decided to write to them. Since I did not know the address, I wrote a request on the envelope for the US Post Office to find the League for me. I waited half a year for a response. Then a letter came from a Mickey in Minnesota. A week later, I got a letter from a young girl in Iowa named Jane. I was as delighted as a child and replied immediately. Two weeks later, I got five letters on the same day from all over America, from boys and girls, Jews and non-Jews (in my letter, I had explained that I was Jewish and had described my situation). I answered them all at length (but not at such great length as before) the next day. Within a few more days, ten additional letters had arrived, and the situation was beginning to look bleak. I was also leading a Jewish Committee youth group, in addition to my job at the Jewish Historical Commission. I started distributing the addresses of American pen pals to anyone who would take them; I soon had 40 of them. I stayed in touch with only the first few correspondents, while tying a ribbon around the rest of the letters and placing them in an old shoe box.

I was writing more and more letters. First of all, I wrote to all my Aryan friends who had helped me during the war. Now, I revealed my true identity. I waited impatiently for their replies. As it turned out, they had all had their suspicions, but had not wanted to show that they knew. These letters were very dear to me. They reaffirmed my faith in people and ensured that many years of close friendship with these people followed.

The circle of correspondents grew and grew. Relatives, friends and classmates began reporting in. They had survived the camps or the ghettos, in Poland and elsewhere. One letter at a time, the shoe box was filled.

I was doing community and community-literary work with young Jewish people. I was a Jew and I wanted to be a Jew. Strong bonds linked me with those starving young Jewish people returning from the German camps and from the Urals. I wrote dozens of articles for all the Jewish magazines then being published in Poland; I edited a monthly for young pioneers preparing to settle in Palestine; I gave lectures on Hebrew culture – with which I myself was only now becoming familiar. Whatever I learned, I immediately passed on to others. Even though I knew the language less than perfectly, I began translating poetry from the Hebrew. Various delegates from Israel who were then in Poland came to my aid. I translated more than a hundred of these poems and gave readings of them from Lodz to Wroclaw, from Walbrzych to Cracow – the works of Bialik, Czernichowski, Rachel, Szymon, Lamdan, Alterman, Melcer and Szlomo. They were not brilliant translations and I knew it, but I did them because I thought I might be the last person who would translate Hebrew poetry into Polish. Little people sometimes think that they are destined for great tasks ...

And the stacks of paper went on growing and growing. I made friends with Yiddish writers, who accepted me into their union despite my Zionist sympathies and ignorance of the Yiddish language. I began learning Yiddish and translating Yiddish poetry into Polish. I acquainted myself with Yiddish theatre, literature and folklore, and threw myself heart and soul into the newly discovered world of Peretz and Sholem Aleichem. A writer once said that you have to love the Jews very, very, very much in order to avoid hating them. That was how I loved the Jews.

At the same time, I was working in the state-owned Film Polski firm, where I was directing Yiddish-language films.

What a paradox in a crazy time when the world was standing on its head! I wrote Polish poetry in the Yiddish writers' union, and made Yiddish films in Film Polski.

I began writing screenplays, short stories and radio programs. I did not hang out in cafés or bars. I did not know what the word 'vacation' meant. I worked day and night, as if I feared that I would not manage to do my life's work, that I would die before I had said what I wanted to say.

What I wrote and said had a transient value. It lived with me, and it vanished with me. Nevertheless, I was living intensely. Something of that intensity, something of that love and delight, reached my audience – made up not of the high and mighty, but of the little people.

One day, I decided to marry. I chose a wife (or perhaps she was the one who did the choosing) and began to think about dotting the i and crossing the t – about realizing my life's goal by returning to the homeland that my ancestors had left so long ago. My wife came from Grodno. Her name, Shulamit, was dear to my heart. She was a geologist by education, and a graduate of a Hebrew secondary school. She helped me translate Hebrew poetry into

Polish, and she was as much in favor as could be of my plans to emigrate to Israel, where she had family. When those plans were ready, we began packing.

And so it was that, five years after the war, I again faced the problem of what to do with my papers. I was permitted to export manuscripts, provided that they bore a stamp from the Ministry of Culture. The same was true of letters, which would have to be censored – despair! To carry a suitcase full of manuscripts to Warsaw, stand in line, submit an application, wait, explain. And the spidery, minuscule handwriting covering all those heaps of paper!

It was more than I was capable of doing, especially since I was working and absorbed in my work up to the very last minute. The departure date was approaching, and I could not think of what I should do. In the end, I decided that I had to reduce the number of papers to the bare minimum, and then smuggle them out.

It was December 1949. I sat down in front of a blazing stove with the intention of tossing all the least important letters into it. I would keep only ten, I thought. Or perhaps 15. I decided to read through them all one last time before carrying out the liquidation. Merry red flames danced in the open door of the stove while I read and read. Each letter, of course brought back warm memories. It would be a shame to throw any of them out. No! I did not have the heart to throw all this into the stove. If I arranged those letters in some sort of compositional order, I could publish them as a novel that would be interesting – no, fascinating. I could already see it in my mind's eye, I had the framework for it.

I decided to pack the letters into a capacious black leather briefcase that was a present from one of the organizations I had worked with. Into it I placed the manuscript of my unfinished work, *On the Mechanisms of Aryan Papers*, along with a sheaf of other manuscripts, as well as reviews and newspaper clippings, posters, invitations, and other mementoes. Then I placed my treasure at the bottom of a wicker basket – I had the right to take one such basket with me. I added ten books. No more were permitted. I gave the rest of my library away to Jewish and Polish friends who were remaining behind. May the will of the heavens be done, I told myself. Let them take what they take; nothing can be done.

My heart was pounding as I waited for the search before

checking my baggage. I was the last in line that day. At around five o'clock, they dragged my basket into the center of the customs clearance area. The customs officers had just removed the cover from the basket when the lights went out. A power failure! Searches by candlelight were tiring, the exhausted customs officers somehow sensed that I was not carrying any great treasures, and they waved me through. They ordered the basket sealed without even looking inside. I heaved a sigh. My papers had been saved.

Just before we left, Shulamit had bought me a big black leather wallet. I shuddered at the sight of it – I have an organic aversion to black leather – but it held a great deal. I could put all my dearest, most beloved photographs, keepsakes and affidavits in it, along with the membership cards that I collected passionately from the Writers' Union, the Historical Commission, Film Polski and the journalists' union, along with my university identification card, my Aryan *kenkart*, my birth certificate and so on. It also contained my baggage claim check, a money order from the PKO bank and other documents connected with the trip.

*

We set out on New Year's Eve, and soon reached Venice. We spent two days in the transit camp on the island of Santa Poelia.

On the evening of the second day, we were taken by motor launch to the ship *Negba*, which was moored in the harbor. Clambering on board, I suddenly clutched at my heart: my wallet was missing. It took me only a moment to realize that I had left it under the mattress of my cot in the camp – I always put my wallet under the mattress before going to sleep, for safety's sake.

I begged a Jewish Agency official to take me back ashore. The ship was not due to sail until the next day. I explained the great value that the wallet had for me, containing as it did my whole past, aside from the claim check, money order and my current documents. He did not want to take me back to the island, but he promised solemnly that he would look for my wallet as soon as he went back, and forward it to Haifa. It would be there before I was – I could count on that 100 per cent! I was furious and unconsoled.

No one, of course, had heard a thing about my wallet in Haifa. To make things worse, I had not taken the name of that Jewish

Agency official. They promised to remember about me should my wallet turn up.

I located numerous acquaintances, friends and comrades from the pioneer movement in Haifa. They helped me to recover my basket, my bundle of bedding, and even the money I had paid into the Polish bank. When we left the transit camp, we moved to the beautiful agricultural settlement of Raanan, where my wife's aunt had a small farm. She put us up in a tiny room – not only too small to unpack the basket in, but even too small for the basket to fit inside. And so the basket made its way to Shulamit's uncle's tool shed.

We never went near that basket during the year that we lived with Shulamit's aunt. Then, our apartment in the Shikun Amidar residential district was ready. At long last! What joy it would be for us to live on our own, for me to be the head of the household! We transferred our humble possessions there, along with the furniture that Shulamit's aunt gave us.

I waited impatiently to unpack the basket. I wanted to get at my papers. After the loss of my wallet, they were my dearest memento of the past, the summing up of a whole period in my life.

One day, I would show them to my children. 'See?' I would say. 'This is what your father looked like back then. He worked like a slave so that ...' So that what? So that he could accumulate this handful of papers?

We had trouble fitting the key into the rusty padlock, but at last the lid of the basket sprang open.

Nothing had been damaged. There was not even any smell of mildew. With a pounding heart, I began tossing out the underwear and the clothes, an old candlestick – itself a memento – and then a rug that shouldn't have been there in the first place, curtains – and then I reached the black leather briefcase. A joy not of this earth washed over me. After all I had been through, I had a right to my doubts about whether it would be there. But it was. I knelt on the floor and lifted it reverently from the bottom of the basket. The clasp was rusty and did not want to open. Or had I perhaps locked it? In the end, I ripped it open impatiently, and an unbelievable sight met my eyes. Instead of sheaves of paper, the briefcase contained something like dry oatmeal flakes or crushed matzo. I went numb. My papers had been eaten by mice, bitten into little strips and scraps of scraps, on which here and there, with great difficulty, I could make out an individual letter. Nothing! There was nothing left! I plunged my hands into those tiny scraps and began sifting the ruins of my works through my fingers, like ashes. The wind, blowing in through the open door, began wafting the grains all over the apartment ...

'What are you doing?' Shulamit asked in irritation.

A hoarse voice tore from my throat and I did not know whether to cry or to laugh ...

Forty years have passed since that time. Once again, the mountains of papers have risen. My annual correspondence, carefully bundled up, fills the entrance way and half the shelves on the balcony. I have written enough poems for five volumes – and have published two. Twenty years of screenplays, film criticism, exhibition reviews, reportage, short stories, articles, essays on the Holocaust, literary portraits. In Polish and in Hebrew.

And then there are my memoirs from the war period, which I have promised to my children and grandchildren. In Hebrew and in Polish. I also owe these to my Polish friends. If I do not manage to see them into print, my heirs will throw them into the trash can. They will be pulped in a paper factory and someone else will write their memoirs and describe their life on that paper.

And perhaps someone's greatness will grow on the grave of my reminiscences.

NOTES

1. NSZ – National Armed Forces – the extreme right-minded, antisemitic clandestine organisation.

14. *Cracow Autumn*

Autumn chestnuts spill from Cracow trees –
But no one hangs them on a Sukkoth booth.
Unchanged, Wawel stands. But near the Dragon's Den
There are no Jewish children.

A carpet of golden leaves bedecks the ground,
As always, sweethearts make dates after class,
But now there are no fraternity scoundrels
Shouting 'Beat the Jews' – for there are no Jews.

St Mary's Church tower and the Cloth Hall still stand,
Mickiewicz from his plinth surveys the Main Square.
The same market stalls, churches, alleys, houses –
But *Nowy Dziennik* is gone from Orzeszkowa street.

Beloved pages of *Nowy Dziennik* –
On Cracow streets, the banner of Zion.
'Jerusalem' and 'The Pogrom in Przytyk',
'Hitler', 'The White Paper', 'Riots in Hebron'.

And ritual slaughter and more politics,
Dykman's translation of verses of Bialik's
And the editorial by Doctor Thon.

Nowy Dziennik is no more, there are no more Jews,
Over Kazimierz hang the ghosts of the past,
The Old Synagogue sinking into the earth,
Out of sorrow, perhaps, out of shame …

On Jozefa, Estery and Dietla Streets,
In the doorways crouch no Jewish beggars;
On Szeroka, Skawinska and Waska Streets,
The wind moans, the wind murmurs.

From Wawel down Stradom
The tram line still runs
Right to Krakowska Street.
Yiddish was spoken here,
Jewish love filled the air,
Where fresh foliage stretched along the Dietla Planty,
Jewish children played here,
Holidays were observed,
With the help of the Lord.

Who Are You, Mr Grymek?

At this season Miodowa Street
Filled with a gala, ceremonious throng
On their way to Ajzyk, Remuh, and the Old Synagogue
And to Temple, where the Reformed went to pray.
In this season in Cracow the shofar blew,
Heartfelt prayers rose unimpeded to heaven.

What we have today
Are profaned Torahh covers
And *azkarot* –
Assemblies of mourning.

Azkarot for Stradom and Kazimierz,
For Jakuba, Jozefa, Szeroka, Miodowa,
Rabbi Meisels and Podbrzezia Streets,
Orzeszkowa, Skawinska, and for Brzozowa
Sleep shrouds the Cracow I can never forget
The Cracow that is no more

For those who rose up in the ghetto to fight,
For the Jewish heroes, the soldiers of hope,
Stones on barricades, erected by God,
In their proper order, going to death
 – For the memory of the Hebrew School
 – For the theatre on Bochenska Street
 – For the years, the months, the days, the weeks
 – For the plenitude of Jewish Cracow
 – For Mizrachi, and for Bejt Jaakov
 – For Makkabi and the Gymnastics Hall.

Where is our Vistula, where is our Cracow?
Where is that country that we called Poland?
Across whole countries our Cracow unfurled,
From Plaszow to Sverdlovsk to the Urals.

We dragged it from Auschwitz to the arctic tundra.
To Paris, London, as far as New York,
All these years, all these years, we still have this:
We meet, reminisce, meet and reminisce.

We are strung together like those Cracow chestnuts
On a thread of memories longer than our sorrow:
Our idyllic Cracovian Jewish childhood,
Our days of rage and triumph, youth, frivolity,
Our days of love and joy, our downfall and our care.
Who knows better than the cobblestones of Cracow
What pained us early, what pains us still:
The Jewish fate given us to fulfill.
Autumn rains soak the chestnuts of Cracow,
Autumn on the Planty, winter in our hearts.
Evening falls. Hurry home. They are locking the gates.